The political economy of American monetary policy

The political economy of American monetary policy

Edited by
THOMAS MAYER
University of California, Davis

CAMBRIDGE
UNIVERSITY PRESS

32 Avenue of the Americas, New York NY 10013-2473, USA

Cambridge University Press is part of the University of Cambridge.

It furthers the University's mission by disseminating knowledge in the pursuit of education, learning and research at the highest international levels of excellence.

www.cambridge.org
Information on this title: www.cambridge.org/9780521446518

First published 1990
First paperback edition 1993

A catalogue record for this publication is available from the British Library

Library of Congress Cataloguing in Publication data

The Political economy of American monetary policy / edited by Thomas Mayer.
p. cm.
Includes bibliographical references.
ISBN 0-521-36316-0
1. Board of Governors of the Federal Reserve System (U.S.)
2. Monetary policy – United States. I. Mayer, Thomas, 1927–
HG2563.P65 1990
332.1′12′0973–dc20 89-23900

ISBN 978-0-521-36316-7 Hardback
ISBN 978-0-521-44651-8 Paperback

Contents

Preface

There is much dispute about the efficacy of countercyclical monetary policy. In part this is due to disagreements about economic theory, or about the size of certain parameters. But much of it reflects different assumptions about the extent to which political pressures prevent the Fed from following appropriate policies, the degree to which its policies are influenced by its own bureaucratic interests, and the efficiency with which it makes policy. Hence, I invited a number of economists and political scientists, most of whom have worked on these problems, to write chapters for a volume dealing with Fed behavior. The resulting chapters cover many aspects of Fed policy, such as its actual independence, its devotion to the public interest, and biases and inefficiencies in its policy-making.

The picture that emerges in these chapters differs sharply from the traditional "textbook" view, which has monetary policy being made by an independent central bank, totally devoted to the public interest, using the most sophisticated tools of economic analysis. In that textbook view, it is only a lack of certain information, such as the absence of reliable forecasts, that constrains the Fed's policy-making. The chapters in this volume show how implausible that textbook view is. Yet this book is not just another exercise in Fed-bashing. It is not the Fed's fault that its actual independence is sharply circumscribed. Nor is the Fed the only organization whose policy-making is influenced by self-interest, by biases, and by cognitive difficulties. I suspect that the Fed has a much better record than do most other government agencies, or the universities, for that matter. But whether or not the Fed is good enough to handle the tasks thrust on it is a more controversial issue.

Davis, California Thomas Mayer

Contributors

Nathaniel Beck, Associate Professor of Political Science, University of California, San Diego

Thomas F. Cargill, Professor of Economics, University of Nevada, Reno

Gerald A. Epstein, Assistant Professor of Economics, University of Massachusetts, Amherst

Roger Frantz, Professor of Economics, San Diego State University

John A. Gildea, Assistant Professor of Economics, Wheaton College

Thomas Havrilesky, Professor of Economics, Duke University

Robert L. Hetzel, Economist and Vice-President, Federal Reserve Bank of Richmond

Michael M. Hutchison, Associate Professor of Economics, University of California, Santa Cruz

Edward J. Kane, Everett D. Rees Professor of Banking and Monetary Economics, The Ohio State University

Nicholas Karamouzis, Economic Advisor, Bank of Greece

Edward Keen, Ph.D. candidate, Claremont Graduate School

Salwa S. Khoury, research student, London School of Economics (Ph.D., University of California, Davis)

Raymond E. Lombra, Professor of Economics, Pennsylvania State University

Thomas Mayer, Professor of Economics, University of California, Davis

William C. Melton, Economist and Vice-President, Investors' Diversified Services

Michael C. Munger, Assistant Professor of Government, University of Texas, Austin

James L. Pierce, Professor of Economics, University of California, Berkeley

William Poole, Professor of Economics and Director, Center for the Study of Financial Markets and Institutions, Brown University

Brian E. Roberts, Assistant Professor of Government, University of Texas, Austin

V. Vance Roley, Ranier National Bank Professor of Banking and Finance, University of Washington

Juliet B. Schor, Assistant Professor of Economics, Harvard University

Robert Schweitzer, Associate Professor of Economics, University of Delaware

Harinder Singh, Assistant Professor of Economics, San Diego State University

Elmus Wicker, Professor of Economics, University of Indiana

Thomas D. Willett, Professor of Economics, Claremont Graduate School and Claremont McKenna College

CHAPTER 1

Introduction

THOMAS MAYER

There are two classic definitions of economics: Alfred Marshall's "a study of mankind in the ordinary business of life" (Marshall 1947, p. 1), and Lionell Robbins's "the allocation of scarce resources among competing ends" (Robbins 1935, pp. 12–15) Marshall focused on the questions that economists try to answer, whereas Robbins focused on the tools they have available.[1] For better or for worse, Robbins's definition won out. But *this* book is Marshallian. It stresses the practical problems that demand answers, rather than those problems that can readily be resolved by the economist's tools. Although the authors of the various chapters in this book – most of whom are economists – use the maximizing model of economic analysis, their focus is on understanding Fed behavior, rather than on refining the tools of economic analysis. They are very much aware that these tools are means to an end, rather than ends in themselves. Hence, they refuse to bypass important economic problems simply because the applicable tools lack elegance and cannot provide rigorously derived answers. Such a problem-oriented focus is now a minority approach among academic economists and hence needs justification.

The problems that fall under the rubric of monetary policy are diverse. Some are problems of economic theory or econometrics, such as the optimal inflation rate or the controllability of the monetary growth rate. These problems rightly receive much discussion in the professional journals, discussion that obviously is necessary to formulate a correct monetary policy. But though such discussion is necessary, it is not sufficient. To gain a complete picture of any government policy, one must also consider the political milieu in which the policy is carried out. Thus, one may recommend one policy if policy-makers are altruistic and open to sound advice from a competent staff, but quite a different policy if they are concerned primarily with their own power and prestige, or if they are ignorant of economics and are unwilling to take the advice of their staff. Hence, to recommend an appropriate policy, one must know the characteristics of the policy-makers as well as the technicalities of policy.

This presents economists with several alternatives. One is to discuss only those aspects of monetary policy for which rigorous answers can be derived. They can then make authoritative statements about particular aspects of monetary policy, but having nothing to say about other important aspects of monetary policy, they can make no statements about monetary policy as a whole. Such self-restraint by economists would certainly be a defensible position.

Defensible, yes, but hardly realistic. Nearly all monetary economists make judgments about monetary policy as a whole. The public, imbued with Marshall's definition of economics, asks economists practical questions about monetary policy, that is, questions requiring knowledge of many aspects of monetary policy, not just questions about those formal problems that economics can resolve unequivocally.

But if economists therefore address broad questions about monetary policy, then they must study, as best they can, all relevant aspects of monetary policy, or else seek the aid of political scientists. However, economists usually act quite differently. There is now a tradition in economics of treating practical problems in the following way: Those components that can be analyzed rigorously, perhaps by formulating them as game-theory problems, are given painstaking and rigorous attention, but the other components are more or less dismissed by arm-waving. It seems as though the familiar principle that a chain is no stronger than its weakest link is turned upside down, as though it were more important to strengthen further the already strong parts of an argument rather than its weaker parts. The result is that, as Herbert Stein (1987, p. 8) has put it, "on many questions of economic policy there is no bridge between theory and decision. Travel between theory and decision is not by bridge but by flight of fancy."

The debates about monetarist policy recommendations illustrate this point. Monetarists have advocated that the Fed should focus on a single variable: the growth rate of money. That has puzzled many Keynesians, who have developed models that demonstrate conclusively that it is better for the Fed to look at many variables rather than just at a single variable. But these models assume that the Fed behaves efficiently and that its policy is not influenced by political pressures, or by the Fed's own bureaucratic interests and aspirations. And it is just those assumptions that monetarists deny. Similarly, the rule that would prescribe a stable monetary growth rate often is criticized as though monetarists were arguing that an efficient central bank, devoted entirely to the public interest, cannot be stabilizing. But that is not what monetarists have actually said. Friedman (Modigliani and Friedman 1977) has stated that "the real argument" for stable money growth "is at least as much political as it is economic." And Karl Brunner (1981) has written that "we should not expect that a monetary authority will naturally pursue the optimal social benefits achievable with cleverly designed stabilization policies." Yet their critics have been reluctant to venture outside the confines of rigorous economic analysis and have thereby ignored much of the monetarist case.[2] Is it any wonder that this debate has become a dialogue of the deaf?[3]

The prevailing disregard for how the Fed actually functions is well illustrated by some studies that at first glance might seem to be exceptions to the rule. In recent years, many papers have used the time-inconsistency principle to argue that discretionary policy is inflationary and undesirable. But that literature simply assumes that the Fed wants output to exceed the amount that agents would supply in equilibrium.[4] It makes that assumption because the level of output that is optimal for each agent as a supplier of productive services is less than the optimal level from a social point of view.

But does the Fed know – and take into account – that equilibrium output is too low? Anyone reading the Federal Open Market Committee (FOMC) minutes will look in vain for such a sophisticated notion. The standard – and usually valid – reply to such an argument based on archives is to say that we should test hypotheses by their implications rather than by their descriptive realism. If the Fed behaves as though it wants to increase equilibrium output, then the fact that it does not actually think in those terms is irrelevant.

But where is the evidence from the implications? The hypothesis implies that the Fed follows an inflationary policy, and so it did in the 1960s and 1970s. But there are many other factors that might explain why monetary policy was then inflationary. And, more seriously, how does the hypothesis explain that monetary policy was not inflationary in the peacetime years between 1920 and 1965 and has been more or less disinflationary since 1980? As Sheffrin (1987) has pointed out, the more specific implications of the hypothesis, such as that inflation is more likely when government debt is high, also do not buttress the hypothesis. Hence, despite their technical virtuosity, the numerous models that have applied the time-inconsistency analysis to monetary policy have added little to our knowledge about Fed behavior.[5]

This book seeks to improve on such a casual treatment of the Fed's motivation by paying attention to the political and bureaucratic context in which monetary policy is made. Some of these issues lend themselves to formal modeling and to econometric testing, but many do not. These have to be treated to some extent outside the positivistic framework that has become the accepted method in economics. That is unfortunate, because positivistic methods are more reliable than the more impressionistic methods that had to be used in some of the chapters in this volume.[6] But surely knowledge about the Fed that does not meet all the positivistic criteria can still be better than the arbitrary assumptions and mere assertions about Fed behavior that often are appended to formal models in the hope of making them policy-relevant. Whether or not studies of the Fed that fail to meet all the positivistic criteria result in "scientific" knowledge is not a central issue – particularly because philosophers of science have not succeeded in drawing an acceptable line between science and nonscience (Caldwell 1982). Surely it is better to provide the best evidence one can than to analyze half of the problem rigorously and dismiss the other half by arm-waving, in an apparent belief that if one cannot be rigorous then one might as well say anything that comes to mind.

In most of economics one can assume that the decision-makers seek to maximize profits, and one can then forecast their actions by seeing what will maximize their profits. There is no need to get entangled in their thought processes. Suppose, for example, that somehow a company president thinks that to maximize profits he should set price equal to twice marginal cost, regardless of the elasticity of demand. Despite this, his firm will not charge twice marginal cost for long; if it tried to do so, it would soon be replaced by a firm that would know better.

But, for three reasons, focusing on the action that will maximize profits will not work as well when analyzing the Fed as it does for the private sector. First, the Fed does not have owners who provide it with an incentive to maximize profits.[7] Indeed, it is difficult to determine what the Fed does maximize. Second, though the Fed may maximize its autonomy and prestige, these are not quantified as easily as are a firm's profits. Third, firms that do not maximize profits usually are driven out of business. But no such Darwinian process applies to the Fed. None of this means that the analysis of self-interested maximizing behavior is entirely inapplicable to the Fed, but it does mean that in studying the Fed, the heuristic rule of "look for the point of maximum profit or utility," though useful, is not as useful as it is in studying the private sector.

An additional difference between analyzing the Fed and analyzing the private sector is that we study the Fed to see whether one of the Fed's main products, discretionary monetary policy, has a positive or a negative value. When studying a firm, we usually do not ask about the value of its product; we let its customers decide. But in the case of the Fed, *we* are the customers, or, more precisely, the customers' advisors, and hence have to evaluate its policy. Ideally, we would evaluate it by determining directly whether or not it has stabilized real income and prices. But that question is difficult to answer directly. Hence, it is useful to supplement any direct test of the Fed's policy with an indirect test that looks at the Fed's motives and at how it formulates policy. It is therefore not surprising that even such a firm believer in the methodology of "as if" as Milton Friedman has analyzed the Fed's motives (Friedman 1982; Friedman and Schwartz 1963). Accordingly, most of the chapters in this book deal with the making of monetary policy, that is, with the Fed's motives, with the political constraints on its policy-making, and with the Fed's efficiency in formulating policy.

The chapters

In Chapter 2, Thomas Willett discusses methodological problems. His position is eclectic; both formal modeling and institutionally oriented work on Fed behavior are useful. Much of his chapter deals with the application of public-choice theory to the Fed. He points out that this approach is much broader than simply the claim that the Fed tries to maximize its own welfare. Though critical of narrow versions of public-choice theory, Willett suggests that Fed behavior is much affected by the self-interest of its political masters.

A standard way of analyzing Fed behavior is to estimate the Fed's "reaction function" by regressing some indicator of the Fed's policy on variables relating to the goals with which the Fed is charged. The next two chapters deal with this topic. In Chapter 3, Salwa Khoury evaluates the numerous Fed reaction functions that have been fitted. Because it is not clear exactly what goals the Fed pursues, various reaction functions have used different variables. They have also been fitted over various periods and with different techniques. Khoury, using a specification search, asks two questions: First, does a useful consensus emerge? Second, are Fed reaction functions robust when subjected to a specification search? In each case the answer is disappointing.

Most Fed reaction functions implicitly assume that the Fed tries to maximize the public's welfare. Gerald Epstein and Juliet Schor challenge that assumption. They consider a reaction function that assumes that the Fed is concerned with the profits of banks and nonfinancial firms, rather than with the public's welfare. Hence, it tries to hold down wage pressures. Their results show that the conventional Fed reaction function is not the only way Fed behavior can be explained; Marxian theory also provides a consistent explanation.

If the traditional reaction-function approach is questionable, is there another way one can infer the Fed's policy? In Chapter 5, William

Melton and Vance Roley suggest that there is. They point out that the market employs Fed-watchers, many of them former Fed officials, who should know what the Fed is doing. The forecasts of these Fed-watchers move interest rates. Hence, Roley and Melton use the behavior of interest rates to track major changes in Fed policy since October 1979.

One cannot understand Fed behavior if one assumes that the Fed is totally autonomous, so that its behavior always represents its own policy choices. To some extent, as Paul Samuelson once remarked, the Fed is a "prisoner of its independence." Accordingly, the next six chapters deal with the extent to which the Fed is independent.

In Chapter 6, Michael Munger and Brian Roberts review the literature on political influences on the Fed. After considering the application of public-choice theory to the Fed, they go on to discuss the evidence regarding the Fed's ability to withstand pressure from the president and from Congress. They find two weaknesses in this literature: One is that an author who finds one type of political influence tends to ignore the influences found by others. The second is that little attention has been paid to the channels through which political influence might operate.

Many economists believe that though the Fed bows to political pressure on occasion, usually it is free to do what is best. But Robert Hetzel argues that the political system is constantly trying to use monetary policy to redistribute income, while the Fed resists. This has three implications: Politicians impose implicit rather than explicit constraints on the Fed. Second, the trend rate for inflation depends not on the mechanics of monetary control but on the demand for inflation. Third, the Fed adopts those procedures that will inhibit political pressure.

Does the president's power over the Fed result in a political business cycle? As Beck points out in Chapter 8, the evidence is conflicting. If one looks at the monetary growth rate, there is evidence for a political business cycle, but not if one looks at the federal-funds rate. Moreover, a historical review of monetary policy does not suggest a political business cycle. Beck's interpretation is that the Fed does not deliberately expand the money supply prior to elections, but that it accommodates the rising demand for money that often occurs prior to an election.

The Fed is not a part of the administration; as members of Congress often remind it, it is a "creature of Congress." But despite its legal status, most observers believe that the Fed is much more responsive to the administration than to Congress, because Congress is not organized to control it. That view was recently challenged by Kevin Grier. In Chapter 9, Nathaniel Beck reworks Grier's analysis and shows that the more recent data reject Grier's results and restore the traditional view of Congress–Fed relations.

The Fed is hardly a political weakling. James Pierce discusses the sources of the Fed's political strength. They include the Federal Reserve's ability to control monetary policy and influence banking legislation, its use of the discount window, its power over bank holding companies, and the influence of the Federal Reserve Bank directors. Not all of this power has accrued to the Fed just by luck. Pierce shows that the Fed works to increase its power. The Federal Reserve's position concerning deregulation of bank holding companies offers a current example.

Economists often criticize the specific instruments and targets used by the Fed, thus giving the impression that the particular techniques used by the Fed are responsible for our sometimes poor macroeconomic performance. One way to evaluate this is to look at another country with similar central-bank techniques. Cargill and Hutchison find that the Bank of Japan uses similar techniques, but that macroeconomic performance is much better in Japan. They explain this by the fact that the Bank of Japan is not subject to the same political pressures as the Fed.

Political pressure for unsound policies is not the Fed's only problem. Like other organizations, it has internal problems and biases that limit its effectiveness. These are discussed in the next five essays.

Raymond Lombra and Nicholas Karamouzis question that the Fed can operate an effective stabilization policy. Such a policy requires reliable forecasts. Using internal FOMC documents, they show that there have been substantial errors in the FOMC's forecasts of real GNP, the GNP deflator, and the monetary growth rate. Furthermore, the FOMC has given inconsistent Directives to the account manager, vacillated on the importance of its monetary targets, and focused on current conditions instead of future conditions.

Decisions at the Fed are made by a small enough group of policymakers for their individual characteristics to matter. Two different questions can be asked about the influence of these characteristics: First, what determined the dissents that were cast during a particular period? Second, what determined whether or not, and in what direction, a particular member would dissent. These two questions differ. In one case the sample consists of votes casts, and in the other the sample consists of the members who voted. The former tells us what drove dissents during a specific period, and the latter tells us what characteristics tended to make particular members dissent. The chapters by Thomas Havrilesky and Robert Schweitzer and by John Gildea deal with these two problems, respectively.

Thomas Havrilesky and Robert Schweitzer model a bureaucracy in which those who dissent face informal sanctions. Whether an FOMC member dissents more on the side of ease or on the restrictive side depends on how closely his or her career is linked to the central government, which Havrilesky and Schweitzer take to favor inflation. Using eight variables that measure linkage to the government, they show that the data confirm this hypothesis.

By contrast, John Gildea deals with the characteristics that make a particular FOMC member vote on one side of a split decision rather than the other. He incorporates career variables and variables pertaining to a member's social background into a politicoeconomic model and finds that a governor's party affiliations can influence dissents, as do the following: a partial-term appointment, an Ivy League education, and a Ph.D. in economics. Whether a member's prior career was at the Fed, elsewhere in the government, or in the private sector also matters.

Harinder Singh and Roger Frantz use X-efficiency theory to analyze Fed behavior. They point out that X-inefficiency is prevalent throughout the economy and that specific conditions inducing policy-makers to adopt a "muddling-through" or X-inefficiency strategy exist at the Fed. Using an X-efficiency framework, they are not surprised that the Fed does not make efficient use of its staff and that policy-makers' prior careers influence their decisions. The Fed's "slack" can also help to explain its proclivity for inappropriate or outdated procedures.

Income and power are not the only arguments in utility functions. In Chapter 16 I explore the implications for Fed policy-making of the assumption that FOMC members wish to minimize the cognitive dissonance that results from realizing that their policy has done harm. This can help to explain why the Fed has multiple goals, makes policy atheoretically, minimizes signs of dissension, tends to stick with its policies, overemphasizes interest rates, and responds in a questionable way to the existence of a lag in monetary policy.

The previously cited chapters discuss Fed policy-making in general. Two other chapters support the findings of many of the preceding chapters with case studies. One examines a particular tool of monetary policy, and the other deals with a specific episode of Fed policy.

Does the discount window – the Federal Reserve's oldest policy tool – have a useful policy role, or should the Fed use it only for the lender-of-last-resort function? William Poole argues that the Fed can control bank reserves more effectively through open-market operations than through the discount window and shows that the announcement effects of discount-rate changes have typically been mistimed. The Fed, he argues, uses the discount window to exercise covert control over banks and to deflect political criticism of its monetary policy.[8]

Unlike the other chapters, Elmus Wicker's Chapter 18 deals with a specific episode: the development of the Fed's thinking in the 1950s. Going back that far has an advantage – our view of those events is less distorted by the passion of current debates. Wicker provides a careful analysis of the behavior of money at a time when the Fed recovered from the trauma of bond pegging and developed its postwar doctrines. He shows that the pro-cyclical behavior of the monetary growth rate resulted from the Fed's failure to distinguish between the supply and demand for free reserves.

Given the problems and pressures that beset Fed policy-making, can, and should, discretionary policy be eliminated? The chapters in this volume provide considerable evidence regarding whether or not that would be a desirable reform. But if that is judged a desirable reform, is it attainable? That is discussed in the final chapter.

In Chapter 19, Edward Kane shows that both politicians and Fed officials have incentives that result in inappropriate Fed policy. Specifically, the current system allows both politicians and Fed officials to avoid adequate accountability. But to advocate that discretionary policy be replaced by a rule is insufficient, because the players have incentives to keep the current game going. Advocates of a rule should therefore look for ways of making a shift to a rule desirable for politicians and Fed officials.

Conclusion

Many, though not all, of these chapters deal with aspects of monetary policy that many economists treat as outside the purview of economics. But a reading of these essays will show that discussion of these topics can be beneficial, that they need not be left to journalists.

Beyond that, this book suggests that neither a simple public-interest interpretation of Fed behavior nor a crude public-choice interpretation will suffice. The Fed does not make policy to maximize public welfare subject to only one major constraint – the technical difficulty of forecasting. It must bend to political pressures, and its policy-makers are subject to biases and limitations on rational behavior. The Fed's concern with its own welfare, stressed by public-choice theorists, is only one of several serious constraints on its policy-making.

Notes

1 This distinction is similar to George Stigler's separation of economic ideas into those "that arise out of the critical examination of the ideas of other economists, and those that seek directly to explain some body of empirical phenomena" (Breit and Spencer 1988, p. 103).

2 Monetarists, too, can be faulted for not discussing their political assumptions in sufficient detail. For a notable exception, see Milton Friedman (1982). In

general, monetarists have relied heavily on the errors that the Fed has made in the past and on the public-choice critique of the Fed, which argues that the Fed is distracted from its stabilization task by its wish to maintain or extend its power, prestige, and autonomy. That approach is discussed in Chapter 15 by Singh and Frantz.

3 For further discussion, see Thomas Mayer (1987).

4 Output is below its socially optimal level because agents do not obtain the full value of their contributions to output. The rise in taxes and the loss of government subsidies, such as unemployment insurance payments, as incomes rise drive a "wedge" between the value of agents' outputs and their net rewards. The term "time inconsistency" comes from the fact that inflationary policies raise output only temporarily. After some time, output falls back to its previous level, while the inflation persists. At that time, the Fed wishes that it had not initiated the inflationary policy. Apart from the objections raised in the text, the argument that time inconsistency induces the Fed to adopt inflationary policies is open to the criticism that the Fed then should know that such a policy is bad (Leijonhufvud 1986). And, as Taylor (1983, p. 125) has pointed out, "in the Barro-Gordon inflation-unemployment model, the superiority of the zero inflation policy is just as obvious to people as the well-recognized patent problem is in the real world. It is therefore difficult to see why the zero inflation policy would not be adopted in such a world." Moreover, if emulation plays a significant role in the utility function, so that my welfare is lowered by an increase in my neighbor's wealth, then equilibrium output may exceed the optimal output despite the wedge, so that the Fed might have no incentive to stimulate output beyond the level desired by agents.

5 By no means all time-inconsistency models imply that the Fed adopts inflationary policies. Some of them argue that the Fed's concern about its reputation as an inflation fighter prevents it from adopting time-inconsistent policies. Can one say that these models are confirmed because in most years the Fed has not followed inflationary policies? No, because that could be due not to the Fed's concern about its reputation but to its not knowing that equilibrium output is below optimal output. The applicability of time-inconsistency models to the Fed must be based either on evidence that the Fed thinks that way or on evidence that it acts as though it did. And neither type of evidence is available.

6 This is not necessarily true of the methods that masquerade as positivism in economics. See Mark Blaug (1980) and Mayer (1980). The methodology used in some of the chapters is Weber's "verstehen," that is, to imagine oneself as the policy-maker or agent whose behavior one wants to understand.

7 Some economists have argued that the Fed does maximize profits, or something closely akin to profits. Thomas Willett's Chapter 2 evaluates that argument.

8 Poole's Chapter 17 is the only one that has already been published.

References

Blaug, Mark (1980). *The Methodology of Economics.* New York: Cambridge University Press.

Breit, William, and Spencer, Roger (1988). *Lives of the Laureates.* Cambridge, Mass.: MIT Press.

Brunner, Karl (1981). "The Case Against Monetary Activism," *Lloyd's Bank Review,* 139(January):95–106.

Caldwell, Bruce (1982). *Beyond Positivism.* London: George Allen & Unwin.

Friedman, Milton (1982). "Monetary Policy and Practice," *Journal of Money, Credit and Banking,* 14(February 1982):98–118.

Friedman, Milton, and Schwartz, Anna (1963). *A Monetary History of the United States.* Princeton University Press.

Leijonhufvud, Axel (1986). "Rules with Some Discretion," in Colin Campbell and William Dougan (eds.), *Alternative Monetary Regimes,* pp. 36–43. Baltimore: Johns Hopkins University Press.

Marshall, Alfred (1947). *Principles of Economics.* London: Macmillan.

Mayer, Thomas (1980). "Economics as a Hard Science: Realistic Goal or Wishful Thinking," *Economic Inquiry,* 18:165–178.

Mayer, Thomas (1987). "The Debate about Monetarist Policy Recommendations," *Kredit und Kapital,* 20:281–302.

Modigliani, Franco, and Friedman, Milton (1977). "The Monetarist Controversy: A Seminar Discussion," Federal Reserve Bank of San Francisco, *Economic Review* (Spring Supplement).

Robbins, Lionell (1935). *An Essay on the Nature and Significance of Economic Science.* London: Macmillan.

Sheffrin, Steven (1987). "Game Theory and Positive Theories of Policy-making," unpublished manuscript.

Stein, Herbert (1987). *Memorandum.* American Enterprise Institute for Public Policy Research, 52(Winter):8.

Taylor, John (1983). "Comments," *Journal of Monetary Economics,* 12:123–6.

CHAPTER 2

Studying the Fed: toward a broader public-choice perspective

THOMAS D. WILLETT WITH EDWARD KEEN

Academic research on the behavior of the Federal Reserve System has accelerated rapidly in recent years. The spread of public-choice analysis has strongly challenged the traditional public-interest view of economic policy-making, opening up exciting new areas of research. In addition, the distinction between the effects of anticipated and unanticipated policy actions emphasized by rational-expectations theory has stimulated additional interest in estimating policy reaction functions.[1] Likewise, the politics of economic policies, both domestic and international, has become a popular topic of research for political scientists. The small band of monetary economists who have long engaged in Fed-watching now has considerable company. This has been a very healthy development.

Monetary policy is determined by the interactions of the preferences and personalities of key government officials with formal and informal institutional structures and the pressures of interest groups and market behavior. This is a highly complex process, and as Tom Mayer emphasizes in his Introduction, its study requires institutional as well as formal mathematical and econometric analysis.

We can learn a great deal from the formal modeling of limited aspects of even very complex situations, but it is essential to keep in mind the distinction between the argument that a particular factor has significant explanatory power and the treatment of that factor as if it were the only important consideration. Both rational-expectations and public-choice theorists have at times failed to be clear on this, dismissing as irrelevant considerations that may have considerable explanatory power.

In public-choice analysis, the tendency of some authors to equate self-interest only with economic gain is a case in point. It is also essential to

Willett is primary author of this chapter. Keen co-authored the section "Some evidence on the political-pressure view." We are indebted to King Banaian, Tom Havrilesky, Mike Kulwein, Steve Marks, Brian Moehring, Clas Wihlborg, and especially Aris Protopapadakis and Tom Mayer for many helpful comments and suggestions on an earlier version of this chapter and to John McArthur for research assistance.

pay careful attention to the institutional environment within which actions are taken. Given current patterns of professional training, such institutional analysis is more natural for political scientists than for economists. It is essential, however, for economists that we not let our increasingly sophisticated technical tools blind us to the traditional interest of economics in understanding the importance of the institutional environment in influencing behavior. This is indeed just an application of two of our most basic truths – incentives matter, and to understand the behavior of individuals we need to examine the incentives facing them, not some larger collectivity.

One of the major contributions of public-choice analysis is its emphasis on the distinction between individual and collective costs and benefits. Unfortunately, however, this insight often has been overlooked in rational-expectations analysis and even in some applications of public-choice analysis. This chapter begins with a brief overview of the public-choice approach and a critique of examples of overly narrow applications of public-choice analysis to the study of the behavior of the Federal Reserve. It then illustrates how the public-choice approach can be used in a broader manner. It is argued that direct rent-seeking by key decision-makers in the Federal Reserve plays relatively little role in the formulation of monetary policy, but that rent-seeking and reelection-seeking by others place strong pressures on the Fed and thus have a substantial indirect influence on monetary policy. Thus, we need a more complex formulation of Fed policy-making than the traditional models of Fed preference maximization subject to the constraints set by the operation of the economy.

It is also suggested that greater attention should be directed to the importance of interest-rate concerns and congressional influence than has been typical in recent literature. Some preliminary empirical support for such emphasis is presented. The chapter concludes with a brief discussion of the implications of positive-political-economy research on determinants of monetary policy for normative analysis of proposals for institutional reforms.

An overview of public-choice analysis

The very success of public-choice analysis in capturing the attention of a wide range of scholars has made it increasingly difficult to give a simple, accurate description of just what public-choice analysis is. Although all public-choice analysis emphasizes distributional considerations, there is no single public-choice theory of government to be contrasted with the public-interest view. For example, though much public-choice analysis makes use of models in which outcomes are determined by the median voter, and that approach is adopted in many models of the political business cycle, there are also many varieties of models in which there can be considerable divergence between voter preferences and policy outcomes.[2] The electoral mechanism is not sufficient to allow effective monitoring of all issues by the public. Furthermore, interest groups have much stronger incentives to make their views known than does the typical voter. Not only may organized interests in both the private and public sectors have disproportionate influence, but rational ignorance on the part of the typical voter may generate popular pressure for the government to adopt policies that will harm the public's longer-term interests.

There is considerable disagreement about the relative importance of various elements in the operation of the political process, yet relatively little systematic empirical research has focused on this issue. It is not clear, for example, whether institutional reforms that give the average voter greater influence should be expected to generate more or less inflation. In the model of government revenue maximization developed by Brennan and Buchanan (1980), and in Friedman's critique (1982) of the Fed for having no bottom line, an increase in accountability to the public would reduce inflation. On the other hand, in models of the political business cycle it is the desire for reelection that pressures the government to inflate. Many popular explanations of government policy-making take for granted some particular model of the political process that is in fact still subject to considerable scholarly controversy. It is not enough to recognize that politics matters. We must give careful attention to the ways in which politics works.

Most public-choice models begin with the assumption that politics is driven by economic interests. Though in that respect they are similar in spirit to Marxist theories of the state, public-choice models typically make quite different assumptions about the nature of economic interests and see class as a much less important element in the formulation of active interest groups. Recent work has emphasized, however, that interests may be far broader than simply economic income. For example, ideological concerns can be important. Frey and Schneider have shown the importance of developing a synthesis of the original models of the political business cycle, based only on concerns with reelection, and the partisan models having ideological or class-based motives.[3]

A critique of some misapplications of public-choice analysis

There is much to be said for starting with simple theories and complicating them only as needed on a case-by-case basis. For example, models based purely on economic rent-seeking have been able to offer considerable insight into the formulation of trade policies, and simple bureaucratic theories of budget maximization do help to explain the growth of governments. However, in my judgment, recent efforts to explain the behavior of the Federal Reserve in these terms have been much less successful.[4] Although some studies did find a significant statistical link between monetary expansion and Fed expenditures, further testing indicated that the relationship was not robust.[5] Though the Fed is funded from its own revenues, and those do tend to rise with monetary expansion, a high and variable portion of those revenues is turned over to the Treasury. As revealed in the annual reports of the Board of Governors, the expenses of the Federal Reserve System averaged less than 10 percent of its income over the period 1970 to 1985. The percentage varied from a high of 10.9 percent in 1972 to a low of 6.2 percent in 1981 around an overall downward trend.

Because there is now no direct relation at the margin between the Fed's monetary expansion and its access to funds for its own activities, such consideration should not be expected to have influenced monetary policy in recent years. Furthermore, though bureaucratic incentives for budget expansion may well be important to managers within the Federal Reserve System, such a consideration seems unlikely to have much influence on the power and prestige of the top officials who make monetary policy, and it certainly does not affect their salaries. Thus, it seems doubtful that bureaucratic budget concerns would have a significant influence on monetary policy under the current U.S. institutional arrangements.

A potentially more relevant link between revenue "needs" and monetary policy is the seigniorage that could be shared with the government as a whole. With no election constraint, a self-interested government might be expected to seek revenue-maximizing rates of inflation. On the other hand, a public-interest-motivated government, or one constrained by an informed electorate, should seek the so-called optimal rate of inflation: the rate that equates the marginal cost of raising government revenue from the inflation tax with that of other forms of taxation. According to traditional calculations, the United States has not approached revenue-maximizing rates of inflation, and indeed has not even inflated enough on optimum tax grounds.[6] From this perspective, the argument that the Fed is dominated by inflationary bias is open to serious empirical challenge. The standard literature on inflationary finance is seriously misleading, however, because of its typical assumption of perfectly anticipated inflation. If, as a good deal of empirical evidence suggests, higher rates of inflation tend to be more variable and generate more uncertainty, then these additional uncertainty costs must be taken into account, and calculations of revenue-maximizing and optimal rates of inflation fall dramatically. From this broader perspective, the optimal rate of inflation for the United States probably is not positive (Banaian, McClure, and Willett 1989). This restores the plausibility of the argument that a serious inflationary bias exists.

Direct versus indirect influences of rent-seeking: the Fed as a passive responder to political pressures

Rent-seeking in the narrow economic sense seems to have relatively little direct influence on Federal Reserve decision-making on monetary policy. Power, prestige, excitement, and fulfillment of a sense of public duty are much more important motivations for top Fed officials. This does not mean, however, that rent-seeking by others has little influence on monetary policy.

The institutional independence of the Federal Reserve from political pressures is far from complete. The president holds important powers of appointment and reappointment, and the current institutional arrangements are legislative provisions, not constitutional provisions. Such legislation is not lightly changed, but the possibility is not so remote that Fed officials have felt free to ignore signals coming from Congress and the executive branch. Ironically, in order to maintain the Fed's independence, Fed officials often have bowed to political pressure. Furthermore, many of the aspects of human psychology discussed in Tom Mayer's chapter in this volume generate a tendency for decision-makers to respond, at least partially, to lobbying, even when direct threats or rewards are not possible. It would take men and women of steel not to be affected by the various pressures brought to bear on the Fed.

Technical studies typically model the Fed as maximizing its (or society's) utility function with respect to inflation, unemployment, and so forth, in the face of various shocks and subject to the constraints imposed by the operation of the economy. A simple public-choice or bureaucratic-theory approach would replace the macroeconomic-oriented objective function with the self-interested utility function of the individual decision-maker. For key Federal Reserve decision-makers, however, their most direct interest in monetary policy decisions may well be the feeling of doing right. This is subject to political as well as economic constraints and realities, however. In this view, the direct utility function of the Fed would be replaced by a function reflecting a weighted average of the objectives of a much broader set of groups and individuals, including the Fed officials themselves. (For an example of analysis along these lines, see the chapter by Hetzel in this volume.) The study of the objectives of this broader set of actors and of the factors that affect their relative influence should be one of the major facets of research on the political economy of the Fed.

In this view, the Fed will be highly political, although typically in a public-spirited, nonpartisan manner. One of the major results of such political pressures is that the Fed will act with a shorter time horizon than if it were unconstrained. Another is that it will treat variables such as interest rates (and also, increasingly, exchange rates) at least partially as objectives, rather than as policy instruments or market prices. Such considerations will interact with each other and with concerns about employment to generate an inflationary bias in decision-making.[7] In the recent literature on time inconsistency, the Fed is assumed to actively generate inflationary surprises to stimulate over-full employment.[8] In practice, the Fed is likely motivated much more by concerns with avoiding high unemployment and high interest rates. In both views, an inflationary bias results from the conflict between short-run and longer-run maximization, but in time-inconsistency models the Fed plays an initiating role in generating inflation, whereas in the view sketched here, the Fed plays primarily an accommodative or sustaining role (Willett and Banaian 1988a).

Given such circumstances, concerns about interest rates can produce politically motivated fiscal behavior by elected officials to induce an election cycle in monetary policy even though the Fed is completely nonpartisan (Beck 1987; Havrilesky 1988b; Laney and Willett 1983). Although such concerns about interest rates frequently are emphasized by economists who have studied the Fed closely (Kane 1980; Poole 1987), they have been downplayed relative to inflation and unemployment in many political models of macroeconomic policy, especially in the literature on political business cycles. Studies that have found a political money cycle in the postwar United States (Grier 1987) have been challenged for finding peaks of monetary expansion much too close to election dates to have the maximum desired effects on employment and output (Beck 1987). Concern with avoiding interest-rate increases prior to elections could account for such timing of monetary expansion.

The likelihood of fiscally-induced election cycles has also been challenged on the grounds that frequently the majority in one or both houses of Congress is not from the president's party (Beck 1987). In such cases there would not be a convergence of partisan interests to generate a political election cycle. However, for many members of Congress, interest in one's own reelection may be stronger than interest in whether or not a member of one's party wins the presidency. Indeed, in the most notorious case of a political business cycle – the Nixon reelection –

Democratic congressmen joined administration officials in pressuring the Fed for monetary ease (Beck 1982).

Emphasis on the importance of Congress is somewhat unfashionable today. Most of the recent literature on the political economy of the Fed argues that the influence of the executive branch is much more important.[9] The executive branch certainly has more expertise in monetary policy than does Congress and has much more frequent contact with Fed decision-makers. Thus, it has a more consistent short-term influence (Havrilesky 1988a). Congress, however, often operates according to the "fire-alarm" principle (McCubbins and Schwartz 1984). Members of Congress focus attention on monetary policy only occasionally, but when they do so, as, for example, when interest rates are "high" before elections, they have considerable clout. As is stressed in the principal–agent literature, an effective agent will not need to be signaled continually. The agent will attempt to learn its principal's wishes and avoid situations in which serious complaints could occur. Because the Fed is influenced by a wide range of pressures, even a fully efficient Fed would not be expected always to manage to avoid annoying its congressional masters, but neither is it likely to consistently ignore pressures from that direction.

It is difficult to determine precisely the influence of Congress on highly responsive bureaus, because the absence of public signaling could reflect either an efficient bureau or an indifferent Congress. We can, however, look for changes in bureau behavior in response to changes in the composition of the power structure of Congress (Grier 1988). Another type of indirect test for the Fed is presented in the following section. The political-pressure view implies that interest rates will tend to be held down before elections. We find some evidence of this occurring before congressional as well as presidential elections. This evidence is at least consistent with the view that more attention should be paid to the role of congressional influences on monetary policy-making.

Some evidence on the political-pressures view: interest-rate behavior prior to elections

Both theoretical and empirical studies of election cycles have paid little attention to the role of interest rates. A notable exception is a study by Beck (1987), who did not find evidence for an election cycle in the federal-funds rate. Here we present alternative evidence that does find an election cycle in Treasury-bill rates. These contradictory findings suggest the need for further research looking at the behavior of a broader array of interest rates.

Besides the choice of interest rates, our study also differs from that of

Beck in the specification of our interest-rate variable. Given the substantial changes in the levels of interest rates over the past several decades, one needs a measure for the height of interest rates that will take into account changes in perception over time of the "normal" level of interest rates. For example, a nominal interest rate of 5 percent would clearly have been seen as high in the 1950s, but low in the inflationary 1970s. This issue of the benchmark for measuring improvement or worsening of economic variables for political analysis is a general problem applying to inflation and unemployment as well (Schneider and Frey 1988).

Beck used quarterly changes in interest rates as his measure. We believe that gave too much weight to the most recent past. Consider, for example, a strategy that would dictate lowering interest rates for the six months before an election. By Beck's measure, no election effect would be recorded, because there would have been no change from the previous quarter. A still crude but better proxy is the quarterly change in interest rate from the average level for the preceding three quarters. (Future research should consider even longer periods for the norm and also should look for possible asymmetries in interest-rate behavior.) Even using this simple measure, however, we do find some evidence of a tendency for lower interest rates before both presidential and congressional elections.

From monthly observations of the 90-day Treasury-bill rate, the quarterly average rate was computed from 1954:1 to 1984:4 (year:quarter). We then generated a variable DQTBILL, which is the difference between the quarter's T-bill rate and its simple average over the prior three quarters.

We ran ordinary-least-squares (OLS) regressions of DQTBILL on a constant and a dummy variable ELECT, which has a value of 1 for the quarters of interest:

$$\text{DQTBILL} = a + b^{*}\text{ELECT}$$

The coefficient of ELECT measures the difference between the mean of DQTBILL for election quarters and for nonelection quarters. The null hypothesis Ho: $b \geq 0$ is that interest rates have no tendency to be lower prior to elections. Rejecting the null hypothesis would suggest that the Fed is not isolated from political concerns about interest rates prior to an election.

It was not clear how far before an election one should expect lower interest rates, so several specifications of ELECT were tested. In some specifications, borderline observations were excluded from the estimation procedures to more clearly distinguish between election and nonelection periods. Results of the OLS regressions are shown in Table 2.1.

Table 2.1. *Behavior of Treasury-bill rates prior to elections: 1954:1 to 1984:4*

Regression	Election quarters: Included	Election quarters: Excluded	Estimates of coefficients: *a*	Estimates of coefficients: *b*	Log of likelihood (LL)
1	3,4 P,C	–	0.2245 (1.836)[a]	−0.3272 (−1.338)	−187.075
2	3 P,C	4 P	0.2245 (1.925)	−0.4856 (−1.574)	−158.560
3	2,3 P,C	–	0.2716 (2.247)	−0.5158 (−2.133)[b]	−185.708
4	3,4 P	3,4 C	0.2245 (1.924)	−0.1732 (−0.5769)	−160.138
5	3,4 P	1,2,3,4 C	0.2912 (2.240)	−0.2400 (−0.7696)	−141.073
6	2,3 P	2,3 C	0.2004 (1.7624)	−0.4329 (−1.390)	−187.004
7	3 P	3,4 C; 4 P	0.2245 (1.943)	−0.4799 (−1.187)	−147.001

Notes: P and C stand for presidential and congressional election years, respectively, and 1–4 are quarters. For example, in regression 2, ELECT = 1 for the 3rd quarters of both presidential and congressional election years. Observations for the 4th quarters of presidential years were thrown out. Data are quarterly averages of monthly 90-day Treasury-bill rates taken from series FYGM3 in the CITIBASE data tape.
[a]*t* ratios are in parentheses.
[b]Significant at the 5% level.

Regression 1 dummies for the 3rd and 4th quarters of both presidential and congressional election years. Although the estimated coefficient of ELECT (hereafter *b*) is not significant at conventional levels, the mean of DQTBILL is positive for nonelection quarters, but negative for election quarters. Regression 2 dummies only for the 3rd quarter of each election year and excludes observations from the 4th quarter of each presidential election year, because elections occur in the first half of the quarter. Our estimate of *b* is still negative and larger than in regression 1, and is closer to conventional significance. Regression 3 looks at the 2nd and 3rd quarters combined. Here the results become significant at the 5 percent level.

In regressions 4–7 we investigate the hypothesis that the cycle is stronger for presidential than for congressional elections by looking at the behavior around presidential elections only. None of the specifications supports the hypothesis. Although the estimated coefficients remain consistently negative, in each regression the *b* coefficient is smaller than in the corresponding equation for both congressional and presidential elections, and the *t* statistics are lower. Although we would not want to draw the inference that congressional elections are more important than presidential elections, these results certainly suggest that congressional elections should not be ignored.

Concluding remarks: some normative implications

Developing a better understanding of the nature of Federal Reserve decision-making is important for a number of purposes. Not the least of these is its relevance for evaluating proposals for institutional reforms to improve monetary policy-making. As Edward Kane stresses in his chapter in this volume, political-economy analysis of Fed behavior suggests strong reasons why the Fed is unlikely voluntarily to support fundamental reforms. Concerns of power and prestige combine to make the preservation of substantial scope for discretionary action an important argument in the Fed's utility function.

Were the bureaucratic-budget-enhancement model an accurate depiction of Fed behavior, then removal of the Fed's independence from the executive branch would reduce an important source of inflationary bias. That does not appear to be the case, however. A more complex set of factors generated the accelerating inflation of the 1960s and 1970s, and more fundamental reforms will be required to assure that such inflationary decades do not reoccur (Willett 1988).

Because the Fed wishes to maintain its discretion, reforms can come only from the outside. To design reforms we need to understand Fed motivation. For example, a major problem with proposals to constrain policy outcomes within a range is that if no attention is paid to the constraint until it is hit, serious problems of dynamic instability may result. Willett (1987) argues, however, that within his constraint proposal, the desire to maintain scope for discretion would lead the Fed to begin adjusting its behavior well before the constraints would become binding, thus reducing the likelihood of serious dynamic instability.

Notes

1 In large part because of the types of political-economy considerations discussed in this chapter, these functions often are quite unstable. See Willett et al. (1988) and the chapter by Salwa Khoury in this volume for references to this literature.

2 For a review of a number of major public-choice models and their implications for macroeconomic policy-making, see Willett and Banaian (1988b).
3 This literature is surveyed in Schneider and Frey (1988).
4 A wide variety of both narrow and broader applications of bureaucratic and public-choice theory to monetary policy-making is conveniently collected in Toma and Toma (1986). Particularly important early examples of a broad approach are the papers by Keith Acheson and John Chant reprinted in that volume.
5 See the analysis and references in Banaian et al. (1988).
6 For analysis and references, see McClure and Willett (1988a).
7 For recent discussions and references to the time-inconsistency literature, see Cukierman (1986), Leijonhufvud (1986), Rogoff (1987), and Mayer's chapter in this volume.
8 For further discussion of the role of short time horizons in generating inflationary pressures, see Cagan (1986) and Willett and Banaian (1988a).
9 See, for example, the analysis and references in Nathaniel Beck's chapter in this volume: "Congress and the Fed." Important exceptions to this view include Grier (1988), Wagner (1986), and Hetzel's chapter in this volume.

References

Banaian, King, et al. (1988). "Subordinating the Fed to Political Authorities Won't Control Inflationary Tendencies," in T. D. Willett (ed.), *Political Business Cycles: The Political Economy of Money, Inflation and Unemployment,* pp. 490–505. Durham, N.C.: Duke University Press.

Banaian, King, McClure, J. Harold, Jr., and Willett, Thomas D. (1989). "Inflation Uncertainty Makes the Inflation Tax Non Optimal," Claremont Working Papers.

Barrow, Robert (1986). "Rules versus Discretion," in C. D. Campbell and W. R. Dougan (eds.), *Alternative Monetary Regimes,* pp. 16–30. Baltimore: Johns Hopkins University Press.

Beck, Nathaniel (1982). "Presidential Influence on the Federal Reserve in the 1970's," *American Journal of Political Science,* 26:415–45.

(1987). "Elections and the Fed: Is There a Political Monetary Cycle?" *American Journal of Political Science,* 31(1):194–216.

Brennan, Goeffrey, and Buchanan, James M. (1980). *The Power to Tax: Analytical Foundations of a Fiscal Constitution.* Cambridge University Press.

Cagan, Phillip (1986). "The Conflict Between Short-Run and Long-Run Objectives," in C. D. Campbell and W. R. Dougan (eds.), *Alternative Monetary Regimes,* pp. 31–7. Baltimore: Johns Hopkins University Press.

Campbell, Colin D., and Dougan, William R. (eds.) (1986). *Alternative Monetary Regimes.* Baltimore: Johns Hopkins University Press.

Cukierman, Alex (1986). "Central Bank Behavior and Credibility: Some Recent Theoretical Developments," *Federal Reserve Bank of St. Louis Review* (May):5–17.

Dorn, James A., and Schwartz, Anna (eds.) (1987). *The Search for Stable Money.* University of Chicago Press.

Friedman, Milton (1982). "Monetary Policy: Theory and Practice," *Journal of Money, Credit and Banking,* 14:98–118.

Grier, Kevin B. (1987). "Presidential Elections and Federal Reserve Policy: An Empirical Test," *Southern Economic Journal,* 52(2):475–86.

(1988). "An Agency Model of Congressional–Fed Interaction," paper presented at the 1988 Public Choice Society meeting, March 18–20, San Francisco.

Havrilesky, Thomas (1988a). "Monetary Policy Signalling from the Administration to the Federal Reserve," *Journal of Money, Credit and Banking,* 20(February):83–101.

(1988b). "Electoral Cycles in Economic Policy," *Challenge,* 31(July/August): 14–21.

Kane, Edward J. (1980). "Politics and Fed Policymaking," *Journal of Monetary Economics,* 6:199–211.

Laney, Leroy O., and Willett, Thomas D. (1983). "Presidential Politics, Budget Deficits, and Monetary Policy in the United States, 1960–1976," *Public Choice,* 40(1):53–70.

Leijonhufvud, Axel (1986). "Rules With Some Discretion," in C. D. Campbell and W. R. Dougan (eds.), *Alternative Monetary Regimes,* pp. 38–43. Baltimore: Johns Hopkins University Press.

McClure, J. Harold, Jr., and Willett, Thomas D. (1988). "The Inflation Tax," in T. D. Willett (ed.), *Political Business Cycles: The Political Economy of Money, Inflation and Unemployment,* pp. 177–85. Durham, N.C.: Duke University Press.

(1988b). "Inflation Uncertainty Makes the Inflation Tax Non Optimal," Claremont Working Papers, Claremont McKenna College.

McCubbins, Mathew, and Schwartz, Thomas (1984). "Congressional Oversight Overlooked: Police Patrols vs. Fire Alarms," *American Journal of Political Science,* 28:165–79.

Poole, William (1987). "Monetary Control and the Political Business Cycle," in J. A. Dorn and A. Schwartz (eds.), *The Search for Stable Money,* pp. 165–79. University of Chicago Press.

Rogoff, Kenneth (1987). "Reputational Constraints on Monetary Policy," *Carnegie-Rochester Conference Series on Public Policy,* 26:141–82.

Schneider, Friederich, and Frey, Bruno (1988). "Politico-Economic Models of Macroeconomic Policy: A Review of the Empirical Evidence," in T. D. Willett (ed.), *Political Business Cycles: The Political Economy of Money, Inflation and Unemployment,* pp. 239–75. Durham, N.C.: Duke University Press.

Toma, Eugenia F., and Toma, Mark (1986). *Central Bankers, Bureaucratic Incentives, and Monetary Policy.* Boston: Kluwer Academic Publishers.

Wagner, Richard E. (1986). "Central Banking and the Fed: A Public Choice Perspective," *Cato Journal,* 6(2):519–38.

Willett, Thomas D. (1987). "A New Monetary Constitution," in J. A. Dorn and A. Schwartz (eds.), *The Search for Stable Money,* pp. 145–62. University of Chicago Press.

(ed.) (1988). *Political Business Cycles: The Political Economy of Money, Inflation and Unemployment.* Durham, N.C.: Duke University Press.

Willett, Thomas D., et al. (1988). "Inflation Hypotheses and Monetary Accommodation: Postwar Evidence from the Industrial Countries," in T. D. Willett (ed.), *Political Business Cycles: The Political Economy of Money, Inflation and Unemployment,* pp. 200–36. Durham, N.C.: Duke University Press.

Willett, Thomas D., and Banaian, King (1988a). "Explaining the Great Stagflation: Towards a Political Economy Framework," in T. D. Willett (ed.), *Political Business Cycles: The Political Economy of Money, Inflation and Unemployment,* pp. 35–62. Durham, N.C.: Duke University Press.

(1988b). "Models of the Political Process and Their Implications for Stagflation: A Public Choice Perspective," in T. D. Willett (ed.), *Political Business Cycles: The Political Economy of Money, Inflation and Unemployment,* pp. 100–28. Durham, N.C.: Duke University Press.

CHAPTER 3

The Federal Reserve reaction function: a specification search

SALWA S. KHOURY

Twenty-five years ago William Dewald and Harry Johnson (1963) published their path-breaking Federal Reserve reaction function. By regressing an indicator of Fed policy on the Fed's goal variables, such as the unemployment rate and the price index, they tried to replace vague talk about the Fed's response to economic conditions with more rigorous econometric procedures. Not surprisingly, their work gave rise to an extensive research effort. Has that effort been successful? One way to approach that question is to see if Fed reaction functions generally have reached similar conclusions, so that one can say that certain results have been well established. Another way is to ask if the results reached by the use of Fed reaction functions are robust with respect to more or less arbitrary differences in specifications. Unfortunately, as this chapter will show, neither of those conditions has been met.

This is unfortunate, because a reliable Fed reaction function is needed for at least three purposes. One obviously is to predict Fed actions. Another is to *evaluate* Fed behavior. This is relevant for the debates about monetary rules and the appropriate degree of Fed independence. A third purpose is to aid in estimating the policy multipliers for econometric models. As Stephen Goldfeld and Allan Blinder (1972), among others, have shown, omitting the central bank's reaction function in an econometric model can lead to serious estimation errors.

There exist two types of reaction functions that answer quite distinct questions. One, which may be called an "intentions function," asks how the Fed *wants* to change aggregate demand when, say, the unemployment rate changes. The other, an "impact function," asks how Fed policy actually affects aggregate demand when the Fed reacts to a change in the unemployment rate. Much of the disagreement about the appropriate dependent variable for a reaction function results from a

I am indebted to Thomas Mayer for his guidance and his revision of this chapter and to Richard Green for his help with the methodology section.

failure to distinguish between these two types of reaction functions. For example, if the variable that best measures the effect of monetary policy is the growth rate of the money supply, but the Fed thinks that it is the funds rate, then both variables can legitimately be used as dependent variables; the money supply belongs in an impact function, and the funds rate in an intentions function. This chapter is concerned primarily with impact functions, because that is what most of the previously fitted reaction functions are.

Reaction functions that have been fitted

Table 3.1 summarizes the results of the 42 reaction functions that are described in Appendix Table 3.1.[1] The first row of Table 3.1 illustrates how much Fed reaction functions differ in the independent variables they use. The most commonly used independent variables are the unemployment rate, the inflation rate, and economic growth, in that order. The variables that are most frequently significant at the 5 percent level are the federal debt and the unemployment rate. Table 3.1 also suggests that the Fed accommodates changes in the rate of economic growth, but that result is not conclusive.

What is disturbing about the results shown in Table 3.1 is that frequently the conclusions reached depend on the particular dependent variable that is used, on the other independent variables that are included, or on the period over which the function is fitted. One who reads just one of these reaction functions may feel convinced that one has learned how the Fed responds to economic conditions, but that seeming knowledge disappears as one reads a large number of these studies. Such a lack of robustness is not uncommon in economics, but all the same, it *seems* as though reaction functions are not robust enough to include them in econometric models or to use them to predict or evaluate Fed behavior.[2]

But such a conclusion should not be based merely on a casual reading of Table 3.1 and Appendix Table 3.1. Edward Leamer (1978) developed a method that can be used for formal testing of the robustness of reaction functions. This method, called "specification search," can test for only one type of robustness – robustness with respect to the inclusion or exclusion of independent variables. Thus, a reaction function might pass the specification-search test and yet be fragile with respect to the sample period or the dependent variables used. But because Table 3.1 suggests that fragility with respect to the independent variables may be a serious problem, Fed reaction functions should be subjected to Leamer's specification test as a necessary, though not sufficient, test of robustness. The next section provides a brief discussion of Leamer's method.

Table 3.1. *Summary of results of reaction functions*

	Growth	U[a]	P[b]	BP/BT[c]	Exchange rate	Deficit	Debt	Interest rate
Number of appearances in Appendix Table 3.1	42	65	56	31	15	27	6	24
Percentage of the time positively significant[d]	36	54	16	13	33	37	83	21
Percentage of the time negatively significant[e]	26	5	39	16	27	19	0	25
Percentage of the time insignificant	33	37	41	61	40	44	17	54

Note: In the first four rows the percentages do not sum to 100% because one author did not specify whether the signs on his significant variables were positive or negative; so his significant-variable results could not be incorporated in this table.

[a]Unemployment rate.

[b]Inflation rate.

[c]Balance of payments or balance of trade.

[d]Refers to expansionary effect.

[e]Refers to contractionary effect.

The method of specification search

To conduct a specification search the researcher first divides the potential independent variables into two groups: "free variables" and "doubtful variables."[3] The former are those variables that the researcher is certain should be included in the regression, and the latter are those concerning which there is doubt. The test then shows how the coefficients of the free variables change as different linear combinations of doubtful variables are added. It is therefore a more general test than traditional regression analysis, which once and for all either includes or excludes all the doubtful variables. Moreover, being a Bayesian test, it combines a priori beliefs with the information provided by the data.

A basic component of a specification search is the "information-contract curve," which pools information from the prior beliefs of the researcher and from the data used in the test. For example, in the case in which two coefficients are being estimated, the prior information can be represented as one set of ellipses, and the information obtained from the data can be represented by another ellipsis. The coordinates of the axes represent possible values of the two coefficients. One point represents the researcher's prior beliefs about the values of the coefficients (e.g., {0, 0} if one is not sure that the variables should be included in the equation), and another point represents the values of the coefficients obtained from the ordinary-least-squares estimates. These points are the centers of two sets of infinite ellipses – one set representing movement away from the researcher's prior beliefs about the values of the coefficients (e.g., {0, 0}), and the other set representing movement away from the ordinary-least-squares results. But these two sets of ellipses meet, and the tangencies between them generate a curve, called the information-contract curve. It represents a set of Pareto-efficient points obtained from pooling two sets of information. The points along the information-contract curve are called "posterior estimates."

Edward Leamer and Herman Leonard (1983b) developed a program called SEARCH that picks a set of 13 points, called Trace 1, on the contract curve. These points vary in the relative weights they assign to the prior information and to the information produced by the data. At one extreme, Trace 1 yields simply the prior estimate, thus making no use of the data under consideration. At the other extreme, Trace 1 disregards the prior information entirely and is just the ordinary-least-squares estimate. The program used here provides 13 posterior estimates obtained by assigning the following standard errors to the priors: 0, 1/16, 1/8, 1/4, 1/2, 2/3, 1, 3/2, 2, 4, 8, 16, and ∞. The prior standard error reflects the strength of the researcher's belief in the prior, as opposed to the information obtained from the data. The smaller the prior standard error, the stronger the researcher's belief in the prior. At the prior location the prior standard error is zero, and at the ordinary-least-squares location the prior standard error is infinite.

The program calculates a *t* statistic for each of the 13 posterior estimates along Trace 1. The behavior of the posterior estimate and its *t* statistic provide information about the fragility of the estimate. If the posterior estimate varies sharply at different points along the contract curve, or if its *t* statistic is not significant, then the traditional least-squares estimate is fragile.

The "extreme-bounds matrix" is another tool produced by SEARCH for testing the fragility of posterior estimates. This matrix summarizes the sensitivity of the posterior estimate to changes in the prior variance–covariance matrix. One sets, or gives bounds to, different possible prior variance–covariance matrices depending on one's beliefs. The diagonal elements of the prior variance–covariance matrix are prior variances and reflect the strength of the researcher's belief in the assigned values of the coefficients. The other elements are prior covariances, and they reflect whether or not the researcher expects different coefficients to be related. Posterior estimates are calculated for different variance–covariance matrices and are reported in the extreme-bounds matrix.

Tables 3.2 and 3.3 provide examples of the extreme-bounds matrices. Each item in the table contains two values: an upper bound (above) and a lower bound (below). These numbers are the uppermost and lowermost values of the posterior estimates for given bounds of the variance–covariance matrix for all the possible linear combinations of doubtful variables. If the upper bound and lower bound of the posterior estimate are close to each other, then the inference is not fragile.

The matrices in Tables 3.2 and 3.3 are calculated for a reaction function in which the dependent variable is M1, the free variables are GNP, unemployment, inflation, the balance of payments, and a constant term, and the doubtful variables are the deficit, the federal debt, and interest rates. The period covered is 1959:I–1973:I, and the regressions are adjusted for serial correlation by the maximum-likelihood procedure. The tables show the upper and lower bounds for GNP and the balance-of-payments coefficients.

In this study the prior variance–covariance matrix is allowed to vary between given upper and lower bounds. The identity matrix and its multiples are chosen as possible prior variance–covariance matrices. The identity matrix (V in the tables) is multiplied by the squares of the

Table 3.2. *Bounds for the posterior estimate of the coefficient on GNP; Prior variance matrix bounded between $V\sigma_L^2$ and $V\sigma_U^2$, where V is the input variance matrix; M1 is the dependent variable*

	σ_U												
σ_L	0	1/16	1/8	1/4	1/2	1/1.5	1	1.5	2	4	8	16	∞
0	0.146	0.146	0.147	0.149	0.150	0.151	0.151	0.151	0.151	0.151	0.151	0.151	0.151
	0.146	0.146	0.146	0.146	0.146	0.146	0.146	0.146	0.146	0.146	0.146	0.146	0.146
1/16		0.146	0.147	0.149	0.150	0.151	0.151	0.151	0.151	0.151	0.151	0.151	0.151
		0.146	0.146	0.146	0.146	0.146	0.146	0.146	0.146	0.146	0.146	0.146	0.146
1/8			0.147	0.149	0.150	0.151	0.151	0.151	0.151	0.151	0.151	0.151	0.151
			0.147	0.147	0.147	0.147	0.147	0.147	0.147	0.147	0.147	0.147	0.147
1/4				0.149	0.150	0.151	0.151	0.151	0.151	0.151	0.151	0.151	0.151
				0.149	0.149	0.149	0.149	0.149	0.149	0.149	0.149	0.149	0.149
1/2					0.150	0.150	0.151	0.151	0.151	0.151	0.151	0.151	0.151
					0.150	0.150	0.150	0.150	0.150	0.150	0.150	0.150	0.150
1/1.5						0.150	0.151	0.151	0.151	0.151	0.151	0.151	0.151
						0.150	0.150	0.150	0.150	0.150	0.150	0.150	0.150

1	0.151	0.151	0.151	0.151	0.151	0.151	0.151
	0.151	0.151	0.151	0.151	0.151	0.151	0.151
1.5		0.151	0.151	0.151	0.151	0.151	0.151
		0.151	0.151	0.151	0.151	0.151	0.151
2			0.151	0.151	0.151	0.151	0.151
			0.151	0.151	0.151	0.151	0.151
4				0.151	0.151	0.151	0.151
				0.151	0.151	0.151	0.151
8					0.151	0.151	0.151
					0.151	0.151	0.151
16						0.151	0.151
						0.151	0.151
∞							0.151
							0.151

Note: V = the unit matrix in this case.

Table 3.3. *Bounds for the posterior estimate of the coefficient on the balance-of-payments variable; prior variance matrix bounded between* $V\sigma_L^2$ *and* $V\sigma_U^2$*, where V is the input variance matrix; M1 is the dependent variable*

	σ_U												
σ_L	0	1/16	1/8	1/4	1/2	1/1.5	1	1.5	2	4	8	16	∞
0	−.139E-03	−.126E-03	−.963E-04	−.368E-04	0.252E-04	0.428E-04	0.586E-04	0.667E-04	0.698E-04	0.728E-04	0.736E-04	0.738E-04	0.739E-04
	−.139E-03	−.145E-03	−.152E-03	−.191E-03	−.231E-03	−.243E-03	−.253E-03	−.259E-03	.261E-03	−.263E-03	−.263 E-03	−.263E-03	−.263E-03
1/16		−.131E-03	−.102E-03	−.423E-04	0.197E-04	0.373E-04	0.530E-04	0.612E-04	0.642E-04	0.672E-04	0.680E-04	0.682E-04	0.683E-04
		−.131E-03	−.145E-03	−.178E-03	−.218E-03	−.230E-03	−.240E-03	−.245E-03	−.247E-03	−.249E-03	−.250E-03	−.250E-03	−.250E-03
1/8			−.115E-03	−.561E-04	0.582E-03	0.234E-04	0.391E-04	0.472E-04	0.502E-04	0.533E-04	0.540E-04	0.542E-04	0.543E-04
			−.115E-03	−.148E-03	−.188E-03	−.208E-03	−.210E-03	−.215E-03	−.217E-03	−.219E-03	−.220E-03	−.220E-03	−.220E-03
1/4				−.690E-04	−.273E-04	−.973E-05	0.591E-05	0.140E-04	0.170E-04	0.201E-04	0.208E-04	0.210E-04	0.211E-04
				−.890E-04	−.129E-03	−.140E-03	−.151E-03	−.156E-03	−.158E-03	−.160E-03	−.160E-03	−.160E-03	−.160E-03
1/2					−.670E-04	−.495E-04	−.338E-04	−.258E-04	−.227E-04	−.197E-04	−.189E-04	−.187E-04	−.187E- 04
					−.670E-04	−.785E-04	−.883E-04	−.941E-04	−.960E-04	−.980E-04	−.985E-04	−.986E-04	−.986E-04
1/1.5						−.610E-04	−.454E-04	−.373E-04	−.343E-04	−.313E-04	−.305E-04	−.303E-04	−.302E-04
						−.610E-04	−.713E-04	.765E-04	−.785E-04	−.805E-04	−.809E-04	−.811E-04	−.811E-04

1	−.557E-04	−.476E-04	−.446E-04	−.415E-04	−.408E-04	−.406E-04	−.405E-04
	−.557E-04	−.609E-04	−.629E-04	−.643E-04	−.653E-04	−.654E-04	−.655E-04
1.5		−.528E-04	−.498E-04	−.468E-04	−.460E-04	−.458E-04	−.457E-04
		−.528E-03	−.548E-04	−.567E-04	−.572E-04	−.574E-04	−.574E-04
2			−.518E-04	−.487E-04	−.480E-04	−.478E-04	−.477E-04
			−.518E-04	−.537E-04	−.542E-04	−.543E-04	−.544E-04
4				−.504E-04	−.499E-04	−.497E-04	−.496E-04
				−.507E-04	−.512E-04	−.513E-04	−.513E-04
8					−.504E-04	−.502E-04	−.501E-04
					−.504E-04	−.505E-04	−.506E-04
16						−.503E-04	−.503E-04
						−.503E-04	−.504E-04
∞							−.503E-04
							−.503E-04

Note: V = the unit matrix in this case.

The balance-of-payments variable used here is the balance-of-payments surplus or deficit divided by GNP.

numbers 0, 1/16, 1/8, 1/4, 1/2, 1/1.5, 1, 1.5, 2, 4, 8, 16, and ∞ to create upper and lower bounds. (In Tables 3.2 and 3.3 the numbers chosen are labeled σ_U and σ_L for upper and lower bounds, respectively.)

Table 3.2 presents posterior estimates of the coefficient of GNP. The lower right-hand corner contains the ordinary-least-squares estimate of the GNP coefficient, 0.151. Here the prior is totally diffuse. At the upper left-hand corner the prior holds tightly. The reported number, 0.146, equals the constrained least-squares estimate when the coefficients on the doubtful variables are constrained to be zero. The number in the center of the matrix, 0.151, is the posterior estimate for GNP when the prior variance–covariance matrix equals the identity matrix. The diagonal elements of the matrix contain posterior estimates of the GNP coefficient when the prior variance–covariance matrix is set to equal different multiples of the identity matrix (i.e., one prior variance–covariance matrix is set by the researcher, rather than setting upper and lower bounds on the prior variance–covariance matrix). The reported numbers in the diagonal elements of the matrix are equivalent to posterior estimates for the GNP coefficient along Trace 1 of the contract curve.

At the upper right-hand corner, σ_U equals infinity, and σ_L equals zero. This means that the prior variance–covariance matrix is bounded from above by infinity and from below by zero. The prior variance–covariance matrix is allowed the most amount of variation at this corner. Thus, the reported numbers, 0.146 and 0.151, represent the widest possible set of bounds for the coefficient of GNP. The set of numbers between (and including) the two numbers at the upper right-hand corner (0.146 and 0.151 here) is called the "extreme-bounds interval." Leamer and Leonard (1983b, p. 43) explain the relevance of the extreme-bounds interval as follows: "If this interval is short enough to be useful it doesn't matter how you play around with the doubtful variables." The size of this interval determines the robustness of the coefficient.

Table 3.3 presents the posterior estimates of the coefficient of the balance-of-payments variable. Because both this variable and GNP are free variables in the same equation, a comparison of the numbers in Tables 3.2 and 3.3 provides a good illustration of how robustness tests are conducted. The extreme-bounds interval for the balance of payments spans zero. One cannot draw conclusions about the sign of the coefficient for the balance of payments. The ordinary-least-squares estimate for the coefficient of the balance of payments has a negative sign, but the sign changes along the extreme-bounds matrix. Therefore, the least-squares estimate for the coefficient of the balance of payments is not robust. For GNP, the extreme-bounds interval is tighter. All the posterior estimates in Table 3.2 show a positive sign for the coefficient of GNP. Despite the different linear combinations of the doubtful variables and all the variations in the prior variance–covariance matrix, the extreme-bounds interval for GNP varies only from 0.146 to 0.151. That differs little from the ordinary-least-squares estimate of 0.151.

Results of the robustness tests

A specification search can now be applied to the reaction-function literature. Because so many reaction functions have been fitted, it is not feasible to test each one individually. Instead, I have used a comprehensive sample of variables that have been employed in these tests, without relating each variable to a specific study that has used it. The eight independent variables selected from the previous studies are GNP, the unemployment rate, the inflation rate, the balance of payments, the exchange rate, the budget surplus or deficit, the federal debt, and the Treasury-bill rate. The dependent variables used are M1, M2, the base (as estimated both by the Board of Governors' staff and by the St. Louis Federal Reserve Bank), total reserves, and the federal-funds rate.[4] However, the Treasury-bill rate cannot be used when the dependent variable is the funds rate, because regressing the Treasury-bill rate on the funds rate would generate a term-structure equation instead of a Fed reaction function.

The sample period is 1959:I–1984:IV. But because of the shift from fixed to flexible exchange rates, it has to be broken into two parts, with the first part terminating in 1973:I. For the first period, the international variable is the balance of payments; for the second it is the exchange rate. This break has the incidental advantage of allowing the data to show a break in the reaction function if one occurred at that time because of the abandonment of fixed exchange rates.

An interesting hypothesis that one might try to test with a reaction function is that the Fed is concerned with economic stabilization. Hence, GNP, unemployment, inflation, and either the exchange rate or the balance of payments are treated as free variables, with the other independent variables used as doubtful variables. Another hypothesis is that the Fed reacts to movements in GNP, debt, the budget surplus, and interest rates. So in another test these four variables are used as free variables, and the other variables are treated as doubtful. Because in preliminary runs, using both ordinary-least-squares and SEARCH procedures, GNP was significant, it is always used as a free variable in this study.

Separate tests were run for the levels and first differences of these variables. Another set of tests was run after correcting for serial correlation by a maximum-likelihood procedure. The variables are used in a form that, except for the inflation rate, makes their expected sign positive.

The resulting output from these tests is too massive to be presented here, but it is available elsewhere (Khoury 1987). To interpret it, some criteria have to be established. One is whether or not the range of the extreme-bounds matrix spans zero. A second criterion is the correctness of the sign. A third criterion is the significance (at the 95 percent level) of the estimates along Trace 1 of the contract curve. Each independent variable is given the chance to appear in a large number of equations, so that the behavior of each variable is examined in numerous trials.

The following conclusions can be drawn, based on the behavior of the variables in the bulk of the runs: GNP is robust for both the periods studied, whereas the federal debt is robust only for the second period, and unemployment seems robust only for the first period.[5]

Finally, one can look at β coefficients to see the extent to which the Fed's reactions to particular variables accounted for the monetary policy it followed during the sample period. The β coefficients are calculated for extreme upper and lower bounds of the free variables. In these tests, GNP dominates the other variables.[6] This is hardly surprising, because the Fed has to accommodate secular increases in GNP.

Conclusion

This chapter first examined 42 previously published reaction functions to see if they would yield consistent results. The results were in disarray. The only independent variables for which they showed consistent and significant results were the federal debt and unemployment. The specification search showed that very few variables were robust in a reaction function, and that was consistent with the lack of robustness in the literature. In a variety of tests, only GNP passed for the entire sample period. The federal debt passed for the flexible-exchange-rate period, and the unemployment rate seemed to pass for the fixed-exchange-rate period.

Notes

1 For definitions of the variables and a discussion of alternative variables, see Khoury (1987, pp. 9–14, 40–6).

2 See Khoury (1987, pp. 35–9). This problem is, of course, not confined to the reaction-function literature (Cooley and LeRoy 1981; Mayer 1980).

3 For details of specification search, see Leamer (1978) and Leamer and Leonard (1983a,b).

4 For specific definitions of the variables, see Khoury (1987, pp. 70–2).
5 The unemployment rate is robust with respect to two criteria: The sign is correct, and the extreme-bounds matrix does not span zero. But the *t* statistic is not always significant at the 5% level.
6 The β coefficient measures the relative importance of the impact that each independent variable has on the dependent variable during the sample period. A variable that fluctuates a great deal can have an important impact even if its regression coefficient is small.

References

Abrams, Richard K., Froyen, Richard, and Waud, Roger N. (1980). "Monetary Policy Reaction Functions, Consistent Expectations and the Burns Era," *Journal of Money, Credit and Banking,* 12(1):30–42.

Allen, Stuart D., and Smith, Michael D. (1983). "Government Borrowing and Monetary Accommodation," *Journal of Monetary Economics,* 12:605–16.

Avery, Robert B. (1979). "Modeling Monetary Policy as an Unobserved Variable," *Journal of Econometrics,* 10:291–311.

Barro, Robert J. (1977). "Unanticipated Money Growth and Unemployment in the United States," *American Economic Review,* 67(2):101–15.

(1978a). "Comment from an Unreconstructed Ricardian," *Journal of Monetary Economics,* 4:569–81.

(1978b). "Unanticipated Money, Output, and the Price Level in the United States," *Journal of Political Economy,* 86(4):549–80.

Barro, Robert J., and Rush, Mark (1980). "Unanticipated Money and Economic Activity," in S. Fischer (ed.), *Rational Expectations and Economic Policy,* pp. 23–48. University of Chicago Press.

Barth, James, Sickles, Robin, and Wiest, Philip (1982). "Assessing the Impact of Varying Economic Conditions on Federal Reserve Behavior," *Journal of Macroeconomics,* 4(1):47–70.

Beck, Nathaniel (1982). "Presidential Influence on the Federal Reserve in the 1970's," *American Journal of Political Science,* 26(3):415–45.

(1984). "Domestic Political Sources of American Monetary Policy: 1955–82," *Journal of Politics,* 46:786–817.

Black, Stanley W. (1984). "The Use of Monetary Policy for Internal and External Balance in Ten Industrial Countries," in J. Frenkel (ed.), *Exchange Rates and International Macroeconomics,* pp. 189–225. University of Chicago Press.

Christian, James (1968). "A Further Analysis of the Objectives of American Monetary Policy," *Journal of Finance,* 23:465–77.

Cooley, Thomas F., and LeRoy, Stephen F. (1981). "Identification and Estimation of Money Demand," *American Economic Review,* 71(5):825–44.

DeRosa, Paul, and Stern, Gary H. (1977). "Monetary Control and the Federal Funds Rate," *Journal of Monetary Economics,* 3:217–30.

Dewald, William G., and Johnson, Harry G. (1963). "An Objective Analysis of the Objectives of American Monetary Policy, 1952–61," in D. Carson (ed.),

Banking and Monetary Studies, pp. 171–89. Homewood, Ill.: Richard D. Irwin.

Epstein, Gerald A., and Schor, Juliet B. (1986). "The Political Economy of Central Banking." Harvard Institute for Economic Research discussion paper no. 1281.

Esaki, Howard Y. (1981). "Interest Rates, Short-Run Monetary Policy, and the Federal Reserve Reaction Function." Ph.D. dissertation, Yale University.

Fair, Ray C. (1978). "The Sensitivity of Fiscal Policy Effects to Assumptions About the Behavior of the Federal Reserve," *Econometrica,* 46(5): 1165–79.

Friedlander, Ann F. (1973). "Macro Policy Goals in the Postwar Period: A Study in Revealed Preference," *Quarterly Journal of Economics,* 87:25–43.

Froyen, Richard T. (1974). "A Test of the Endogeneity of Monetary Policy," *Journal of Econometrics,* 2:175–88.

Goldfeld, Stephen M. (1966). *Commercial Bank Behavior and Economic Activity.* Amsterdam: North Holland.

Goldfeld, Stephen M., and Blinder, Alan S. (1972). "Some Implications of Endogenous Stabilization Policy," *Brookings Papers on Economic Activity,* 3:585–640.

Gordon, Robert J. (1977). "World Inflation and Monetary Accommodation in Eight Countries," *Brookings Papers on Economic Activity,* 2:409–77.

Hamburger, Michael J., and Zwick, Burton (1981). "Deficits, Money and Inflation," *Journal of Monetary Economics,* 7:141–50.

(1982). "Deficits, Money, and Inflation, Reply," *Journal of Monetary Economics,* 10:279–83.

Havrilesky, Thomas (1967). "A Test of Monetary Policy Action," *Journal of Political Economy,* 75:299–304.

Havrilesky, Thomas, Sapp, Robert, and Schweitzer, Robert (1975). "Tests of the Federal Reserve's Reaction to the State of the Economy: 1964–1974," *Social Science Quarterly,* 55:835–52.

Hosek, William R. (1975). "A Test of the Targets of Monetary Policy," *Applied Economics,* 7(1):17–24.

Keeley, Sam R. (1976). "A Note on Estimating the Temporal Stability of Reaction Functions of the Monetary Authorities," *Journal of Monetary Economics,* 2:419–23.

Keran, Michael W., and Babb, Christopher T. (1969). "An Explanation of Federal Reserve Actions (1933–68)," *Federal Reserve Bank of St. Louis Review,* 51(7):7–20.

Khoury, Salwa S. (1987). "The Federal Reserve Reaction Function: A Specification Search." Ph.D. dissertation, University of California, Davis.

Leamer, Edward (1978). *Specification Searches, Ad Hoc Inference with Nonexperimental Data.* New York: Wiley.

(1982). "Sets of Posterior Means with Bounded Variance Priors," *Econometrica,* 50:725–36.

Leamer, Edward, and Leonard, Herman (1983a). "Reporting the Fragility of Regression Estimates," *Review of Economics and Statistics* (May):306–17.

(1983b). *User's Manual for SEARCH.* SEARCH version 6.

Levy, Mickey D. (1981). "Factors Affecting Monetary Policy in an Era of Inflation," *Journal of Monetary Economics,* 8:351–73.

Lombra, Raymond, and Moran, Michael (1980). "Policy Advice and Policymaking at the Federal Reserve," in K. Brunner and A. H. Meltzer (eds.), *Monetary Institutions and the Policy Process,* pp. 9–68. *Carnegie-Rochester Conference Series on Public Policy,* Vol. 13. Amsterdam: North Holland.

McMillin, Douglas W. (1981). "A Dynamic Analysis of the Impact of Fiscal Policy on the Money Supply," *Journal of Money, Credit and Banking,* 13(2):221–6.

McMillin, Douglas W., and Beard, Thomas R. (1980). "The Short Run Impact of Fiscal Policy on the Money Supply," *Southern Economic Journal,* 47:122–35.

(1982). "Deficits, Money and Inflation," *Journal of Monetary Economics,* 10:273–7.

McNees, Stephen K. (1986). "Modeling the Fed: A Forward-Looking Monetary Policy Reaction Function," *New England Economic Review,* (November–December):3–8.

Mayer, Thomas (1980). "Economics as a Hard Science: Realistic Goal or Wishful Thinking?" *Economic Inquiry,* 18:165–78.

Moore, Basil J. (1979). "The Endogenous Money Stock," *Journal of Post Keynesian Economics,* 2(1):49–70.

Niskanen, William A. (1978). "Deficits, Government Spending and Inflation," *Journal of Monetary Economics,* 4:591–602.

Perryman, M. Ray (1982). "Causality and the Temporal Characterization of Monetary Responses," in O. D. Anderson and M. R. Perryman (eds.), *Applied Time Series Analysis.* Amsterdam: North Holland.

Potts, Glenn T., and Luckett, Dudley G. (1978). "Policy Objectives of the Federal Reserve System," *Quarterly Journal of Economics,* 92(3):525–34.

Sheehan, Richard G. (1985). "The Federal Reserve Reaction Function: Does Debt Growth Influence Monetary Policy?" *Federal Reserve Bank of St. Louis Review,* 67(3):24–33.

Teigen, Ronald L. (1969). "An Aggregated Quarterly Model of the U.S. Monetary Sector, 1953–1964," in K. Brunner (ed.), *Targets and Indicators of Monetary Policy,* pp. 195–216. San Francisco: Chandler Publishing.

Witte, Willard E. (1984). "Cyclical Variation in the Short-Run Federal Reserve Reaction Function, 1969–1978," *Journal of Macroeconomics,* 6(4):457–64.

Wood, John W. (1967). "A Model of Federal Reserve Behavior," in G. Horwich (ed.), *Monetary Process and Policy,* pp. 135–66. Homewood, Ill.: Richard D. Irwin.

Appendix Table 3.1. *Summary of reaction functions*

Study	Time period	Dependent variable	Form	Data frequency	Growth	U	P	BP/BT	Exchange rate	Deficit	Debt	Interest rate
Dewald-Johnson (1963)	1952:I–1961:IV	M1	Levels	Q	+	+	0	0				
Goldfeld (1966)	1950:III–1962:II	Potential demand deposits	Levels	Q	0	+	0	0				0
	1950:III–1962:II	Potential demand deposits	Logs	Q	+	0	0	0				–
Havrilesky (1967)	1952:I–1965:IV	Total reserves (adjusted)	Levels	Q	+	+	–	0				
Wood (1967)	1952:I–1963:IV	Federal holdings of government securities	Levels and change	Q	– 0	0	–	0 +		0	+	
Christian (1968)	1952:I–1966:IV	M1	Change	Q	+	+	–	+				
	1952:I–1966:IV	Free reserves			+	0	–	0				
	1952:I–1966:IV	Treasury-bill rate			+	0	–	0				
Keran-Babb (1969)	1933:III–1939:IV	Monetary base	Central difference and first	Q						–		+ 0
	1940:I–1952:IV	Monetary base	difference							+		0
	1953:I–1968:IV	Monetary base								0		+

Teigen (1969)	1953:I–1964:IV	Unborrowed reserves plus currency	Percentage change and levels	Q	± 0	0	0					+ 0
Friedlander (1973)	1954:I–1964:IV	Net free reserves	Deviation from desired level	Q	+	0	+	0		0		0
Froyen (1974)	1953:2–1961:1	Monetary base	Deviations, levels, and change	M	+	+	0	0		0	0	0
	1961:2–1969:1	Monetary base			+	+	−	0		+	+	0
	1969:2–1972:12	Monetary base			+	+	0	+		0	+	0
Havrilesky et al. (1975)	1964:1–1966:11	Federal-funds rate	Levels	M		0	−		−			
	1966:12–1967:11 and 1968:7–1968:12	Federal-funds rate				+	−		0			
	1969:1–1970:1 and 1967:12–1968:6	Federal-funds rate				0	−		0			
	1970:2–1971:7	Federal-funds rate				+	+		−			
	1971:8–1972:9	Federal-funds rate				0	−		+			
	1972:9–1974:2	Federal-funds rate				+	−		−			
Hosek (1975)	1972:I–1971:IV	Total reserves	Levels	Q		+	0					
	1972:I–1971:IV	Free reserves				+	−					
	1952:I–1971:IV	Money supply				0	0					
	1952:I–1971:IV	Bank credit				+	+					

Appendix Table 3.1. *(cont.)*

Study	Time period	Dependent variable	Form	Data frequency	Growth	U	P	BP/BT	Exchange rate	Deficit	Debt	Interest rate
Keeley (1976)	1951:I–1969:IV	Money supply	Levels	Q	√	√	√	√				
	1951:I–1969:IV	Short-term interest rate			0	√	0	√				
	1961:I–1969:IV	Index of money-market tightness			√	√	√	√				
Barro (1977)	1941–1973	Systematic money growth	Differenced logs and logs	Y		+						
DeRosa and Stern (1977)	1967:3–1969:12	Federal-funds rate	Percentage change	M	0							
	1970:12–1974:12	Federal-funds rate			–							
Gordon (1977)	1958:3–1973:1	M1	Percentage change, change, and level	Q	0			$\bar{0}$		–		
	1958:3–1976:4	M1			0			0		–		
Barro (1978a)	1941–1976	Systematic money growth	Differenced logs, logs, and level	Y		+				–		
	1946–1976	Systematic money growth				+				–		

Barro (1978b)	1941–1976	Systematic money growth	Differenced logs and logs	Y		+					
Fair (1978)	1954:I–1976:II	Three-month Treasury-bill rate	Percentage change and levels	Q	0	+	0				
Niskanen (1978)	1948–1976	M1	Percentage change and level	Y	0		–			0	
Potts and Luckett (1978)	1956:1–1975:12	Intended policy: tight or easy	Levels and change	M	–	+	0	0			
	1956:1–1961:1	Intended policy: tight or easy			–	0	–	0			
	1961:2–1969:1	Intended policy: tight or easy			–	+	0	0			
	1969:2–1975:12	Intended policy: tight or easy			0	+	0	0			
Avery (1979)	1955:1–1975:4	Six indicators of unobserved monetary policy	Derivations about means (of the change)	M	0	+	–	+			
Moore (1979)	1951:2–1977:2	Monetary base	Levels, logs	M		0	+		+		0
	1952:II–1976:II	Monetary base	First difference and percentage change	Q	+	–	+		+		–

Appendix Table 3.1. *(cont.)*

Study	Time period	Dependent variable	Form	Data frequency	Growth	U	P	BP/BT	Exchange rate	Deficit	Debt	Interest rate
Abrams et al. (1980)	1970:3–1977:3	Federal-funds rate	Levels	M		+	–		–			
Barro and Rush (1980)	1941–1977	Systematic money growth	Differenced logs and logs	Y		+						
	1941–1977	Systematic money growth		Y		+						
	1941–1977	Systematic money growth		Y		+						
	1941:I–1978:I	Systematic money growth		Q		+						
Lombra and Moran (1980)	1971:I–1973:IV	Federal-funds rate target	Levels and change	Q	–	+	0					
McMillin and Beard (1980)	1953:I–1976:IV	Unborrowed reserves (adjusted)	Levels	Q	+		0					
Esaki (1981)	1974:3–1979:9	Midpoint of Federal-funds rate target range	Change and levels	M		+	0		+			

Hamburger and Zwick (1981)	1954–1976	Systematic money growth	Differenced logs, logs, and levels	Y		0			0		
	1961–1974	Systematic money growth							+		
Levy (1981)	1952:I–1978:IV	Monetary base (adjusted)	First difference	Q	0	0	+		+	+	0
McMillin (1981)	1953:I–1976:IV	Unborrowed reserves (adjusted)	Levels	Q	+		+				–
Barth et al. (1982)	1953:1–1978:2	Monetary base (unadjusted)	Deviations from means (linear and polynomial form)	M	+	+	–		+		0
Beck (1982)	1970:3–1979:8	Federal-funds rate	Levels and change	M		0	–	0			
	1970:3–1979:8	Short-run target for M1				0	+	0			
	1970:3–1974:7	Federal-funds rate				0	–	0			
Hamburger and Zwick (1982)	1961–1974	Systematic money growth	First differenced logs and levels	Y					+		
	1961–1981	Systematic money growth							+		
McMillin and Beard (1982)	1961–1978	Systematic money growth	First differenced logs and levels	Y					0		

Appendix Table 3.1. *(cont.)*

Study	Time period	Dependent variable	Form	Data frequency	Growth	U	P	BP/BT	Exchange rate	Deficit	Debt	Interest rate
Perryman (1982)	1953:I–1975:IV	M1	Levels	Q	0	0	+	–				
	1953:I–1975:IV	Noncyclical indicator:M1*			–	0	0	–				
	1953:I–1975:IV	Noncyclical indicator:M2*			–	0	0	–				
Allen and Smith (1983)	1954:I–1974:IV	Systematic monetary-base growth	Differenced logs, logs, and levels	Q						+		
	1954:I–1980:IV	Systematic monetary-base growth								0		
	1961:III–1978:IV	Systematic monetary-base growth				0				0		
	1961:III–1978:IV	Systematic money growth				0				0		
Beck (1984)	1955:II–1982:IV	Total reserves (adjusted)	Percentage change and levels	Q		–	0	0		+		–
Black (1984)	1964:1–1979:11	Central-bank discount rate	Levels and change	M		+	–	0				
	1963:2–1979:11	Unborrowed reserves (adjusted)				0	0	$\overline{0}$				

Witte (1984)	1969:2–1978:11	Federal-funds rate	First difference of the logs and change	M	–		–				
Sheehan (1985)	1958:I–1984:III	M1	Log difference form and level	Q		–					–
	1958:I–1984:III	Federal-funds rate				+	0			+	
	1958:I–1983:III	M1				0			+		0
	1958:I–1983:III	Federal-funds rate				+	0				0
Epstein and Schor (1986)	1966:I–1983:IV	Federal-funds rate	Change and levels	Q	–		–	+	0		
McNees (1986)	1970:III–1986:II	Federal-funds rate	Change and levels	Q	0	+	0				+
	1970:III–1986:II	Federal-funds rate				+		0			+

Notes: In the cases in which more than one sign is shown for a given variable, more than one definition for that variable or more than one form of the equation was used, and each case gave a different result.

For more detailed explanations of the methods of different authors, see Table 2-1 and its footnotes in Khoury (1987, pp. 19–34).

The check marks shown for Keeley (1976) denote temporal stability without specifying the sign. The signs are not available in the article.

CHAPTER 4

Corporate profitability as a determinant of restrictive monetary policy: estimates for the postwar United States

GERALD A. EPSTEIN AND JULIET B. SCHOR

Current debates over international coordination of macroeconomic policy pose interesting conundrums for our understanding of domestic monetary policy. For a number of years the United States has been exerting pressure on Japan and West Germany to pursue an easier monetary policy, and particularly in the case of the West Germans the United States has been unsuccessful. German officials cite fear of inflation as their rationale for a restrictive policy. Yet, last year, consumer prices fell in West Germany, casting suspicion on either the sincerity or wisdom of the German government's stance.

An alternative explanation, now recognized by economists and other observers, is that macroeconomic expansion is thought by the German government to be incompatible with maintenance of corporate profitability in West Germany (Llewellyn 1983). The German case suggests the need to rethink traditional approaches to understanding macroeconomic policy in general and monetary policy in particular.

This chapter attempts such a rethinking. Using the case of the United States, we investigate the hypothesis that the Federal Reserve's monetary policy is motivated by a concern for corporate profitability. We reinterpret the standard evidence on the determinants of monetary policy in light of this hypothesis. The results are consistent with the view that the Federal Reserve is acting so as to maximize the (weighted) profitability of finanical and nonfinancial corporations. Furthermore, there is no evidence that the Fed independently attempts to promote labor's interests.

We thank Lexa Edsall and Emily Kawano for research assistance, Richard G. Davis, John Gildea, Modesty Johnson, Maureen LeBlanc, and Ross Waldrop for data, David Gordon for helpful discussion, Samuel Bowles and Thomas Mayer for helpful comments on a previous draft, and the World Institute for Development Economic Research of the United Nations University for financial assistance. We are responsible for any remaining errors.

Theories of monetary policy

It is well established that the Federal Reserve responds to inflation and the growth of output by leaning against the wind. Reaction-function studies such as that of McNees (1986) support this proposition. The dominant explanation for this evidence is the "liberal" approach, of which standard Keynesianism is the best example. According to this perspective, the central bank acts in the interests of society as a whole.

The liberal theory is subject to several criticisms. First, liberal theory is not consistent with the experiences of independent central banks. Independent banks, as defined by their statutory relationship to the government, pursue tighter monetary policy than banks that are not independent (Bade and Parkin 1980; Epstein and Schor 1986). Yet, in the liberal theory there is no reason why an independent bank would pursue a different policy than a nonindependent bank. Why does the bank need to be independent of the constituency it represents? A second problem with the liberal theory is specifying the relation between one of the central bank's main target variables, inflation, and social welfare. It is widely assumed that inflation reduces social welfare. Yet this assumption is rarely justified. Economic theory suggests that expected inflation should have little effect on social welfare, with the exception of menu or shoe-leather costs, which cannot plausibly be considered large, particularly in comparison with the traditional costs of inflation reduction.

Of course, unexpected inflation has distributional effects that impose costs on particular groups within society. Unexpected inflation adversely affects holders of cash and bonds. However, these groups represent a small minority of the population. For example, the Federal Reserve's "Survey of Consumer Finances" shows that 97 percent of American families own no bonds at all, and 40 percent own $1,000 or less in liquid assets.[1]

Yet the Federal Reserve appears to think it should respond to rentier (saver) interests. In our earlier work on the Federal Reserve–Treasury Accord of 1951, we noted that Allan Sproul, the influential president of the Federal Reserve Bank of New York, took that position. Sproul's notes contained the following:

> The interests of "savers" including insurance policy holders are [a] legitimate concern of the Federal Reserve System. A credit policy entered into with the deliberate intention of driving down rates of interest on savings to very low levels, or keeping them there, would have to have very strong justification on other grounds. That was one of the questions and doubts we had continually in mind while we were pegging the price of long term Government bonds [during and immediately after] the Second World War.[2]

In addition to harming rentiers, inflation adversely affects the profitability of financial corporations, as they tend to be net creditors (Federal Reserve Bank of New York 1985). Of course, financial corporations represent a small minority relative to both the population and the total number of businesses in the economy. Nevertheless, there is a growing body of evidence that the U.S. central bank maintains a special relationship with the financial sector (Epstein and Schor 1986).

By contrast, the evidence suggests that neither nonfinancial corporations nor workers are systematically harmed by inflation. Nonfinancial corporations tend to hold net monetary liabilities, whose value is reduced by unexpected inflation. Workers' interests are mixed. Wages are, of course, ceteris paribus reduced by unexpected inflation; yet ceteris is not paribus. Historically, growth and inflation have been correlated, and workers benefit from growth. For example, Schor (1985) showed that real wages followed a pro-cyclical pattern in nine Organization for Economic Cooperation and Development (OECD) countries from 1955 until roughly 1970.

Though not conclusive, a review of the evidence on the distributional effects of inflation casts doubt on the traditional claim that the central bank's inflation aversion is attributable to its desire to maximize the general welfare.

Of course, many would argue that the liberal theory is wrong and that the central bank merely fulfills its (often statutory) function: It is the guarantor of a sound currency. That may be true. Nevertheless, the functional explanation brings us no closer to understanding the priority accorded antiinflation policy, because it begs the question why the central bank was given that statutory requirement in the first place.

The second major approach to understanding central-bank policy is bureaucracy theory, which includes many monetarists among its adherents. Bureaucracy theory sees the state as a Leviathan, power-hungry and independent, acting against the interests of civil society. Such treatments argue that the central bank's primary goal is to increase its power and prestige. This tradition argues that monetary policy has an inflationary bias due to the central bank's desire to maximize its income by buying income-earning government securities. There are several problems with this approach. For one, it has difficulty explaining restrictive policy. More fundamentally, it does not adequately specify the central bank's objective function. To understand how the central bank would maximize its utility according to this theory, it is necessary to understand what policy it could take to enhance its prestige. Yet the determinants of the central bank's prestige are left unexamined. In fact, the central bank's prestige is probably related to its reputation among important groups within civil society, such as the financial community. Thus, bureaucracy theory is misleading when it suggests that the central bank makes policy in its "own" interest, unconnected to the interests of important groups within society.

The foregoing suggests that neither the liberal approach nor the bureaucratic approach yields a satisfactory theory of the determinants of central-bank behavior. We are therefore led to consider an alternate explanation that emphasizes the influence of corporate interests on monetary policy.[3] In particular, *we suggest that the Federal Reserve is primarily responsive to corporate and rentier interests, rather than the general interest or its own narrow interest.* More concretely, we hypothesize that the Federal Reserve acts as if it maximizes a weighted combination of the profit rates of financial and nonfinancial corporations. In equilibrium, assuming neither group is sated in profits, it will make policy to balance the demands of the two groups, depending on their ability to influence central-bank policy as reflected in the weights the central bank assigns to their respective profit rates.[4]

With this perspective, important historical anomalies are easily interpreted. For example, the Federal Reserve's failure to reflate the economy in 1932, otherwise inexplicable as a rational act, was due to the adverse impact that reflation would have had on bank profitability (Epstein and Ferguson 1984). Similarly, the Fed's reluctance to maintain low interest rates during and after World War II was an example of its preference for the interests of rentiers over the interests of the general public (Epstein and Schor 1986; Samuelson 1945).[5]

Our hypothesis provides an explanation for why independence is so important, both in terms of its effect on the stance of policy and in the minds of central bankers. Without it, as our previous research on the United States and Italy has shown (Epstein and Schor 1986, 1989a,b), the central bank has a difficult time enacting its occasionally unpopular optimal policy. The importance of independence suggests a rationale for a strong claim of our hypothesis, which is that business influence on the central bank is large, whereas labor influence is small. Although we have not found that to be the case in all countries, in the United States the combination of an independent Fed, a low rate of unionization, and the absence of a labor-dominated political party has resulted in little labor influence on monetary policy-making.

To investigate our theory's claims, we use a traditional approach to modeling central-bank behavior. We then estimate some parameters of that model and suggest that our theory is at least as compatible with the evidence as are the other theories.

The model

The traditional approach to modeling policy-making is to assume that policy-makers minimize a quadratic loss function of policy targets subject to a model of the economy.[6] The weights that the policy-maker places on these targets represent the policy-maker's preferences. As applied to monetary policy, economists have assumed that the central bank has targets for traditional macroeconomic variables such as the unemployment rate, the inflation rate, and GNP growth (McNees 1986).

In practice, these preferences are rarely estimated. Instead, a "reaction function," a regression estimating the central bank's response to macroeconomic variables, is calculated. The coefficients of the reaction function are amalgams of the preferences and reduced-form coefficients of the economic model itself. Generally speaking, economists have not tried to determine what the ultimate monetary policy targets are. They have typically assumed that the targets themselves are the same variables that appear in the reaction functions. However, just because the central bank reacts to inflation and GNP growth does not necessarily mean that those variables are of ultimate interest.

It is important to note that a model that assumes that the central bank minimizes a loss function of a combination of bank profits and nonfinancial profits will yield a reaction function very similar to traditional reaction functions. The result will be a reaction function in which the Federal Reserve reacts to macroeconomic variables such as inflation and real GNP growth, even though its ultimate targets are bank and nonfinancial profits. The reaction-function coefficients will be combinations of weights the central bank places on the bank profits and nonfinancial profits, the reduced-form coefficients relating macroeconomic variables to the two profit rates, and the reduced-form coefficients relating the federal-funds rates to the macroeconomic variables. In this context, if the economist knows these reduced-form coefficients, then the relative weights that the Fed places on these two targets can be estimated. If, however, the economist assumed that the Fed's ultimate goals were the macroeconomic variables themselves, the economist would calculate the policy weights incorrectly by taking the intermediate variables to be the final ones.

In this chapter we shall show that the reaction-function coefficients we estimate are consistent with our view that the central bank responds to financial and nonfinancial profitability.

In order to interpret the reaction function, it is essential to know the signs, if not the magnitudes, of the key parameters relating policy, macroeconomic variables, and targets. There have been several attempts to investigate the effects of macroeconomic variables on bank profits (Federal Reserve Bank of New York 1985). Most of these have suggested that bank profits are harmed by unexpected inflation because banks are net creditors. Moreover, because banks tend to value customer relations, their interest rates may be sticky. So actual inflation may harm bank profits as well. Increases in the rate of growth of GNP would be expected to increase the demand for loans and therefore increase bank profits, ceteris paribus. However, increases in GNP growth may also increase short-term interest rates, which may reduce profits in the short run because of sticky loan rates. Finally, even though labor costs represent a small percentage of the costs of bank operations, reductions in labor costs may improve bank profits.

This formulation suggests that bank profits should be determined by the rate of unexpected inflation (p_u), actual inflation (p), a measure of aggregate economic activity, such as the rate of real GNP growth (y), and a measure affecting labor costs, the cost of job loss (w^*), which we describe later.

$$P = P(p_u, p, y, w^*) \tag{4.1}$$

The rate of profit for nonfinancial corporations has undergone intense theoretical scrutiny, but relatively less empirical investigation (Bowles, Gordon, and Weisskopf 1987). Generally speaking, the rate of profit is determined by a Keynes process in which low levels of aggregate demand reduce the rate of capacity utilization and thus lower the rate of profit, by a Wicksell process, in which nonfinancial corporations, as net debtors, should gain from inflation, and by a Marx process, in which the greater the power of labor, the lower will be the rate of profit.

The arguments concerning the Marx process are less widely known. According to Marx, profit is a residual after the costs of depreciation, raw materials, and labor are accounted for. The costs of labor are not determined by workers' technical productivity per se, but by their strength in a bargaining process. Changes in workers' power affect work intensity and wages and therefore profitability. Following Schor and Bowles (1987), we argue that workers' bargaining power depends on the options available to them outside the employment relation, in particular, on the cost of job loss. The cost of job loss (hereafter w^*), is defined as the difference between income on the job and expected income after employment termination. When the cost of job loss rises (falls), workers' power declines (increases), wages fall (rise), and work intensity rises (falls).[7] The cost of job loss affects productivity (Bowles et al. 1983), the profit rate (Bowles et al. 1987, 1989), and work intensity (Schor 1987).

According to these arguments, the rate of profit for nonfinancial cor-

Table 4.1. *Determinants of bank profits, 1961–85*

	C	Independent variables UXINF	RGNPG	RINFL	w^*	$\bar{R}^2$	D.W.	S.E.R.
1.	.07	−.5	−.0004			.29	1.24	.01
	(15.3)	(−2.9)	(−.3)					
2.	.034	−.44			1.4D−05	.39	1.53	.01
	(1.85)	(−3.0)			(1.9)			
3.	.09	−.49	−.002	−.26		.56	2.03	.01
	(13.9)	(−3.5)	(−2.2)	(−3.7)				
4.	.09	−.48	−.002	−.26	2D−07	.53	2.03	.01
	(3.7)	(−3.3)	(−2.0)	(−3.0)	(.03)			

Notes: t statistics in parentheses. All data are annual. Dependent variable: rate of return on bank capital, all insured U.S. banks, adjusted for inflation. Independent variables: UXINF, unexpected inflation, based on ARIMA(2, 1, 0) forecast of CPI rate of change; RGNPG, rate of growth of GNP, lagged one period; RINFL, rate of CPI inflation, lagged one period; w^*, cost of job loss, lagged one period. $\bar{R}^2$, multiple-correlation coefficient corrected for degrees of freedom; D.W., Durbin-Watson statistic; S.E.R., standard error of regression. For complete definitions and sources, see data appendix, available from the authors on request.

porations should be determined by a measure of aggregate economic activity, say real GNP growth (y), unexpected and possibly actual inflation (p_u, p), and the cost of job loss (w^*).

$$r = r(w^*, y, p, p_u) \tag{4.2}$$

These macroeconomic variables, in turn, are assumed to be affected in traditional ways by monetary policy. Increases in the interest rates reduce inflation, lower the rate of growth of GNP, and increase the cost of job loss, primarily by increasing unemployment duration.[8]

Empirical results

In order to interpret the coefficients of the Federal Reserve's reaction function, it is necessary to have estimates of the reduced-form coefficients relating monetary policy instruments to macroeconomic variables, and macroeconomic variables to the ultimate target variables. We shall concentrate on estimating the effects of macroeconomic variables on bank and nonfinancial corporate profit rates. Then we shall estimate a reaction function for the Federal Reserve and interpret the results in the light of our results on the determinants of profitability, using other

Table 4.2. *Determinants of nonfinancial corporate profits, 1950–85*

	Independent variables							
C	RGNPG	RINFL	w^*	$w^* \times$ Time	ar(1)	$\bar{R}^2$	D.W.	S.E.R.
8.9	.22	−.06	.1	−.05	.67	.86	1.8	.81
(5.1)	(5.5)	(−.8)	(3.3)	(−3.3)	(4.3)			

Notes: t statistics in parentheses. All data are annual. Dependent variable: rate of return on capital, nonfinancial corporate business sector. Independent variables: RGNPG, rate of growth of real GNP; RINFL, rate of CPI inflation; w^*, cost of job loss; $w^* \times$ Time, w^* times an index of time; ar(1), first-order autoregression coefficient. For complete definitions and sources, see data appendix, available from the authors on request.

estimates of the relationships between policy instruments and macroeconomic variables (Fair 1984; Gordon 1988).

Table 4.1 presents the results of several estimates of the determinants of bank profits. The dependent variable is the profit rate of all insured commercial banks, adjusted for the effects of inflation on banks' earnings from 1961 to 1985 (Federal Reserve Bank of New York 1985).[9] The independent variables are the unexpected rate of inflation (UXINF), which is calculated from a time-series forecast of inflation, the rate of growth of real GNP (RGNPG), a measure of aggregate economic activity, the actual rate of inflation (RINFL), and the cost of job loss (w^*). Both the unexpected rate and the actual rate of inflation have a negative effect on bank profits.

Increases in the rate of growth of real GNP appear to hurt bank profits. Increases in the cost of job loss are positively associated with bank profits, but not always significantly so. These results suggest that reductions in the rate of inflation help bank profits and that increases in the rate of GNP growth may harm bank profits. Increases in the cost of job loss may also increase bank profits, though their effects are problematic.

If the Fed minimized a quadratic loss function and were concerned only with bank profits (assuming interest rates had their traditional effects), one would find a reaction function in which the central bank would act countercyclically: Increases in the rate of growth of GNP would harm bank profits, and so the central bank would raise interest rates to increase profits; increases in the rate of inflation would also harm bank profits, and so the central bank would again raise interest rates; reductions in the cost of job loss might harm bank profits, and so the Federal Reserve would raise interest rates.[10]

Turning to the interests of nonfinancial corporations, Table 4.2 pres-

Table 4.3. *Federal Reserve reaction function (federal-funds rate), 1966:1–1983:4*

		Independent variables								
	C	RGNPG	RINFL	*w**	*U*	*EG*	$\bar{R}^2$	D.W.	S.E.R.
1.	−1.7 (−2.8)	146.9 (4.4)	46.5 (1.8)				.29	1.85	1.24
2.	−.38 (−.3)	203.4 (5.2)	64.9 (2.6)	−.001 (−1.8)			.37	2.10	1.16
3.	−1.0 (−1.0)	123.9 (1.7)	55.7 (1.9)		−.11 (−1.0)		.28	1.98	1.24
4.	.8 (.7)	257.5 (5.9)	46.3 (1.39)	−.002 (−2.5)		−.59 (−1.2)	.39	2.12	1.18

Notes: t statistics in parentheses. All data are quarterly. Dependent variable: change in the federal-funds rate. Independent variables: all independent variables are third-order-polynomial distributed lags, lagged five periods, with no end-point constraints; RGNPG, quarterly rate of growth of real GNP; RINFL, quarterly rate of CPI inflation; *w**, cost of job loss; *U*, civilian unemployment rate; *EG*, real spendable weekly earnings of production workers. For complete definitions and sources, see data appendix, available on request from the authors.

ents estimates of the determinants of nonfinancial corporate profit rates, measured as before-tax profit divided by tangible assets. The signs are generally as expected. Increases in the rate of growth of real GNP increase corporate profit rates, ceteris paribus, presumably through the Keynes process. The rate of inflation, however, seems to have no significant effect on the rate of profit. Increases in the cost of job loss increase profit rates, as expected (the Marx process), though the effectivity of the cost of job loss appears to have decreased through time (the negative coefficient on $w^* \times$ Time).[11]

Combining the results of the two tables, a central bank concerned with a weighted average of bank and nonfinancial profits would, ceteris paribus, raise interest rates in response to an increase in GNP growth to raise bank profits and lower nonfinancial profits, and it would also raise interest rates in response to increases in inflation to increase bank profits. Thus, monetary policy would operate countercyclically as in the standard reaction-function studies. In addition, we would expect monetary policy to react to w^*.

Table 4.3 presents the results of several estimates of a Federal Reserve reaction function. The dependent variable is the change in the federal-funds rate. Though the Fed may have changed its operating procedures during the period under study, there is substantial evidence that the Fed has consistently used the federal-funds rate as a major policy instrument.[12] The time period chosen was 1966:1 to 1983:4 because of data limitations. The dependent variables include those discussed already (real GNP growth, rate of inflation, cost of job loss) and two others, earnings growth and unemployment, which will be described later. Equations 1–3 in Table 4.3 suggest that the Fed reacts to offset increases in the rate of inflation, in the rate of GNP growth, and in the cost of job loss. Equations that include the cost of job loss explain about 40 percent of the variance of the dependent variable.

These results suggest that as the rate of inflation increases and bank profits are reduced, the Federal Reserve raises interest rates to restore them. When real GNP increases, bank profits fall, and nonfinancial profits rise; so the Fed raises interest rates to restore equilibrium in the relationship between the two profit rates by raising bank profits and lowering nonfinancial profits. The cost of job loss is also a significant and quite robust variable in the reaction function. To determine if the cost of job loss may simply be a proxy for the unemployment rate, we substituted the unemployment rate (U) for the cost of job loss. However, it was not significant (equation 3 in Table 4.3).

The final equation investigates whether or not the Fed reacts to a variable of interest to workers: the rate of growth of real spendable earnings (EG). The results do not support the hypothesis that the Fed does so, as the coefficient on EG is not significant at conventional levels.

Conclusion

We have argued that the liberal and bureaucratic theories of the Federal Reserve are theoretically and empirically problematic. We have proposed an alternate theory of Federal Reserve policy that suggests that the Fed is primarily concerned with financial and nonfinancial profitability. This concern explains the Fed's strong inflation aversion and restrictive policies undertaken by the Federal Reserve to reduce the power of labor by increasing the cost of job loss.

Much work remains to be done to test our hypothesis fully. However, if the Fed is motivated as we suggest, it would seem important to place the issue of Federal Reserve independence on the political agenda, for if the Federal Reserve, as currently structured, does not try to make policy in the interests of all segments of society, then that structure is difficult to justify in a liberal democracy such as ours.

Notes

1 Unexpected inflation may have additional negative effects; yet empirical evidence does not seem to have found large effects for moderate rates of inflation. For a survey, see Fischer and Modigliani (1978).

2 Sproul files, Federal Reserve Bank of New York, marked E/C 3/25/54-AS.

3 In the formulation of our approach we have benefited greatly from the related work of Ferguson (1984) and Hall (1986).

4 Though we suggest that the Federal Reserve's ties to the financial community are particularly strong, there have been long periods of time in the postwar period when large segments of the financial and nonfinancial business communities have shared a strong common interest (Ferguson 1984).

5 During the war, in its negotiations with the Treasury, the Federal Reserve pushed for a higher interest rate on long-term bonds than the Treasury wanted. As Samuelson put it toward the end of the war, "this war is a 2% war. It should have been a 1% war" (Samuelson 1945, p. 26).

6 Notice that the quadratic loss function, which makes our results comparable to those in the Federal Reserve reaction-function literature, is a special case of the maximization problem described in the preceding section.

7 The cost of job loss, arbitrarily defined over a period of one year, is $w^* = w - [ud \cdot ui + (1 - ud) \cdot wn]$, where w is current earnings; ud is the expected unemployment duration expressed as a fraction of a year, ui is the social-welfare benefit available to the unemployed worker, and wn is expected earnings in the worker's next job. The cost of job loss is defined for an average worker in the private economy; see Schor and Bowles (1987).

8 Fair's model (Fair 1984) shows that a one-percentage-point increase in the Treasury-bill rate sustained for 12 quarters resulted in a decrease in real GNP of 1.51%, an increase in the unemployment rate of 0.51 percentage point, and a fall in the GNP deflator of 0.92% (p. 323). In the model of Bowles et al. (1987) there is a positive relationship between interest rates and the cost of job loss (communication from David M. Gordon).

9 For a complete description of data and sources, see the data appendix, available from the authors on request: Prof. G. A. Epstein, Department of Economics, University of Massachusetts, Amherst, MA 01003; Prof. J. B. Schor, Economics Department, Harvard University, Cambridge, MA 02138.

10 These and all other comparative static results reported in this chapter are derived quite simply from minimizing the loss function and assuming the signs of the reduced-form equations reported in the tables and text.

11 $W^* \times$ Time was also tried in the bank profit equation, but it was not significant. We also tried unexpected inflation in the equation for nonfinancial corporate profit, but it performed no better than actual inflation.

12 Changes in the federal-funds rate are highly correlated with a measure of monetary policy decisions (tighten, loosen, stay the same) that John Gildea gleaned from the minutes of Federal Reserve meetings.

References

Bade, Robin, and Parkin, Michael (1980). "Central Bank Laws and Monetary Policy," mimeograph, University of Western Ontario.

Bowles, Samuel, Gordon, David M., and Weisskopf, Thomas (1983). "Hearts and Minds: A Social Model of Productivity," *Brookings Papers on Economic Activity,* pp. 381–441.

(1987). "Power and Profits: The Social Structure of Accumulation and the Profitability of the Postwar U.S. Economy," *Review of Radical Political Economics,* 18(1&2):132–7.

(1989). "Business Ascendancy and Economic Impasse: A Structural Retrospective on Conservative Economics, 1979–1989," *Journal of Economic Perspectives,* 3(1):107–34.

Epstein, Gerald, and Ferguson, Thomas (1984). "Monetary Policy, Loan Liquidation and Industrial Conflict: The Federal Reserve and the Open Market Operations of 1932," *Journal of Economic History,* 64(4):957–98.

Epstein, Gerald, and Schor, Juliet B. (1986). "The Political Economy of Central Banking," Harvard Institute for Economic Research discussion paper 1281.

(1989a). "Macropolicy in the Rise and Fall of the Golden Age," in Stephen A. Marglin and Juliet B. Schor (eds.), *The Golden Age of Capitalism.* New York: Oxford University Press.

(1989b). "The Divorce of the Banca D'Italia and the Italian Treasury: A Case of Central Bank Independence," in Peter Lange and Marino Regini (eds.), *State, Market and Social Regulation: New Perspectives on the Italian Case.* Cambridge University Press.

Fair, Ray C. (1984). *Specification, Estimation, and Analysis of Macroeconomic Models.* Cambridge, Mass.: Harvard University Press.

Federal Reserve Bank of New York (1985). *Recent Trends in Commercial Bank Profitability; A Staff Study.* New York: Federal Reserve Bank of New York.

Ferguson, Thomas (1984). "From Normalcy to New Deal: Industrial Structure, Party Competition and American Public Policy in the Great Depression," *International Organization,* 38(Winter):41–94.

Fischer, S., and Modigliani, F. (1978). "Towards an Understanding of the Real Effects and Costs of Inflation," *Weltwirtschaftliches Archiv,* 114(4):810–32.

Gordon, David M. (1988). "Laying Theory in Concrete: First Steps Toward a Left Macroeconometric Model of the Postwar U.S. Economy," mimeograph, New School for Social Research.

Hall, Peter (1986). *Governing the Economy: The Politics of State Intervention in Britain and France.* Oxford University Press.

Llewellyn, John (1983). "Resource Prices and Macroeconomic Policies: Lessons from Two Oil Shocks," *OECD Economic Studies,* 1(1):197–212.

McNees, Stephen (1986). "Modeling the Fed: A Forward-Looking Monetary Policy Reaction Function," *New England Economic Review* (November–December):3–8.

Samuelson, Paul (1945). "The Effect of Interest Rate Increases on the Banking System," *American Economic Review,* 35(March):16–27.

Schor, Juliet B. (1985). "Changes in the Cyclical Variability of Real Wages: Evidence from Nine Countries, 1955–1980," *Economic Journal,* 95(378): 452–68.

(1987). "Does Work Intensity Vary with Macroeconomic Variables? Evidence from British Manufacturing, 1970–1986," mimeograph, Department of Economics, Harvard University.

Schor, Juliet B., and Bowles, Samuel (1987). "Employment Rents and the Incidence of Strikes," *Review of Economics and Statistics,* 69(4):584–92.

CHAPTER 5

Federal Reserve behavior since 1980: a financial-market perspective

WILLIAM C. MELTON AND V. VANCE ROLEY

Knowledge of actual Federal Reserve behavior is important in studies of monetary policy and financial markets for at least two reasons. First, the interpretation of variables chosen to represent the monetary policy process may be marred if they do not correspond to variables actually used by the Federal Reserve to implement monetary policy or to gauge its performance. Accordingly, the Federal Reserve's choices regarding targets, intermediate targets, and instruments may play a key role in research design.[1] Unfortunately, information regarding these choices is not always easy to obtain. Relevant Federal Reserve policy statements, such as an FOMC policy directive, are released after substantial delays and often are ambiguous.[2] Thus, additional knowledge regarding actual Federal Reserve behavior may have a methodological payoff.[3]

Second, the recurrent issue of policy credibility requires an assessment of the extent to which Federal Reserve statements find a reflection in the beliefs and behavior of economic agents. Although credibility potentially has a variety of interpretations, all would seem to require that a shift in stated policy objectives and instruments be associated with at least some change in market behavior. Thus, additional knowledge regarding Federal Reserve behavior, and the financial market's reaction to it, may help illuminate the credibility issue.

This chapter examines actual Federal Reserve behavior from a financial-market perspective. Movements in interest rates are used as the metric in this exercise. The underlying presumption is that financial-market participants fully understand Federal Reserve behavior. This position is sensible for two reasons. First, many financial-market participants are former Federal Reserve officials and economists. Second, given the key role of the Federal Reserve in influencing interest rates in at least the

We are grateful to Thomas Mayer for helpful comments, to Steven R. Thorley for research assistance, and to the National Science Foundation (grant no. SES-8408603) for research support.

short run, market participants have a strong incentive to study Federal Reserve behavior.

Following this introductory section, a framework for examining monetary policy is presented. Within that framework, several different types of monetary policy regimes are distinguished. In the next section, the implications of the different monetary policy regimes for the behavior of interest rates are discussed. The following section presents empirical results on actual Federal Reserve behavior. The period beginning in 1980 and ending in early 1987 is considered. That period is interesting in that Federal Reserve statements indicate that monetary policy changed several times. Thus, specific instances of Federal Reserve behavior can be analyzed in terms of the credibility of policy-makers. The main conclusions are summarized in the final section.

The monetary policy framework

Several aspects of monetary policy are reviewed in a stylized framework in this section. The long-run objectives of monetary policy are first considered. These long-run objectives involve both the targets and intermediate targets of policy over a given year. Next, several features pertaining to short-run monetary policy are discussed. It is argued that to interpret Federal Reserve behavior correctly, the short-run implementation of monetary policy must be examined. Different types of short-run policies are distinguished both by the type of operating procedure implemented by the Federal Reserve and by the desire to offset deviations from the targets.

Monetary policy objectives

The uncertainties facing the Federal Reserve make monetary policy a particularly challenging task, even apart from outside political pressures. The first choice facing policy-makers is to decide whether policy should be based directly on a set of ultimate targets, such as output, employment, inflation, and foreign exchange rates, or on an intermediate target. Potential intermediate targets include monetary and credit aggregates, as well as other indicators from financial markets, including interest rates.

In the middle to late 1970s, the intermediate-target procedure was progressively made a more formal part of Federal Reserve policy. Coinciding with that adoption, the Federal Reserve initiated a series of annual targets for monetary and credit aggregates. That procedure was formalized further under the Humphrey-Hawkins Act in 1978, which imposed a single, nonoverlapping calendar-year policy period on the Federal Reserve.

By the early 1980s the intermediate-target procedure was firmly entrenched. Nevertheless, some ambiguities were apparent. One area of ambiguity involved the appropriate weights to be placed on the various intermediate targets, particularly M1 and M2, in formulating policy. A second area involved uncertainties about the proper definition of the narrowly defined money stock, M1. Despite problems in determining an appropriate definition for M1 and the related problem of erratic M1 velocity, M1 was the main focus of monetary policy. One reason for the use of M1 was its timeliness. Preliminary M1 data are available weekly, with a lag of about 1.5 weeks, whereas data on broader monetary aggregates are available only monthly. However, many of the components of the broader aggregates are available weekly. A second reason was that M1 was the traditionally preferred monetary aggregate because of its intended link with transactions balances. Another reason was that the reserve requirements applied to non-M1 components of the broader aggregates are either zero or very low, implying a potentially loose relationship between reserves and the broader aggregates.

Because of the continuing erratic behavior of M1 velocity, the Federal Reserve virtually abandoned its intermediate-target procedure by the mid-1980s. In the record of policy actions at the November 2, 1987, FOMC meeting, for example, the FOMC's domestic policy directive listed the behavior of the monetary aggregates last among four items that could cause the Federal Reserve to change current pressure on reserve positions. The first three items were the strength of the business expansion, inflationary pressures, and developments in foreign-exchange markets. Thus, policy-makers were looking directly at measures of economic performance. It is also noteworthy that the items on the list occasionally change order. Developments in foreign-exchange markets, for example, had been listed first a few months earlier.

The foregoing is clearly a casual interpretation of monetary policy objectives in the 1980s. It does, nevertheless, suggest several hypotheses about Federal Reserve behavior. These hypotheses are tested in a later section. However, to interpret Federal Reserve behavior more precisely, the short-run implementation of policy must be considered.

Short-run monetary policy

The Federal Reserve's short-run monetary policy can be described in terms of two factors. The first concerns the rate at which the Federal Reserve attempts to offset any deviation from its target or intermediate target. The second is the type of operating procedure adopted. This latter area involves the choice of an instrument, or operating target, to conduct monetary policy.

The view of monetary policy advanced here is that the Federal Reserve does not initiate short-run shocks to the monetary aggregates; it merely reacts to them. This view seems particularly appropriate prior to February 1984, when contemporaneous reserve requirements (CRR) were adopted. Under the system of lagged reserve requirements (LRR) in effect from 1968 to that time, there was no direct link between bank reserves and M1 in a given week. As a consequence, the money stock was essentially demand-determined, and monetary shocks reflected shifts in the public's demand for money.[4]

Given that observed monetary shocks represent new information to both the public and the Federal Reserve, the relevant issue for policymakers is to determine the desired adjustment toward the monetary target. Casual evidence suggests that this adjustment speed may have changed at least twice since the late 1970s. In particular, the Federal Reserve committed itself more closely to M1 targets in October 1979, implying that any deviation from the monetary targets would be offset more quickly than before. In October 1982 the Federal Reserve deemphasized its monetary targets, implying slower adjustment speeds.

At the same time that the Federal Reserve changes adjustment speeds, it may also change its operating procedures. The choice of operating procedures, however, is logically independent of the desired rate of adjustment. That is, any of the three most prominent types of operating procedures – that is, the procedures based on the federal-funds rate, nonborrowed reserves, and borrowed reserves – can potentially yield virtually the same rate of adjustment.[5] Nevertheless, the adoption of an operating procedure based on the federal-funds rate or money-market conditions frequently is interpreted as an abandonment of monetary targets. Similarly, the adoption of the nonborrowed-reserves procedure, or reserves-aggregate procedure, in October 1979 often is viewed as being consistent with a greater desire to offset monetary shocks. As discussed in the next section, actual interest-rate behavior can be used to infer both the type of operating procedure adopted by the Federal Reserve and the desired rate at which monetary shocks are offset.

Implications for interest rates

Market interest-rate data are used to represent the actions of financial-market participants. It is further assumed that market participants fully understand Federal Reserve behavior. As a consequence, the Federal Reserve's reaction function can be inferred under this rational-expectations assumption. Moreover, changes in the estimated reaction function can be used to infer changes in monetary policy regimes.

Three aspects of interest-rate behavior are considered here: the volatility of interest rates, the response of interest rates to weekly M1 announcements, and the response of interest rates to new information about inflation, economic activity, and exchange rates. Differences in the volatility of interest rates in different periods are used to infer changes in Federal Reserve operating procedures. Similarly, changes in the response of interest rates to M1 announcements also are used to infer changes in operating procedures, as well as different degrees of emphasis on M1 targets. Finally, the response of interest rates to other economic information is used to infer the targets of monetary policy during a particular period.

Volatility of interest rates

The volatility of the federal-funds rate depends on disturbances affecting the market for reserves, Federal Reserve intervention in the reserves market through open-market operations, and the market's perception of the type of operating procedure being used. If the market believes that the Federal Reserve will offset shocks affecting the reserves market through open-market operations, and the shocks are in fact offset fairly quickly, the federal-funds rate will be relatively stable over a short period, such as a week. If disturbances in either the demand for or supply of reserves are not expected to be offset, however, the federal-funds rate will move quickly to clear the reserves market. Different operating procedures imply different behavior for the federal-funds rate through these channels.[6]

Under the procedure based on the federal-funds rate, the Federal Reserve offsets most shocks affecting the reserves market to keep the federal-funds rate relatively stable over a given period, such as a week. Even under this procedure, however, the federal-funds rate will be expected to exhibit some volatility over time. In particular, to offset deviations from the targeted money growth, the Federal Reserve may initiate discretionary changes in the rate. Nevertheless, in comparison with the other operating procedures discussed later, the federal-funds rate should be relatively more stable under this procedure.

Under the nonborrowed-reserves procedure, most disturbances affecting the reserves market, and therefore the federal-funds rate, are not offset. Instead, the nonborrowed-reserves path is maintained over a given period, and the federal-funds rate fluctuates in response to shocks either to the demand for reserves or to the supply of reserves. As a result, the federal-funds rate will be expected to be more volatile under this procedure.

The final procedure considered is the borrowed-reserves procedure. Under this procedure, the Federal Reserve can be characterized as attempting to achieve a certain level of discount-window borrowing over a given period. In this case, unanticipated changes in either required or excess reserves are accommodated by changing nonborrowed reserves. If the demand for required reserves is higher than expected, for example, the federal-funds rate rises initially, and borrowing increases to equate supply and demand in the reserves market. To offset the increase in borrowing, nonborrowed reserves are increased until the federal-funds rate falls to its previous level. In contrast, if a shock originating in the demand for borrowed reserves occurs in which borrowing is higher than expected at every level of the federal-funds rate, this disturbance is, at most, partially offset, and the federal-funds rate falls. The decline in the federal-funds rate serves to reduce the demand for borrowed reserves. So this source of disturbances in the reserves market causes fluctuations in the federal-funds rate. In comparison with the other procedures, the borrowed-reserves procedure implies more short-run volatility in the federal-funds rate than does the federal-funds-rate procedure, and less volatility than does the nonborrowed-reserves procedure.[7]

The volatility of other interest rates, such as the three-month Treasury-bill yield, also depends on the type of operating procedure employed by the Federal Reserve, although to a lesser extent. The three-month Treasury-bill yield depends on both the current federal-funds rate and the rate expected in future weeks. If the current week's federal-funds rate fluctuates, then some of this volatility is reflected in the Treasury-bill yield.

Treasury-bill yields also fluctuate if financial-market participants change their assessments about the federal-funds rate in future weeks. Monetary targets are important in examining this link. If new information about either money or the economy suggests, for example, that the future level of the money stock will be higher than previously expected, the Treasury-bill yield may rise if the market expects the Federal Reserve to offset this increase. In this instance, the market expects the Federal Reserve to attempt to achieve a particular monetary target, and the magnitude of the increase in interest rates reflects the desired speed of short-run adjustment back to the target level. Alternatively, if the Federal Reserve places little or no weight on a particular monetary target, the market will expect future levels of the federal-funds rate to be as previously predicted. So, for a given monetary disturbance, the greater the Federal Reserve's commitment to achieve a particular monetary target, the greater the coinciding fluctuation in longer-term yields.

Responses to money and economic announcements

The response of interest rates to money and economic announcements provides futher evidence for the type of operating procedure adopted by the Federal Reserve, as well as the degree of emphasis placed on various targets and intermediate targets of policy. In particular, the response of the federal-funds rate depends on the type of operating procedure. The response of longer-term yields depends somewhat on the operating procedure, but it depends more importantly on the intermediate target or target of policy. The responses to M1 announcements and other economic announcements will be considered separately.

First, consider the response of the federal-funds rate to weekly M1 announcements. The response depends directly on the type of operating procedure employed by the Federal Reserve. In particular, the response depends on whether or not the corresponding shock to the market for reserves is offset. The reserves market is affected by unanticipated announced changes in M1 initially through the market's assessment of the demand for required reserves. Under the LRR system in effect before February 1984, required reserves depended on the level of the money stock two weeks previously, the statement week corresponding to the current week's money-announcement data. Under the CRR system adopted in February 1984, required reserves depend on the current money stock, with a lag of two days.[8] As a consequence, the money-announcement data under CRR do not coincide with the current reserves periods. Unanticipated announced changes in M1 may still affect the demand for reserves, however, if the unanticipated changes have persistent effects on future levels of the money stock. That is, the current week's demand for reserves will be affected if a positive money-announcement surprise causes market participants to raise their assessments of the current week's money stock.

Under the federal-funds-rate procedure, the federal-funds rate should not respond to money-announcement surprises. In this case, market participants expect the Federal Reserve to accommodate the implied shock in the reserves market. In contrast, the federal-funds rate should increase in response to a positive money-announcement surprise under the nonborrowed-reserves procedure. This rise is due to a higher assessment of the demand for reserves that is not expected to be accommodated through Federal Reserve open-market operations. Similar to the federal-funds-rate procedure, the federal-funds rate should not respond to money-announcement surprises under the borrowed-reserves procedure. This behavior follows because the Federal Reserve accommodates shocks to the demand for reserves under this operating procedure.

The response of Treasury-bill yields and other longer-term yields to money-announcement surprises depends partly on the response of the federal-funds rate. Most of the response, however, depends on the extent to which the market expects the Federal Reserve to offset the shock in the future. In particular, the response is greater the more quickly the Federal Reserve acts to offset the money surprise. So the response of the Treasury-bill yield to money-announcement surprises can be used to determine whether the Federal Reserve is perceived to be attempting to achieve its M1 target.[9]

The response of Treasury-bill yields to unanticipated announced changes in economie activity and inflation may operate through the same channels as money announcements if these other economic announcements provide information useful in predicting money demand. In particular, if either real economic activity or inflation is higher than expected, the market may raise its assessment of the current and future weeks' demand for money. Interest rates, then, would be expected to rise in response to this new information about the domestic economy if the market does not expect the Federal Reserve to accommodate the increased demand. A similar direct link between exchange-rate movements and the demand for money is not evident.

The primary effect of new information about economic activity, inflation, and foreign-exchange rates on interest rates is likely due to the direct value of this information. That is, if policy-makers are placing more weight on their targets, and less weight on their intermediate monetary targets, new information about the economy and exchange rates may cause immediate interest-rate movements. If inflation is announced to be higher than expected, for example, policy-makers may adopt more restrictive policies, causing interest rates to rise immediately. The effect could be the same for an unexpectedly large increase in economic activity, especially during the later stages of an economic expansion, when concern about future inflation is growing. Moreover, if the Federal Reserve is focusing directly on the value of the dollar in currency markets, new information about exchange rates may lead to immediate interest-rate movements. Depending on the Federal Reserve's emphasis on this type of direct information about its ultimate targets, the responses of interest rates may have varied over different periods.

Empirical results

The various aspects of interest-rate behavior discussed in the preceding section will be used to test hypotheses about the behavior to the Federal

Reserve in conducting monetary policy. Three separate periods are examined, beginning in 1980. The first actually began in October 1979, when the Federal Reserve announced a new operating procedure along with an increased emphasis on the monetary aggregates. That new procedure corresponded to the nonborrowed-reserves procedure discussed earlier. The second period began in October 1982, when the Federal Reserve announced the abandonment of the nonborrowed-reserves procedure in favor of the borrowed-reserves operating procedure. At that time, somewhat less emphasis also may have been placed on the monetary aggregates – specifically M1 – as intermediate targets. The third period began in February 1984, coinciding with the implementation of CRR. Because of the uncertainties regarding the effects of CRR, among other factors, the Federal Reserve may have deemphasized the role of the monetary aggregates further in that period.[10] Another period, beginning in October 1977 and ending in October 1979, also is examined to compare the monetary policy regimes in the 1980s with monetary policy in the late 1970s. Prior to October 1979, the federal-funds-rate procedure was in effect.

Volatility of interest rates

The volatilities of the federal-funds rate and the three-month Treasury-bill yield are examined over four periods in Table 5.1. As is apparent in the table, the weekly volatility of the federal-funds rate is consistent with the changes in operating procedures hypothesized previously. In particular, in comparison with the pre–October 1979 period, the standard deviation of weekly percentage changes in the federal-funds rate was about four times as large in the October 1979–October 1982 period. That behavior was consistent with a switch to the nonborrowed-reserves procedure from the federal-funds-rate procedure. The volatility then declined to about half of the October 1979–October 1982 period in both of the periods after October 1982. Despite that decline, the volatility since October 1982 has been significantly larger than that experienced prior to October 1979, suggesting that the Federal Reserve did not return to the federal-funds-rate procedure.[11] Instead, the evidence is consistent with the adoption of the borrowed-reserves procedure.

Similar to the volatility of the federal-funds rate, the volatility of the three-month Treasury-bill yield increased significantly following October 1979. In contrast to the federal-funds rate, however, volatility after October 1982 returned to pre–October 1979 levels. Though some portion of the volatility of the Treasury-bill yield should reflect the volatility of the federal-funds rate, a larger part can be attributed to changes in the

Table 5.1. *Volatility of interest rates*

	Standard deviations of weekly percentage changes			
Interest rate	Oct. 1977– Oct. 1979	Oct. 1979– Oct. 1982	Oct. 1982– Feb. 1984	Feb. 1984– Feb. 1987
Federal-funds rate	0.019	0.077	0.037	0.043
$F(m, n)$[a]	–	16.89[b] (150, 99)	4.36[b] (150, 64)	1.37[b] (154, 64)
p value		0.00	0.1×10^{-12}	0.05
Three-month Treasury-bill yield	0.027	0.058	0.026	0.021
$F(m, n)$	–	4.62[b] (150, 99)	5.08[b] (150, 64)	1.53[b] (64, 154)
p value		0.2×10^{-13}	0.9×10^{-15}	0.01

Notes: The interest-rate quote on the day following each week's money announcement is used to form weekly percentage changes. The number in the first row and first column, for example, denotes a standard deviation of weekly percentage changes of 1.9%. The last weekly observation of each year is deleted to avoid the influence of excessive year-end interest-rate movements.

[a]$F(m, n)$, F statistic with (m, n) degrees of freedom for the hypothesis that the variance is the same as that in the previous period.

[b]Significant at the 5% level.

market's expectation about future monetary policy. As a result, the increased volatility of the Treasury-bill yield in the October 1979–October 1982 period was consistent with a greater commitment of the Federal Reserve to offset a given shock affecting the money stock, whereas the decline in volatility after October 1982 suggests the opposite. Other evidence, however, allows more direct inference about this possible shift.

Responses to money and economic announcements

To provide further evidence on changes in the operating procedures regarding monetary policy, hypotheses discussed in the preceding section concerning the response of the federal-funds rate to money-announcement surprises are first tested. Then, to determine the market's assessment of the Federal Reserve's targets and intermediate targets, the response of the three-month Treasury-bill yield to money and other economic announcements is examined empirically.

Table 5.2. *Responses of the federal-funds rate to M1 announcements*

Estimation period	Coefficient estimates			Summary statistics			
	Constant	UM1	EM1	$\bar{R}^2$	SE	DW	$F(m, n)$
Jan. 1980– Oct. 1982	0.0277 (0.0515)	0.0994[a] (0.0228)	−0.0121 (0.0291)	0.11	0.59	2.70	–
Oct. 1982– Feb. 1984	0.0413 (0.0272)	0.0137 (0.0128)	0.0016 (0.0122)	−0.01	0.20	1.76	10.71[a] (1,203)
Feb. 1984– Feb. 1987	−0.0872[a] (0.0191)	0.0103 (0.0103)	−0.0089 (0.0055)	0.01	0.22	1.97	0.04 (1,219)

Notes: The precise estimation-period dates are January 1, 1980 to October 5, 1982, October 6, 1982 to February 1, 1984, and February 2, 1984 to February 28, 1987. Observations in the last week of each year are deleted to avoid the influence of excessive year-end interest-rate movements. Numbers in parentheses are standard errors of estimated coefficients. Equations are estimated in the form $\Delta RFF_t = b_0 + b_1 UM1_t + b_2 EM1_t + e_t$, where b_0, b_1, and b_2 are estimated coefficients and e_t is a random-error term. ΔRFF_t, change in the federal-funds rate from the day of the money announcement to the next business day; UM1, money-announcement surprise, defined as M1 − EM1, where M1 is the announced change in the narrowly defined money stock, in billions of dollars; EM1, expected announced change in the narrowly defined money stock, based on the survey measure provided by Money Market Services, Inc.; $\bar{R}^2$, multiple-correlation coefficient corrected for degrees of freedom; SE, standard error; DW, Durbin-Watson statistic; $F(m, n)$, F statistic with (m, n) degrees of freedom for the hypothesis that the response coefficient, b_1, is the same as that estimated in the previous period (in this test, the estimated equations are weighted by their standard errors).
[a]Significant at the 5% level.

The usual efficient-markets model is used to estimate the responses of both the federal-funds rate and the three-month Treasury-bill yield. This model relates daily changes in interest rates to unanticipated announced changes in money and other economic variables. With the exception of the exchange-rate variable, unanticipated changes are measured as the difference between announced and expected values. The expected values are taken from a survey conducted by Money Market Services, Inc. The survey data are further adjusted, however, to take into account information from the time of the survey to the time of the announcement.[12] If the Federal Reserve – and therefore the market – views new information about a particular variable as being relevant for policy, the estimated response of interest rates should be significant.

The estimated responses of the federal-funds rate to the unanticipated component of weekly M1 announcements are reported in Table 5.2. The only statistically significant response occurred in the January 1980–

October 1982 period, consistent with the nonborrowed-reserves procedure.[13] In the two post–October 1982 periods, the responses were insignificantly different from zero, consistent with either the federal-funds-rate procedure or the borrowed-reserves procedure. Although estimates are not reported here, previous studies found that the response also was insignificantly different from zero prior to October 1979 (Roley and Walsh 1985). Combined with the evidence from Table 5.1, these results support the hypothesis that the Federal Reserve operated under a federal-funds-rate procedure prior to October 1979, and then implemented the nonborrowed-reserves procedure during the October 1979–October 1982 period. After October 1982, the combined evidence from Tables 5.1 and 5.2 suggests that the Federal Reserve adopted the borrowed-reserves procedure.

To determine the relative importance of various targets and intermediate targets of monetary policy, the responses of the three-month Treasury-bill yield to a set of economic variables are estimated in Table 5.3. In addition to weekly M1 announcements, the unanticipated components of monthly announcements of the producer price index, consumer price index, industrial production, and the unemployment rate are considered. Daily changes in the yen/dollar exchange rate also are included to estimate the significance of foreign-exchange-rate factors. Yen/dollar rate changes are measured as the difference in closing and opening quotes in the Tokyo market each day. Thus, such movements in the Tokyo market can be regarded as news to traders in New York, because these movements are recorded when the New York market is closed.

The results in Table 5.3 indicate that the role of M1 targets successively decreased over the three periods since 1980, and the differences across periods were significant at the 5 percent level. Moreover, since February 1984, the response of the three-month Treasury-bill yield to weekly M1 announcements has been insignificantly different from zero.[14] Whereas the role of M1 has decreased, the results suggest that the effect of direct information about the domestic economy has increased over time. As indicated by the reported F statistics, the hypothesis that new information about inflation, unemployment, and output does not affect interest rates can be rejected at the 5 percent level for the February 1984–September 1986 period. The most significant variable during this latter period was industrial production, suggesting that the Federal Reserve was looking directly at the performance of the economy in conducting policy. Finally, yen/dollar exchange-rate movements are not estimated to have had significant effects overall, though intermittent effects cannot be ruled out.[15]

Table 5.3. *Responses of the three-month Treasury-bill yield to new economic information*

Estimation period	Constant	Unanticipated change in: PPI	CPI	IP	UNEM	M1	YEN	Summary statistics $\bar{R}^2$	SE	DW	Tests $F_1(m, n)$	$F(m, n)$
Jan. 1980– Oct. 1982	−0.0079 (0.0107)	0.0290 (0.1620)	−0.2048 (0.1929)	0.0305 (0.1084)	−0.1964 (0.2438)	0.0842[a] (0.0109)	0.0029 (0.0112)	0.07	0.28	1.70	–	0.48 (4,694)
Oct. 1982– Feb. 1984	0.0033 (0.0047)	−0.0921 (0.0763)	−0.2048 (0.1651)	0.0558 (0.0751)	−0.1758 (0.1358)	0.0346[a] (0.0055)	0.0100 (0.0067)	0.11	0.09	1.55	16.59[a] (11,024)	1.34 (4,330)
Feb. 1984– Sept.1986	−0.0058[a] (0.0029)	−0.0075 (0.0443)	−0.0056 (0.1066)	0.1820[a] (0.0431)	−0.0800 (0.0689)	0.0019 (0.0043)	−0.0069 (0.0051)	0.02	0.08	1.89	21.95[a] (1,992)	4.85[a] (4,662)

Notes: See the notes to Table 5.2. The last period ends on September 19, 1986, because of the availability of yen/dollar exchange-rate data. Equations are estimated in the form $\Delta RTB_t = b_0 + b_1 UPPI_t + b_2 UCPI_t + b_3 UIP_t + b_4 UUNEM_t + b_5 UM1_t + b_6 YEN_t + e_t$, where the U's indicate that only the unanticipated components of the data are included. Unanticipated values of the first five variables are calculated using survey data provided by Money Market Services, Inc.; ΔRTB_t, change in three-month Treasury-bill yield from 3:30 p.m. to 3:30 p.m. on the subsequent business day; PPI, percentage change in the producer price index; CPI, percentage change in the consumer price index; IP, percentage change in the industrial production index; UNEM, percentage of labor force unemployment; YEN, change in the yen/dollar exchange rate from open to close in the Tokyo market on day *t*; $F_1(m, n)$, *F* statistic with (m, n) degrees of freedom for the hypothesis that the response coefficient, b_5, is the same as that estimated in the previous period (the relevant estimated equations are weighted by their standard errors); $F_2(m, n)$, *F* statistic with (m, n) degrees of freedom for the hypothesis that $b_1 = b_2 = b_3 = b_4 = 0$.

[a]Significant at the 5% level.

Conclusions

This chapter has exploited the financial market's understanding of Federal Reserve behavior in considering changes in monetary policy. In particular, both interest-rate volatility and the financial market's perception of the Federal Reserve's reaction function have been used to examine several monetary policy regimes over the last decade. One regime began in October 1979, when the Federal Reserve adopted a nonborrowed-reserves operating procedure and placed greater emphasis on M1. Prior to October 1979, the federal-funds-rate operating procedure was in effect. In Otober 1982, monetary policy shifted to a borrowed-reserves operating procedure and a diminished role for M1. Finally, in February 1984, still less weight was placed on M1 as an intermediate target of policy, with more weight placed directly on the performance of the domestic economy. These different periods correspond to Federal Reserve statements about changes in policy, and, as a whole, the evidence suggests that actual changes were made. To that extent, the evidence suggests that policy was credible.

To analyze the motives surrounding the Federal Reserve's formulation and implementation of monetary policy, it seems particularly worthwhile to study these specific episodes on a case-study basis. Such a study may reveal the relative importance placed on political and economic factors influencing Federal Reserve behavior. In brief, it appears that both factors are important. The change in policy in October 1979, for example, was driven by the desire to increase interest rates to defend the dollar in foreign-exchange markets and to reduce inflation in the United States. A slowdown in the growth of the monetary aggregates also was desired to reduce inflation in the future. Under the federal-funds-rate procedure in effect prior to October 1979, the Federal Reserve would be blamed for a sharp rise in interest rates. To deflect such criticism, policy-makers adopted a procedure in which "the market determines rates," the nonborrowed-reserves procedure. At the same time, there was some hope that that procedure would allow closer control of M1 and hence reduce the prospects of continued high inflation.

Similar economic and political choices were made in 1982. In particular, by October 1982 the behaviors of both M1 and the economy seemingly were becoming more unpredictable, and the Federal Reserve's independence was being threatened by the Congress. Policy-makers decided to weaken the link between M1 and interest rates, thereby reducing interest-rate volatility. Nevertheless, the advantage of some interest-rate volatility due to market factors was that no blame attached to the Federal Reserve for a particular level of interest rates. As a consequence, the borrowed-reserves procedure was adopted, in which the federal-funds rate fluctuated in response to errors in the borrowings function. In that sense, the Federal Reserve could continue to claim that it was not targeting a particular level of interest rates. A macroeconomic justification for the borrowed-reserves procedure is not, however, readily apparent, as the added volatility of interest rates created by random shifts in discount-window borrowing creates no clear benefit.[16]

The third regime in the 1980s appears to have been due primarily to an economic decision based on the uncertainties of the economic environment. In particular, the implementation of CRR in February 1984 had the potential to affect the behavior of an already unpredictable money stock, as well as to alter the previous relationships between reserves and money. That change was a delayed product of the nonborrowed-reserves regime, as closer monetary control was more likely under CRR than under LRR. Because of the added uncertainties surrounding CRR and the continuing erratic behavior of M1 velocity, policy-makers deemphasized their monetary targets further, and the borrowed-reserves procedure was maintained.

In sum, the behavior of the Federal Reserve in conducting monetary policy is best described by considering the Federal Reserve's operating procedures, targets, and desire to achieve its targets. Changes in those factors led to at least three different policy regimes in the 1980s.[17] In those regimes, the importance to the Federal Reserve of tight monetary control increased initially and subsequently became negligible. The lasting inheritance of the regime shift that began in October 1979 is the Federal Reserve's substantially greater willingness to tolerate interest-rate volatility. Regardless of the specific details of the operating procedures adopted, there apparently has been no reversion to the federal-funds-rate procedure employed in the late 1970s.

Notes

1 The terminology used here for targets, intermediate targets, and instruments of policy follows Friedman (1975).

2 Mayer (1987) and Goodfriend (1986) discuss issues relating to the disclosure of the FOMC's policy directive in detail.

3 One example, among many possible illustrations, would be the avoidance of confusion between use of an interest-rate instrument to achieve a particular policy target and interest-rate targeting, where the level of an interest rate itself is the policy objective.

4 For further discussion on this issue, see LeRoy (1979), Hetzel (1982), and Roley (1987).

5 The nonborrowed-reserves procedure is potentially slightly faster because of

federal-funds-rate movements in the current week. This property is discussed further in the next section. Also see Roley (1987).

6 For a more detailed discussion of these operating procedures, see Roley (1987).

7 A variant of the federal-funds-rate procedure, which apparently was introduced following the sharp decline of the stock market on October 19, 1987, is intermediate between the federal-funds-rate procedure described earlier and the borrowed-reserves procedure. In contrast to the earlier funds-rate procedure, in which the Federal Reserve entered the reserves market almost daily to add or drain reserves in order to keep the funds rate close to target, open-market operations under the variant procedure are relatively sparse and generally limited to adding or draining reserves, but not both, during a reserves-maintenance period. In this regard, the variant resembles the borrowed-reserves procedure. The main difference is that there is no explicit target for borrowed reserves, so that shocks to banks' demand for borrowed reserves do not (in principle) affect the funds rate. Some market participants have described the variant procedure as a "fuzzy" funds-rate target, because the allowable deviation of the actual rate from the target is larger than under the earlier funds-rate procedure. The Federal Reserve has announced its intention to revert to the borrowed reserves procedure at some point in the future.

8 Also, reserve computation and maintenance periods are two weeks in length, whereas they lasted one week under LRR. The response under two-week CRR is examined in detail by Roley (1987).

9 Considerable evidence suggests that the response of the Treasury-bill yield to M1 announcements is a response in a real rate, not expected inflation. One type of evidence is from the response of foreign-exchange rates to M1-announcement surprises. In particular, the dollar appreciates in response to positive money-announcement surprises. See, for example, Cornell (1982), Engle and Frankel (1984), and Hardouvelis (1984).

10 The introduction of CRR introduced at least two uncertainties. First, the previous relationship describing the demand for reserves changed, leading to uncertainties about the effects of various shocks on the federal-funds rate. Second, the stochastic behavior of the money stock itself was potentially affected, as it was no longer entirely demand-determined in a given week.

11 The test of the hypothesis that the two post–October 1982 periods have the same volatility as the pre–October 1979 period yields F statistics of 3.88 (64, 100) and 5.29 (154, 100), which are significant at the 5% level.

12 The change in the Treasury-bill yield over the previous five business days is used as a proxy for this information. See Roley (1983).

13 The results are qualitative the same when the estimation period starts in October 1979 instead of January 1980. See Roley and Walsh (1985). To conform with the results in Table 5.3, the January 1980 starting period was used. That date was chosen because of the availability of data for the exchange-rate variable used in Table 5.3.

14 In a specification analogous to that used in Table 5.2, the response of the Treasury-bill yield to money-announcement surprises also was examined over additional subperiods. In particular, starting with September 29, 1977, the response was estimated for overlapping 26-week periods, beginning every 13 weeks. The first two estimation periods, for example, were September 29, 1977 to March 23, 1978 and December 29, 1977 to June 22, 1978. The results from these regressions generally support the beginning and ending dates of the subsamples used in the tables. In particular, all responses after the June 1982–December 1982 period were estimated to be smaller than those of this period. Moreover, the responses in both the June 1983–December 1983 and September 1983–March 1984 periods were statistically significant at the 5% level, but the estimated responses starting with the December 1983–June 1984 period were not significant. This result is consistent with a change in the response around the beginning of 1984.

15 Positive and negative movements also were considered separately, but the statistical significance of the results did not change.

16 The borrowed-reserves procedure was implemented under LRR. Under CRR, however, this procedure may be capable of offsetting shocks from money and factors supplying reserves. See, for example, Roth and Seibert (1983).

17 And, as mentioned in note 7, a fourth regime may have begun following the October 19, 1987, stock-market crash.

References

Cornell, Bradford (1982). "Money Supply Announcements, Interest Rates, and Foreign Exchange," *Journal of International Money and Finance,* 1(August):201–8.

Engle, Charles, and Frankel, Jeffrey (1984). "Why Interest Rates React to Money Announcements: An Explanation from the Foreign Exchange Market," *Journal of Monetary Economics,* 13(January):13–39.

Friedman, Benjamin M. (1975). "Targets, Instruments and Indicators of Monetary Policy," *Journal of Monetary Economics,* 1(October):443–73.

Goodfriend, Marvin (1986). "Monetary Mystique: Secrecy and Central Banking," *Journal of Monetary Economics,* 17(January):63–82.

Hardouvelis, Gihas (1984). "Market Perceptions of Federal Reserve Policy and the Weekly Monetary Announcements," *Journal of Monetary Economics,* 14(September):225–40.

Hetzel, Robert L. (1982). "The October 1979 Regime of Monetary Control and the Behavior of the Money Supply in 1980," *Journal of Money, Credit and Banking,* 14(May):234–51.

LeRoy, Stephen F. (1979). "Monetary Control Under Lagged Reserve Accounting," *Southern Economic Journal* (October):460–70.

Mayer, Thomas (1987). "Disclosing Monetary Policy," Saloman Brothers Center for the Study of Financial Institutions, New York University, monograph 1987-1.

Roley, V. Vance (1983). "The Response of Short-Term Interest Rates to Weekly Money Supply Announcements," *Journal of Money, Credit and Banking,* 15(August):344–54.

(1987). "The Effects of Money Announcements under Alternative Monetary Control Procedures," *Journal of Money, Credit and Banking,* 19(August): 292–307.

Roley, V. Vance, and Walsh, Carl E. (1985). "Monetary Policy Regimes, Expected Inflation, and the Response of Interest Rates to Money Announcements," *Quarterly Journal of Economics, Supplement,* 100:1011–39.

Roth, Howard L., and Seibert, Diane (1983). "The Effects of Alternative Discount Rate Mechanisms on Monetary Control," *Federal Reserve Bank of Kansas City Economic Review,* 68(March):16–29.

CHAPTER 6

The Federal Reserve and its institutional environment: a review

MICHAEL C. MUNGER AND BRIAN E. ROBERTS

Introduction

The Federal Reserve System is perhaps the most controversial non-elected element of the government of the United States. Journalists and voters vilify it, Congress and the president seek to dominate it, and scholars argue about it. Our focus is on the literature that considers the political accountability and responsiveness of the U.S. monetary authority.[1] This body of work has undergone a clear evolution over time, going from a view of the Fed that took for granted its autonomy toward a perspective that debates the agency's independence and seeks to illuminate the avenues of political influence on it.

Because of the importance of the Fed in shaping monetary and overall economic policy, it is a powerful weapon. If political actors could gain control of it and learn how to use it effectively, there is little question that the executive, the Congress, and other external actors could better their own lot by providing useful service to grateful constituents. The question is, can political actors influence the Fed, and if so, how? The literature contains some hints that both the Congress and the executive have at least occasionally succeeded in influencing monetary policy, presumably to their electoral benefit. But these results are controversial, and the only real agreement to date is that there exists no consensus on their validity.

We shall not presume in this brief setting to describe at length the issues in this controversy or to take a position on them. Instead, our goal is to trace the evolution of scholarly work on the Federal Reserve's political accountability. Our reasons are two: First, as events have given us greater historical perspective on the regularities and turning points of monetary policy, the literature has been shaped by these events, as both economists and political scientists have sought to explain them. Second, an improved understanding of political and economic processes has allowed us to create new and more complete explanations for previous events, and therefore a more prospective and predictive, rather than simply descriptive, analytical framework.

These two observations imply a clear mechanism for organizing our review of the literature. The general outlines follow the actual chronological development of events, with each section internally organized according to where different papers fit in attributing accountability or autonomy to the Fed's conduct of monetary policy. In particular, we consider the Fed in its relation as an autonomous agent to its potential political principals, the executive and the Congress.

This outline is an apt characterization of the actual sequence of events, where first considerable freedom of action apparently followed the Fed–Treasury Accord of 1951, and that was the perspective taken in the literature reviewed in the first section. However, it became clear that monetary policy differed across presidential administrations and that presidents could seek to influence the Fed through appointments and moral suasion. The second section examines the relations between the Fed and the executive, particularly the Treasury.

Finally, at least from a historical perspective, Congress made concerted efforts throughout the middle 1970s to force the Fed to accept the wishes of its ovesight committees and to state general, clear economic goals. This literature, reviewed in the third section, is the most controversial and the most divergent in its evidence and conclusions about Fed accountability. The fourth and final section considers the effectiveness of the principal–agent model in informing the literature on the Federal Reserve and offers some tentative conclusions.

The autonomous Fed

We begin our review of the political economy of Federal Reserve decision-making with models of bureaucratic behavior. Early work on the Fed, particularly that focusing on the period before the Accord (e.g., Bach 1950, 1971; Wicker 1966), had generally taken a "public-interest" view in explaining Fed behavior, or at least in describing bureaucratic motives.[2] That is, early work assumed that Fed officials sought what was best for the country, thwarted though they may have been by other political actors. The more recent, and more useful, view is based loosely on the now formalized principal–agent model and draws heavily on the links among individual incentives, institutional structure, and public policy.[3] The advantage of organizing our survey in this way is that virtually all the relevant literature either, explicitly or implicitly, makes assertions about Fed accountability to external actors.

Although we tend to associate this perspective with more contemporary accounts of Fed behavior, it emerges quite clearly in an early piece by Michael Reagan (1961). In the first article in a political science journal on the subject of Fed accountability, Reagan observes that "public policy is not self-generating; it emerges from institutions," drawing immediate attention to the role of organizational design (rather than personalities) in the shaping of Fed policy.[4]

Institutional structure is, of course, endogenous (Riker, 1980). It derives from secular choice, in this case from the collective decision of Congress (a social-choice problem we shall not explore). In designing the Fed, Congress was clearly well aware of the political vulnerability of a central monetary authority. We should not, however, be too hasty to congratulate Congress on its success, as many other authors have done. As we shall see, it seems unlikely that Congress ever actually sought to create a truly independent Fed. Instead, there appear to exist carefully considered attempts at putting political constraints on Fed behavior. The issue that divides the literature on Fed accountability is whether or not such political constraints actually influence Fed behavior in any material way.

Bureaucrats

The bureaucratic autonomy model, whose creation can best be attributed to Niskanen (1971), provides a useful benchmark in the accountability debate. In its simplest form, it asserts that there exist few, if any, binding political constraints on Fed behavior. Monetary policy therefore derives from the preferences of utility-maximizing bureaucrats who take advantage of their comparative expertise and the fact that it is costly for congressional oversight committees to monitor the Fed's behavior effectively. Fed officials can therefore eschew concern for the "public interest," or in fact any other politically induced objective functions, in their prosecution of monetary policy.

The first research explicitly applying the bureaucratic autonomy model to monetary policy examined the central bank of Canada. In two related articles, John Chant and Keith Acheson (Chant and Acheson 1972; Acheson and Chant 1973) suggest that bureaucratic preference for the "maintenance of autonomy and self-preservation" dictates the choice of goals, instruments, and techniques in monetary policy management. The model predicts an equilibrium policy systematically different from that preferred by the public. In particular, Chant and Acheson claim there should exist an institutional inflationary bias arising from narrowly focused bureaucratic self-interest.

A similar thesis has been used to address U.S. central-bank behavior

(Frey and Schneider 1978; Friedman 1982; Toma 1982; Shughart and Tollison 1983; Chappell and Keech 1985; Fand 1986; Wagner 1986; Toma and Toma 1986). Often labeled the public-choice model of Fed policy-making, it is implicitly based on Niskanen's thesis that bureaucrats maximize their own utility, which generally translates into maximizing the agency's budget. Toma focuses on the funding of the Fed's budget: the interest earned on the Fed's portfolio of government bonds. He asserts that the bureaucratic preference for budget maximization leads to an inflationary bias in Fed policy as it seeks to increase its interest earnings. Shughart and Tollison go a step further and suggest that Fed earnings (proxied by growth in the monetary base) are immediately dissipated by increased size (number of employees) of the Fed, explaining bureaucratic incentives to inflate in order to create a larger, more powerful bureau, as Niskanen predicts.

Models of Fed behavior predicated on a theory of bureaucracy provide insights important to an understanding of Fed behavior, but their partial-equilibrium perspective on incentives to shirk discounts or ignores potentially important political constraints that may limit shirking. The simple prediction that "bureaucrats always win" is based on only one aspect of the incentives for monetary policy formation, reducing such models' predictive usefulness. Regardless of the extent of shirking (which we would naturally expect to exceed zero in equilibrium if enforcement is costly), it is imperative that an explanation be offered for why a legislature would permit such behavior. Congress created, and the president approved, the Fed and the attendant opportunities for its officials to shirk. The unanswered question in this literature remains: Why would an institution composed of rational actors tolerate such activities by an agent when it could be prevented?[5]

One answer is provided by Wagner (1980, 1986). He claims that legislative acceptance of a Fed with an inherent inflationary bias (Toma 1982) is explained by the electoral benefits deriving from the real effects of a sustained inflationary environment: "It is the distributional consequences of alternative monetary institutions and their processes of monetary expansion that will be the primary element in explaining the choice and persistence of particular institutions" (Wagner 1986, p. 531). Wagner asserts that the Fed would not exist as we know it if not for its ability to deliver the desired inflation and consequent constituent benefits through reducing the real quantity of debt and expanding output. To extend the principal–agent analogy, the apparent shirking of Fed officials leading to persistent inflation may actually be consistent with congressional wishes, but achieved through a decentralized institutional design.[6]

The chairman

Whatever the objectives of Fed bureaucrats in general, the preferences of the chairman are always singled out for special treatment. The agenda power, staff control, and influence with the White House exercised by the chairman have established him in the eyes of many as a virtual dictator of Fed policy. Literature that has taken this view implicitly or explicitly accepts the extreme form of Niskanen's autonomous bureaucrat theory and ascribes almost all power to a single individual.

The role of the chairman has changed dramatically over the history of the Fed, so that the single-actor bureaucratic autonomy view is truly applicable (if at all) only in recent years. The centralized decision-making process that emerged from New Deal reforms (particularly the 1933 and 1935 Banking Acts) expanded the influence of the Fed chair at the expense of the district bank presidents (Maisel 1973). Heralded by some as an important step toward increased political accountability, others viewed the ascendancy of the chair as a frightening concentration of power.[7] With the latter view in mind, Whitlesey (1963, p. 43) observes that "in a society based upon government by laws rather than men, monetary policy seems to be governed more by men than by laws." In the context of our principal–agent discussion, such a conclusion taken on its face implies either a failure in the design of the Fed as an institution or the success of an inexplicable goal of elected officials, simply abdicating all power over monetary policy.

Actually, however, the implications for the question of political accountability that follow from an institutionally powerful chairman are not clear-cut (Borins 1972). If the Fed is as autonomous as the bureaucratic models suggest, then a dictatorial chairman may pose an alarming threat to public policy. If, however, the Fed is subject to binding political constraints, an internally omnipotent but externally manipulable chairman may prove an ideal channel for political influence on policy. Although anecdotes abound, empirical efforts to substantiate either of these scenarios have not met with much success (Pierce 1979; Ersenkal, Wallace, and Warner 1985).

The FMOC

Another important institutional innovation of the 1935 Banking Act relating to the intramural decision-making of the Fed was the creation of the Federal Open Market Committee (FOMC) (see the chapter in this volume by Havrilesky and Schweitzer). In a unique set of articles,

Yohe (1966, 1974) and Canterbery (1967) use the voting behavior of FOMC members to infer policy preferences within the Fed. Both authors focus on the relative influence of the chair in light of persistent claims (e.g., Whitlesey 1963) that the chair, particularly Chairman Martin, had assumed dictatorial powers over Fed decisions. The empirical evidence amassed by the authors fails to support such claims. We are therefore left with no compelling reasons to accept the claims made in earlier work that the chairman or the FOMC possesses the political autonomy from external control ascribed to them by the bureaucratic dominance model.

Studies such as these should not be discarded simply for failing to paint a complete picture of the policy process. As they stand in historical context, these models provided the critical insights that moved the literature beyond simple public-interest models to consider individual bureaucratic incentives and pointed the way toward an examination of the realistic responses of agents with such motivations to external efforts at interference. This approach has led to a more sophisticated view of the politics of monetary policy formation. Woolley (1984), in a comprehensive overview of the Fed in its relations with political actors and interest groups, offers the thesis that the strategies and effectiveness of outside actors will be determined by the resources they control. We now turn sequentially to the literature that considers the two most important external actors: the executive and the Congress.

The executive

If the quantity of literature taking a single perspective on Fed accountability is to serve as a guide, there is little question that the executive branch, manifested either as the president or as the Treasury Department, is the most important source of extramural policy guidance confronting Fed officials. Hypotheses concerning the political origins of monetary policy generally fall into one of two categories, and we shall consider each in turn.

The first, based partly on early work by Douglas Hibbs (1977) on the relationship between political parties and macroeconomic policy, finds the political origins of economic policy in the preferences of the constituencies of competing political parties. For our purposes, this theory suggests that monetary policy is generally expected to be tighter under conservative administrations than under liberal administrations.[8] We label this view of presidential influence the "accommodation theory." Such research (e.g., Bach 1971; Maisel 1973) portrays the Fed as passively accommodating administration fiscal policy in an effort to avoid confrontation, rather than as succumbing to explicit political pressure.

The second hypothesized political origin of monetary policy derives from the electoral imperative of politicians. Though apparently similar in origin, this perspective is profoundly different in its predictions: Rather than focusing on competition between parties, the electoral imperative view pits incumbents against challengers. To enhance their re-election prospects, politicians manipulate the money supply to ensure expansion in the months preceding an election. Thus, money growth is a function of the time before the next election; this cycle differs from that implied by accommodation theory in that the electoral cycle will exist regardless of the overall fiscal policies the executive pursues. The monetary cycle theory is conceptually analogous to the political business cycle literature (Nordhaus 1975; Tufte 1978; Alt and Crystal 1983), though in this case we are concerned with the existence of a political monetary cycle (PMC). The degree of manipulation implied by a PMC requires that, contrary to the conclusions in the literature, the Fed is extremely malleable politically.

Reaction function models have been used to test both the accommodation theory and the PMC theory. The first important paper in this area was by Potts and Luckett (1978), and it falls in the former category. Most subsequent work, however, deals with the more controversial topic of the PMC (Luckett and Potts 1980; Golden and Poterba 1980; Maloney and Smirlock 1981; Pollard 1983; Grier 1984, 1987; Beck 1984, 1987; Wallace and Warner 1984; Allen 1986; Havrilesky 1988). The results of these studies are no more convincing than those advanced in support of the more general political business cycle. A notable exception is the work of Kevin Grier, who discovers strong cyclical trends in money growth that coincide with presidential elections.[9]

As with other diviners of political monetary cycles, however, Grier does not identify the linkage or incentives that motivate systematic Fed acquiesence to the desires of politicians (whose motivations were never in doubt). Whether the result of conscious manipulation or not, the very appearance of political accommodation may threaten the viability of the Fed as a central bank (Meiselman 1986; Gutfeld 1988).

One still-nascent explanation for the existence of monetary cycles draws attention to fiscal policy initiatives. As noted by Laney and Willett (1983), depending on the choice of how deficits are financed, "an election cycle in fiscal policy would induce an election cycle in monetary policy also, even if the Fed were entirely apolitical in a partisan sense" (p. 54). Grier and Neiman (in press) provide further empirical support for a deficit/money growth relationship, but suggest the existence of some partisan influence. In particular, they detect significant cycles under Democratic administrations.

Presidential administrations do appear to bear upon the course of monetary policy. This influence is manifested in differences in money growth rates across administrations (Potts and Luckett 1978; Beck 1982a, 1982b; Havrilesky 1987). These results do not revitalize claims for the existence of political monetary cycles, however, as the observed changes in money growth rates are not generally found to be cyclic within electoral terms. Instead, except for the work of Grier and Neiman, they are found to vary from one administration to the next, calling into question whether or not in fact an incumbent president can dictate policies to his own advantage.

Congress

The origin of the scholarly interest in Congress as an influence on the Fed after the act of creating the agency can be traced back as far as the full employment act of 1946 and its (admittedly weak) attempt to change the direction of Fed policy. Following the Fed–Treasury Accord in 1951, the United States had a monetary authority whose mandate was to lean against the wind, implying an unprecedented discretionary choice of how much monetary growth was too much, and how little was too little.

These events created a situation where it was for the first time plausible to ask if Congress might enjoy any systematic influence. The first examination of this question by a political scientist was that by Bibby (1967). His work recounts two episodes (1955 and 1958) when the Senate Banking and Currency Committee successfully brought pressure to bear upon the Fed to pursue a more expansionary policy. These two case studies lent some credibility to the proposition that Congress could extract some marginal concessions from the Fed, but their anecdotal nature could hardly allow any general conclusions about the effectiveness of the principal–agent relation from the perspective of the legislature.

Maisel (1973) sought to clarify the terms of the agency relationship, concluding that Congress and its oversight committees have little day-to-day influence because of the absence of active oversight. Once monetary policy strays far enough from the desired path to begin to generate constituent mail, however, oversight committees do appear to become concerned (McCubbins and Schwartz, 1984, call this "fire alarm" oversight). Although the evidence once again is subjective and anecdotal, Maisel's conclusion was that once Congress awakes, "what concerns individual congressmen in the monetary field automatically concerns the Federal Reserve" (1973, p. 154).

The next stage of research interest was once again precipitated by events, this time a major wave of attempts at congressional interference following what was perceived as an overly restrictive Fed monetary policy in 1974. Congress responded in three stages. First, hearings were held and harsh statements issued threatening statutory emasculation. Second, the House passed Concurrent Resolution 133, which called for semiannual appearances of Fed officials before Congress to present projections of money growth and to defend those projections as part of a coherent national economic policy. Finally, the provisions of Resolution 133 were made binding by the passage of the 1978 Humphrey-Hawkins (Balanced Budget and Growth) Act.

This sudden surge of congressional activity prompted renewed academic interest in congressional oversight of the Fed. In 1978, a series of invited papers on congressional influence was published in the *Journal of Monetary Economics.* Without exception, those papers concluded that congressional meddling in the mid-1970s had failed to alter the policy preferences of the Fed, if in fact influence rather than simple position-taking had ever been the meddlers' true goal. Paul Volcker (1978), then president of the New York Fed, acknowledged continuing Fed concerns over congressional desires, but discovered nothing in the flurry of legislative activity of that period that unusually heightened such concern.

Other work in that volume is no less skeptical of claims of congressional power. Pierce (1978) unequivocally entitles his article "The Myth of Congressional Supervision of Monetary Policy." He argues that members of Congress lack the expertise to debate monetary policy with the Fed, and more important, they permit Fed officials to obfuscate their presentations before the committees so much that projected money growth rates are virtually meaningless. Pierce concludes that the legislative activity of the 1970s was little more than face-saving: "Congress has salved its conscience by passing a resolution [House Concurrent Resolution 133] and then a law [the Humphrey-Hawkins Act] but it showed little interest in providing meaningful oversight of monetary policy" (p. 364).

Weintraub (1978) argues, in perhaps the most famous article in that collection, that monetary policy is dominated by the president, and the Congress plays only a marginal role. This observation is important because Weintraub was himself a long-time staff member of the House Banking Committee and had a personal, if subjective, set of experiences on which to draw.

A parallel development in the study of the agency relationship between Congress and bureaus has recently called these conclusions into question. In particular, a "congressional dominance" theory of bureaucratic behavior has been developed (Weingast and Moran 1983; McCubbins and Schwartz 1985; Weingast 1984; McCubbins and Page 1986; Weingast and Marshall 1988). The theory has two premises: First, Congress voluntarily delegates policy-making authority to a bureau only when it is to the advantage of Congress to do so. Second, specialized monitoring institutions evolve within Congress to control shirking: "It makes no sense to let bureaucrats capture all the political rewards when an agency's policy could reasonably be used to enhance electoral prospects" (Weingast 1984, p. 154). The implicit monitoring mechanisms include responses to complaints of constituents who possess both the knowledge and incentive to monitor, control over appointments, and the threat of institutionally painful sanctions in the event of continued agency malfeasance.

As we have seen, Congress has attempted, particularly in the mid-1970s, to use such devices to exert influence over the Fed. The question is whether or not such attempts have been effective. This is particularly crucial because previous work has found some significant influence attributable to presidential terms of office, which after all coincide with congressional elections. To the extent that Congress influences Fed policy, the coincidence of presidential and congressional elections may have confounded the results of previous studies claiming to isolate presidential influence. Grier (1984) finds evidence that a proxy for preferences of Senate Banking Committee members (particularly the chair) over the period 1961–80 is a statistically significant explanatory variable for money supply growth (M1). The comparative statics prediction of the congressional dominance model for which Grier finds support is that a change in the composition of the relevant oversight committee causes a change in policy and in the direction of the change in policy preferences implied by the new membership compared with the old. Wagner (1986) offers a similar conclusion, though with less systematic evidence. A slightly different interpretation of the same events is offered by Kane (1974, 1980, 1982). He claims that while it may appear Congress is distant and aloof from monetary policy, this insulation serves a useful purpose by allowing Congress to claim credit for success and blame the Fed as a scapegoat for failure, or even for economically sound but politically damaging stabilization policy.

Nathaniel Beck, in an article in this volume, replicates Grier's results, but finds that the estimated coefficients are not robust, losing significance and changing sign in response to the inclusion of more recent data (1980–7). This is not surprising, however, because the new data cover an era in which the Fed employed new targeting procedures and redefined monetary aggregates. Although Beck offers several theoretical reasons why congressional preferences should not prove important in Fed policy-making, the question is now an empirical one, and the debate remains alive.

Conclusions

The attention garnered by the Fed is easily explained as a consequence of its unique institutional position within the economic policy process. In no other single institution resides such powerful weapons for unilateral influence over the course of economic policy. The visibility attending such power understandably attracts questions about its susceptibility to the political or personal agendas of bureaucrats and politicians.

The literature we have reviewed is far from conclusive in characterizing the political pressures bearing upon the conduct of monetary policy. Although the motives of the principals are rarely in doubt, the avenues of manipulation of the Fed as an agent have never been clearly mapped. The whole question of these linkages is more often than not skirted entirely in the empirical literature. This is truly unfortunate, for it distracts from what otherwise may be convincing evidence of a political dimension to monetary policy, and it represents the most important lacuna in the existing literature. One problem, of course, is that even if such direct links exist (meetings with no minutes, conversations at which no notes were taken, etc.), they will almost certainly be invisible to observers. Nonetheless, our understanding of U.S. monetary policy will be woefully incomplete unless we can either identify the links or demonstrate their nonexistence.

The question of the specific paths of influence aside, the literature also suffers from a fundamental lack of integration arising from the lack of an explicit treatment of the overall relation of the Fed to its potential principals. Authors' convictions that they have identified *the* source of political pressure on Fed decision-making all too often lead to ignoring competing hypotheses in the formulation of empirical models. The fact that separate studies have found evidence (however weak) of political influence emanating from disparate sources suggests the strong need for broader, more encompassing studies of the political environment of monetary policy.

Notes

1 Although this essay is restricted to the political dimensions of Fed policy, questions concerning Fed accountability certainly extend beyond the realm of politics, most notably to the financial community (Havrilesky 1987).

2 For historical overviews of early events shaping U.S. monetary policy, see Epstein and Ferguson (1984), Friedman and Schwartz (1963), Hammond (1957), and Peretz (1983).

3 The formal literature on bureaucracy, as yet unapplied to the specific case of the Federal Reserve, is replete with principal–agent models (Moe 1984; Bendor 1987).

4 Economists have generally had little interest in the question of accountability, focusing instead on optimal policy and the conflict between rules and discretion in achieving the desired results. However, the question of accountability clearly arises, as in the exchange between Barro (1986) and Cagan (1986). Also, see Friedman (1977) for a broader economics perspective.

We might also note that the pioneering work of Reagan, though often itself the target of criticism (too "critical," Yohe; "overly legalistic," Beck 1982a), stood alone for many years within the political science literature as the sole examination of the relation between the structure of the Fed and its actual policy choices.

5 Toma (1982) baldly asserts that "Congress does not monitor the activities of the Fed." Such a tolerance of shirking must rely on an insoluble incentive incompatibility or information asymmetry. Because Congress *can* clearly measure outputs (money supply growth, inflation, etc.), this is an open question.

6 In a comment on Wagner (1986), Grier (1986) supports Wagner's contention that Congress represents an important factor in Fed decision-making, but suggests that presidential influence must also be accounted for. We take up the issue of presidential influence in a separate section.

7 To this day, one of the most persistent recommendations for reform of the Fed is to have the terms of the U.S. president and the Fed chair coincide.

8 In an interesting study reexamining the original work of Hibbs (1977), Beck (1982b) finds that inflation and unemployment rates exhibit remarkable differences across administrations, but that these differences are largely independent of which party is in power.

9 Beck (1987) partially replicates Grier's results, though he questions their validity.

References

Acheson, Keith, and Chant, John F. (1973). "Bureaucratic Theory and the Choice of Central Bank Goals," *Journal of Money, Credit and Banking,* 5:637–55.

Allen, Stuart (1986). "The Federal Reserve and the Electoral Cycle," *Journal of Money, Credit and Banking,* 18:62–6.

Alt, James E., and Crystal, K. A. (1983). *Political Economics.* Los Angeles: University of California Press.

Bach, George L. (1950). *Federal Reserve Policy Making.* New York: Knopf.

Bach, George L. (1971). *Making Monetary and Fiscal Policy.* Washington, D.C.: Brookings Institution.

Barro, Robert J. (1986). "Rules versus Discretion," in C. D. Campbell and W. R. Dougan (eds.), *Alternative Monetary Regimes,* pp. 16–30. Baltimore: Johns Hopkins University Press.

Beck, Nathaniel (1982a). "Presidential Influence on the Federal Reserve in the 1970's," *American Journal of Political Science,* 26:415–45.

Beck, Nathaniel (1982b). "Parties, Administrations, and American Macroeconomic Outcomes," *American Political Science Review,* 76:83–93.

Beck, Nathaniel (1984). "Domestic Political Sources of American Monetary Policy," *Journal of Politics,* 46(3):786–817.

Beck, Nathaniel (1987). "Elections and the Fed: Is There a Political Monetary Cycle?" *American Journal of Political Science,* 31(1):194–216.

Bendor, Johnathon (1987). "Formal Models of Bureaucracy: A Review Essay," paper presented at the annual meeting of the American Political Science Association, Chicago.

Bibby, John F. (1967). "The Senate Committee on Banking and Currency," in J. F. Bibby and R. Davidson (eds.), *On Capitol Hill,* pp. 170–96. New York: Holt, Rinehart & Winston.

Borins, Sanford F. (1972). "The Political Economy of the Fed," *Public Policy,* 30:175–98.

Cagan, Phillip (1986). "The Conflict between Short-run and Long-run Objectives," in C. D. Campbell and W. R. Dougan (eds.), *Alternative Monetary Regimes,* pp. 31–7. Baltimore: Johns Hopkins University Press.

Canterbery, E. R. (1967). "A New Look at Federal Open Market Voting," *Western Economic Journal,* 6:25–38.

Chant, John F., and Acheson, Keith (1972). "The Choice of Monetary Instruments and the Theory of Bureaucracy," *Public Choice,* 12:13–34.

Chappell, Henry W., and Keech, William R. (1985). "The Political Viability of Rule-Based Monetary Policy," *Public Choice,* 46(2):125–40.

Epstein, Gerald, and Ferguson, Thomas (1984). "Monetary Policy, Loan Liquidation, and Industrial Conflict: The Federal Reserve and the Open Market Operations of 1932," *Journal of Economic History,* 4:957–983.

Ersenkal, Caryl, Wallace, Myles S., and Warner, John T. (1985). "Chairman Reappointments, Presidential Elections and Policy Actions of the Federal Reserve," *Policy Sciences,* 18(2):211–25.

Fand, David I. (1986). "Federal Reserve Hegemony and Monetary Surprises," *Cato Journal,* 6(2):581–6.

Frey, Bruno S., and Schneider, Friedrich (1978). "An Empirical Study of Politico-Economic Interaction in the United States," *Review of Economics and Statistics,* 60:174–83.

Frey, Bruno S., and Schneider, Friedrich (1981). "Central Bank Behavior: A Positive Empirical Analysis," *Journal of Monetary Economics,* 7:291–315.

Friedman, Milton (1977). "Nobel Lecture: Inflation and Unemployment," *Journal of Political Economy,* 85:461–72.

Friedman, Milton (1982). "Monetary Policy: Theory and Practice," *Journal of Money, Credit and Banking,* 14:98–118.

Friedman, Milton, and Schwartz, Anna J. (1963). *A Monetary History of the United States, 1867–1960.* Princeton University Press.

Golden, David G., and Poterba, James M. (1980). "The Price of Popularity: The Political Business Cycle Reexamined," *American Journal of Political Science,* 24(4):696–714.

Grier, Kevin B. (1984). "The Political Economy of Monetary Policy," doctoral dissertation, Department of Economics, Washington University, St. Louis, Mo.

Grier, Kevin B. (1986). "Monetary Policy as a Political Equilibrium," *Cato Journal,* 6(2):539–43.

Grier, Kevin B. (1987). "Presidential Elections and Federal Reserve Policy: An Empirical Test," *Southern Economic Journal,* 54(2):475–86.

Grier, Kevin B., and Neiman, Howard E. (in press). "Deficits, Politics and Money Growth," *Economic Inquiry.*

Gutfeld, Rose (1988). "Greenspan Criticizes Top Treasury Aid for Attempting to Influence Fed's Policy," *Wall Street Journal,* February 25, p. 4.

Hammond, Bray (1957). *Banks and Politics in America from the Revolution to the Civil War.* Princeton University Press.

Havrilesky, Thomas (1986). "The Effect of the Federal Reserve Reform Act on the Economic Affiliations of Directors of Federal Reserve Banks," *Social Science Quarterly,* 67(2):393–401.

Havrilesky, Thomas (1987). "A Partisanship Theory of Fiscal and Monetary Regimes," *Journal of Money, Credit and Banking,* 19(3):308–25.

Havrilesky, Thomas (1988). "Monetary Policy Signaling from the Administration to the Federal Reserve," *Journal of Money, Credit and Banking,* 20(1):83–101.

Hibbs, Douglas A. (1977). "Political Parties and Macroeconomic Policy," *American Political Science Review,* 71:1467–87.

Kane, Edward J. (1974). "The Re-Politization of the Fed," *Journal of Financial and Quantitative Analysis,* 9:743–52.

Kane, Edward J. (1980). "Politics and Fed Policymaking," *Journal of Monetary Economics,* 6:199–211.

Kane, Edward J. (1982). "External Pressure and the Operations of the Fed," in R. E. Lombra and W. E. Witte (eds.), *Political Economy of International and Domestic Monetary Relations,* pp. 211–32. Ames: Iowa State University Press.

Laney, Leroy O., and Willett, Thomas D. (1983). "Presidential Politics, Budget Deficits, and Monetary Policy in the United States, 1960–1976," *Public Choice,* 40(1):53–70.

Luckett, Dudley G., and Potts, Glenn T. (1980). "Monetary Policy and Partisan Politics," *Journal of Money, Credit and Banking,* 12:540–6.

McCubbins, Mathew, and Page, Talbot (1986). "The Congressional Foundations of Agency Performance," *Public Choice,* 51:173–90.

McCubbins, Mathew, and Schwartz, Thomas (1984). "Congressional Oversight Overlooked: Police Patrols vs. Fire Alarms," *American Journal of Political Science,* 28:165–79.

Maisel, Sherman (1973). *Managing the Dollar.* New York: Norton.

Maloney, Kevin J., and Smirlock, Michael L. (1981). "Business Cycles and the Political Process," *Southern Economic Journal,* 48:377–92.

Meiselman, David I. (1986). "Is There a Political Monetary Cycle?" *Cato Journal,* 6(2):563–79.

Moe, Terry (1984). "The New Economics of Organization," *American Journal of Political Science,* 28:739–77.

Niskanen, William (1971). *Bureaucracy and Representative Government.* Chicago: Aldine-Atherton.

Nordhaus, William D. (1975). "The Political Business Cycle," *Review of Economic Studies,* 42:169–90.

Peretz, Paul (1983). *The Political Economy of Inflation in the United States.* University of Chicago Press.

Pierce, James (1978). "The Myth of Congressional Supervision of Monetary Policy," *Journal of Monetary Economics,* 4:363–70.

Pierce, James (1979). "The Political Economy of Arthur Burns," *Journal of Finance,* 34:485–96.

Pollard, Walker A. (1983). "Presidential Elections: Cyclical and Distributional Economic Effects," *Public Finance Quarterly,* 11:217–36.

Potts, Glenn T., and Luckett, Dudley G. (1978). "Policy Objectives of the Federal Reserve System," *Quarterly Journal of Economics* (August): 525–34.

Reagan, Michael D. (1961). "The Political Structure of the Federal Reserve System," *American Political Science Review,* 55:81–103.

Riker, William (1980). "Implications from the Disequilibrium of Majority Rule for the Study of Institutions," *American Political Science Review,* 74: 432–46.

Shughart, William F., and Tollison, Robert D. (1983). "Preliminary Evidence on the Use of Inputs by the Federal Reserve System," *American Economic Review,* 73:291–304.

Toma, Eugenia, and Toma, Mark (1986). *Central Bankers, Bureaucratic Incentives and Monetary Policy.* Boston: Kluwer Academic Publishers.

Toma, Mark (1982). "Inflationary Bias of the Federal Reserve System: A Bureaucratic Perspective," *Journal of Monetary Economics,* 10:163–90.

Tufte, Edward R. (1978). *Political Control of the Economy.* Princeton University Press.

Volcker, Paul A. (1978). "The Role of Monetary Targets in an Age of Inflation," *Journal of Monetary Economics,* 4:329–39.

Wagner, Richard E. (1980). "Public Choice, Monetary Control and Economic Disruption," in P. Whiteley (ed.), *Models of Political Economy,* pp. 201–20. New York: Sage.

Wagner, Richard E. (1986). "Central Banking and the Fed: A Public Choice Perspective," *Cato Journal,* 6(2):519–38.

Wallace, Myles S., and Warner, John T. (1984). "Fed Policy and Presidential Elections," *Journal of Macroeconomics,* 6(1):79–88.

Weingast, Barry R. (1984). "The Congressional-Bureaucratic System: A Principal-Agent Perspective (With Applications to the SEC)," *Public Choice,* 44:147–92.

Weingast, Barry R., and Marshall, William J. (1988). "The Industrial Organization of Congress; or, Why Legislatures, Like Firms, are not Organized as Markets," *Journal of Political Economy,* 96:132–63.

Weingast, Barry R., and Moran, Mark J. (1983). "Bureaucratic Discretion or Congressional Control? Regulatory Policy-making by the Federal Trade Commission," *Journal of Political Economy,* 91:765–800.

Weintraub, Robert E. (1978). "Congressional Supervision of Monetary Policy," *Journal of Monetary Economics,* 4:341–62.

Whitlesey, C. R. (1963). "Power and Influence in the Federal Reserve System," *Economica,* 45:123–35.

Wicker, Elmus R. (1966). *Federal Reserve Monetary Policy 1917–1933,* pp. 192–221. New York: Random House.

Woolley, John T. (1984). *The Federal Reserve and the Politics of Monetary Policy.* Cambridge University Press.

Yohe, William P. (1966). "A Study of Federal Open Market Committee Voting, 1955–64," *Southern Economic Journal,* 12(April):98–117.

Yohe, William P. (1974). "Federal Reserve Behavior," in W. J. Frazer (ed.), *Crisis in Economic Theory,* pp. 189–200. Gainesville: University of Florida Press.

CHAPTER 7

The political economy of monetary policy

ROBERT L. HETZEL

In general, the art of government consists in taking as much money as possible from one class of citizens to give to the other.

Voltaire, "Money," *Philosophical Dictionary* (1764)

From time immemorial, the major source of inflation has been the sovereign's attempt to acquire resources. . . . Inflation has been irresistibly attractive to sovereigns . . . because it is a tax that can be imposed without specific legislation. It is truly taxation without representation.

Milton Friedman, "Using Escalators to Help Fight Inflation," *Fortune* (1974)

This chapter advances an analytical framework for the current monetary regime based on the self-interest of the political system. The basic character of the existing monetary regime is determined by the willingness of the political system to use inflation (or to reserve the potential to use inflation) to affect the distribution of income and to raise revenue. Monetary policy emerges out of the interaction between the Federal Reserve and the other agents of the political system: Congress and the executive branch. This framework yields three empirical implications. First, the political system will impose implicit, rather than explicit, constraints on the Fed. Second, the trend rate of inflation reflects the demand for inflation by the political system. Third, the Fed chooses its procedures for formulating and implementing monetary policy in order to render costly any pressure from the political system. The first section describes the Phillips curve that summarizes the way inflation affects real variables. The last two sections describe, respectively, the self-interests of the political system and the Fed.

This chapter is a revision of a paper written in the early 1980s. I gratefully acknowledge useful criticisms of the earlier paper from William Dewald, Michael Dotsey, Milton Friedman, Marvin Goodfried, Denis Karnosky, Robert King, Richard Lang, Robert Laurent, David Lindsey, Raymond Lombra, Bennett McCallum, Thomas Mayer, Allan Meltzer, Alan Stockman, Roy Webb, and John Woolley. The views in this chapter are solely those of the author and do not necessarily represent the views of the foregoing individuals, the Federal Reserve Bank of Richmond, or the Federal Reserve System.

Table 7.1

Expectations-adjusted Phillips curve

$$D_n - D_t = a(\pi_t - \pi_t^e) \qquad (a > 0) \tag{7.1}$$

Political system

Political system's cost function:

$$C_t = b(D_t - k_t D_n)^2 + c(\pi_t)^2 + d(P_t) \qquad (0 < k_t \leq 1, \qquad b, c, d > 0) \tag{7.2}$$

Political system's view of Fed reaction function:

$$\pi_t = \phi(P_t) \qquad (\phi' > 0) \tag{7.3}$$

Form of cost function minimized by political system:

$$C_t = b\{[D_n - a(\phi(P_t) - \pi_t^e)]^2 - 2k_t D_n[D_n - a(\phi(P_t) - \pi_t^e)] + k_t^2 D_n^2\} + c[\phi(P_t)]^2 + d(P_t) \tag{7.4}$$

Political system's first-order condition:

$$P_t = \chi(k_t, \pi_t^e) \tag{7.5}$$

Federal Reserve System

Fed's cost function:

$$F_t = b(D_t - D_n)^2 + c(\pi_t)^2 + f(P_t) \qquad (f > 0) \tag{7.6}$$

Fed's view of political system's reaction function:

$$P_t = \psi(\pi_t) \qquad (\psi' < 0) \tag{7.7}$$

Form of cost function minimized by Fed:

$$F_t = b[-a(\pi_t - \pi_t^e)]^2 + c(\pi_t)^2 + f[\psi(\pi_t)] \tag{7.8}$$

Fed's first-order condition:

$$\pi_t = \omega(\pi_t^e) \tag{7.9}$$

Note: D_t, actual income of groups adversely affected by inflation; D_n, income of same groups in absence of inflationary distortions; π_t, inflation rate; π_t^e, inflation rate expected and incorporated into institutional arrangements; k_t, measure of pressure on political system to redistribute income; P_t, pressure by political system on Federal Reserve to inflate.

The influence of inflation on income distribution

In Table 7.1, equation (7.1) summarizes the way in which inflation interacts with real variables. Equation (7.1) is an expectations-adjusted Phillips curve, but with expectations defined to include not only the public's contemporaneous expectation of inflation but also the expectation of inflation incorporated into existing institutional arrangements at the time of their inception. More specifically, the United States entered the 1960s with a set of institutional arrangements shaped by the assumption that inflation would be minimal. Those institutional arrangements allowed for two primary sorts of monetary nonneutralities. One sort derived from government price-fixing in the form of legal ceilings on interest rates, for example, Regulation Q (Reg Q). The other derived from a tax code specified in nominal terms, rather than indexed to the price level. In the 1960s and 1970s, the major revenue gain from inflation came through the lack of indexing in the tax code, rather than through the tax imposed on the holding of high-powered money.

$D_n - D_t$ in (7.1) is a proxy for the extent to which monetary policy actions affect the distribution of income. D_t is the percentage of national income that goes to groups adversely affected by inflation, the losers when the political system redistributes income through inflation. D_n is the percentage of national income that goes to those same groups when institutions have been completely adapted to the actual inflation rate. That is, it is the income distribution that obtains when inflation exercises no influence on the allocation of resources because of distortions in the price system or in the tax system (other than the tax on high-powered money).

An actual inflation rate, π_t, that differs from the inflation rate expected by the public and incorporated into institutional arrangements, π_t^e, causes D_t to diverge from its natural value, D_n. When actual inflation exceeds expected inflation, $D_n - D_t$ rises. There is a rise in the share of national income that is redistributed through the political system to groups with political clout. In time, however, expected inflation will adjust to actual inflation, and the redistribution effected by inflation will disappear. For example, Reg Q, which imposed ceilings on the interest rates that financial institutions could pay on their time and savings deposits, was enacted in 1933 when deflation prevailed. The inflation of the 1960s and 1970s interacted with Reg Q ceilings to lower the real rate of return received by small savers. Initially, high fixed costs prevented small savers from entering the competitive money market. Over time, however, the emergence of money-market funds allowed them to circumvent Reg Q and purchase money-market instruments. Reg Q then lost its ability to affect real variables and was repealed.

Until the indexing of the tax code in 1985, inflation pushed individuals into higher tax brackets and increased real revenues. When they realized that their taxes were being increased by inflation, the political advantage of an inflation tax, which is that it does not have to be explicitly legislated, was lost. The political system then lowered tax rates in order to offset the effects of past inflation. It is, nevertheless, important to note that between periodic adjustments of tax rates, the political system gained additional revenue with which to compensate groups lobbying for a redistribution of income. The revenue gain from inflation also bought time for the political system to determine whether or not a political consensus could be established to redistribute income in ways demanded by particular constituencies.

The political system

Inflation and the distribution of income

Under the Constitution, Congress is responsible for determining the monetary regime. The choices of institutional arrangements that determine the monetary regime must be in accord with the self-interest of Congress. In a discussion of the choice of monetary regime, the cost function for the political system, equation (7.2) in Table 7.1, can be thought of as the cost function of Congress (Hetzel 1986). Of course, Congress and the executive branch may possess different objectives with respect to monetary policy. In a historical explanation of particular monetary policy actions, often it would be more useful to identify the objective function of the political system with that of the executive branch. In an explanation of the institutional arrangements that determine the monetary regime, however, a useful simplification is to consider (7.2) as representative of the objectives of Congress. It is Congress, after all, that possesses the authority to terminate the Fed's autonomy.

The various groups directly affected by the income redistributions caused by unexpected inflation possess different incentives and costs to organizing in order to influence the political system. Also, the various groups affected by the income redistributions effected through fiscal policy possess different incentives and costs to organizing in order to influence the political system. In dealing with pressures arising from this latter source, the political system may turn to inflation as a temporary expedient for raising revenue while it searches for a political consensus over the income redistributions desired by particular constituencies. As a consequence, the political system has possessed, at times, an incentive to pressure the monetary authority for positive monetary enterprises. In equation (7.2), k_t is a random variable that measures the incentive of the political system to use monetary policy actions to influence the distribution of income. A realization of k_t less than 1 implies a preference on the part of the political system for an income redistribution effected through inflation. The second term on the right in (7.2) measures the cost to the political system of inflation. This cost derives both from a general dislike by the public for inflation and from the reaction of groups adversely affected by inflation. The final term measures the cost of exerting pressure on the Fed to inflate. This cost is discussed later.

The character of the monetary regime is determined by whether or not the potential exists for the political system to use monetary policy to redistribute income. At one extreme, the political system develops ways of precommitting to a k_t always equal to 1, for example, a gold standard or a fixed-exchange-rate regime. At the other extreme, k_t is highly variable; that is, the political system regularly turns to inflation to deal with pressure to redistribute income. Movement from the former to the latter monetary regime decreases the coefficient a in (7.1). As government control of economic activity such as price fixing increases, the value of a increases. In societies where government intervention in the marketplace is common, legal constraints may impede significantly the adaptation of institutional arrangements to different inflation rates. For example, periodic application of wage and price controls, combined with a variable inflation rate, can produce significant income redistributions even in a society accustomed to variable inflation.

If a monetary regime is characterized by discretion rather than precommitment, the political system will take π_t^e as given (Barro and Gordon 1983). There will then be an incentive for groups to organize to influence the inflation rate. The intensity of the lobbying to which the political system is subject to redistribute income (k_t) evolves randomly over time. In the absence of price-fixing and nonneutralities in the tax code, monetary surprises that redistribute income to politically influential groups will be offset over time by surprises that redistribute income away from these groups. Although positive and negative monetary surprises net out over time, the political system will still derive a net political benefit from the positive surprises because they coincide with low realizations of k_t. The political system will value the ability to pressure the monetary authority for monetary surprises at times of "low" realizations of the random variable k_t; see Barro (1983) and Cukierman and Meltzer (1986).

The evolution of k_t

Under the Bretton Woods system of fixed exchange rates, k_t had been constrained to be 1. It became variable and began to assume values less than 1 after the middle of the 1960s. Two kinds of political pressures have determined the evolution of k_t since the 1960s. First, in the 1960s and 1970s, investors, as represented by the home-construction industry, purchasers of homes with fixed-rate mortgages, owners of small businesses, and farmers, exercised more political clout than did small savers. In that situation, a reduction in the real rate of interest would have only a small effect on the individual incomes of the large number of small savers. On the other hand, even a transitory reduction in the real rate of interest could substantially affect the incomes of the smaller number of investors. Groups representing investors, therefore, expended more resources in order to influence the political process than did groups representing savers. In the mid-1960s, k_t fell as a consequence of an increase in the political influence of the savings-and-loan (S&L) and home-construction industries. In 1966, Reg Q was extended to S&L deposits, and regulators set the ceiling on S&L deposits below the ceiling on bank deposits as a way to allocate credit to housing. The Fed then came under political pressure to keep market rates below Reg Q ceilings in order to keep S&Ls from losing deposits through disintermediation.

In the 1960s and 1970s, Congress was extremely sensitive to the way in which monetary policy actions affected the distribution of income by influencing interest rates. At times, Congress exhibited that sensitivity directly, for example, through support for Reg Q and the two-tier prime rate in 1973. In general, congressional sensitivity over interest rates appeared in the pattern of its criticism of the Fed. Congress readily criticized the Fed over "high" rates of interest, but never over "low" rates of interest. This asymmetry of concern over the behavior of interest rates suggests a concern for the distributional implications of monetary policy, rather than the implications for macroeconomic stabilization. Members of the banking committees in Congress became interested in monetary policy when it was possible to rally significant public support from groups who felt that their economic interests had been adversely affected by "high" interest rates. Poole (1985) comments: ". . . political pressures on the Federal Reserve are concentrated on interest rate issues [and] the institution is politically safe as long as interest rates are trending down. In reconciling a sound monetary policy with the political realities, interest rates are *the* issue" (p. 695, italics in original).

The second kind of political pressure that has determined the evolution of k_t since the 1960s has been the way in which inflation influences government revenue. There are three avenues through which inflation raises government revenue (Friedman, 1985). First, there is the straightforward seigniorage tax of inflation on high-powered money. Congressional concern over this source of revenue was evidenced by passage of the Monetary Control Act in 1980. That act, by extending reserve requirements to nonmember banks, ended the exodus of banks from the Fed that threatened the base of the tax constituted by non-interest-bearing reserves (Goodfriend and Hargraves 1983). Congress showed no interest in a solution to the member-bank problem that entailed payment of interest on reserves. Second, there is the reduction in the value of government bonds outstanding produced by unanticipated inflation. The steadfast opposition of the Treasury to bonds indexed to the rate of inflation is evidence that the political system is unwilling to foreclose the possible use of this source of effective revenue. Third, to the extent that the tax code is not indexed to the price level, increases in nominal income and wealth are taxed when the price level rises. Before the partial indexation of the tax code in 1985, a given positive inflation rate produced a continuous increase in government revenue relative to GNP.

The collegial character of Congress allows congressmen to vote for programs that distribute benefits to politically active constituent groups without, at the same time, assuming responsibility for the aggregate level of expenditure that results. It is difficult for Congress to reach a political consensus over the acceptability of the aggregate total of expenditure on programs considered politically desirable individually. The more difficult the achievement of this consensus, the more attractive an inflation tax becomes. The reason is that an inflation tax can be imposed without an explicit vote by Congress. This phenomenon is most clearly evident in the extreme cases of third-world countries, where governments are under pressure to redistribute income to particular interest groups, but lack a mechanism for producing a political consensus over the total share of national income to redistribute through the public sector.

A value of k_t less than 1 measures the incentive of the political system to reduce the value of its debt through unanticipated inflation. It also measures the incentive to finance government expenditures in part through inflation, that is, through a tax that does not need to be explicitly legislated. Again, an inflation tax is attractive to the political system when it is under pressure to redistribute income to particular constituencies, but there is no political consensus that such a redistribution is desirable. In the mid 1960s, k_t fell because of the combined fiscal pressures created by the Vietnam War and by the expansion of income-transfer programs, motivated in part by the increased political influence of older voters. The resort to inflation to increase revenue purchased the political system additional time to reach a consensus over the desirability of an expansion of such programs. [The arguments in this section are developed by Hetzel (1988). For other discussions of inflation in a public-choice context, see Buchanan and Wagner (1977, pp. 111–21), Gordon (1975), and Meltzer (1982).]

Fed institutional autonomy

An understanding of the current monetary regime requires, in addition to an explanation of the preferences of the political system, an explanation for why Congress has created an institutionally distinct monetary authority, with a preference function that differs from its own. The institutional autonomy of the Fed can be explained by the collegial, partisan character of Congress. Congressional decision-making, which requires the formation of coalitions yielding a majority, is too cumbrous for the regular conduct of monetary policy. Congress is jealous of its constitutional prerogatives, however, and is unwilling (except during wartime) to hand over control of monetary policy to the executive branch. The conduct of monetary policy, consequently, has been turned over to an institutionally autonomous Fed.

Given the institutional autonomy of the Fed, it is also necessary to explain the fact that Congress influences monetary policy through informal pressure on the Fed, rather than through an explicit mandate to guide the conduct of monetary policy. This informal pressure is exerted through threats to limit the Fed's institutional autonomy and regulatory responsibilities. Most frequently, pressure is exerted through hearings on legislation that would limit the budgetary autonomy of the Fed or submit its budget to congressional audit (Woolley 1984, Chapter 7). This characteristic of congressional behavior arises from the political inefficiency of redistributing income through monetary policy actions (Hetzel 1986). The cost – inflation – is not hidden. (In contrast, tariffs and import quotas are efficient means of redistributing income because the costs they impose are hidden.) Current institutional arrangements allow individual congressmen to exert an influence on monetary policy actions without, at the same time, accepting responsibility for inflation. More specifically, if monetary policy were directly under the control of Congress, the costs to nonincumbent politicians of creating a public awareness of the association between inflation and congressional actions would be lowered. Creation of such a public awareness with current institutional arrangements would entail substantial investment by nonincumbent politicians in the economic literacy of the public. Consequently, it becomes more difficult for nonincumbent politicians to place the blame for inflation on incumbents. [This explanation for the institutional autonomy of the Fed is in the spirit of Kane (1975, 1980, 1982a,b, 1984). Kane, however, assumes that the Fed's objective function is a simple reflection of that of the political system.]

It is assumed that since the 1960s, k_t has varied randomly over the interval (0, 1]. In response to variations in k_t, Congress varies the extent to which it exerts pressure (P_t) on the Fed to produce inflation. (Of course, no congressman thinks in these terms. Congressional pressure on the Fed, which takes the form of criticism of "high" rates of interest, is restrained by the cost of inflation. At times of low realizations of k_t, this cost is less, and congressional criticism of "high" rates increases.) In Table 7.1, equation (7.3) summarizes the view of Congress of the relationship between the pressure it exerts and the choice by the Fed of the inflation rate. Congress minimizes its cost function indirectly by influencing the Fed's choice of the inflation rate. Substitution of (7.1) and (7.3) into (7.2) yields (7.4), which is the cost function of Congress expressed in terms of its choice variable, P_t. P_t is chosen in order to minimize (7.4), yielding the first-order condition (7.5), where the optimal P_t is expressed in terms of the given variables, k_t and π_t^e. Low realizations of k_t lead to high values of P_t and to positive inflationary shocks, and vice versa. Note, finally, that exerting pressure on the Fed is costly to Congress. The costs are discussed below.

The Federal Reserve System

Explication of the Fed's cost function usefully begins with discussion of the selection procedure for the chairman. The views of serious candidates will be described in terms such as "pragmatic" and "eclectic." That is, a Fed chairman who would formulate policy according to an abstract economic paradigm, rather than in a pragmatic, judgmental way would be unacceptable to the political system. Attributes that promote an individual's candidacy for chairman include a distinguished career of public service, recognition in financial markets, recognition by key politicians (especially the chairmen of the House and Senate Banking Committees), and acceptability to presidential political advisors. On the one hand, this selection process ensures that a Fed chairman will take seriously the concerns of the political system. On the other hand, it also ensures that the chairman will be acceptable to a variety of diverse groups and to the financial community. As a consequence, whoever is selected as chairman will not represent the views of a particular political constituency and, especially, will not share the distributive objectives that motivate Congress. An institutionally autonomous Fed, then, imposes on Congress a cost, which is a lack of complete control over monetary policy. That cost, however, is balanced by a benefit, which is a degree of insulation from attack over inflation.

Congressional pressure on the Fed is motivated by the way in which inflation influences the distribution of income, either directly through the revenue it generates or indirectly through the redistribution it effects among groups. It is natural, therefore, for the Fed, in organizing support for its institutional autonomy, to appeal to groups antipathetic to the income redistribution deriving from inflation. Because the chairman of the Fed does not share the distributive objectives of Congress, it is natural for him to identify the preferences of the Fed with the preferences of these latter groups. The Fed's cost function can then be viewed as typical of the particular groups to which the Fed looks for support on the basis of their hostility to the income redistributions of inflation. For example, in the 1960s and 1970s, Congress attempted to allocate credit to politically influential constituencies like the housing industry. There was then a coincidence of self-interest between the Fed and the commercial and banking sectors that would be adversely affected by that credit allocation. The Fed's regional organization and boards of directors allowed contact with these natural allies.

The cost function of the Fed, equation (7.6), contrasts with that of Congress by the absence of the variable k_t, which measures the incentive of Congress to redistribute income through inflation. The Fed, however, owes its existence to Congress and cannot pursue a policy that ignores the congressional preferences expressed in (7.2). The Fed then views itself as trying to minimize the first two terms of its cost function (7.6), subject to constraints imposed by the political system. These constraints are captured by the term $f(P_t)$ that reflects congressional pressure. The Fed views congressional pressure (P_t) as influenced by its choice of inflation, π_t, as shown by (7.7). Substituting (7.1) and (7.7) into (7.6) yields (7.8), the Fed's cost function expressed in terms of its choice variable π_t. Minimization of (7.8) by the Fed yields the first-order condition for the optimal inflation rate, (7.9). At a high level of abstraction, monetary policy actions can be viewed as reflecting the compromises reached by the political system between groups benefiting from the redistribution of income deriving from unanticipated inflation, whose preferences are expressed in (7.2), and groups harmed by such income redistributions, whose preferences are expressed in (7.6). The spirit of the model is captured by a quotation from Arthur Burns. The role of the Fed is to continue "probing the limits of its freedom to undernourish . . . inflation" (Burns 1979, p. 16).

The Fed's independence of Congress varies directly with the magnitude in (7.2) of the coefficient *d,* which measures the cost to Congress of influencing the Fed. In part, the magnitude of *d* is given to the Fed. For example, the Monetary Control Act of 1980, by ending the exodus of banks from Fed membership, eliminated a problem for the Fed whose solution required congressional assistance. It can be plausibly inferred that the value of *d* increased as one source of congressional leverage on the Fed was removed. To an extent, however, *d* is under the control of the Fed. The Fed chairman chooses procedures for formulating and implementing policy in order to increase the value of *d.*

The responsibility for increasing the autonomy of the Fed, summarized by the value of *d,* falls to the chairman. This responsibility accounts for the dominant role he plays within the Federal Open Market

Committee. In a broad sense, Fed chairmen come up through the political system and view themselves as possessing specific human capital that allows them to increase the value of *d*. This human capital can consist of an astute awareness of politics that endows a chairman with skill in preventing the formation of political coalitions capable of threatening Fed autonomy. A discussion of this aspect of policy-making would require extending the model to include the executive branch as well as Congress. A good relationship with the executive branch, with its veto power, becomes important when Congress threatens Fed autonomy.

Also, the chairman can take advantage of the news-media coverage he is accorded to increase the cost to the political system of pressuring the Fed. Congressional criticism of the Fed usually centers on "high" interest rates. In order to parry these threats, the chairman can associate "high" interest rates with deficit spending, rather than monetary policy. Also, he can simply criticize deficit spending. Such criticism makes the Fed appear as a fiscally responsible, apolitical organization. Attacks on the Fed then become politically risky, as they look like scapegoating of the only apolitical and fiscally responsible organization in Washington. [See the discussion of political gaming by Poole (1985).] More generally, the chairman appeals for public support for an institutionally autonomous Fed by arguing that such autonomy permits a politically nonpartisan monetary policy.

Empirical work

The framework outlined earlier yields a number of testable implications. It is assumed that the character of the existing monetary regime is determined by the unwillingness of the political system to put into place institutional arrangements that would preclude it from influencing inflation in order to affect the distribution of income. One implication is that Congress will not formulate an explicit mandate to guide monetary policy, but rather will retain the ability to influence the inflation rate indirectly. In this way, it becomes more costly for nonincumbent challengers to blame incumbent congressmen for inflation. The Fed, for its part, will not formulate explicit goals against which the actual behavior of monetary policy can be assessed. A second implication is that changes in the trend rate of inflation can be explained by changes in pressure on the political system to control the distribution of income and by the adaptation of institutional arrangements that alter the influence of inflation on the distribution of income. A third implication follows from the existence of different cost functions for the political system and the Fed. The

Fed will choose procedures for formulating and implementing monetary policies that will increase the cost to the political system of influencing Fed policy actions.

The second implication mentioned earlier is that the inflation rate emerges out of a concern by the political system for the way in which inflation redistributes income between the public and private sectors and among groups within the public. The objective of empirical work is to provide an explanation of changes in the inflation rate in terms of changes in the incentive of the political system to use inflation to affect the distribution of income. Given the major movements of the inflation rate since the Korean War, it is necessary to explain a rise in the trend rate of inflation beginning in the mid-1960s and a fall beginning in the 1980s. Within these trends, it is necessary to explain two surges in inflation, one from 1973 to 1975 and the other from 1977 to 1981. In the work of Hetzel (1988), that behavior of inflation is explained by political pressure to allocate credit to politically influential constituencies and by the difficulty in reaching a political consensus over the financing of the income-transfer programs that expanded significantly after the mid-1960s.

The third implication mentioned earlier is that the Fed will choose procedures for formulating and implementing monetary policy that will increase the cost to the political system of influencing its behavior. There has been considerable consistency over time in the way the Fed formulates and implements monetary policy. It is contended that this consistency derives from the desire by the Fed not only to pursue macroeconomic objectives but also to increase its independence of political pressures. Consistency in monetary policy derives from its discretionary, judgmental character. Policy evolves under the assumption that an optimal long-run policy will result from a concatenation of policy actions, each of which appears optimal within the context of a short time horizon. No systematic procedure is imposed whereby long-run objectives would constrain these policy actions. In each period the policy-maker retains the freedom to alter the relative priorities assigned to the achievement of objectives of ultimate concern, such as inflation and unemployment. In sum, policy avoids precommitment. It is discretionary.

In principle, a discretionary monetary policy could be model-based. Model-based procedures, however, require explicit formulation of objectives. This explicitness would increase the ability of the political system to influence policy. Consequently, a judgmental framework is utilized for determining the values of policy variables, as opposed to a framework in which explicit numerical targets are set for ultimate objectives and a model of the economy is utilized to derive settings on policy variables. In practice, the funds rate is moved judgmentally away from its prevailing value on the basis of a subjective, ongoing evaluation by the Fed of the relative priorities to assign to its qualitative ultimate objectives. The priorities that emerge from this subjective evaluation are dominated by the contemporaneous state of the economy and the general political environment. This procedure, which has been termed "leaning against the wind," produces changes in the Fed's policy variable, the funds rate, that appear to address the contemporaneously most pressing problem of the economy (Hetzel 1985).

Model-based decision-making procedures, as opposed to the Fed's judgmental procedures, would make monetary policy easier to monitor. Policy actions taken within a model-based framework would require numerical specification of ultimate objectives. Explicit objectives would constrain the ability of the Fed to change the priorities assigned to its objectives, becuse changes would serve as focal points for pressure from vocal, well-organized groups in Congress. If an objective were revised in a way that a particular group considered undesirable, the explicitness of the previous objective would facilitate accusations of a lack of resolve and consistency on the part of the Fed. Also, explicit specification of ultimate objectives would encourage their congressional review, which might allow Congress to dictate those objectives.

At times, model-based procedures would call for changes in the funds rate that would conflict with the desire to alter that variable in accord with the "leaning against the wind" procedure. Changes in the funds rate might not appear justifiable in light of the contemporaneous behavior of the economy. In addition, model-based procedures for decision-making would cause the Fed's preference for moderate, gradual changes in the funds rate to appear adventitious. It is useful to spread out over time a change in the funds rate in order to create the impression of not making a clear choice between conflicting goals, but rather of shading the emphasis of policy. In this way, monetary policy actions are packaged in order to avoid serving as a lightning rod for the criticism of potential opposition. Finally, explicitness about the relationship between ultimate objectives and operating targets would facilitate challenges to the Fed over whether or not the actual choice of operating targets would in fact achieve the stated ultimate objectives.

Summary

The framework exposited here for understanding the current monetary regime makes explicit the self-interest of the agents in this regime and the constraints that circumscribe the pursuit of that self-interest. The first in the hierarchy of these agents is Congress, because constitutionally it is charged with determining the monetary regime. The self-interest of congressmen lies in enhancement of their electoral prospects. The revenue and distributive consequences of inflation create both electoral pressures and opportunities. The constraint faced by Congress is the inherent political inefficiency of inflation for affecting the distribution of income. The effects of monetary policy actions on real variables are transitory, and the cost – inflation – is not hidden. Congress has dealt with these constraints by endowing the Fed with institutional autonomy, but not with a guarantee of that autonomy. On the one hand, then, congressmen can pressure the Fed for particular policy actions when it is politically expedient. On the other hand, they can dissociate themselves from the undesirable side effects of such pressure. For example, individual congressmen can exert pressure for expansionary monetary policy actions by criticizing "high" rates of interest, without also accepting responsibility for the inflation rate.

The Fed identifies its self-interest with the self-interest of groups antipathetic to the redistribution of income associated with unanticipated inflation. It can then appeal to these groups when its institutional autonomy is threatened. The Fed chooses procedures for formulating and implementing monetary policy that allow it to defend its institutional autonomy by rendering criticism from the political system costly. It can also appeal for public support with the argument that its institutional autonomy removes the conduct of monetary policy from partisan politics. The absence of a constitutional guarantee of Fed autonomy or of an explicit, substantive mandate from Congress to guide the formulation of monetary policy, however, means that the Fed must be sensitive to the concerns of the political system. The trend rate of inflation provided by the Fed is at the level demanded by the political system. Monetary policy emerges as part of the general democratic decision-making process, rather than out of the economic paradigms of economists.

References

Barro, Robert J. (1983). "Inflationary Finance under Discretion and Rules," *Canadian Journal of Economics,* 16(February): 1–16.

Barro, Robert J., and Gordon, David B. (1983). "A Positive Theory of Monetary Policy in a Natural Rate Model," *Journal of Political Economy,* 91(August): 589–610.

Brunner, Karl, and Meltzer, Allan H. (1984). *The Federal Reserve's Attachment to the Free Reserve Concept.* House Committee on Banking and Currency, Subcommittee on Domestic Finance. Washington, D.C.: U.S. Government Printing Office.

Buchanan, James M., and Wagner, Richard E. (1977). *Democracy in Deficit: The Political Legacy of Lord Keynes.* New York: Academic Press.

Burns, Arthur F. (1979). *The Anguish of Central Banking.* Belgrade, Yugoslavia: Per Jacobsson Foundation.

Cukierman, Alex, and Meltzer, Allan H. (1986). "A Theory of Ambiguity, Credibility and Inflation under Discretion and Asymmetric Information," *Econometrica,* 54(September): 1099–128.

Friedman, Milton (1985). "Monetary Policy in a Fiat World," keynote address, Second International Conference of The Institute for Monetary and Economic Studies, Bank of Japan. May 29.

Goodfriend, Marvin, and Hargraves, Monica (1983). "A Historical Assessment of the Rationales and Functions of Reserve Requirements," *Federal Reserve Bank of Richmond Economic Review* 69(March–April): 3–21.

Gordon, Robert J. (1975). "The Demand for and Supply of Inflation," *Journal of Law and Economics,* 18(December): 807–36.

Hetzel, Robert L. (1985). "The Formulation of Monetary Policy," Federal Reserve Bank of Richmond working paper, October.

(1986). "A Congressional Mandate for Monetary Policy," *Cato Journal,* 5(Winter): 797–820.

(1988). "The Political Economy of Inflation," Federal Reserve Bank of Richmond working paper.

Kane, Edward J. (1975). "New Congressional Restraints and Federal Reserve Independence," *Challenge,* 17(November–December): 37–44.

(1980). "Politics and Fed Policymaking," *Journal of Monetary Economics,* 6(April): 199–211.

(1982a). "External Pressure and the Operations of the Fed," in Raymond E. Lombra and Willard E. Witte (eds.), *Political Economy of International and Domestic Monetary Relations,* pp. 211–32. Ames: Iowa State University Press.

(1982b). "Selecting Monetary Targets in a Changing Financial Environment," in *Monetary Policy Issues of the 1980s,* Federal Reserve Bank of Kansas City.

(1984). "Fedbashing and the Role of Monetary Arrangements in Managing Political Stress," in *Monetary Reform and Economic Stability,* hearings before the Joint Economic Committee, 98th Cong., 2nd sess., May 16 and June 5, 1984, pp. 45–8. Washington, D.C.: U.S. Government Printing Office.

Lombra, Raymond E., and Moran, Michael (1980). "Policy Advice and Policymaking at the Federal Reserve," *Carnegie-Rochester Conference Series on Public Policy,* 13:9–68.

Mayer, Thomas (1982a). "A Case Study of Federal Reserve Policymaking," *Journal of Monetary Economics,* 10(November): 259–71.

(1982b). "Federal Reserve Policy in the 1972–1975 Recession: A Case Study of Fed Behavior in a Quandary," in Paul Wachtel (ed.), *Crisis in the Economic and Financial Structure,* pp. 41–83. Lexington, MA: Lexington Books.

Meltzer, Allan H. (1982). "Politics and Economics at the Federal Reserve," in

Raymond E. Lombra and Willard E. Witte (eds.), *Political Economy in International and Domestic Monetary Relations,* pp. 233–5. Ames: Iowa State University Press.

Poole, William (1986). "Monetary Control and the Political Business Cycle," *Cato Journal,* 5(Winter):685–99.

Woolley, John T. (1984). *Monetary Politics: The Federal Reserve and the Politics of Monetary Policy.* Cambridge University Press.

CHAPTER 8

Political monetary cycles

NATHANIEL BECK

There are rhythms in American political life. There is the regular four-year electoral rhythm, as well as the more irregular rhythm of party alternation in control of the White House. It would be surprising if economic policy and outcomes did not resonate with these rhythms. Much empirical research has been done on this question. As is typical, there are contradictory findings, but it seems quite clear that economic policy and outcomes do vary with control of the White House, and it is likely that policy and outcomes vary with the electoral calendar.[1] Are there similar rhythms in monetary policy? The answer is less clear. The Fed, after all, was set up to be insulated from these political rhythms. In this chapter I shall look at some arguments and some evidence for electoral or partisan rhythms in the making of monetary policy.[2]

I take as uncontroversial that presidents wish to be reelected; if one is not eligible for reelection, one prefers that the White House remain with one's party. Presidents may have other goals, and they may even rank those other goals more highly, but no one achieves the presidency without some interest in being elected. It follows from this that presidents will prefer policies that will help them get reelected, at least insofar as those policies do not conflict with other goals. We need not view the president as being willing to do anything to get elected in order to believe that he evaluates policies at least partially in terms of their effects on the next election.

The timing of elections has consequences for the political desirability of various economic policies. In particular, incumbents will favor policies whose benefits will come before the election, but whose costs will be paid after the election. This is true even if the electorate is sophisticated; it is not a mark of naiveté for voters to weigh events that have already occurred more heavily than those that might occur.[3] This does not mean that the president will risk economic ruin after the election to bring about a temporary boom before the election (although he might); it does mean that the president will take timing into account in choosing economic policies.

The issue of the timing of elections and its effect on (politically) optimal economic policy goes under the rubric of "political business cycles" (PBCs). This literature, whose modern incarnation is in the work of William Nordhaus (1975), and whose popularity is largely due to Edward Tufte (1978), stresses that policies that create booms before elections, even if they have bad consequences after elections, may help the president's reelection effort. If there is a (short-run) Phillips-curve type of trade-off between unemployment and inflation, and if the employment consequences of policy are felt before the inflationary consequences, and if voters do not make forecasts about postelection inflationary costs, then there is room for political manipulation of the economy.

The Tufte version of the PBC has the president simply "gunning" the economy as the election nears. The benefits of that gunning come before the election and hence affect voting behavior; the inflationary costs come after the election and hence have no electoral consequences. The Tufte PBC consists of a sharp turn toward economic ease in the electoral year, producing sharp increases in output, real income, and employment during that year; the next year sees a sharp tightening of policy, producing declines in output and income and an increase in inflation.

The Nordhaus PBC is a four-year cycle: Early in his term, the president induces a recession to lower inflationary expectations. Then a preelection boom is engineered, with the inflationary costs of that boom deferred because of low inflationary expectations.[4] After the election, the reelected incumbent will then induce another recession to drive down (high) inflationary expectations, and so on. Unlike Tufte, Nordhaus predicts policy and outcome consequences over the entire four-year period.

There has been much controversy about whether or not PBCs exist in the United States. Political scientists, in general, have found scant evidence for such cycles. However, the most recent and most technically sophisticated evidence, that of Haynes and Stone (1988), indicates that there is a PBC. They find a four-year cycle in both unemployment and inflation. The unemployment cycle troughs in the electoral quarter, and the inflation cycle peaks a year later. These findings are quite consistent with the Nordhaus theory.[5] The evidence for PBCs probably will never be totally persuasive.[6] I shall assume for the purposes of this chapter, given the evidence of Haynes and Stone and the inherent theoretical attraction of PBCs, that such cycles do exist. If that is the case, then they must be created by some set of policies. Are they created by monetary policy? Does the Fed cause a "political monetary cycle" (PMC)? The next section of this chapter deals with that question.

Once a president is elected, I take it that he will make some attempt to carry out his program. Economic policies affect different portions of the electorate in different ways. This has led to a literature that emphasizes the linkage between the party of the president and economic outcomes and policies. The linkage is, presumably, that Democratic presidents, who must rely on working-class voters, are particularly concerned with high unemployment, whereas Republican presidents, who rely on a more middle-class constituency, worry more about inflation. The political scientist best known for studying the linkage between political party and economic policy is Douglas Hibbs (1977, 1987).

It seems fairly clear that there is some relationship between the president's party and the economic outcomes observed. Although I think that Hibbs may have overstated the long-term effect of having a Democrat in the White House, and though I believe that there have been differences among Democratic presidents that have been almost as large as the differences between Democratic and Republican presidents, there is no question that unemployment has been lower, and inflation higher, under Democratic presidents.[7]

The impact of party on unemployment and inflation is larger, according to Hibbs, the longer a party is in power. But as a party stays in power, agents come to expect the policies offered by that party. Rational expectations would then tell us that the impact of party should not grow during its time in office. Rational-expectations theorists, such as Chappell and Keech (1986), Havrilesky (1987), and Alesina and Sachs (1988), model the party/policy/outcome linkage differently than does Hibbs. They predict that the impact of party on real outcomes (output and employment) will be maximal early in a presidential term, whereas the impact of party on inflation may grow over the course of a term.

Both Chappell and Keech and Alesina and Sachs specifically claim that the only surprise in policy is right after an election. Before the election, there is uncertainty about who will win and what policies will be pursued. Thus, agents expect a lottery over tight versus easy policy, with the probability of each policy determined by forecasts about the result of the election. The election then picks a single policy. That policy is a surprise and hence has real consequences. After a Republican takes the White House, policy, including monetary policy, will be surprisingly tight, and hence output will decrease; just the opposite happens after a Democratic victory. But the only surprise in policy is right after an election, and so over the course of an administration, though there still will be a link between party and policy, there will be no long-term link between party and output. Both sets of authors provide some evidence of this short-term party/output linkage, but neither clearly examines the party/policy linkage.[8]

The Havrilesky argument is different. He argues that liberal governments must create monetary surprises to offset disincentives created by their redistributive policies. These surprises are part of deliberate, but unanticipated, electorally motivated policies pursued by all governments. The Havrilesky theory makes a different prediction than do the other two rational-expectations theorists, namely, that monetary surprises will occur only when Democrats replace Republicans in the White House, and they will always be in the direction of easing the money supply. He finds some (modest) empirical support for this proposition. It should be noted that Havrilesky provides a direct test of the impact of party on monetary policy.

All of these theorists posit a link between party control of the White House and economic outcomes. If there is to be such a link, then the parties must pursue different economic policies and, in particular, different monetary policies. Both Hibbs and the rational-expectations theorists assume that presidents can obtain the monetary policies they desire. Given the formal independence of the Fed, that is not obviously the case. In the third section of this chapter I shall examine the theoretical underpinnings of that assumption, as well as some empirical evidence. The fourth section concludes with a brief discussion of some open questions about PMCs.

Electoral monetary policy

Does the Fed manipulate the money supply to aid the incumbent president's chance of being reelected? We should, before looking at some evidence, ask if such manipulation would be expected on theoretical grounds. The formal independence of the Fed might lead us to ask why the Fed would engage in such manipulation. But given the enormous power of the president, it would not be surprising if the Fed found it in its own interest to aid the incumbent. What are the interests of the Fed in this matter?

I have argued at greater length elsewhere (Beck 1987, 1988) that the Fed's power comes from its legitimacy, which derives from its appearance of engaging in politically neutral, technical implementation of policy. In the absence of such legitimacy the Fed would be powerless to induce major recessions (or, more correctly, such decisions would soon be overturned in other parts of the government). If that is true, the Fed would be crazy to be caught being involved in electoral manipulations of the money supply. Nothing could be so likely to erode the Fed's legitimacy.

The Fed's own understanding of its role would make it difficult for it to deliberately engage in electoral manipulation. The language of the Fed is either the language of the economist or the language of the banker, not the language of the politician. This is not to say that elections are not important to the leaders of the Fed, but rather that they cannot explain their decisions, either to themselves or to their peers, in the language of partisan electoral politics.

There might be another cost to electoral manipulation of the money supply. The incumbent might lose in spite of the best efforts of the Fed. The new president might be unhappy with the role played by the Fed and might take steps to bring in new leadership. Of the three recent chairmen whose terms spanned presidential administrations, all wished to be (or were) reappointed. Electoral manipulation would have great cost if one were on the losing side.[9]

PMCs may exist whether or not I think them plausible. Before turning to the existence of a cycle in general, it seems useful to look at a few specific elections, starting with 1968. Monetary policy was very easy before the 1968 election. Was that to help the Democrats hold the White House, or for other reasons? Former Governor Maisel (1973) attributed the ease (and overease) to a miscalculation of the effectiveness of the tax surcharge. His account is surely plausible, and I see no evidence of anyone in 1968 claiming that monetary policy was electorally inspired. Prosperity, after all, was hardly the major issue in that election. Also, the chairman of the Fed, William Martin, was not a close confidant of the president. But we should also remember that Maisel had been appointed by Lyndon Johnson, and so we might take his account with at least one grain of salt.

The situation in 1972 was almost exactly the opposite. Chairman Arthur Burns had been a key advisor to President Nixon, and back in 1959 he had warned Nixon (then vice-president) about the electoral dangers of a bad economy. Nixon was certainly concerned about having a good economy on election day, and indeed it was good. Monetary policy clearly was not tight before the election.

But even here it is not obvious that the Fed eased to help the president. Woolley (1984) argues that Burns kept interest rates down to keep them from being subject to price controls. And though insider accounts clearly showed the White House putting great pressure on the Fed, none of those accounts tells the juicier story of the Fed caving in to that pressure.[10] My own research (Beck 1982a) found no clear changes in the way the Fed pegged the federal-funds rate before the election. I estimated a reaction function for the monthly change in the funds rate during the period when Nixon was president and Burns was chair

(March 1970 through July 1974). There was no apparent shift in that reaction function for the preelectoral period, regardless of how that period is defined.

We shall never know if Arthur Burns eased monetary policy to help Richard Nixon's election. It is clear that many observers thought he did so, and that thinking clearly hurt the Fed. Until 1972 the press had virtually ignored the Fed. But in 1974 *Fortune* magazine ran a major attack on the Fed and Arthur Burns (Rose 1974). The centerpiece of the story was Burns's manipulation of the money supply to aid Nixon's reelection. According to Rose, at some (unspecified) meeting, the FOMC balked about easing. Burns supposedly adjourned the meeting; on returning, he announced that he had just been on the phone to the White House. With that, the FOMC capitulated and gave Nixon his easy monetary policy.

That story is instructive for two reasons. First, we can see the cost to the Fed of engaging in that type of activity. (The cost of being caught in that way was so great as to cause Governors not known to be allied with the chair to write angry denials to *Fortune*. That was, to my knowledge, the first time the Fed ever defended itself in public.[11]) But perhaps more important, we should see that the Rose account was implausible. Could any member of the FOMC have been ignorant of Nixon's desires? And would any professional economist or banker change policy after hearing that the president was unhappy? Again, I would think it likely that one of the reasons that policy was easy in 1972 was because everyone knew that such a policy would make the president happy, but I find it hard to believe either that Burns would have used that as a public argument or that anyone on the FOMC would have acceded to that argument.[12] Rose's conclusions may or may not have been correct, but his supposed mechanism for presidential control seems unlikely. However, 1972 was marked by a confluence of circumstances most favorable to a PBC: a president who thought a robust preelection economy vital and a chairman of the Fed who was a close political confidant of the president. If any election was ever going to produce a PMC, it was 1972, but even there the evidence is not overwhelming.

No one accused the Fed of electoral manipulation in either 1976 or 1980. Of course, 1980 was the election in which the Fed induced a recession in March, just in time to sink Jimmy Carter's chance of reelection. That recession, surprisingly enough, was induced at the behest of the president. The end of the campaign saw Carter attacking the Fed for tightening policy, but the Fed did not ease in response (Greider 1987). In any event, by October the damage was already done.

Monetary policy was extremely tight during the first half of the Reagan administration. During the summer of 1982 the Fed eased, and Ronald Reagan enjoyed a healthy economy and a healthy victory in 1984. Did the Fed ease to help Ronald Reagan? Greider's scathing critique of the Fed during that period spends little time on that question; I assume that if he had found evidence of electoral manipulation of the money supply, he would have reported it. There were many reasons for the Fed to ease in mid-1982. Volcker had already put the economy through the wringer, and inflation had fallen. Velocity, moreover, was lower than had been anticipated. At such a point monetary ease is not unreasonable, especially because the growth rate of the money supply had slowed.

M1 began to grow rapidly in September of 1982. In its October meeting, the FOMC decided that for technical reasons having to do with financial deregulation, M1 was not a reliable indicator, and so they decided to focus on M2 for the rest of the year. That allowed the FOMC to continue its policy of relative ease, which allowed the recovery to continue. Again, Reagan was clearly a beneficiary of that decision in 1984. Was the October decision electorally motivated?

It may have been politically motivated without having been electorally motivated. Congress was clamoring for ease, and, more importantly, Mexico was threatening bankruptcy. The costs of retightening would have been great. One of those costs might have been the collapse of the American financial system; another cost might have been to the reelection effort of Ronald Reagan. Given the confluence of all those political factors, it is not surprising that the Fed eased. We can never know the importance of electoral politics in that ease, but there is no reason to conclude that policy in 1982 was principally motivated by a desire to aid Reagan's reelection.

I think that a more nearly correct way to read 1982 (and 1968) is that the Fed operates in a world of great uncertainty. That is hardly a controversial statement. Sometimes this uncertainty is so great that the FOMC comes close to tossing a coin (although decisions are justified in other ways). In this extreme uncertainty, if one outcome will help the incumbent and another will hurt him, does it not seem reasonable that the Fed will choose the former? Had tightening been clearly indicated in October of 1982, perhaps the Fed would have done so despite the electoral consequences. But given all the plausible (nonelectoral) reasons to continue ease and the (at best) very uncertain case for tightening, was it foolish for the Fed to take the politically expedient course? I think not.

This strategy of choosing a policy to help the incumbent if there is no clear choice is also politically fairly safe. There is no problem if the incumbent wins. But if he loses, his successor may be fairly happy with a

Fed that adheres to that type of policy. Such a policy may be the best that a president can get from the Fed, and given the other resources of the incumbent, it may be enough. "Cause no electoral harm" may be the monetary oath.

Is there evidence of a general political monetary cycle? Meiselman (1986), looking simply at plots of M1, claims that the growth of money peaks about six months before most elections. Tufte (1978), also looking at M1, claims that the money supply grows more rapidly in the preelection biennium. Both analyses are fairly primitive, and my work (Beck 1982a) casts doubt on the Tufte finding. There is, however, more sophisticated evidence available.

If we look for the type of manipulation suggested by Tufte, that is, a sudden move toward ease right before the election, it does not appear to exist. Looking at monetary outcomes, Hibbs (1987) found no tendency for M1 to increase in the year before an election. Turning to instruments, I found no tendency for adjusted reserves to increase in the year before an election (Beck 1984). Both Hibbs and I also looked at specific elections. The only elections showing any signs of monetary manipulation were 1968 and 1972. A general theory is not built on one (or two) elections.

Kevin Grier (1987) has recently argued that it is a mistake simply to look for changes in policy right before the election. Monetary policy changes slowly, and so, if there is a PMC, it should show up as a four-year cycle. Grier finds such a cycle in M1, with monetary growth being maximal in the election quarter, declining for the next year, and then rising regularly over the ensuing three years.[13]

Grier's results on the timing of the cycle are puzzling. M1 growth is maximal in the fourth quarter of the election year; yet the election takes place only one-third of the way through that quarter. Presumably the electorate does not care about M1, but its consequences, and it takes time for increased M1 to temporarily stimulate the economy. Analysts vary in their estimates of the outside lag, the time from when policy is implemented to when it takes effect, but all agree that it is long. The simplest monetarist models, such as the St. Louis model, give the shortest lags, but the more sophisticated models, such as that of Sims (1982), show a lapse of almost a year before an increase in the money supply has its maximal impact on output. In their text, Hall and Taylor (1988, p. 350) state that "the peak effect of monetary expansion on GNP probably occurs between one and two years after the expansion."

The lag before monetary expansion has its peak political effect may be even longer. Voters appear to care more about unemployment than about output growth. Unemployment is a lagging indicator, and so the maximal political impact of monetary expansion may well not come for almost two years. Any monetary growth before the election probably is helpful to the president, but if the Fed is really creating PMCs, why not start the printing presses a year or two before the election?[14]

Perhaps the answer is that the Fed is not creating the cycle in M1. The money supply is not directly controlled by the Fed. I looked at whether or not there is a cycle in two policy instruments: adjusted reserves and the federal-funds rate (Beck 1987). Using either reaction functions or autoregressions, there is no evidence of an electoral cycle, of any kind, in either of these two instruments. How can there be a cycle in M1 but not in the instruments of monetary policy?

As the economy heats up, the demand for money increases. The Fed has no control over this demand. The Fed does control the supply of money, but if the Fed fails to accommodate this demand, then the economy must contract. If the president is creating a boom that will peak on election day, the demand for money will peak in the electoral quarter. Thus, the increase in M1 that peaks in the electoral quarter may be demand-driven, not supply-driven.

We should then distinguish between an "active" PMC, created by Fed policy, and a "passive" PMC, driven by forces outside the Fed, but acquiesced to by the Fed. This distinction makes it possible to reconcile the contradictory empirical findings. A cycle in M1 will appear if there is either a passive or an active PMC; a cycle in the instruments will appear only if there is an active PMC. Thus, the evidence seems to favor a passive PMC.

If the cycle in M1 is being caused by increased demand for money driven by a political business cycle, then it will take great political power for the Fed not to accommodate that demand. The president may not be sufficiently powerful to force the Fed to create a PMC, but the Fed may not be so powerful as to undertake actions to offset presidential manipulations. This is especially true because the Fed feels that it should, in general, cooperate with the president. It is one thing not to help a president be reelected, but quite another to harm that effort. This story is consistent with the observed facts.

If there are PBCs, and they are not being created by the Fed, they must be created by some other economic policy. Fiscal policy appears to follow an electoral rhythm. I found (Beck 1987) that the high employment deficit is about one point greater in the electoral quarter than it is a year later. If the Fed monetizes this politically inspired deficit in the same proportion that it monetizes all deficits, then there will be a passive PMC.

To study this question, we can add the high employment deficit to either an autoregression or a reaction function for M1. About half of the impact of an election on the money supply disappears when fiscal policy is held constant (Beck 1987). Other researchers (Allen 1986; Laney and Willett 1983) have argued that PMCs occur through the Fed's accommodation of politically motivated fiscal policy. Neither of these researchers found any direct Fed electoral manipulation of the economy, but both found evidence of accommodation of easy fiscal policy, whether electorally motivated or not.

My research found no tendency for the Fed to accommodate electorally motivated fiscal policy in any manner different than they accommodate all fiscal policy. Both Allen and Laney and Willett did find some hints of extra accommodation of politically motivated fiscal policy. But it is hard to measure what portion of fiscal policy is politically motivated, and so both the Allen and Laney and Willett findings can only be taken as suggestive. It is this linkage between politically inspired fiscal policy and monetary policy that I think will be the most promising area for future research into PMCs. But at present it does not appear as though Fed policy echoes electoral rhythms, although the money supply may do so. Let me now turn to the monetary impact of the second type of rhythm, that of a change in the party in control of the White House.

Partisan monetary policy

Is monetary policy easier under Democratic presidents than under Republicans? That appears to be the case. Hibbs (1987, chapter 7.5) modeled the growth of M1 as a distributed lag of the difference between realized and target unemployment. He found that M1 grew one point more for every point decrease in target unemployment, and target unemployment under Democratic presidents was about two points lower than the similar figure under Republican presidents. Thus, M1 grew, on average, about 3.5 points faster under Democratic presidents. Because M1 is not completely controlled by the Fed, we also should look at the policy instruments controlled by the Fed. I found that reserves grew about two points faster under Democratic presidents (Beck 1984).[15]

Why should that happen, given the independence of the Fed? Part of the answer is clearly that the Fed is not completely independent of the president. The president does appoint both the chair and the members of the Board of Governors. Although the Governors were given long (14-year) terms to make them independent of the president, in practice they serve much shorter terms, and many appointments are made simply to fill out unexpired terms. The chair serves only a four-year term; so every president gets to designate a new chair if he desires. In practice, presidents get to nominate different numbers of Governors; Carter, for example, had appointed six of the sitting governors by 1980; Reagan had only one such appointment by 1984, although he did have six appointees by the end of 1987.

The power to reappoint the chair every four years is more critical. Most observers (Maisel 1973) give the chair tremendous power. Chairs who wish to be reappointed had better do what the appointer desires. Though it is difficult to find systematic evidence of chairs who changed policy to secure reappointment (Ersenkal, Wallace, and Warner 1985), anecdotal evidence abounds of how two chairmen, Martins and Burns, adapted to the needs of differing presidents.

More important than the appointment power is the legitimacy of the president vis-à-vis the Fed. The president is elected to carry out a program; the Fed is not elected and is barely perceived by much of the electorate. A president who finds his economic policies thwarted by the Fed should have little trouble taking his case before the people. That is not to say that the Fed is powerless. It has powerful support in the financial community and can use that support to its advantage.

Two examples illustrate the extremes of this relationship. Lyndon Johnson was determined to finance the war in Vietnam without raising taxes. That would have the obvious inflationary consequences. The Fed raised the discount rate in 1965. Johnson, furious, summoned Martin to Johnson's ranch to let Martin know who was in charge.[16] The Fed made no further attempts to stop inflationary financing of the war. There, as in World Wars I and II, the president, not the Fed, made the key decisions about war finance.[17]

The opposite extreme was the relationship between Carter and Volcker in 1979 and 1980. The dollar was rapidly falling, and there were doubts about Carter's ability to manage the economy. The Carter administration opposed the September 1979 change in Fed operating procedures; that did not deter Volcker (Greider 1987, pp. 116–23). After a period of "Democratic" easy money under Chairman Miller, monetary policy was much more "Republican" under Chairman Volcker, even with the same Democrat in the White House. That was not completely without the consent of the president: Credit controls and the subsequent monetary contraction were, after all, introduced at the behest of the president. But the perceived incompetence of Carter, particularly in the financial community, combined with the perceived threat of inflation and the devaluation of the dollar, gave the chairman of the Fed a very strong hand. A president more singlemindedly devoted to easier money might still have gotten his way, but given an ambivalent president, and no issues of war finance, the Fed was at its most powerful. How long that situation would have remained that way is anyone's guess, but the election in 1980 brought a committed antinflationary Republican to the White House (and also gave Republicans control of the Senate). "Republican" tight money was no longer anomalous.

These examples illustrate the power of the president vis-à-vis the Fed, but they also show that presidential control is not total. My guess is that if the president wants to win a struggle with the Fed, he can, and the Fed, knowing that, will give in without a struggle. But the cost to the president of doing that may be high, and so he may give the Fed some latitude. How much, and under what circumstances, are questions that we still need to answer. But changes in administration, and particularly changes in party control of the White House, should be expected to lead to changes in monetary policy. Whether or not these different policies will have effects late in a presidential term, when they are no longer surprises, is an open question. The answer to this question depends on an overall evaluation of the policy-ineffectiveness argument of the rational-expectations school. But rational expectations do not challenge the party/monetary policy linkage.[18]

Conclusion

We know a lot more about PMCs than we did five years ago. M1 does appear to grow faster before elections, and it does appear to grow faster under Democratic presidents. New theories of the PBC have been able to square these empirical findings with modern macroeconomics. The major issue now is why the Fed either produces or allows these cycles.

Current models of PMCs, whether party- or election-oriented, essentially assume that the president can get the monetary policy he desires. At that point, the study of PMCs is just the study of PBCs, and there is nothing special about money. These models of PMCs are improvements over the PBC models that deal only with outcomes, because they provide an account of how presidents might provide those outcomes, but they still ignore the institutions of monetary policy. The president does not directly control the Fed, and so PMCs are not just a subset of PBCs.

To understand PMCs we need to understand the incentives of the Fed and the relative powers of the Fed and the president. There have been several attempts to deal with the first, although none remarkably successful. By now, no one seems to believe the public-interest view of the Fed, and the public-choice view of the Fed as maximizing bureaucrats seems limited.[19] One new approach that may be promising is to look in more detail at what the White House is telling the Fed. Havrilesky (1988) has had some success here, and his approach appears to be reasonable. We cannot know if the Fed is doing what the president wants without knowing what the president wants.

The second question of the relative powers of the president and Fed may be even more difficult to resolve. Perhaps we can do a better job looking at formal control mechanisms, such as appointments. This has been investigated with limited success (Ersenkal et al. 1985), but more needs to be done. Modeling the Fed as being in a principal–agent relationship with either the president or Congress is a promising possibility (Grier 1984, 1987), but at present this approach assumes that the agent is completely controlled by the principal and hence ignores institutional details.[20] Workers in the "new institutionalist" school of political science may be able to give a more satisfactory principal–agent account of monetary policy than has been given, but that remains a project for the future.

Notes

1 I make no attempt to review the nonmonetary literature here. A good review of the literature through the early 1980s can be found in Alt and Crystal (1983, chapters 5–7). More recent work on the impact of party control is that of Hibbs (1987), and the most recent statement of electoral cycles is that of Haynes and Stone (1988).

2 Most of the literature on this question through 1986 has been surveyed elsewhere (Beck 1988a). Here I only selectively cite a few of the more important and/or recent studies. By "partisan monetary policy" I mean policy that varies with the party of the president.

3 There is debate on how sophisticated the electorate is when it comes to evaluating economic policy. Chappell and Keech (1985) find the electorate quite sophisticated, whereas my research (Beck 1989) finds a (rationally) naive electorate.

4 Nordhaus assumes adaptive expectations. It is difficult, although perhaps not impossible, to square the Nordhaus theory with rational expectations.

5 Most political scientists who have looked for a PBC have used the Tufte version, whereas Haynes and Stone tested the Nordhaus version. That may account for the difference in findings.

6 Haynes and Stone, using quarterly data, find a cycle of four years, plus or minus at least one year. My (unpublished) spectral analysis of monthly unemployment rates finds a 2.5-year to 3-year cycle, again plus or minus some months. (Quarterly averaging enhances the contributions of the lower frequencies.) Given the uncertainties and lags in economic policy-making, it would be surprising to find an exact four-year cycle. This is especially true becasue we have a sample period of at most 11 post-war elections, hardly enough data to firmly settle any question. But the data certainly do not rule out a four-year economic cycle, although my findings are not nearly as favorable as Haynes and Stone's to the PBC hypothesis.

7 My hesitations about the Hibbs model have been published (Beck 1982b). There I argued that intraparty differences in outcomes (say between the Johnson and Carter or Eisenhower and Nixon administrations) were as large as the observed interparty differences. No claim was made in that article that party differences were unimportant, although I did find party differences to be only half of the Hibbs (1977) estimate.

8 Alt (1985a,b) argues that building a reputation causes parties to follow different policies right after an election. He finds, both in the United States and in Western Europe, a tendency for outcomes to diverge in the expected way after an election, but for that divergence to die out before the next election. Alt looks only at outcomes, not policies.

9 Of course, failing to help the incumbent has consequences if the incumbent wins. But that strategy seems to have fewer immediately awful consequences for the Fed, especially as the Fed can defend itself by saying that it is not supposed to engage in electoral politics. Note also that I am not saying that the Fed should go out of its way to hurt the incumbent's chances, only that it should not actively aid the incumbent.

10 There are dozens of accounts by White House insiders that came out after Watergate. The clearest statement on economic policy is Ehrlichman (1982, Chapter 14), who goes into great detail about pressure on the Fed, but never once accuses the Fed of doing anything to help Nixon's reelection. Maisel's account (1973) is similar. Maisel was off the Board well before election day.

11 Newton (1983) reported that Rose claimed that the Fed engaged in other, less defensible behavior in reaction to the Rose story. That only confirms the cost to the Fed of engaging in electoral manipulations, whether or not the original Rose story was accurate.

12 I may be giving the members of the FOMC too much credit for political sophistication. Some of the Governors and Bank Presidents may have come from sheltered environments.

13 He holds other factors constant by including nine lagged values of M1 as well as the cyclic variable. Grier's results were through 1982, but my work shows that the result holds up through 1984 (Beck 1987). My replication shows that the Grier result, like others reported here, holds whether we use autoregressions or reaction functions.

14 To go back to the discussion of 1984, the key decision to ease was in 1982, not 1984. All of this is not to argue that ease that increases M1 in the electoral quarter may not help the incumbent, especially if forecasts matter, but simply that a monetary peak in the electoral quarter is far from optimal. If the estimated peak were only a quarter off, we might simply chalk that up to imprecision of estimation, but with the estimated peak being a year or more off, I think that something else is going on here.

15 This is based on a reaction function holding constant the usual macroeconomic variables, with the dependent variable being totally adjusted reserves (using the St. Louis series). Only about one-third of this effect is due to Fed accommodation of easier Democratic fiscal policy.

16 See Woolley (1984, pp. 120–3) or Greider (1987, pp. 331–2) for details.
17 Even this story is not one of total presidential dominance. The Fed did raise the discount rate, knowing that this would not endear it to the president. And after being called to the ranch, Martin did not lower the discount rate. Thus, even there, the Fed had some latitude.
18 In fact, it strengthens the linkage. If Democrats continue to foster "normally" easy money, then eventually that has no output consequences. But if they tighten, or even ease less than normal (for a Democrat), they then induce a surprise that will lead to recession, something the theory assumes they do not want. If Democrats want to lower unemployment later on in their term, they will have to resort to surprisingly easy policy, that is, policy that is easier than normal by Democratic standards.
19 For a less cryptic view of my position on these two schools, see Beck (1988a).
20 More details are provided in my chapter on Congress and the Fed elsewhere in this volume.

References

Alesina, A., and Sachs, J. (1988) "Political Parties and the Business Cycle in the United States, 1948–1984," *Journal of Money, Credit, and Banking,* 20: 63–82.

Allen, S. (1986). "The Federal Reserve and the Electoral Cycle," *Journal of Money, Credit and Banking,* 18:62–6.

Alt, J. (1985a). "Political Parties, World Demand and Unemployment: Domestic and International Sources of Economic Activity," *American Political Science Review,* 79:1016–40.

(1985b). "Party Strategies, World Demand, and Unemployment in Britain and the United States, 1946–1983," in H. Eulau and M. Lewis-Beck (eds.), *Economic Conditions and Electoral Outcomes: The United States and Western Europe,* pp. 32–61. New York: Agathon.

Alt, J., and Crystal, A. (1983). *Political Economy.* Berkeley: University of California Press.

Beck, N. (1982a). "Presidential Influence on the Federal Reserve in the 1970s," *American Journal of Political Science,* 26:415–45.

(1982b). "Parties, Administrations and Macroeconomic Outcomes," *American Political Science Review,* 76:83–93.

(1984). "Domestic Political Sources of American Monetary Policy, 1955–1982," *Journal of Politics,* 46:787–815.

(1987). "Elections and the Fed: Is There a Political Monetary Cycle?" *American Journal of Political Science,* 31:194–16.

(1988a). "Politics and Monetary Policy," in T. Willett (ed.), *Political Business Cycles: The Political Economy of Money, Inflation and Unemployment,* pp. 366–97. Durham, N.C.: Duke University Press.

(1989). "Presidents, the Economy and Public Opinion: A Principal–Agent Perspective," in P. Brace, C. Harrington, and G. King (eds.), *The Presidency in American Politics,* pp. 121–56. New York University Press.

Chappell, H., and Keech, W. (1985). "A New View of Political Accountability for Economic Performance," *American Political Science Review,* 79:10–27.
(1986). "Party Differences in Macroeconomic Policies and Outcomes," *American Economic Review: Papers and Proceedings,* 76:71–4.
Ehrlichman, J. (1982). *Witness to Power.* New York: Simon & Schuster.
Ersenkal, C., Wallace, M., and Warner, J. (1985). "Chairman Reappointments, Presidential Elections and Policy Actions of the Federal Reserve," *Policy Sciences,* 18:211–25.
Greider, W. (1987). *Secrets of the Temple: How the Federal Reserve Runs the Country.* New York: Simon & Schuster.
Grier, K. (1984). "The Political Economy of Monetary Policy," unpublished Ph.D. dissertation, Washington University.
(1987). "Presidential Elections and Federal Reserve Policy: An Empirical Test," *Southern Economic Journal,* 54:475–86.
Hall, R., and Taylor, J. (1988). *Macroeconomics,* 2d ed. New York: Norton.
Havrilesky, T. (1987). "A Partisanship Theory of Fiscal and Monetary Regimes," *Journal of Money, Credit and Banking,* 19:308–25.
(1988). "Monetary Policy Signaling from the Administration to the Federal Reserve," *Journal of Money, Credit and Banking,* 20:84–101.
Haynes, S., and Stone, J. (1988). "Does the Political Business Cycle Dominate United States Unemployment and Inflation? Some New Evidence," in T. Willett (ed.), *Political Business Cycles: The Political Economy of Money, Inflation and Unemployment,* pp. 276–93. Durham, N.C.: Duke University Press.
Hibbs, D. (1977). "Political Party and Macroeconomic Policy," *American Political Science Review,* 71:1467–87.
(1987). *The American Political Economy: Macroeconomics and Electoral Politics in the United States.* Cambridge, Mass.: Harvard University Press.
Laney, L., and Willett, T. (1983). "Presidential Politics, Budget Deficits and Monetary Policy in the United States, 1960–1976," *Public Choice,* 40: 53–69.
Maisel, S. (1973). *Managing the Dollar.* New York: Norton.
Meiselman, D. (1986). "Is There a Political Monetary Cycle?" *Cato Journal,* 6:563–79.
Newton, M. (1983). *The Fed.* New York: Times Books.
Nordhaus, W. (1975). "The Political Business Cycle," *Review of Economic Studies,* 42:169–90.
Rose, S. (1974). "The Agony of the Fed," *Fortune,* 90(July): 90–3, 180–90.
Sims, C. (1982). "Policy Analysis with Econometric Models," *Brookings Papers on Economic Activity,* 1:107–64.
Tufte, E. (1978). *Political Control of the Economy.* Princeton University Press.
Woolley, J. (1984). *The Federal Reserve and the Politics of Monetary Policy.* Cambridge University Press.

CHAPTER 9

Congress and the Fed: why the dog does not bark in the night

NATHANIEL BECK

"The Fed is a creature of Congress." So Senator Paul Douglas told William McChesney Martin during his confirmation hearings. Senator Douglas went so far as to suggest that Martin paste that slogan on his mirror so that he would see it every morning while shaving. The slogan has some merit. The Federal Reserve was created by a simple act of Congress in 1913. The act has had at least one major set of amendments (during the New Deal), as well as numerous more minor changes. Congress debated, in 1975, the possibility of making major structural changes in Fed–Congress relationships.[1] At any time, by a simple act of Congress, the Fed could be radically changed, or even disbanded. Careful observers (Pierce 1978; Roberts 1978; Weintraub 1978; Woolley 1984) have noted, however, that Congress gives the Fed an unusually free rein.

These observers noted that at least through the 1970s, Congress appeared to play no role in the making of short-run monetary policy.[2] The Fed's legislative mandate appears to be to "make monetary policy in the public interest." The reforms of 1975 simply mandate that the Fed tell Congress what it did and what it is doing, and why it did not do what it said it would do. Congress gives the Fed a similar free rein in regulating the banking industry. The amendments to the Bank Holding Company Act of 1970 and 1976 give the Fed tremendous latitude to pass on bank-holding-company mergers and acquisitions, as well as to determine the

I would like to thank Gary Cox, John Ferejohn, Morris Fiorina, John Goodman, Thomas Havrilesky, Gary Jacobson, David Laitin, Matt McCubbins, Thomas Mayer, Barry Weingast, and John Woolley for sharing their knowledge of Congress and/or monetary politics with me. This chapter draws on some ideas first presented at a Conference on the Political Economy of Regulation at Stanford University, May 1984, organized by Roger Noll and James Rosse. The discussant on my presentation, Barry Weingast, attempted to educate me about the correct way to view Congress, although his success was at best mixed. Finally, I am most grateful for the comments and suggestions given me in response to a presentation at the Working Group on Comparative Monetary Policy, Center for European Studies, Harvard University, March 1987. The conclusion of this chapter owes much to that seminar, and particularly to Mo Fiorina.

legitimate scope of the activities of banks and bank holding companies. In spite of the efforts of Representative Fernand St. Germain, the chair of the House Banking Committee, Congress refused to take a stance on the "nonbank bank" controversy for almost five years.

If we think of Congress and the Fed as being in a relationship of principal and agent, this wide grant is perhaps not surprising. The Fed, after all, deals with issues that either are highly technical or require very quick action, or both. It may make sense for Congress to give its agent wide latitude in this type of situation. But principals usually keep some form of control mechanism over their agents. The typical form of congressional control is the budgetary process, where agents must justify their previous activities to get what they desire, a larger budget. But Congress allows the Fed to control its own budget, paying for its operations out of its large earnings on its portfolio.[3]

The principal–agent approach has also been used, in a recent series of papers by Barry Weingast and collaborators (Weingast 1984; Weingast and Moran 1983; Calvert, Moran, and Weingast 1987), to argue the opposite, namely, that, in general, such appearances may be deceiving. The Weingast perspective is that congressional inactivity is as consistent with congressional dominance as with congressional impotence. Agencies will recognize congressional power and accede to congressional demands without the appearance of a struggle. Agencies, according to Weingast, fear "the big club behind the door." The appearance of political struggle indicates two politically powerful antagonists; the absence of struggle indicates dominance, but tells nothing about which party is dominant.

This perspective has been applied to the Fed in an interesting series of papers by Weingast's student, Kevin Grier (1984, 1985). After repeating the Weingast argument that the absence of congressional struggle is deceiving, Grier presents evidence of indirect congressional control of the Fed. He finds that shifts in the growth rate of the money supply can be explained by shifts in the membership of the Senate Banking Committee.

The finding in this chapter is that the observational evidence is not deceiving: There is little evidence of congressional control over monetary policy. Moreover, there are good reasons for this lack of control. From the Weingast-Grier perspective it is puzzling why Congress has not dramatically modified its 1913 grant of authority to the Fed. This puzzle is an interesting one, and prior to Weingast and Grier it went unnoticed. Here I take notice of the puzzle posed by the new perspective and show that there are good reasons why Congress has not radically modified its 1913 grant of authority.

Congress and the Fed

Since David Mayhew's path-breaking book (1974), it has been common to look at members of Congress (MCs) as being electorally motivated. Though MCs clearly have other motives too (Fenno 1973), it is necessary for an MC to be reelected if he or she wishes to pursue any of those other motives. Electorally motivated MCs pursue three types of activities: position-taking, credit-claiming, and advertising. Providing collective goods, such as good policy, has little, if any, electoral payoff. Agency oversight also has little payoff; it is time-consuming, and one cannot claim credit for the improved policy. Appearing at highly publicized oversight hearings, making speeches attacking an agency and getting agencies to provide individual goods for a district all will have electoral payoffs. But the outcome of an oversight hearing – good policy – is not of great moment from this perspective.

Woolley (1984, Chapter 7), building on the work of both Scher (1963) and Mayhew, argues that MCs have no specifically electoral incentive to supervise the making of monetary policy. When interest is high, that is, when interest rates are high, MCs do attend oversight hearings. A spot on the evening TV news attacking the devil himself, or his agent Paul Volcker, is never to be turned down, but there is no electoral reason for any MC actually to care about whether monetary policy is too tight or too easy.

This idea has been buttressed by several studies of the impact of House Concurrent Resolution 133 on the making of monetary policy. HCR133 was passed in 1975 in the midst of the 1974–75 recession. As Woolley shows, the final bill was a substantially watered-down version of several bills that would have mandated a money-supply growth rate. HCR133 (whose essential provisions were more or less enshrined intact in the Humphrey-Hawkins bill) demanded only that the Fed report to the House and Senate Banking Committees on a quarterly (later semiannual) basis. At those hearings, the Fed was forced to specify its future targets, as well as report on its success (or, more typically, failure) in hitting previous targets. Whereas commentators such as Milton Friedman (1982) originally saw HCR133 as a milestone in responsible monetary policy, most studies (Pierce 1978; Roberts 1978; Weintraub 1978) did not find it to have much effect. In a time of high interest rates the monetary hearings were well attended, and the chairman of the Fed was told in no uncertain terms that high interest rates were intolerable, but little else seems to have happened. Chairman Arthur Burns, according to Pierce, had little difficulty explaining to Congress why the Fed had missed most of its monetary targets, emphasizing the importance of whatever target the Fed had actually managed to hit.

Even the considerable monetary tightness and recession of 1981–2 seemed to have little impact on congressional control of the Fed. Yet, while Congress emitted more rumblings than usual, and several bills were proposed, Congress did very little. This is not to say that Congress would have remained inactive if tight policy had continued, but by the time the Fed eased in the summer of 1982, Congress had done nothing.[4]

We know less about congressional inactivity in the bank regulatory area. The various amendments to the Bank Holding Company Act give the Fed wide discretion in approving bank mergers, as well as in regulating the appropriate activities of bank holding companies. I have not been able to discern MCs playing an important role in that process for their constituent banks. Informed observers to whom I have talked, both inside and outside the Fed, agree with this observation. MCs may write cover letters introducing their important constituents to the Fed. But if they have any weight they can throw around at the Fed, they do not appear to use it, and the Fed does not seem worried about the congressional response when it makes regulatory decisions.[5]

If we look at the legislative history of congressional attempts to deal with nonbank banks, we see that legislation either died in committee or was blocked by the House Rules committee. Some of that failure was due to wrangling between Chairman St. Germain of the House Banking Committe and his counterpart in the Senate, Jake Garn, and part of it was due to St. Germain's wrangling with Rules Committee member Claude Pepper. But Congress did not take a stand on nonbank banks (either pro or con) from the time the issue broke in 1982 until the middle of 1987. And the eventual action came about only because of a crisis in the thrift industry that Congress could not ignore. Chairman St. Germain took advantage of that crisis to tack on to the critical FSLIC bailout bill a bill regulating nonbank banks.

This position is consistent with the "shift-of-responsibility" argument of Fiorina (1982). Congressional actions cause both goods and bads, and usually there is asymmetry between the political responses of those who get the goods and those who suffer the bads. Fiorina argues that electorally motivated MCs are risk-averse, because, in the absence of serious mistakes, they are quite likely to win reelection. Congress will, therefore, legislate (that is, make explicit rules) in areas where the (electoral) benefit of making policy exceeds the cost, and it will shift onto an agency (via a wide grant of authority) those policy concerns that inevitably cause (electoral) harm. Monetary policy appears to be of the latter type. Tight money hurts the housing and automobile industries, and those groups seem likely to remember such hurt on the next election day. Those who gain from a decline in inflation are a more diffuse group and are not likely to be terribly thankful to their MCs on election day. This is particularly true because no MC can claim credit for bringing down inflation.

The regulation of financial institutions probably also shows a similar diversity of constituency interests. Even the smallest of constituencies contains a large number of different types of financial institutions. Regulatory issues either pit classes of institutions against each other (Can thrifts sell life insurance?) or pit firms of the same type against each other (for every bank that fears out-of-state competition, there is another bank that wants to be taken over, at an inflated price, by an out-of-state bank). MCs might gain by favoring or opposing any given regulation, but given the risks, it probably is quite sensible for MCs to avoid taking any position on many issues involving bank regulation.

Kane (1980) argues, with similar reasoning, that Congress uses the Fed as a "whipping boy." Given the Fed's seeming independence, Congress (or MCs) can blame the Fed for bad economic times. Thus, he takes Fiorina one step further: Not only does the Fed get a broad grant of authority, but it actually appears to get independence. But, for Kane at least, that independence is a chimera. When monetary policy starts to hurt, and Congress gets pressure from the "low-interest lobby," the Fed caves in. It does that because Congress controls what the Fed wants: independence. Thus, there is a charade in which the Fed preserves the appearance of independence by doing what Congress wants, and Congress allows the Fed independence because that serves congressional needs.

Neither the Fiorina argument nor the Kane argument can explain the lack of budgetary control by Congress over the Fed. In Fiorina's analyses, Congress has no difficulty in shifting responsibility onto agencies over which it has budgetary control, and there is no reason why Congress cannot maintain the charade that hard economic times are to be blamed on the Fed, even if the Fed has not controlled its own budget. (If the consumers of the charade are voters, then they are unlikely even to be aware of Fed independence. And it seems unlikely that the charade could possibly work for sophisticated observers of Congress.)

The Kane argument was honed for the 1970s, to explain why the Fed continually eased too early (in terms of fighting inflation). There are many reasons for the Fed to ease during a downturn in the business cycle (especially if the Fed believed, as it at least seemed to, that it could fine-tune the economy). There are lots of forces, both inside and outside Congress, that desire low interest rates. The Fed often may have eased too soon, but that does not allow one to conclude that the Fed acceded to congressional pressures for lower interest rates. It is difficult, using empirical means, to validate the Kane argument. It would be interesting to know, for example, what would have happened in Congress had the Fed not turned to ease in 1982, but we shall never know the answer to that question. It is clear that many in Congress desired easier money in the summer of 1982, but they were not the only actors, both inside and outside the United States, with such preferences.

It may, indeed, be the case that the countercyclical nature of monetary policy is what keeps Congress from getting involved in monetary policy. It takes a while for constituents to complain about high interest rates, and it takes a while for Congress to gear up to do anything. This is particularly true for a technical area like monetary policy. Given the support for the Fed in various parts of the financial community, no congressional attack on the Fed is going to be easy. But business cycles inevitably turn down, and unemployment inevitably appears as important as inflation to the Fed.[6] Thus, the Fed will inevitably lower interest rates before Congress takes any serious action, and so there will be little impetus for major institutional reform.

A stronger variant of Kane's argument is embodied in the Weingast-Grier principal–agent model of the Congress–Fed relationship. In contrast to most principal–agent relationships, here the principal holds all the cards. As for Kane, the key card is the congressional grant of independence. The Fed, knowing that it will lose what it most prizes if it goes against Congress, divines the policy desired by its principal and follows that policy. Weingast stresses the critical role of congressional committees; so the desires of Congress are the desires of the relevant committees and subcommittees, and particularly the leadership of those committees and subcommittees. It is difficult to come up with a definitive test of the Weingast model because its critical implication is that congressional dominance and congressional impotence are observationally equivalent with respect to congressional activity. Thus, the argument must turn on the indirct evidence of the relationship between some observable change in Congress and an observable change in agency output. Weingast has managed to show that the comparative-statics predictions of his theory have been upheld for several different agencies.

Weingast himself has not looked at the Fed, but Grier has done so. His studies make innovative use of several different kinds of evidence. Looking at the events of 1975, which most observers have seen as an example of congressional lack of power, Grier sees congressional strength. As various bills limiting Fed independence found their way to the floor, the Fed eased policy. At that point, strenuous congressional action became unnecessary, and we ended up with the relatively innocuous HCR133. Where observers like Woolley see congressional passivity, Grier sees congressional power.

Perhaps more persuasive is his demonstration that under Volcker, monetary policy tightend, not with the coming of the new procedures of October 1979, but with the election of 1980, which gave conservatives control of the Senate and the Senate Banking Committee. But there are problems with attributing the tightening of policy to Republican control of the Senate, because an important new actor occupied the White House. Any single historical event is going to be subject to several different explanations and hence cannot be decisive for discriminating between explanations.[7] Thus, Grier's argument must rest on his econometric evidence.

Before turning to that evidence, let me briefly consider the reasonableness of the Weingast-Grier perspective. Weingast stresses budgetary control as the key power of the principal. In fact, in most of his empirical analyses, he uses the relevant subcommittee of the Appropriations Committee, not the substantive committee, as his indicator of congressional preference. Yet the Fed is not subject to budgetary control. If Congress wishes to control its principal, why does it not at least move toward budgetary control of the Fed? Why should a principal give up a relatively low-cost means of controlling its agent? Budgetary review could be cursory, in which case it would be of little value, but of low cost; alternatively, it could be interventionist, but costly. But why give up the mechanism altogether and rely only on "the big club behind the door" (removal of Fed independence)?

Econometric evidence[8]

Grier shows that Senate preferences, as measured by the liberalism of the leadership of the Senate Banking Committee [operationalized as the Americans for Democratic Action (ADA) scores of the committee chair and relevant subcommittee chairs] Granger causes monetary policy, operationalized as growth in M1. Specifically, he shows that if the growth of M1 is regressed on nine lags of itself and the Senate-liberalism variable lagged two quarters, there is a significant impact of the Senate variable on M1. (The results are weaker, but still quite significant, for other lags.) This is impressive evidence, because M1 is measured quarterly, but the Senate variable is fixed over the year.

Grier makes a few arguments for looking only at Senate preferences. His strongest argument is that only the Senate confirms new members of the Board. But the only time the confirmation process ever seems to generate any excitement is when the chair of the Fed is being either appointed or reappointed. Given the long term of Board members, the confirmation power probably is not the strongest tool for congressional sanction. Looking at legislative histories, much of the action on bills attacking the Fed has been in the House. This is particularly true for the Patman era, but it also holds for the Reuss chairmanship. There is no reason to believe that the Grier argument ought not to hold as well for the House as the Senate.

I replicated and extended Grier's results, making a few minor changes in method.[9] Committee liberalism is operationalized as the difference between "Conservative Coalition Opposition" and "Conservative Coalition Support" scores for the Banking Committee chair and relevant subcommittee chairs.[10] Monetary policy is measured by the percentage growth in M1 from the previous year. As in the Grier formulation, the best autoregression for M1 is of the ninth order. As in Grier's work, I then added to the autoregressions a variable measuring House or Senate Banking Committee liberalism; various lags for this variable were tried, with two-, four-, and eight-quarter lags reported here (other lags are consistent with the reported results). All data used are quarterly, with economic data obtained from Citibase.[11]

Grier's evidence is for the period 1961–80. He finds that increased liberalism of the Senate Banking Committee led to a higher growth rate in M1. In Table 9.1, I show a similar finding. An increase in Senate Banking Committee liberalism of, say, 20 points, a large but not atypical increase, led to a 2-point increase in M1, with a lag of either half a year or one year (or a 2.6 percent increase in M1 two years later, if one prefers the two-year-lag specification). Given the autoregressive model for M1, this increase will then feed through the system in a complicated way. But there is no question that for the period 1962–80 there appears to have been a relationship between Senate Banking Committee liberalism and monetary policy, as measured by the growth of M1.

A longer sample period is now available than Grier could have used in his dissertation. A simple replication for the period 1962:II–1987:II shows that, if anything, increased Senate liberalism actually led to a lower growth in M1. In any event, the estimated coefficients are not much larger than their standard errors, and their signs are clearly inconsistent with the Weingast-Grier hypothesis.

It would seem as though House Banking Committee liberalism should also increase the growth in the money supply. But it does not, either for the Grier sample period or for my longer period. (For the shorter sample period, House liberalism entered with a lag of seven quarters is marginally significant, but no other lag is close to being significant. In

Table 9.1. *Regression results*

Variable	1962:II–1987:II b	SE	1962:II–1980:IV b	SE
Dependent variable: percentage growth in M1; ninth-order autoregression				
LibSen (lag 2)	−.0080	.0021	.0089	.0038
LibSen (lag 4)	−.0024	.0021	.0106	.0041
LibSen (lag 8)	−.0026	.0022	.0134	.0050
LibHouse (lag 2)	.0027	.0058	−.0007	.0051
LibHouse (lag 4)	.0033	.0058	.0041	.0051
LibHouse (lag 8)	−.0007	.0047	.0045	.0041

Variable	1961:III–1987:II b	SE	1961:III–1980:IV b	SE
Dependent variable: change in Federal-Funds rate; sixth-order autoregression				
LibSen (lag 0)	.0035	.0047	−.0013	.0044
LibSen (lag 1)	.0048	.0027	.0030	.0044
LibSen (lag 2)	.0082	.0027	.0045	.0044
LibSen (lag 4)	.0065	.0031	.0055	.0045
LibSen (lag 8)	.0057	.0034	.0052	.0046
LibHouse (lag 0)	.0090	.0077	.0086	.0063
LibHouse (lag 1)	.0092	.0078	.0111	.0063
LibHouse (lag 2)	.0128	.0079	.0110	.0065
LibHouse (lag 4)	.0035	.0068	.0039	.0056
LibHouse (lag 8)	.0023	.0055	.0052	.0046

the absence of a compelling argument as to why a lag of seven quarters should be chosen on a priori grounds, this finding must be dismissed as a quirk in the sample data.) This result is inconsistent with the Weingast-Grier hypothesis. In the absence of a compelling argument as to why the Senate should have greater control over the Fed than does the House, and I can think of no such argument here, this would seem to indicate that the Grier finding is artifactual. (Artifactual results are common in the analysis of time series, particularly if lag lengths are empirically determined.)

Most observers will not be surprised at the lack of congressional influence on the money supply. If MCs are concerned about what troubles their constituents, then they will be sensitive to high interest rates, not the money supply. Because the Fed directly controls the shortest interest rate, the federal-funds rate, if Weingast and Grier are correct we should see a strong congressional impact on that rate. Although the link between liberalism and interest-rate sensitivity may not be as strong as the link between liberalism and preference for easy money, because all MCs may prefer low interest rates, there still should be such a link (because those who prefer monetary soundness and low inflation must be more willing to pay the temporary costs of higher interest rates).

To test whether or not congressional liberalism is related to lower interest rates, I ran analyses similar to that for the growth in M1, using as the dependent variable the simple change in the federal-funds rate. A sixth-order autoregression proved best. Autoregressions were fit for both the 1962–80 and 1962–87 sample periods. The results are shown in Table 9.1. Because the Fed can control the federal-funds rate almost instantaneously, I checked for immediate as well as longer lag impacts of changes in congressional liberalism on the federal-funds rate.

For neither sample period, and for no lag, whether short or long, is there any evidence that either House or Senate committee liberalism led to lower interest rates. In fact, liberalism was associated, slightly, with increasing interest rates. Because congressional liberals are more likely to take positions opposing high interest rates, this is strong evidence against the Weingast-Grier position.[12]

The principal–agent theory of Congress and the Fed is not supported by the quantitative evidence. It should be stressed that the evidence is hardly conclusive, and, as noted earlier, it is unlikely that we will ever find the proverbial "smoking gun." The quantitative evidence, when combined with all the qualitative evidence, does seem to favor the conclusion that Congress is not very important in the short-run making of monetary policy.[13] This is not to say that the comparative-statics results of Grier are incorrect. An increase in congressional liberalism could hardly be expected to lead to tighter monetary policy. But before the work of Grier, no one thought that effect to be very large, and the evidence presented here indicates that the earlier view may well have been correct.

Why the dog does not bark in the night[14]

It is not hard to understand why Congress gives the Fed a broad mandate for regulating the financial industry. Bank regulatory issues often will set constituents against other constituents rather than constituencies against other constituencies. That increases the risk of congressional action either way. Even an issue like interstate banking, which at first glance appears to pit money-center districts against all the others, is actually a fight within most of the other constituencies. If large out-of-state banks enter markets by acquiring smaller banks, rather than by chartering a bank de novo, and that has been the pattern thus far, then those being acquired (usually at an inflated price relative to book value) have an interest in interstate banking. Some constituents, such as farmers or owners of small businesses, may worry about their access to credit under interstate banking. But some important constituents – (some) local financial institutions – may favor interstate banking.[15]

Other issues that arise under the Bank Holding Company Act, such as intrastate acquisitions or the scope of permissible activities for bank holding companies, can also be seen as risky from the perspective of MCs.[16] Banks do not want competition from thrifts, but some thrifts want to compete with banks. Banks want to be able to do what insurance companies do, but insurance companies do not want that. Although most banks in a locality may fear the entry of a large bank holding company into their market, I would presume that the bank being acquired would favor such entry.

It is not that taking a position one way or the other would not help, but rather that there is enough uncertainty that a risk-avoiding member probably would prefer to score electoral points in another arena. The financial arena is particularly problematic because the intraconstituency split probably is not along party lines. Congress, after all, frequently intervenes in arenas such as labor relations, where there are also divisions within every constituency. But even in the most divided constituencies, Democratic and Republican representatives have a fairly good idea where their electoral interests lie when taking positions in the labor area. Such is not the case for financial matters, which do not pit labor against management, or consumers against producers, but rather pit one set of financial institutions against another set in each district. An incumbent MC is a fairly safe bet for reelection unless he or she makes a serious miscalculation. The financial arena is one in which such a miscalculation could easily occur.

It seems just as easy to explain congressional inactivity in the making of monetary policy *as currently implemented.* The electoral imperative leads MCs to pursue activities for which they can claim credit. Monetary policy is a collective good, and it is difficult for any MC to use good monetary policy to his or her electoral advantage. MCs cannot go home to their districts and say "I brought down interest rates." Even if they could, there is, again, diversity in most districts on this issue. If an MC claiming credit for low interest rates also had to shoulder the burden of being blamed for high inflation, would it be worth it? Perhaps, but perhaps not. Voters may not readily see the link between interest rates and inflation, but the president, or a clever opponent in the next election, might educate the voters. In a world in which MCs have many things to do that are clearly attractive from an electoral standpoint, why engage in an activity whose electoral payoffs are a good deal more uncertain?

It is, however, not necessary to have monetary policy be a collective good. Fiscal policy provides individual goods to congressional districts, as well as a collective good (or bad): the deficit. Congress does not simply tell the Internal Revenue Service to collect taxes in a manner conformable with the public interest. Monetary policy could similarly be used to aid individual MCs. Why do we not make policy in this manner? In other word, why is monetary policy in the United States not credit allocation? Why does monetary policy consist of manipulating aggregates such as total credit (or its price), either through manipulating some interest rates or through manipulating the overall supply of money?

In other nations, such as France, monetary policy has consisted of credit allocation. The government of France, by setting lending ceilings for banks, but then allowing different types of loans to count differentially against those ceilings, was able to move money toward certain favored sectors.[17] If the United States were to engage in credit allocation, MCs could aid their electoral chances by getting credit moved to important industries in their constituencies. Why do we not do this?

One answer is that to some extent we do. The housing sector is an important part of almost every constituency, and we subsidize the price of credit for housing. This is done not through the Fed, but, at least until very recently, through the thrift industry.[18] In return for making mortgage loans at below market rates, the thrifts were given an advantage in the interest rates they could pay small savers, as well as various tax advantages. Interest-rate ceilings on financial institutions then shielded the thrifts from competition, allowing the thrifts to survive while charging below market interest rates. That system made it possible for the American home-building industry to thrive and for many Americans to own their own homes.

We also subsidize credit in another politically sensitive sector: agriculture. Much of current agricultural policy is designed to allow farmers to borrow at below market rates, or to allow farmers to value their security – their crops – above market valuation. Farmers have always wanted cheap credit, and American agricultural policy provides that cheap credit. (To see the size of the credit subsidy, one need only consider the current $6 billion bailout of the Farm Credit System being considered in Congress.)

But both of these forms of credit allocation are handled outside of the Fed. With the exception of the disaster of March 1980 (and the disaster of 1929), the Fed typically has not attempted to say that credit should be used for some purposes and not others.[19] Why does Congress not go further and attempt to get the Fed to move credit toward sectors that would aid reelection efforts? The original bills in 1975 made noises in that direction, but that idea never made the final version of HCR133 (Woolley 1984, Chapter 7). Why?

Two answers suggest themselves. The first is that the Fed is not being formed de novo. Monetary policy is made within a set of rules dating from 1913, and amended several times since. Those rules set up an environment that would be costly to change. Although individual MCs might gain from credit allocation, they might not gain from expending effort to get the Fed to move toward credit allocation. If the Fed were being designed today from scratch, we might see more credit allocation. But that is not the case.

Monetary policy is quite technical, and it would take MCs a long time to come up to speed on this issue. Getting the Fed to engage in credit allocation is a collective good to Congress, and there is no reason for any MC to engage in this activity. Such a move would clearly generate opposition, both from the Fed and the "Fed family" and from financial institutions that prefer the current arrangements.[20] (Support for the Fed from the financial institutions may derive from self-interest. A bank never knows when it may need the help of the Fed.) And these supporters of the Fed are going to be important constituents of at least one MC. Could a typical MC gain enough from credit allocation to make the fight worthwhile? It seems doubtful, and the events of 1975 are consistent with this.

This also explains why Congress has not gone even so far as to impose budgetary control on the Fed. In the short run, such a move might be politically costly to many MCs, and the long-run electoral gains from such a move might not be realized by current MCs who might lose their seats. In a risk-averse electoral environment, reform of the Fed might not be a winning issue.[21] Again, it seems clear to me that if the Fed were being created today, there would be congressional budgetary control, but that is of little moment given that the history of the Fed already spans three-quarters of a century.

The second answer is more general. Particularistic fiscal policy already gives MCs any advantage they might derive from credit allocation. If they cannot help move credit toward an important constituent or sector, they can certainly do more or less the same thing via particularistic taxation or spending. If fiscal policy were made in a nonparticularistic manner, then credit allocation would be helpful, but only one particularistic type of economic policy is politically necessary, and we already have that in fiscal policy. In general, we might expect to see nations engage in either credit allocation or particularistic fiscal policy, but not both.

Normatively, a particularistic fiscal policy probably has fewer macroeconomic consequences than does a particularistic monetary policy. From a macroeconomic perspective, the critical effect of particularistic fiscal policy is on spending. There are clearly particularistic elements of U.S. taxation policy, but their consequences are primarily microeconomic. If, as Weingast, Shepsle, and Johnsen (1981) argue, particularistic spending policy leads the government to spend too much, some of this bad effect may be offset by tax policy. There is no such revenue-raising counterpart to offset the bad effects of particularistic monetary policy. Credit allocation probably would lead to an increase in overall credit (in nominal terms), rather than a simple reallocation of existing credit (the latter might be politically painful). The consequences of that for monetary discipline could be disastrous.[22]

It may appear as though MCs could use monetary and banking issues to further their careers, but on closer examination that strategy is either unnecessary or unnecessarily risky. In addition, it would be costly to change institutions so as to bring that advantage about. If Congress were creating the Fed de novo, it might do things differently, but it is not doing that. If there were more of an electoral advantage to incurring that cost of change, MCs might choose to do it. But the apparent advantages of credit allocation may be chimerical. Congress may be retaining the current institutions for making monetary policy not because those institutions lead to better policies but because the current arrangement is simply the by-product of congressional (electoral) self-interest.

Notes

1 I refer here to the debate over what eventually became the watered-down House Concurrent Resolution (HCR) 133. See Woolley (1984, Chapter 7) for a discussion of the legislative history of HCR133.

2 There has been much less study on the role of Congress during the Volcker period. Greider's journalistic account (1987) of the Volcker period is consistent with the standard account of the earlier period.

3 The best discussion of control mechanisms for Congress is that of McCubbins and Schwartz (1984). They argue that Congress sets up "fire alarms," that is, mechanisms that allow constituents to make it quite clear when an agency is doing something that might cause MCs electoral harm. This is generally more efficient for Congress than engaging in costly direct oversight. But budgetary control is a fairly efficient method of direct oversight, and one that we would not expect Congress to scorn.

The origin of budgetary independence is the initial Act of 1913, which was a compromise between those who wanted the Fed to be a "banker's bank" and those who wanted it to look like any other agency. Under that compromise, the Federal Reserve Bank would look like private corporations, with stock held by the member banks. Those member banks would receive a dividend (up to 6%), with the remainder of profits used to pay for bank operations, and any remaining profits going into a special fund. In some sense the initial Act set up two sets of entities: the Federal Reserve Board in Washington, whose members were appointed by the president and confirmed by the Senate, and the Federal Reserve Banks, which were essentially private structures loosely tied to the Board.

It was originally thought that the Federal Reserve Banks would finance their operations out of rediscounting profits, but those proved insufficient. They then moved to manage their portfolio so as to increase revenues. That led, eventually, to the current Federal Open Market Committee. Open-market operations are now the principal tools of monetary policy. See Chandler (1958) for a good discussion of this history.

Matt McCubbins has suggested to me that Congress may have known what it was doing in 1913, although my own reading of history is that financing the Fed was not a major issue. In general, the Act of 1913 did not give Congress much of a supervisory role over the Fed. That was partly because the Fed was simply seen as performing a technical banking function (rediscounting eligible paper) and partly because it was seen as behaving without discretion (the real-bills doctrine). It is obvious that the Fed always made policy, but the Fed was not viewed as an important maker of economic policy until, at the earliest, the Employment Act of 1946. But even that Act scarcely took notice of the Fed as an economic policy-maker.

4 See Greider (1987, pp. 472–5, 512–15) for a discussion of congressional unhappiness with monetary policy in 1981–2 and Volcker's lack of concern with congressional demands. He goes into great detail about the lack of success of Senator Robert Byrd's attempt to mandate lower interest rates with the Balanced Monetary Policy Act of 1982. According to Greider (1987, pp. 513–14), by the time the bill was introduced in August, it was an "empty threat. . . . House Democrats might have conceivably passed the bill, but it was never evident that Senate Democrats could muster a majority . . . to enact such a fundamental reform. It would require Congress to take responsibility for monetary policy . . . responsibility that many in Congress preferred to keep at a mysterious distance in the central bank. *More to the point, the falling interest rates and the stock market rally . . . simply collapsed the congressional zeal for Fed bashing*" (emphasis added).

5 This paragraph is based on interviews I conducted in 1981–3 with current and former Fed staff. Those interviews were not for attribution and were not so systematic that I can be sure of the conclusions of this paragraph. Weingast argues that Congress is so powerful that it does not need to put any pressure on the Fed and, conversely, that the Fed knows what is required without being explicitly told. It is almost impossible to gather evidence to show that position false (or true), but my own discussions with people whom I believe to be knowledgeable do not lead me to believe in the Weingast position.

6 This may be because of outside actors putting pressure on the Fed, but I would argue that these outside actors are much more likely to be in the executive branch than in the legislative branch of government.

7 Moreover, it is not even obvious that monetary policy was tightened in 1981 and not 1979. It is difficult to compare Volcker's policies under Carter and Reagan. The post–October 1979 Carter years were marked by roller-coaster monetary policy, primarily as a result of the March 1980 experiment with credit controls and their subsequent lifting. That made monetary growth in the second quarter of 1980 exceptionally small, but growth in the next two quarters quite large. Overal, M1b grew by about 7.4% in the last 15 months of the Carter administration and by 7.7% in the first 15 months of the Reagan administration. These are the simple growth rates from beginning to end of the period. If one averages, as Grier did, the quarterly periods, one finds that growth was faster under Carter (8.5% as compared with 7.4%). The discrepancy between these two calculations is due to the different impacts given to the decline and subsequent growth of M1 due to credit controls and their lifting. It is not trivial to settle the issue, but the assertion about when monetary policy was eased is problematic.

8 The evidence here is inevitably going to be far from conclusive. It is hard to get a good measure of what Congress wants monetary policy to look like. Moreover, the entire thrust of the Weingast-Grier argument is that Congress does not have to do much to get the Fed to go along. Thus there will not be a lot of activity that can be analyzed. There were, for example, no roll-call votes that could shed light on the controversy.

The only point of this section is to argue that the quantitative evidence regarding the Weingast-Grier view is far from conclusive and is, if anything, contradictory to their view. But we shall never be certain on purely empirical grounds that the Weingast-Grier view is incorrect. Only the critical econometric results are presented here; complete econometric results are available, on request from the author: Prof. Nathaniel Beck, Department of Political Science, University of California, San Diego, La Jolla, CA 92093.

9 It does not appear as though any of my minor changes led to results different from those of Grier, because my results for the 1962–80 sample period are qualitatively similar to his.

10 The score is as reported in various issues of the *Congressional Quarterly.* It is superior to the ADA score used by Grier in that it takes a consistent set of issues over time, whereas the ADA score is sensitive to Vietnam during the 1960s. In addition, the ADA does not distinguish between opposition and abstention; for example, Senator Edward Kennedy does not always appear quite so liberal by the ADA standard.

General liberalism might not correctly reflect preferences for easy money. As Tom Mayer has pointed out to me, Patman's attitudes on race may have had nothing to do with his feelings about the Fed. Given the paucity of votes on monetary (or economic) issues, there is nothing that can be done about this problem. The "Conservative Support" score is more sensitive to economics than is the ADA score, and so, at a minimum, Grier's results are more sensitive to this problem than are mine.

11 The Citibase data set is from August of 1987. M1 is the "new M1" (Citibase FM1), seasonally adjusted. M1 is available from 1959; so the yearly growth rate is available from 1960. It is this and the number of lagged values of the dependent variable that determine the start of the sample period. The beginning of Grier's sample period is slightly different, but that difference does not appear to have had any impact. (Grier measured growth rates from quarter to quarter; so he had three earlier quarters of data. That slight measurement change had no substantive impact.) The first difference in the federal-funds rate, used later, is calculated from Citibase's FYFF, which is not seasonally adjusted.

12 The relationship between liberalism and preferences for low interest rates is not completely clear-cut. Supply-side conservatives, such as Representative Jack Kemp, joined liberals in opposing high interest rates (Greider 1987, pp. 607–8). Note that most of the opposition to Fed-induced high interest rates in both 1974–5 and 1981–2 came from the Democratic side of the aisle (Woolley 1984, Chapter 7; Greider 1987, pp. 513–14).

Note also that if that Democratic position-taking was merely posturing, then the Weingast-Grier position is still tenable. One would need to make a case as to why the Democrats claimed to be opposed to high interest rates when they were not, and such a case has not been made. If such a case were made, it would invalidate all of Grier's quantitative evidence and leave us in a position from where it would be impossible to evaluate the Weingast view. Finally, none of the evidence presented here rejects the Kane view about a congressional preference for low interest rates, with a subsequent impact on the Fed, because in Kane's view that preference among MCs is essentially universal. Again, this makes the Kane thesis essentially untestable.

13 Havrilesky (1988) also presented quantitative evidence showing congressional impotence in the making of monetary policy. He coded "signals" from both the White House and Congress on their desired directions for monetary policy. Whereas the White House signals were good predictors of Fed policy, the congressional signals were of no value in predicting policy. The Havrilesky study is for a very limited period (not surprising, given the difficulty of doing the coding); it also is concerned primarily with executive–Fed relationships. But it is interesting that its empirical finding about Congress–Fed relationships is completely consistent with the view presented here.

14 The reference is to the Sherlock Holmes story "Silver Blaze," in which Holmes was able to infer that the horse had been stolen by an insider because the dog had not barked.

15 My observations indicate that Congress also gives the FDIC and the comptroller of the currency broad discretion in bank regulation. This is consistent with my view of the Fed. I am not aware of good studies of congressional control of the FDIC or the comptroller, and so all we have is fairly casual observation.

16 There will be times when constituency interests are clear. Representative Pepper of Florida, for example, used his position on the House Rules Committee to block the St. Germain nonbank banking bill from coming to the floor because, according to the *Congressional Quarterly,* of how it treated a provision of the Florida interstate banking compact.

17 It would require a monograph to describe French monetary policy. Until the reforms of the mid-1960s, the Bank of France did not use traditional central-bank means to control the money supply. Selective credit controls played a major role in French monetary policy from the end of World War II until the reforms of the mid-1960s (Dieterlen and Durand 1973). While the Bank of France moved toward control of the money supply in the 1970s, policy from 1973 until 1981 was implemented via credit expansion ceilings, with some loans either counting less toward those ceilings or not counting at all (Aftalion 1983). That system became obsolete with the nationalization of the banking system under Mitterand. Monetary policy in the 1980s was driven largely by France's commitment to the European Monetary System, which forced the franc to stay within a narrow band around a central parity.

18 The recent deregulatory movement has changed this somewhat. But the bailout of the Federal Savings and Loan Insurance Corporation in 1989 must mean that the thrifts are being subsidized (albeit somewhat covertly). For a good discussion of credit allocation via deposit insurance, see Kane (1985). There are, in addition, tax incentives for the thrifts to continue making mortgage loans at what must be less than market rates.

19 In March of 1980 the Fed suggested that member banks not increase their total loan portfolios, regardless of the soundness of their doing so. That led to the largest single-period decline in M1 since the Great Depression. The reference to 1929 is, of course, to the Fed's attempt to separate credit being used for "sound" purposes from credit being used for stock-market speculation. On the futility of doing that, see Chandler (1958). More generally, Tom Mayer has suggested to me that Regulation A, limiting the eligibility of what paper can be discounted, is also a form of credit allocation. He has also told me of an instance in which Arthur Burns covertly told banks that only some types of lending would find favor at the discount window.

After the Penn Central failure, the Fed announced that the discount window would be open to banks making business loans. I am unsure whether that was credit allocation or an attempt to make it easy for bank loans to replace commercial paper. Kane (1974, pp. 845–6) argues that the Fed has subsidized smaller banks by allowing them special access to the discount window through seasonal borrowing privileges. But according to Kane, that was done to keep those banks in the Federal Reserve System, not to move credit to smaller towns. The Fed also used credit controls during World War II and the Korean War.

It is certainly possible that the Fed could have used moral suasion, or access to the discount window, to encourage or discourage certain types of loans. But that does not appear to have been a major undertaking of the Fed (as contrasted with, say, French policy).

20 The Fed family is the group of people who once were associated with the Fed. Many former Fed personnel now hold key positions in the financial community.

21 Cyclicity of monetary policy may also aid the Fed here. As tight money leads to pressure for reform, the inevitable downturn in the business cycle allows the Fed to ease, relieving that pressure.

22 In his recent book, Greider (1987) completely disagrees with this conclusion. He argues that we should use credit allocation and that it should be controlled by Congress. His argument is based on the undemocratic nature of the Fed and the idea that current policy-making benefits the few at the expense of the many. Though one might respect Greider's journalistic skills, I am less sure about his command of economics. The subtitle of his book also makes me nervous about his political analysis.

References

Aftalion, F. (1983). "The Political Economy of French Monetary Policy," in D. Hodgman (ed.), *The Political Economy of Monetary Policy: National and International Aspects,* pp. 52–69. Federal Reserve Bank of Boston.

Calvert, R., Moran, M., and Weingast, B. (1987). "Congressional Influence over Policymaking: The Case of the FTC," in M. McCubbins and T. Sullivan (eds.), *Congress: Structure and Policy,* pp. 493–522. Cambridge University Press.

Chandler, L. (1958). *Benjamin Strong Central Banker.* Washington: Brookings Institution.

Dieterlen, P., and Durand, H. (1973). "Monetary Policy in France," in K. Holbik (ed.), *Monetary Policy in Twelve Industrial Countries,* pp. 135–202. Federal Reserve Bank of Boston.

Fenno, R. (1973). *Congressmen in Committees.* Boston: Little, Brown.

Fiorina, M. (1982). "Legislative Choice of Regulatory Process: Legal Process or Administrative Process," *Public Choice,* 39:33–66.

Friedman, M. (1982). "Monetary Policy: Theory and Practice," *Journal of Money, Credit and Banking,* 14:98–118.

Greider, W. (1987). *Secrets of the Temple: How the Federal Reserve Runs the Country.* New York: Simon & Schuster.

Grier, K. (1984). "The Political Economy of Monetary Policy," unpublished Ph.D. dissertation, Washington University.

(1985). "Congressional Preference and Federal Reserve Policy," unpublished working paper, Center for the Study of American Business, Washington University.

Havrilesky, T. (1988). "Monetary Policy Signaling from the Administration to the Federal Reserve," *Journal of Money, Credit and Banking,* 20:83–101.

Kane, E. (1974). "All for the Best: The Federal Reserve Board's *60th Annual Report,*" *American Economic Review,* 64:835–50.

(1980). "Politics and Fed Policy-making: The More Things Change, the More They Remain the Same," *Journal of Monetary Economics,* 6:199–212.

(1985). *The Gathering Crisis in Federal Deposit Insurance.* Cambridge, Mass.: MIT Press.

McCubbins, M., and Schwartz, T. (1984). "Congressional Oversight Overlooked: Police Patrols versus Fire Alarms," *American Journal of Political Science,* 28:165–79.

Mayhew, D. (1974). *Congress: The Electoral Connection.* New Haven: Yale University Press.

Pierce, J. (1978). "The Myth of Congressional Supervision of Monetary Policy," *Journal of Monetary Economics,* 4:363–70.

Roberts, S. (1978). "Congressional Oversight of Monetary Policy," *Journal of Monetary Economics,* 4:543–56.

Scher, S. (1963). "Conditions for Legislative Control," *Journal of Politics,* 25:526–51.

Stein, H. (1984). *Presidential Economics.* New York: Simon & Schuster.

Weingast, B. (1984). "The Congressional–Bureaucratic System: A Principal–Agent Perspective," *Public Choice,* 44:147–91.

Weingast, B., and Moran, M. (1983). "Bureaucratic Direction or Congressional Control: Regulatory Policymaking by the Federal Trade Commission," *Journal of Political Economy,* 91:765–800.

Weingast, B., Shepsle, K., and Johnsen, C. (1981) "The Political Economy of Benefits and Costs: A Neoclassic Approach to Distributive Politics," *Journal of Political Economy,* 89:642–64.

Weintraub, R. (1978). "Congressional Supervision of Monetary Policy," *Journal of Monetary Economics,* 4:341–62.

Woolley, J. (1984). *Monetary Politics: The Federal Reserve and the Politics of Monetary Policy.* Cambridge University Press.

CHAPTER 10

The Federal Reserve as a political power

JAMES L. PIERCE

There is growing awareness that political considerations play an important part in determining the Federal Reserve's monetary policy and regulatory actions. As a result, economists and political scientists are becoming increasingly interested in the Fed's political role. This chapter is concerned with how the Federal Reserve uses its regulatory functions, its role as lender of last resort, and other means to amass political power. It is argued that when these sources of political strength interact with the tremendous influence derived from being the agency of monetary policy, the Federal Reserve emerges as a formidable source of political power within the U.S. government. The Federal Reserve's position concerning expanded powers for banks is an example of how it works to increase its political power.

The Federal Reserve's political role

Studies of the Federal Reserve's political role are slowly accumulating, but the work is still at a rudimentary stage. Several chapters in this volume contribute to that literature, and they provide references to earlier studies. Some studies have attempted to show that the Federal Reserve's independence of Congress or the president is more apparent than real. For example, Kane, in this volume and elsewhere (Kane 1980, 1982), argues that Congress makes the Fed appear more independent than it really is by using the central bank as a scapegoat or whipping boy: Congress engages in "Fed-bashing" when it is politically desirable to do so. Other studies have documented instances in which the Federal Reserve's monetary policies were influenced by presidents or powerful members of Congress. Still others have pointed to principal–agent considerations to explain why the Fed at times can act independently of Congress.

Though useful, those studies appear to have mistaken the trees for the forest. All elements of government engage in the political role-playing attributed to the Federal Reserve. Congress often serves as a whipping boy for the president, and there have been presidents who have done the same for Congress. Furthermore, powerful presidents influence Congress, and powerful members of Congress influence presidents. All of this is part of the political process.

What is remarkable is the extent to which the Federal Reserve is able to play in this tough and complex game. The Fed has amassed sufficient political power to hold its own with the executive and legislative branches. Legally, the Fed is the creation of Congress and is therefore its agent. Practically, however, it has sources of political power that allow it to go far beyond the "shirking" that might be expected of an agent.

Perhaps the best single indication of the Federal Reserve's political power is its ability to continue to avoid budgetary control by Congress. If Congress had budgetary control over the Federal Reserve, Congress could influence the central bank and still avoid being held accountable for unpopular monetary policies. The reasons for originally exempting the Fed from the budgetary process are buried in the confusions and politicking over establishing a central bank. But the exemption continues to this day because the Federal Reserve has sufficient political power to beat back attempts in Congress to eliminate it.

Exempting the Federal Reserve from budgetary control involves, in part, the whipping-boy or scapegoat process described by Kane. The Federal Reserve does carry out much of the dirty work, and it is subjected to congressional and presidential criticism (Fed-bashing) when it pursues policies with which elected politicians do not want to be identified. It is mighty handy for these politicians to have someone to blame when things do not go right. It is also true that the Federal Reserve receives much in return for being bashed. It is free to conduct monetary policy as it sees fit within very wide limits, and it enjoys great prestige. The Fed is, of course, part of government, and so it bends and alters its policies if criticism becomes too broad-based and serious. But the limits can be wide, as the events of 1979–82 indicate.

There is a sort of unholy alliance between the Federal Reserve and the elected politicians, but why have the politicians given up so much? Surely at some point some chair of some appropriate congressional committee would find it in his or her political interest to "save" the nation from the Fed's monetary policies. Some president, sometime, would launch a serious attack on a Federal Reserve whose policies were threatening his chances of reelection. Members of Congress would surely at some time discover that their whipping boy had developed into a potential monster whose policies could deprive them of reelection. It would be prudent for politicians to have the power to affect Fed policies should that prove expedient. There probably could be no more effective means than through control over its budget. A Federal Reserve threatened with large budget cutbacks would be a more docile Federal Reserve.

There appears to be no escaping the proposition that the Fed possesses sufficient political power to prevent Congress and the executive branch from putting it on a shorter leash. Many of its sources of power are subtle and indirect, but when added together they are formidable.

The chairman

Every year or so some national magazine carries an article arguing that the current chairman of the Federal Reserve is the second most powerful person in Washington. Whether or not that is truly the case, there is nonetheless widespread recognition that the chairman of the Fed is an immensely powerful person. Because of his influence on monetary policy, his contacts with national and international leaders – including foreign heads of state – and his virtually universal treatment in the news media as the one true foe of inflation and champion of financial stability, the chairman of the Fed is in a position to injure enemies and reward friends. In the final analysis that is largely what politics is all about. A favorable word from a Fed chairman concerning some member of Congress is potentially equivalent to sizable campaign contributions and many votes. Criticisms, on the other hand, can be costly. In addition, a member of Congress or a president who wants a piece of banking legislation passed knows that success or failure often will depend on whether or not the chairman supports it. Furthermore, the chairman's position on any type of economic legislation, either domestic or foreign, often is crucial in determining the fate of a specific bill.

The Federal Reserve as regulator

It might appear that the Fed really is not all that powerful as a regulator. After all, it has primary responsibility only for regulating state-chartered member banks. National banks are regulated by the Office of the Comptroller of the Currency, and state-chartered nonmembers by the Federal Deposit Insurance Corporation (FDIC) and state regulators. But the Fed's power comes much less from the banks it regulates than from the fact that it alone is responsible for regulating bank holding companies.

Because all large banks and many smaller ones are affiliated with a bank holding company, the Federal Reserve's influence stretches far beyond state member banks. Acquisitions of banks within holding companies, and operation of new activities by nonbank affiliates, must be approved by the Federal Reserve. Furthermore, the Federal Reserve regulates and supervises the activities of the bank holding company itself and its nonbank affiliates, including their transactions with banks in the holding company, irrespective of what agency happens to regulate the banks within the holding company. In effect, the Fed's regulatory powers extend to any institution that is a bank holding company or happens to be affiliated with one.

The Federal Reserve is also authorized by Congress to determine within wide guidelines what activities are allowable for a bank holding company. For example, can a bank holding company have finance companies as affiliates, or can a bank holding company underwrite commercial paper? This authority gives the Federal Reserve great power to affect the competitive positions of bank holding companies *vis-à-vis* other financial entities, such as securities firms, giving it influence over both bank holding companies and these other entities. Provision of brokerage services by bank holding companies is an example.

Finally, the Federal Reserve has tremendous influence over proposed legislation concerning the powers of bank holding companies. In effect, it has virtual veto power over bills it does not like, and it has a strong voice in formulating legislation it does like, including active and often dominant participation in drafting legislation. As an example of this power, the Federal Reserve successfully opposed entry of bank holding companies into those areas of the securities business from which they are currently prohibited by law, despite support for entry from the Reagan administration and the Senate Banking Committee.[1] As will be discussed later, with its new chairman, Alan Greenspan, now reversing the Fed's position to favor such activity, it is only a matter of time before bank holding companies will have that power. The president and the chair of a banking committee had better have the Fed on their side if they want to succeed in liberalizing banking powers.

It is in the self-interest of operators of banks and bank holding companies to stay on the good side of the Fed. Those who neglect that principle and incur the ire of the Federal Reserve can encounter uncommon difficulty in having holding-company applications approved, much to the detriment of their profits. If bank holding companies are to obtain expanded powers, they had better curry the favor of the Federal Reserve.

Federal Reserve Bank directors

The Federal Reserve also amasses political power through the boards of directors of the 12 Federal Reserve banks and their 25 branch offices. Included as directors are not only bankers but also prominent business persons and other leaders in the community. Members of the boards of directors tend to identify with and support the Federal Reserve. This gives the Fed important contacts that extend beyond banking. The boards of directors are natural vehicles for the Fed to influence elected politicians. The Federal Reserve is fully aware of the political importance of the Federal Reserve Banks' boards of directors. This importance explains why the Fed has vehemently and successfully opposed attempts to eliminate them.

Using the sources of power

Armed with its control over banks and bank holding companies, and its legions of Federal Reserve Bank boards of directors, the Federal Reserve can, and does, bring forth tremendous lobbying efforts by its constituents in opposition to attempts by Congress to put the Fed on a shorter leash. Members of Congress who threaten the Federal Reserve too much run the risk of being damaged politically. Those who support the Fed look forward to a more friendly atmosphere. Thus, the Federal Reserve's relationship with Congress is not merely a matter of acting as a whipping boy. It is also grounded in old-fashioned power politics. The Federal Reserve possesses great political power and wields it with considerable skill. Often as not the Fed can give as good as it gets in a political fight. Both the Congress and presidents are well aware of this.

The lender-of-last-resort function as a source of power

Over the past 20 years or so, the Federal Reserve has fundamentally changed the role of the discount window in ways that have added to both its power and prestige. This has made the Fed an even more potent political power. In changing the role of the discount window, the Federal Reserve has (unwittingly) reduced the stability of the financial system.

When the Federal Reserve was reformed in the 1930s, it joined the newly established FDIC in extending a federal "safety net" to protect the monetary system. Through open-market operations and provision of funds through the discount window, the Federal Reserve assured that currency withdrawals during bank runs would not drain reserves from the system and that solvent banks confronting liquidity strains could receive funds directly from the central bank.

Though open-market purchases of securities can prevent the declines in aggregate reserves, money, and credit that otherwise would occur during bank runs and currency drains, the discount window serves as an additional safeguard. Should a solvent bank experiencing large losses of deposits encounter adjustment problems (i.e., be unable to borrow enough in the interbank market or be unable to sell enough assets without substantially reducing their prices), it can turn to the Federal Reserve for a loan. As long as the discount rate is a penalty rate (i.e., above prevailing market interest rates), the bank will use the discount window only when other forms of adjustment are unavailable. Under these circumstances, the discount window is a useful and potentially important part of the federal safety net because it protects the system from market failures that hamper the adjustment of individual banks. The panic that could be produced by such adjustment problems is avoided by allowing solvent banks access to the discount window.

After the FDIC was established, the Fed has not been called on to offset the effects on bank reserves of massive withdrawals of currency. Rather, on the relatively few occasions when the public has become concerned about the safety of its funds, this has involved the imminent failure of a particular bank or thrift, not a panic over the safety of depositories in general. When such concerns arise, the public transfers funds from a troubled institution to safer ones. Currency holdings do not rise, and there is no need to provide additional reserves. Private markets take care of the problem.

One might think that the discount window has become an unimportant tool of the Federal Reserve because it rarely, if ever, has to be used to meet bank liquidity crises. That is not the case, however. The discount window has evolved into an instrument for subsidizing certain banks and for aiding troubled banks and other institutions. This change in the use of the discount window has increased the political power of the Federal Reserve, making it an even more potent force in the economy. It has also eliminated important market discipline and in the process has reduced financial stability.

The discount rate usually is not a penalty rate, but rather is below the federal-funds rate. With the discount rate acting as a subsidy, banks find it profitable to borrow. In order to keep this borrowing under control, the Fed rations credit through the discount window, attempting to limit access to "emergencies" and other accepted uses. In practice, rules have been established policing and limiting both the size and frequency of borrowing by individual institutions. Through these rules, the Fed has the ability to punish banks by cutting off their access to discount-window subsidies. This power could be applied not only to banks that borrow too much but also to those that fail to give the Federal Reserve their political support.

In the 1960s the Federal Reserve became concerned about the fact that small banks did not want to be member banks. As an inducement to these banks, the Fed began to make funds available through the discount window to meet their seasonal and other needs. That was a boon to small agricultural banks that did not have to obtain funds from more costly and less reliable private sources. Thus, access to the discount window was extended beyond what had come to be its normal use as essentially an emergency source of funds. That move helped retain small banks within the Federal Reserve System and helped maintain the Fed's political base.

A major change in the use of the discount window came in 1970 following failure of the Penn Central Railroad. There the Fed spread the safety net under the commercial-paper market. With the failure of Penn Central, there was fear that many substantial and highly solvent firms would not be able to roll over their commercial paper. The Fed let it be known that banks should provide the credit and that they could turn to the discount window for funding. Reasonable people differ over whether or not Fed intervention was necessary. Schwartz (1986), for example, called that a "pseudo-financial crisis," arguing that intervention was not necessary because there was not a flight to currency, only a temporary reshuffling of credit. Furthermore, most of the panic concerned loans to large but weak borrowers. In contrast, Maisel (1973) argued that the Federal Reserve's actions averted financial panic: The Fed clearly decided that it would not be worth it to find out whether or not intervention was necessary; it intervened. In the process, the Federal Reserve got in the business of using the discount window to stabilize financial markets generally.

Following the "panic," creditors in the commercial-paper market insisted that borrowers have formal credit lines at banks that could be drawn on should another panic develop. That private action was beneficial because it helped stabilize the market. Unfortunately, the process did not stop there. Banks began issuing irrevocable standby letters of credit to businesses borrowing in the commercial-paper market. Those letters of credit obligated the issuing bank to pay off the commercial paper should the borrower default. In effect, banks assumed the credit risk of borrowers in the commercial-paper market. With widespread use of those letters of credit, the federal safety net was extended indirectly to the commercial-paper market.

Jumping ahead for a moment in our chronology, following the stock-market collapse of October 19, 1987, the Fed again moved to protect a market and individual firms within it. The Federal Reserve not only engaged in open-market operations to provide liquidity generally but also encouraged banks to lend to securities firms using the discount window as a source of funds.

In 1974, in the case of the Franklin National Bank, the Fed began the practice of making the discount window available to large, failing banks. When it became clear to holders of large-denomination certificates of deposit (CDs) and other major creditors of Franklin National that the bank either was or soon would be insolvent, those creditors demanded payment at maturity for their instruments, rather than rolling them over. There was a "silent run" by uninsured depositors and creditors. Note that the run was not a flight to currency from a solvent bank, but rather a withdrawal of uninsured funds from a failing institution for redeposit elsewhere. Fearing that the silent run would spread to other banks, and wanting the FDIC to have enough time to arrange a merger, the Fed opened up the discount window to Franklin National. In order to avoid closure of Franklin National, the Fed replaced disappearing CDs and other sources of funds with money provided through the discount window. All private creditors of the bank were therefore protected, not just insured depositors. The Federal Reserve became Franklin National's largest creditor.

The Federal Reserve intervened again in a major way during the failure of Continental Illinois in 1985, making the discount window available to replace lost funds. Loans through the discount window helped the bank stay afloat until a massive bailout by the FDIC could be arranged. As in the case of Franklin National, Federal Reserve officials expressed the fear that a general run on banks would occur, again failing to note that such "runs" would not constitute a flight to currency, but only a redirection of funds to other banks. Any solvent bank could replace lost funds through the interbank market or, failing that, through the discount window. In an effort to avert these "runs," the federal bank regulators announced not only that creditors of Continental Illinois would be protected from any losses but also that no large bank would be allowed to fail. Whatever discipline large uninsured depositors had imposed on the risk-taking of large banks was undermined by that announcement. In effect, federal protection was extended to all depositors and creditors of large banks. The process continues to this day. At this writing, the discount window has been opened up again, this time to offset the silent runs occurring at the banks of RepublicBank Corporation of Dallas, which are being kept afloat by massive FDIC assistance. Again, all depositors and creditors of the banks in the holding company have been assured that their funds are safe.

One of the reasons that the Federal Reserve makes loans available to failing banks is to accommodate the FDIC, which is frantically trying to keep them open. Another reason is that Federal Reserve officials apparently believe that if a large bank were allowed to fail, a loss of confidence in solvent large banks in general would ensue, triggering runs on their uninsured liabilities. That is a strange fear, because unless the uninsured depositors opt to hold currency – a highly unlikely event, to put it mildly – the funds will be redeposited in banks. The system as a whole cannot lose reserves as long as depositors do not demand currency. There would be a reallocation of reserves among individual banks, and that might cause temporary adjustment problems meriting use of the discount window. But the banks doing the borrowing would be solvent banks that would temporarily lose funds to other banks during the pseudocrisis.

Surely the Federal Reserve understands this. If it forgets, it is reminded when it has to engage in offsetting sales of securities to remove the reserves provided to failing banks through the discount window. Why, then, does the Fed continue to make massive loans to failing banks? One interpretation is that it adds to its power and prestige by doing so. It gains influence with, and support from, the FDIC, because without loans from the discount window, the FDIC's misguided efforts to keep failing institutions in operation would fail. Furthermore, the Federal Reserve comes across in the news media as the champion of financial stability.

The Federal Reserve received favorable reviews in the press and elsewhere for its bailouts of the commercial-paper market and stock market. Furthermore, its actions in lending to Franklin National, Continental Illinois, and the banks of RepublicBank Corp. were seen as necessary evils to avert general panics. Whether or not the public's perceptions are correct is not the point here. The fact of the matter is that the Federal Reserve is viewed as the champion of financial stability, preventing crises from developing. That perception gives the Fed a tremendous amount of political leverage. Fed officials are able to threaten that any attempts to lessen its independence or its regulating authority would weaken its ability to avert panics. That is powerful stuff that few members of Congress or presidents want to take on.

The Federal Reserve's role in financial deregulation

The Federal Reserve has played a powerful and often dominant role in the politics of bank deregulation. Its strategy in this process has been skillfully crafted to maintain its power, at a minimum, and more likely to increase further its power and influence. It is instructive to review its activities not only to illustrate how the Fed uses its power but also to argue that its quest for power and influence, if successful, could seriously weaken the stability of the financial system.

Until Alan Greenspan replaced Paul Volcker as chairman, the Federal

Reserve opposed any substantial increase in banking powers and any significant integration of banking with other financial activities. In effect, the Fed endorsed the Glass-Steagall Act, which keeps banks out of many facets of the securities business, as well as provisions of the Bank Holding Company Act, which keeps banks out of most forms of insurance and other financial activities not closely related to banking and thus separates banking from commerce. The Fed used arguments concerning financial stability, conflicts of interest, risk, and concentration of economic power in stating its preference for the status quo. It came forward with remarkably little evidence to support its position, apparently preferring to appeal to conventional wisdom. As mentioned earlier, the Fed's opposition was sufficient to block any expansion of powers, despite the efforts of the Reagan administration and several influential members of Congress.

Furthermore, as pressure built to eliminate Glass-Steagall and liberalize the Bank Holding Company Act, the Fed steadfastly resisted notions that the fortune ("safety") of banks could be separated from that of nonbanking affiliates within a holding company. It stuck to the position that all elements of the holding company have to be regulated in order to protect banks and that a holding company should "serve as a source of strength" for its banking affiliates. Thus, nonbanking affiliates and the holding company itself should support banking affiliates should the need arise.

Why would the Fed cling to the assertion that banks cannot be separated from other elements of their holding companies when there is strong evidence to the contrary in the doctrine of corporate separateness (Chase 1987)? After all, insurance companies often are parts of conglomerates, but corporate separateness protects them from the misfortunes of their affiliates. Furthermore, if the Federal Reserve fears that existing law does not insulate banks from their affiliates, why does it not propose legislation to correct the situation? The answer seems to lie with fears by the Fed that if insulation of banks from other elements of the holding company were successful, it would lose power. If securities and other activities were conducted by holding-company affiliates whose affairs were separate from those of the banks, there would be no justification for Federal Reserve regulation of the nonbank affiliates or the holding company. Over time, an increasing amount of activities would be conducted by nonbank affiliates and less by banks; the Fed would have diminished influence.

The chairmanship of Alan Greenspan has seen some modification of the Federal Reserve's position; the Fed has discovered a way to allow expanded powers for banking organizations while adding to its political power. In recent testimony, Greenspan has endorsed elimination of Glass-Steagall, but a holding company with securities affiliates would still be regulated by the Fed, and it would still have to be a source of strength for banking affiliates. He opposes allowing banking institutions into insurance (which enjoys corporate separateness) and endorses keeping banking separate from commerce.

Greenspan's position exhibits two elements that are keys to understanding what the Federal Reserve's future role is likely to be. First, the Fed will spread its regulatory net to include activities of securities firms that are affiliated with banks. Over time this will allow the Federal Reserve's influence to extend to the securities industry. With securities firms dependent on Federal Reserve largess, their support will add to the Fed's political power. Second, the Fed is likely to spread the federal safety net under securities activities.

By viewing a bank holding company as a source of strength for its banks, the Fed has an interest in the profitability and viability of securities affiliates of holding companies. The Fed will seek to regulate securities affiliates on the grounds that this is necessary to assure their soundness, which in turn is important in protecting the holding company and its banks.[2] Furthermore, if a securities affiliate encounters financial difficulties, the Fed will have an incentive to bail it out so as not to weaken the holding company. It can use the banks in the holding company to act as conduits for channeling funds (loans) made available through the discount window to troubled securities affiliates. Section 23a of the Federal Reserve Act places limits on loans by banks to their holding-company affiliates. This constraint can be avoided by pressuring banks that are not affiliated with a securities firm to make loans to it, using funds made available through the discount window. Finally, the Fed can lend directly to the affiliate using its emergency powers.

It is not even farfetched to suppose that the Fed will become concerned about the fortunes of securities firms that are not affiliated with banks. Its logic probably would run as follows: If a nonaffiliated securities firm fails, the public will question the viability of securities firms in general. This could cause panic, threatening bank-affiliated securities firms and the banks themselves. These threats can be avoided by coming to the assistance of the securities firms that are not affiliated with banks. This is precisely the kind of logic that leads it to bail out failing banks in order to "protect" other banks.

There is little doubt that elimination of Glass-Steagall will be just the first step in the process of deregulating financial markets. Over time, banking organizations will become involved in a growing list of activities, and many kinds of firms will acquire banks. If matters go on as they have, the Federal Reserve will regulate an ever-growing number of activities and firms. This not only will extend its political power but also will involve extension of the federal safety net to more and more activities and firms. There are a few economists and other observers who believe that such would be good public policy.

Where to go from here?

The path that deregulation has begun to follow is dangerous because of the increasingly perverse role that the Federal Reserve is likely to play. On the one hand, the Fed will amass even greater political power as its regulatory activities reach further and further beyond conventional banking. On the other hand, its extension of the safety net will make the financial system increasingly vulnerable to shocks. With the Fed ultimately standing ready to bail them out, an increasing number of players in financial markets will have an incentive to take on risk. As has become painfully clear in the case of deposit insurance, this adds to instability and forces periodic panic-control measures by the Fed. Because the private incentives to assess, control, and charge for risk will be undermined, more and more of the burden will fall on the Fed. Not only will such a course be inefficient; it will be dangerous. The Fed's prestige and political power will increase as it rises to meet financial "crises." With an increasing part of the financial system dependent on Federal Reserve bailouts, the stability of the financial system will depend on swift and wise actions by a few persons. Slow and/or unwise actions could bring the system crashing down. That is simply too much power to bestow on a handful of mortals, no matter how well-intentioned.

There is a dire need for economists and policy-makers to rethink and evaluate the role of the federal safety net and the part that the Federal Reserve plays in it. What should be protected, and how? What is the appropriate role of the discount window? It currently plays a crucial role in providing protection to several elements of the financial system. Are those protections appropriate?

Most serious students of the subject agree that it is desirable to allow banking to be integrated with other financial activities. This should not come at the price of increasing the political power of the Fed, and it should not come at the price of trying to protect everything just to protect the monetary functions of banks. But as long as the Federal Reserve retains its political power, and as long as it retains the policy of trying to ensure stability by protecting institutions from failure, there is little hope that the issues will be resolved in a satisfactory fashion.

Despite this rather distressing prospect, there are possibilities for legal reforms that are feasible, as financial integration continues, and they could limit increases in the Fed's power and in the coverage of the safety net. Congress must see to it that banks are insulated from the misfortunes of their nonbanking affiliates. Failure of a nonbanking affiliate should not spill over to the bank. This can be accomplished by imposing the doctrine of corporate separateness – creditors of the nonbanking affiliates should have no claim on the bank. An additional important reform would be to require that the separate nonbanking affiliates of banks have formal and extensive credit lines with banks outside their holding companies. These lines would not be of the standby letter-of-credit variety, but rather conventional borrowing authorizations subject to "material change in condition" restrictions. The idea here is to have machinery in place whereby securities firms and other affiliates that are solvent but illiquid can borrow from banks. The Federal Reserve would be authorized to provide funding through the discount window for the loans on an emergency basis. Exercise of these emergency powers would be rare, because banks themselves would be required to establish credit lines with other banks. That would make it easier for an individual bank to raise funds to honor its lending obligations. It would also make it less easy for the Federal Reserve to become involved. Only during a general liquidity crisis would the Fed have to provide reserves through the discount window.

The extensive use of credit lines would also have the advantage of "privatizing" a great deal of regulation. A nonbank affiliate of a holding company would have passed the market test of risk evaluation in determining the size and terms of its credit lines. Risky institutions would have smaller and costlier lines than less risky ones. The same goes for banks.

These issues are important because in the absence of outside pressure, the Federal Reserve's position will hold sway. The nation likely will drift into a situation in which its central bank will be expanding its regulatory and safety-net coverage, vainly trying to protect everything in the interest of protecting "banks." The tremendous power it will come to wield not only will be harmful to the structure of the financial system but also will make the Fed an even more formidable foe to those inside and outside the government who believe that it is too powerful already.

Notes

1 Currently, banks and bank holding companies can engage in many securities activities, including full investment banking overseas, underwriting of the general-obligation bonds of states and municipalities, dealing in government

securities, securities brokerage, and "underwriting" of commercial paper. Under the Glass-Steagall provisions of the Banking Act of 1933, they are generally excluded from such activities as the domestic underwriting of corporate securities and of municipal revenue bonds, and from offering mutual funds. For a more complete discussion see Pierce (1985).

2 Some proposed legislation would appear to adopt "functional" regulation, assigning responsibility for securities subsidiaries to the Securities and Exchange Commission (SEC). This is largely without content, however, because the Fed would continue to be responsible for the parent holding company, which would be used as a "source of strength" for banking affiliates.

References

Chase, Samuel B. (1987). "Insulating Banks from Risks Run by Nonbank Affiliates," Chase, Laub and Company, Washington, D.C.

Kane, Edward J. (1980). "Politics and Fed Policymaking: The More Things Change the More They Remain the Same," *Journal of Monetary Economics,* 6(April):199–211.

(1982). "External Pressure and the Operations of the Fed," in R. Lombra and W. Witte (eds.), *Political Economy of International and Domestic Monetary Relations,* pp. 211–32. Ames: Iowa State University Press.

Maisel, Sherman J. (1973). *Managing the Dollar.* New York: Norton.

Pierce, James L. (1985). "On the Expansion of Banking Powers," in I. Walter (ed.), *Deregulating Wall Street,* pp. 13–34. New York: Wiley.

Schwartz, Anna J. (1986). "Real and Pseudo-Financial Crises," in F. Capie and G. Wood (eds.), *Financial Crises and the World Banking System,* pp. 11–31. New York: St. Martin's Press.

CHAPTER 11

Monetary policy and political economy: the Federal Reserve and the Bank of Japan

THOMAS F. CARGILL AND
MICHAEL M. HUTCHISON

The monetary experience of Japan over the past decade provides an example of a nation that has effectively stabilized its domestic inflation rate in the face of major internal and external shocks, while simultaneously avoiding recession. Japan did experience a short period of double-digit inflation around the time of the 1973 oil price shock that was higher and initially more disruptive than in the United States. However, Japan's response to that experience was the introduction in 1973 and 1974 of an explicit price stabilization strategy that quickly reduced the nation's "core inflation" to the lowest among the major industrial countries.

Four important aspects of the relative performances of the U.S. and Japanese economies since 1975 are shown in Figure 11.1. The panels on the left show that monetary growth and inflation in Japan have been more stable than in the United States. The panels on the right show that Japan has experienced a smaller degree of disruption in the real and financial sectors, as reflected by the unemployment rate and the gap between unregulated and regulated interest rates.[1]

This chapter focuses on the differing monetary policy experiences of the United States and Japan as an explanation for the differences between the two nations' macroeconomic performances.[2] We attempt to isolate reasons for the differences in monetary policy experiences. In particular, we argue that the differences cannot be found in the technical characteristics by which the Federal Reserve (FR) and the Bank of Japan (BOJ) formulate and execute monetary policy; rather, the differences are more fundamentally rooted in the institutional and political environments in which the two central banks operate. Our analysis fol-

Cargill's research was supported in part by funds provided by the Hoover Institution at Stanford University and by the U.S.-Japan Friendship Commission. Hutchison's research was partly supported by a Pacific Basin Research Funds grant by the President's Office of the University of California.

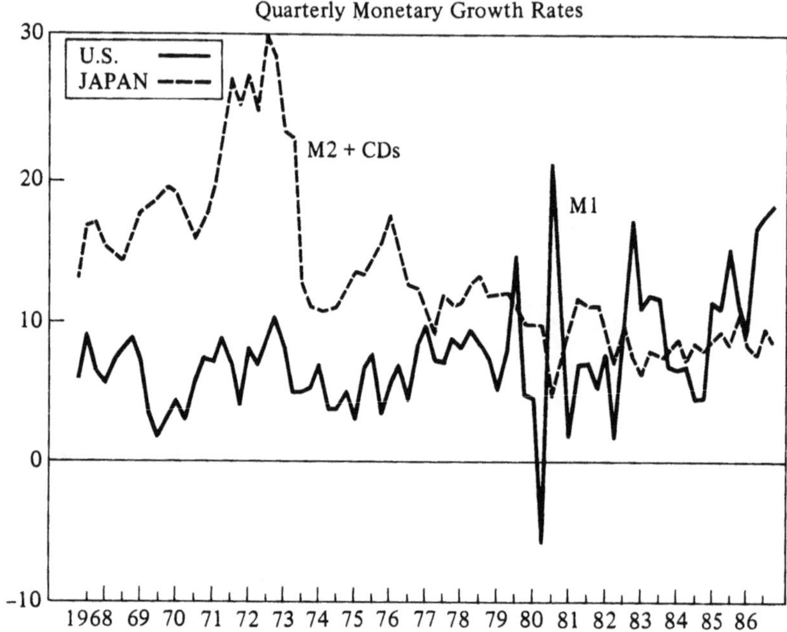

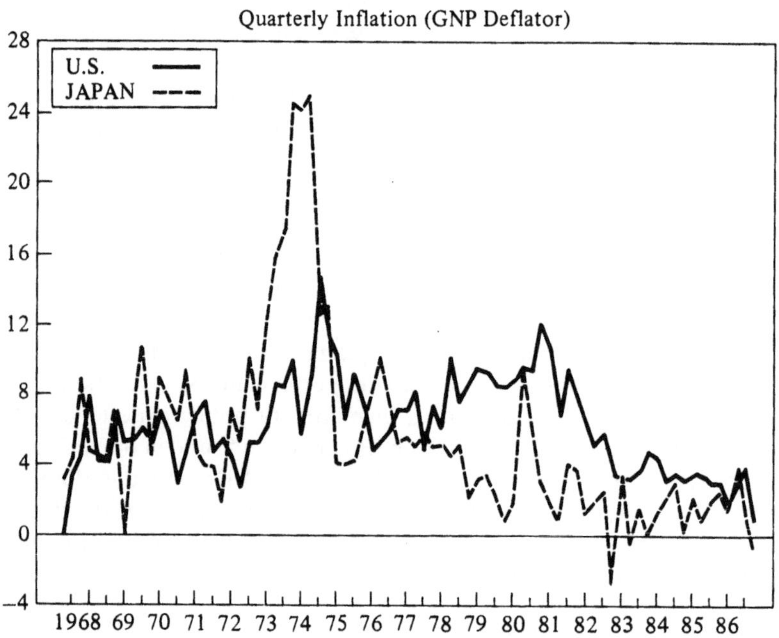

Figure 11.1. Relative performances of the U.S. and Japanese economies since 1975

Quarterly Unemployment Rates
U.S.
JAPAN
11
9
7
5
3
1
1968 69 70 71 72 73 74 75 76 77 78 79 80 81 82 83 84 85 86

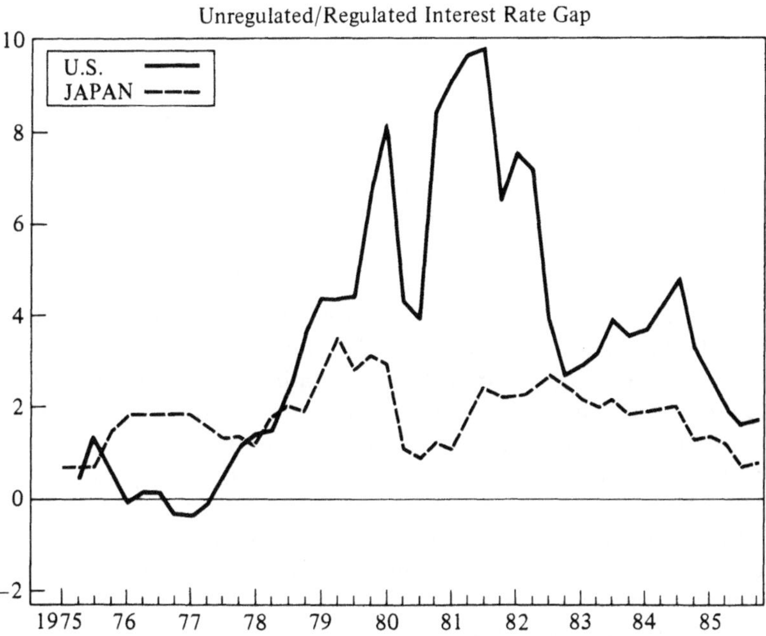
Unregulated/Regulated Interest Rate Gap
U.S.
JAPAN
10
8
6
4
2
0
−2
1975 76 77 78 79 80 81 82 83 84 85

lows a two-level approach to understanding the sources of inflation. The first level is largely technical and focuses on the link, over long periods of time, between money growth and core inflation and on central-bank control over the long-run trend in money growth. The second level analyzes macroeconomic policies, and the nation's commitment to noninflationary policies in particular, as the outcome following an equilibrating political process involving government, the monetary authority, and the public. Our analysis of inflation and monetary policy in Japan and the United States attempts to integrate various aspects of political economy in the two nations with technical monetary economics.[3]

Technical explanations for the differences in performances

Inferences about the technical differences are available from research that has directly compared BOJ and FR policies during the past decade. This research strongly suggests that one cannot easily attribute differences in central-bank performances to differences in operating procedures, differences in the degree of regulatory and market financial innovations, or differences in the stability of the demand and supply functions for money.

Operating procedures

BOJ procedures have gradually been altered since 1975 in response to financial reform (Fukui 1986); however, the basic operating strategy of BOJ policy remains essentially unchanged (Cargill 1986). Dotsey's comparison of BOJ and FR short-run operating procedures that focus on interest rates strongly suggests that the BOJ interest-rate-focused procedures are essentially the same as those employed by the FR in the mid-1970s (Dotsey 1986). Hutchison (1986, 1988) provides empirical evidence to substantiate the claim that the BOJ's short-run operating procedures are interest-rate-focused. In fact, the operating strategy of the BOJ differs little from that employed by the FR in the mid-1970s, and although the FR has shifted operating strategy at least two times in the past decade (October 1979 and late 1982), the FR has returned to an operating strategy that focuses in the short run on interest-rate behavior (Rasche 1985).

Thus, if anything, the BOJ has clearly shown that an interest-rate-focused policy is capable of sustaining noninflationary monetary growth as long as the central bank is willing to vary the interest rate in the required amount.[4] The BOJ showed its willingness to permit high rates of interest to support its commitment to price stability during the second oil price shock in 1979–80.

Financial innovation

A second technical difference between the FR and BOJ performances in monetary control cited by Suzuki (1985) was the more rapid pace of financial reform in the United States as compared with Japan. Consistent with Suzuki's view, the FR frequently has voiced concern that market and regulatory innovations in the financial system since the mid-1970s have rendered monetary policy more difficult. Although there is some merit to that argument (Judd and Scadding 1982), the rapid pace of regulatory and financial market innovations in the United States has been at least partly attributable to past inflationary experience and its association with monetary policy (Cargill and Royama 1988). Moreover, the BOJ has been required to adapt to a changing financial environment that in several respects has involved greater relative changes than those experienced by the FR. In particular, the process of interest-rate deregulation and the increasing openness of the Japanese financial system after the 1980 official decision to remove constraints on capital flows have greatly increased the ease with which domestic and foreign assets can be substituted (Frankel 1984; Otani and Tiwari 1981; Pigott 1983). That has represented a more significant departure for Japan from its traditional financial structure (tightly controlled interest rates and regulated capital flows) than has the process of financial reform and innovation in the United States over the past decade.

Stability in the demand for and supply of money

The difficulties resulting from market and regulatory financial innovations are likely to manifest themselves by influencing the stability of the demand and supply functions for money. Without attempting to get into the largely econometric and technical literature on this issue, both the United States and Japan have clearly experienced shifts in the demand function for money over the past decade (Judd and Scadding 1982; Rasche 1987; Suzuki 1985). However, the FR and the BOJ appear to have fairly similar records in their accuracy of forecasting money growth (Hutchison and Judd 1987).

On balance, however, the technical literature suggests that instability of the money demand probably has been a less significant problem in Japan than in the United States, and the BOJ has a somewhat better record in forecasting the money supply. At the same time, despite the major market and regulatory innovations of the past decade in the United States, the evidence remains unclear whether or not the demand and supply functions for money have been rendered so unstable as to seriously impede long-run stable money growth.[5] Although that may offer a partial technical reason for the differing monetary-control experiences of the FR and the BOJ, two considerations suggest that the relative stability of the demand and supply functions for money cannot offer a satisfactory explanation for the different monetary-control performances of the FR and the BOJ. First, the differences in the stabilities of the money demand and supply functions have not been overwhelming. Second, and most important, the FR must accept at least part of the responsibility for any instability in the demand for and supply of money, because it was associated with the rise of inflation in the 1970s.

The political economy of inflation and monetary control

Technical considerations of FR and BOJ monetary control do not provide a complete explanation for the difference between inflation and output fluctuations in the United States and Japan. However, once one relaxes the implicit assumption that the monetary authority acts alone as an independent authority with the primary macroeconomic objective of price-level stabilization, another question is raised. In particular, the success or failure of the monetary authority in achieving price stability may be determined less by technical differences than by the institutional and political environment in which monetary policy functions. Moreover, technical changes in operating procedures, such as the October 1979 FR announcement or the establishment of projections for the money supply by the BOJ in 1978, need not result in major differences in the general course of monetary policy unless they reflect fundamental changes in central-bank objectives. From this perspective, what differences in the political and economic environments of the two nations could account for a higher weight, on average, being assigned to price stability in the BOJ's objective function over an extended period, as compared with the FR?

The political-economy characteristics of the United States and Japan represent a complex set of factors that may influence the inflation bias of each country's monetary authority. Several major differences in the institutional and political environments of the United States and Japan can be readily identified, however. Following Gordon (1975), these characteristics can be analyzed within a framework that regards inflationary monetary policy as an equilibrium outcome of this interaction between "the demand for inflation" and the "supply of inflation."

The demand for inflation emerges from a variety of sources ranging from public resistance to tax increases to efforts by various groups to increase their shares of the national income or wealth at the expense of other groups. Moreover, the central bank or other governmental authority may view a level of output above the market-clearing "natural" equilibrium rate as the social optimum. That, in turn, could induce an inflationary bias to the economy.

The supply of inflation, or, more appropriately, the nature of the government response to a given demand for inflation, depends on such factors as the election cycle, the structure of labor markets, insulation of the central bank from political pressure, and the distribution of gainers and losers from inflation.

The interaction between the demand for and supply of inflation, directly and indirectly, influences the conduct of monetary policy and hence the behavior of the money supply. The monetary authority does not formulate policy in a political or institutional vacuum. Given that the money supply (more specifically, high-powered money) is the only major macroeconomic variable controllable by the monetary authority in the long run, the path of monetary growth necessarily reflects a balance between the forces of the demand for and supply of inflation.

With this in mind, what differences exist between the United States and Japan that permit the monetary authority in one country to consistently pursue long-run noninflationary monetary growth, while the monetary authority in the other country is more prone to generate a long-run inflationary path of monetary growth?

Demand for inflation

There are several factors that suggest that the demand for inflation in the United States has been more important in determining the course of monetary policy than in Japan. First, the degree of unionization often has been identified as one potential determinant of the extent to which wages exert a "cost push" influence on the general course of monetary policy (Hayek 1959; Gordon 1975, 1977). Wage increases beyond productivity growth in the absence of an accommodative monetary policy will raise real wage costs to the firm and put upward pressure on the unemployment rate. That could result in the monetary authority monetizing the nominal wage increase and thereby generating a higher inflation rate than previously.[6] Several institutional characteristics of the labor market in Japan suggest one reason that may permit the BOJ to more easily pursue a noninflationary policy. Although the degree of unionization in Japan is not appreciably smaller than that in the United States (Weiner 1987), labor unions in Japan generally have not demanded nominal wage increases beyond productivity growth. That could be associated with the sense of cooperation shared by Japanese workers and firms, reflecting in part a different union orientation. Japanese unions are organized along enterprise lines, not occupational lines, and blue-collar and white-collar employees belong to the same union. That has strengthened firm identity, which in turn has been one factor leading to more moderate wage increases in Japan than in the United States (Hamada and Kurosaka 1986; Tachibanaki 1986; Weiner 1987). The pressure on the BOJ to monetize nominal wage hikes has thus been less than that on the FR in the case of the United States.

Second, other institutional features in the Japanese labor market make nominal wages more flexible than in the United States (Gordon 1982; Grubb, Jackman, and Layard 1983). Greater nominal wage flexibility, in turn, could be an important factor behind the lesser demand for inflation in Japan, as the central bank would not have as strong an incentive to induce real wage flexibility via price-level changes. Gordon (1982), for example, finds that Japanese wages are 5 to 10 times more responsive to economic conditions than are U.S. wages (measured either as the standard deviation of wages relative to hours worked or as the ratio of the respective response coefficients of wages and hours worked to changes in GNP). The fact that union contracts in Japan normally have a duration of one year and are effectively synchronized across industries in the "spring wage offensive" (*Shunto*), as opposed to the typical three-year duration and unsynchronized nature of U.S. labor contracts, is one institutional factor for the Japanese relative wage flexibility.

Moreover, wage flexibility in Japan is also facilitated by the nation's unique bonus system. Large firms in Japan typically pay their regular employees a biannual bonus representing about 20 percent of income, on average. The bonus payments usually are tied to firm profitability (Okuno 1984), and econometric evidence supports the view that bonuses are more responsive to profits than are base wages (Freeman and Weitzman 1987; Wadhwani 1987). Profit sharing in the United States is much less widespread and in quantitative terms accounts for a much smaller proportion of total earnings (Summers and Wadhwani 1987).

The role of the housing sector, combined with the extent of explicit and implicit government subsidies to support housing, produces a third major political and economic difference between Japan and the United States that could account for differences in the demand for inflation. Although U.S. inflation from 1965 through the early 1980s imposed costs on the economy as a whole, the housing sector was a major beneficiary of the inflationary process, for several reasons (Minarik 1979, 1980): (1) housing was the only inflation hedge available to many people, (2) the deductibility of mortgage interest increased in real value as the inflation rate increased, and (3) financial regulation (favorable tax treatment of thrift institutions, portfolio restrictions on thrifts, and Regulation Q), government efforts to subsidize the establishment of secondary markets in mortgage instruments, and the institutionalization of the long-term fixed-rate mortgage assured a steady flow of credit to support the housing sector at favorable terms. These factors combined to confer considerable transfers of wealth to home ownership during the 1970s (Wolff 1979). Given the size of the housing sector in the U.S. economy and the political power housing plays throughout all levels of government, the housing sector may be argued to be a major demand force for inflationary monetary policy.

In Japan, housing traditionally has not had the political support and as a consequence has not received the same level of government subsidy as in the United States (Cargill 1987; Mills and Ohta 1976). The relatively shorter maturity of mortgage loans, the inability to treat mortgage interest as an income deduction, the lower leveraged position of home ownership, and the lower turnover rate of home ownership (Japanese households, unlike those in the United States, typically do not attempt to "move up" in value after an initial purchase and thereby increase the demand for housing) all suggest that the housing sector is not an important component of the demand for inflation.[7]

Fourth, Japan's greater dependence on exports and international trade in general than in the United States could also exert an important restraint on the public's demand for inflation. In particular, to the extent that nominal exchange rates do not fully adjust to domestic wage and price inflation, a nation's internationally competitive position deteriorates. Export markets would be lost as a consequence, and in a nation as export-dependent as Japan, the potential benefits of inflationary policies would be hard set against the costs imposed on the export-dependent sectors of the economy.

These arguments suggest that institutions and structural features in the two economies have likely generated a lower demand for inflation in Japan than in the United States. Limited empirical work on the importance of price stability and unemployment as determinants of the government's popularity seems to support this judgment. Schneider and Frey (1988) have surveyed a wide range of evidence and concluded that for the United States, inflation, unemployment, and real income growth significantly influence election outcomes and the popularity of the administration. In addition, the evidence strongly suggests that unemployment and/or the growth of income dominate the popularity function. There has been only a limited amount of comparable research on these issues for Japan; however, on the basis of a study by Inoguchi (1980), inflation and real income growth appeared equally important in the popularity function, but in stark contrast there was no evidence that the economic situation influenced the election outcome.

Supply of inflation

A number of models based on Nordhaus (1975) suggest that the government can exploit the short-run Phillips curve prior to elections to maintain power while permitting disinflation during the first part of the new term. To the extent that unemployment dominates political concern, the government will have an incentive to pursue an asymmetrical approach to the political business cycle, and as a consequence, a tendency on average toward expansionary policy could impart an inflationary bias to monetary policy. The possibility of political business cycles and the bias toward inflationary policies suggest that monetary policy in the United States is likely to be more inflationary than in Japan. Four considerations support this statement.

First, Japan's political structure, until recently, had not offered the diversity of governments with a reasonable chance of being elected that one sees in the case of the United States. The Liberal Democratic Party (LDP) has dominated Japanese politics throughout most of the postwar period, and the alternative contenders for power have offered radical positions on noneconomic issues that have overshadowed concerns for the condition of the economy (Pempel 1987). In addition, the opposition has been hard pressed to offer economic alternatives that could significantly improve Japan's economic performance. In contrast, the two-party system in the United States provides two alternatives with almost equal probabilities of winning an election in which economic issues are offered as major distinctions.

Second, the U.S. political system is characterized by periodic elections that offer the government in power a fixed point in time on which to formulate macroeconomic policy. Although the absence of fixed election periods, as in the parliamentary system of Japan,[8] does not rule out the political-cycle phenomenon, it may remove the dominant periodic nature of such cycles.

Third, the structure of the economic system in Japan suggests that the short-run Phillips curve is steeper than in the United States (Hamada and Hayashi 1985). Models of the political business cycle imply that the steeper the short-run Phillips curve, the less ability the government has to manipulate the economy and induce a political business cycle (Nordhaus 1975).

Fourth, the evidence for a political business cycle in the United States has not yet produced a consensus; however, studies (Whiteley 1980;

Willett 1988) suggest that it would be difficult to reject the hypothesis that the monetary authority does not engage in some type of systemic policy for reasons other than price stability. On the basis of some brief evidence for Japan provided by Nordhaus (1975) and the more extensive studies by Inoguchi (1980) and Ito and Park (1988), there appears to be little empirical evidence of a political business cycle in Japan. Additional work is needed, however, to determine if a political-business-cycle phenomenon exists in Japan or exists to a lesser degree in Japan than in the United States.

A final point distinguishing the different responses to the demand for inflation by the FR and the BOJ concerns their real or imagined independence from their respective finance ministries and other branches of government. The FR is directly accountable to the U.S. Congress and is formally independent of the U.S. Treasury and the executive branch of government. At times, its policies are clearly at odds with the wishes of the U.S. Treasury and the executive branch of government. However, the Board of Governors is appointed by the president, and a great deal of political pressure may be brought to bear on the FR to support an administration's economic policies. This often leads to a delicate political balance for the FR.[9]

The BOJ, in contrast, is legally subordinate to the Japanese Ministry of Finance (MOF), and no claims of formal independence are suggested. Although in practice the BOJ does have some independence in the policy realm, little political gain could be made by the MOF or the current government in Japan by pressuring the BOJ for expansionary policies while simultaneously insisting it accept responsibility for inflationary tendencies. In Japan, the government agencies, viewed in their entirety, take responsibility for economic policies, and hence political trade-offs between agencies based on manipulation of the economy are not commonplace.

Concluding comments

The main conclusions of our study can be briefly stated as follows: (1) The performances of the U.S. and Japanese economies since 1975 have diverged, especially in terms of the level and stability of the inflation rate. (2) Analyses of FR and BOJ policies suggest little difference in the ability of each to control the money supply; in fact, the short-run operating procedures of the two monetary authorities are both examples of an interest-rate-focused monetary policy. (3) The differences in the institutional and political environments of the United States and Japan offer a more reasonable explanation of the differing monetary policy performances.

Notes

1 Unregulated and regulated interest rates in Japan are measured as the long-term secondary-bond rate and the one-year time-deposit rate, respectively. In the United States, unregulated and regulated interest rates are measured as the three-month Treasury-bill rate and the Regulation Q ceiling on commercial-bank savings deposits, respectively.

2 Cargill and Royama (1988), Cargill and Hutchison (1988), Dotsey (1986), Friedman (1985), Greenwood (1984), and Meltzer (1986) have suggested that BOJ policy deserves major credit for the more stable and sustained economic performance of the Japanese economy and for a smoother and more gradual financial reform process. The results of BOJ policy reflected by almost any measure – monetary control, price stability, economic growth, credibility and predictability, and the pace of financial change – strongly suggest that the BOJ policy has been more successful than has FR policy.

3 The past decade has witnessed rapid growth of research on the political economy of inflation, monetary policy, and business cycles. A sample of the studies adopting the political-economy approach include Nordhaus (1975), Whiteley (1980), and Willett (1988). The volumes edited by Whiteley and Willett contain a number of interesting papers that survey the political-economy approach from many aspects and also incorporate extensive references on the subject. Schneider and Frey (1988), Locksley (1980), Wagner (1980), and Willett and Banaian (1988) have provided particularly useful surveys of the literature.

4 The inflationary monetary growth permitted during the 1970s by the FR was not the result of a short-run "interest-rate-focused" policy but rather the result of not increasing interest-rate targets high enough and fast enough (Mayer 1988). In contrast, the BOJ has shown willingness to increase interest rates rapidly, so that the BOJ's short-run interest-rate-focused policy has produced a noninflationary monetary growth path since 1975.

5 Judd and Treban (1987) provided evidence that M1 targeting is no longer useful; however, M2 and M3 targeting provides a meaningful operating framework. Rasche (1987) provides evidence that M1 targeting continues to provide a reasonable framework for the FR.

6 There is debate surrounding the role that unions have historically played in generating inflation in the United States and other nations. The empirical evidence on the combined direct and indirect effects of unions on price inflation is mixed. Freeman and Medoff (1984) and Hirsch and Addison (1986) provide good summaries of this literature. Hirsch and Addison argue that unions are not primary proximate determinants of inflation, but appear to influence significantly the mechanics of the process.

7 The relative importance of the housing sector in Japanese society is growing, however, and could exert stronger inflationary force on the political process in the future. For example, the subsidy to housing through the two primary government agencies, the Housing Loan Corporation and the Japanese Hous-

ing and Urban Development Corporation, has increased in both absolute and relative terms over the past two decades (Lincoln 1988). As a percentage of funds in the Fiscal Investment and Loan program, housing grew from 11% in 1965 to 25% by 1980, while the share to the Japan Development Bank and the Eximbank (lending exclusively to the corporate sector) declined. Government loans as a percentage of total housing investment also grew from 3.6% in 1966 to 31.4% in 1983 (Lincoln 1988).

8 A description of Japan's political structure is provided by Koichi (1982).

9 Kettl (1986) provides a good discussion of FR independence.

References

Barth, James R., Bisenius, Donald J., Brumbaugh, R. Dan, Jr., and Sauerhaft, Daniel. (1986) "The Thrift Industry's Rough Road Ahead," *Challenge* 28(September–October):38–43.

Cargill, Thomas F. (1986). "Flows of Funds Shifts and Monetary Policy in Japan," *Federal Reserve Bank of San Francisco Economic Review,* 3(Summer):21–32.

(1987). "A Perspective on Trade Imbalances and U.S. Policies Toward Japan," *Columbia Journal of World Business,* 22(Winter):55–60.

Cargill, Thomas F., and Garcia, Gillian G. (1985). *Financial Reform in the 1980s.* Stanford, Calif.: Hoover Institution Press.

Cargill, Thomas F., and Hutchison, Michael M. (1988). "The Bank of Japan's Response to Macroeconomic and Financial Change," in Hang-Sheng Cheng (ed.), *Challenges to Monetary Policy in Pacific Basin Countries,* pp. 227–46. Norwell, Mass: Kluwer Academic Publishers.

Cargill, Thomas F., and Royama, Shoichi. (1988). *The Transition of Finance in Japan and the United States: A Comparative Perspective.* Stanford, Calif.: Hoover Institution Press.

Dotsey, Michael. (1986). "Japanese Monetary Policy: A Comparative Analysis," *Bank of Japan Monetary and Economic Studies,* 4(October):105–28.

Fischer, Stanley. (1987). "Monetary Policy and Performance in the U.S., Japan, and Europe, 1973–86," Paper presented at the Third International Conference sponsored by the Institute for Monetary and Economic Studies, the Bank of Japan, Tokyo, June 3–5.

Frankel, Jeffrey (1984). *The Yen-Dollar Agreement: Liberalizing Japanese Capital Markets.* Washington, D.C.: Institute for International Economics.

Freeman, Richard B., and Medoff, James L. (1984). *What Do Unions Do?* New York: Basic Books.

Freeman, Richard B., and Weitzman, Martin L. (1987). "Bonuses and Employment in Japan," *Journal of the Japanese and International Economies,* 1:168–94.

Friedman, Milton (1956). "The Quantity Theory of Money – A Restatement," in Milton Friedman (ed.), *Studies in the Quantity Theory of Money,* pp. 3–21. University of Chicago Press.

(1985). "Monetarism in Rhetoric and in Practice," in Albert Ando, Hidekazu Eguchi, Roger Farmer, and Yoshio Suzuki (eds.), *Monetary Policy in Our Times,* pp. 15–28. Cambridge, Mass.: MIT Press.

Fukui, Toshihiko (1986). "Recent Developments of the Short-Term Money Market in Japan and Changes in Monetary Control Technics and Procedures by the Bank of Japan," Bank of Japan, Research and Statistics Department, Special Paper No. 130, January.

Gordon, Robert J. (1975). "The Demand for and Supply of Inflation," *Journal of Law and Economics,* 18(December):807–36.

(1977). "World Inflation and Monetary Accommodation in Eight Countries," *Brookings Papers on Economic Activity,* 2:409–68.

(1982). "Why U.S. Wage and Employment Behavior Differs from That in Britain and Japan," *Economic Journal,* 92(March):13–44.

(1983). "A Century of Evidence on Wage and Price Stickiness in the United States, the United Kingdom, and Japan," in J. Tobin (ed.), *Macroeconomics, Prices and Quantities,* pp. 85–133. Washington, D.C.: Brookings Institution.

Greenwood, John (1984). "The Japanese Experiment in Monetarism, 1974–1984," *Manhattan Report on Economic Policy,* 4.

Grossman, H., and Haraf, W. (1983). "Shunto, Rational Expectations, and Output Growth in Japan," National Bureau of Economic Research working paper no. 1144.

Grubb, D., Jackman, R., and Layard, R. (1983). "Wage Rigidity and Unemployment in OECD Countries," *European Economic Review,* 21:11–39.

Hamada, Koichi, and Hayashi, Fumio (1985). "Monetary Policy in Postwar Japan," in Albert Ando, Hidekazu Eguchi, Robert Farmer, and Yoshio Suzuki (eds.), *Monetary Policy in Our Times,* pp. 83–121. Cambridge, Mass.: MIT Press.

Hamada, Koichi, and Kurosaka, Yoshio (1986). "Trends in Unemployment, Wages, and Productivity: The Case of Japan," *Economica,* 5:275–96.

Hayek, F. A. (1959). "Unions, Inflations, and Profits," in Phillip D. Bradley (ed.), *The Public Stake in Union Power,* pp. 46–62. Charlottesville: University of Virginia Press.

Haynes, Stephen, Hutchison, Michael M., and Mikesell, Raymond F. (1986). *Japanese Financial Policies and the U.S. Trade Deficit,* Essays in International Finance no. 162, International Finance Section, Princeton University.

Hirsch, Barry T., and Addison, John T. (1986). *The Economic Analysis of Unions: New Approaches and Evidence.* Boston: Allen & Unwin.

Hutchison, Michael M. (1986). "Japan's 'Money Focused' Monetary Policy," *Federal Reserve Bank of San Francisco Economic Review,* 3(Summer): 33–47.

(1988). "Monetary Control, Interest Rates and Exchange Rates: The Case of Japan, 1973–1986," *Journal of International Money and Finance,* 7:261–71.

Hutchison, Michael M., and Judd, John P. (1987). "Monetary 'Targeting' in Japan and the U.S.: Which Is More Accurate?" Federal Reserve Bank of San Francisco working paper 87-10.

Inoguchi, Takashi (1980). "Economic Conditions and Mass Support in Japan, 1960–1976," in Paul Whiteley (ed.), *Models of Political Economy,* pp. 121–54. London: Sage.

Ito, Takatoshi, and Jin Hyuk Park (1988). "Political Business Cycles in the Parliamentary System," *Economic Letters,* 27:233–8.

Judd, John P., and Scadding, John (1982). "The Search for a Stable Money Demand Function," *Journal of Economic Literature,* 20 (September):993–1023.

Judd, John P., and Trehan, Bharat (1987). "Portfolio Substitution and the Reliability of M1, M2, and M3 as Monetary Policy Indicators," *Federal Reserve Bank of San Francisco Economic Review* (Summer):5–30.

Kasman, Bruce (1987). "Japan's Growth Performance Over the Last Decade," *Federal Reserve Bank of New York Quarterly Review* (Summer):45–55.

Kettl, Donald (1986). *Leadership at the Fed.* New Haven: Yale University Press.

Koichi, Kishimoto (1982). *Politics in Modern Japan.* Tokyo: Japan Echo Inc.

Lincoln, Edward J. (1988). *Japan: Facing Economic Maturity.* Washington, D.C.: Brookings Institution.

Locksley, Gareth. (1980). "The Political Business Cycle: Alternative Interpretations," in Paul Whiteley (ed.), *Models of Political Economy,* pp. 177–200. London: Sage.

Mayer, Thomas (1988). "Federal Reserve Policy Since October 1979: A Justified Response to Financial Innovations?" in Stephen Frowen (ed.), *Monetary Policy and Financial Innovations in Five Leading Industrial Countries.* London: Macmillan.

Meltzer, Allan H. (1986). "Lessons from the Experience of Japan and the United States under Fixed and Floating Exchange Rates," *Bank of Japan Monetary and Economic Studies,* 4(October):129–45.

Mills, Edwin S., and Ohta, Katsutoshio (1976). "Urbanization and Urban Problems," in Hugh Patrick and Henry Rosovsky (eds.), *Asia's New Giant,* pp. 673–752. Washington, D.C.: Brookings Institution.

Minarik, Joseph J. (1979). "The Size Distribution of Income During Inflation," *Review of Income and Wealth,* 25(December):377–92.

(1980). "The Distributional Effects of Inflation and Their Implications," in *Stagflation: Causes, Effects and Solutions.* Joint Economic Committee, U.S. Congress.

Nordhaus, W. (1975). "The Political Business Cycle," *Review of Economic Studies,* 42:169–90.

Okuno, M. (1984). "Corporate Loyalty and Bonus Payments," in M. Aoki (ed.), *The Economic Analysis of the Japanese Firm.* Amsterdam: North Holland.

Otani, Inchiro, and Tiwari, Siddharth (1981). "Capital Controls and Interest Rate Parity: The Japanese Experience, 1978–81," *International Monetary Fund Staff Papers,* 28:793–815.

Pempel, T. J. (1987). "The Unbundling of 'Japan, Inc.': The Changing Dynamics of Japanese Policy Formation," *Journal of Japanese Studies,* 13:271–306.

Pigott, Charles (1983). "Financial Reform in Japan," *Federal Reserve Bank of San Francisco Economic Review,* 1(Winter):25–46.

Rasche, Robert H. (1985). "Interest Rate Volatility and Alternative Money Control Procedures," *Federal Reserve Bank of San Francisco Economic Review,* 2(Summer):46–63.

(1987). "M1-Velocity and Money Demand Functions: Do Stable Relationships Exist?" Department of Economics, Michigan State University.

Schneider, Friedrich, and Frey, Bruno S. (1988). "Politico-Economic Models of Macroeconomic Policy," in Thomas D. Willett, (ed.), *The Political Business Cycle,* pp. 239–75. Durham, N.C.: Duke University Press.

Sorrentino, C. "Japan's Low Unemployment: An In-Depth Analysis," *Monthly Labor Review,* 107(March):18–27.

Summers, Lawrence H., and Wadhwani, Sushil B. (1987). "Some International Evidence on Labour Cost Flexibility and Output Variability," Centre for Labour Economics working paper no. 981.

Suzuki, Yoshio (1985). "Japan's Monetary Policy Over the Past 10 Years," *Bank of Japan Monetary and Economic Studies,* 3(September):1–10.

(1986). *Money, Finance, and Macroeconomic Performance in Japan.* New Haven: Yale University Press.

Tachibanaki, Toshiaki (1986). "Labour Market Flexibility in Japan in Comparison with Europe and the U.S.," Kyoto Institute of Economic Research, Kyoto University.

Taira, Koji (1983). "Japan's Low Unemployment: Economic Miracle or Statistical Artifact?" *Monthly Economic Review,* 106(July):3–10.

Wadhwani, S. (1987). "The Macroeconomic Implications of Profit Sharing: Some Empirical Evidence," *Economic Journal,* 97(Supplement):171–83.

Wagner, Richard E. (1980). "Public Choice, Monetary Control and Economic Disruption," in Paul Whiteley (ed.), *Models of Political Economy,* pp. 201–20. London: Sage.

Weiner, Stuart E. (1987). "Why Is Japan's Unemployment Rate So Low and So Stable?" *Federal Reserve Bank of Kansas City Economic Review,* 72(April): 3–18.

Whiteley, Paul (ed.) (1980). *Models of Political Economy.* London: Sage.

Willett, Thomas D. (ed.) (1988). *The Political Business Cycle.* Durham, N.C.: Duke University Press.

Willett, Thomas D., and Banaian, King (1988). "Models of the Political Process and Their Implications for Stagflation: A Public Choice Perspective," in Thomas D. Willett (ed.), *The Political Business Cycle,* pp. 100–28. Durham, N.C.: Duke University Press.

Wolff, Edward N. (1979). "The Distributional Effects of the 1969–1975 Inflation on Holdings of Household Wealth in the United States," *Review of Income and Wealth,* 25(June):195–207.

CHAPTER 12

A positive analysis of the policy-making process at the Federal Reserve

RAYMOND E. LOMBRA AND
NICHOLAS KARAMOUZIS

A major purpose of this volume is to identify and focus on the most significant problems that demand answers if researchers are to make more progress in understanding, modeling, and assessing the procedures and performance of the Federal Reserve. Of course, many volumes and papers on nearly all facets of the policy process already exist. Normative analyses of policy, in particular, are seldom in short supply; yet progress has been disturbingly slow and limited. As Brunner argues, "a wide gulf separates the reality of stabilization policy from the official claims [of policy-makers] and academic rhetoric" (1985, p. 224).

In this chapter we aim to bridge the gulf between the rigors of monetary theory and the realities of monetary policy with a largely positive analysis designed to complement the other chapters in this volume. In general, we focus on the process governing the formulation and implementation of monetary policy in the United States. More specifically, we examine the economic analysis producd by the Federal Reserve staff, its role in the policy-making process, and the strategy and tactics employed by the Federal Open Market Committee (FOMC). We proceed by, in effect, asking a series of questions reminiscent of those once asked by Howard Baker:[1] What did the FOMC know or believe that it knew when it was making decisions? What were the properties and overall quality of the information it had? What did it do in light of the available informa-

This is part of a larger study of Federal Reserve policymaking. For a more comprehensive examination of many of the issues discussed here, the interested reader is urged to consult Karamouzis and Lombra (1989). We would like to express our deep appreciation to Normand Bernard, special assistant to the Federal Reserve Board, for his assistance in securing the Federal Open Market Committee documents used in this research and to Brian Madigan of the Federal Reserve Board staff, Roy Weeb of the Federal Reserve Bank of Richmond staff, and Stephen McNees of the Federal Reserve Bank of Boston staff for kindly providing us with some of the key data sets analyzed. We would also like to thank Adrienne Kearney and Jeff Butler for their invaluable research assistance and Thomas Mayer for his usual penetrating comments on an earlier draft.

Table 12.1. *Nonfinancial forecast errors: Fed staff, 1973–82*

Variable and period	Mean error	Mean absolute error	Root-mean-square error
Nominal GNP			
Next quarter	0.33	3.62	4.78
Year ahead	0.16	2.16	2.60
Real GNP			
Next quarter	−0.54	3.54	4.39
Year ahead	−0.68	2.00	2.53
Deflator			
Next quarter	0.86	1.68	2.26
Year ahead	0.91	1.55	1.95

Notes: Forecast errors are defined in percentage points as actual minus predicted values. Forecasts are taken from the Greenbooks prepared for the first FOMC meeting within a quarter. Actual values are taken from the most recent *Business Conditions Digest: Historical Series.* "Year ahead" is the forecast over the entire interval from the current quarter through four quarters ahead. All data are expressed as seasonally adjusted rates. There are 40 observations for each variable and forecast horizon.

tion? Why did it do what it did? What can we infer about received theory, empirical work, and policy-making from the answers to these questions?

How good are the staff's nonfinancial forecasts?

The Fed's staff is charged with developing an overall, integrated assessment of past, present, and future economic and financial developments, laying out consistent and feasible policy alternatives for consideration by policy-makers, and making specific policy recommendations to the FOMC. In discharging its responsibility, the staff prepares forecasts of GNP and its various components for each FOMC meeting, using both "judgmental" and "econometric" techniques.[2]

As Brunner (1985) and Meltzer (1987) have recently emphasized, forecast accuracy and knowledge about structural relationships define the *limits* of stabilization policy, especially in a world characterized by lags between policy actions and effects. Accordingly, we begin by examining the accuracy of the staff's forecasts for economic growth (real GNP) and inflation (GNP implicit price deflator) over the 1973–82 period.[3]

Table 12.1 presents the standard set of diagnostic statistics summarizing the characteristics of the Fed staff's nonfinancial forecast errors. The

Table 12.2. *Year-ahead forecast errors: Fed staff vs. McNees sample, 1973–82*

Variable and error	Fed	McNees
Real GNP		
Mean error	−0.68	−0.51
Mean absolute error	2.00	1.83
Root-mean-square error	2.53	2.39
Deflator		
Mean error	0.91	0.31
Mean absolute error	1.55	1.44
Root-mean-square error	1.95	1.80

Notes: The Fed data are from the year-ahead rows in Table 12.1. The McNees data are the median of the one-year-ahead forecasts made by 11 well-known forecasting organizations (such as Chase, DRI, and Wharton) and as reported by McNees (1985). The forecasts were made in 1973:2–1982:4 and cover the yearly periods ending in 1974:2–1983:4. All data are in percentage points at seasonally adjusted annual rates. See also the notes in Table 12.1.

mean absolute errors for the next quarter certainly are not small, but are attenuated somewhat over a longer projection horizon by partially offsetting quarterly errors when the entire year-ahead interval is evaluated. The sizes and signs of the mean errors for real GNP and the deflator suggest that, on average, the staff, like other forecasters, has difficulty pinning down the slope and position of the short-run Phillips curve, tending to overestimate real growth and underestimate inflation. Table 12.2 provides further evidence of that tendency and compares the Fed staff's forecasting performance to the performances of other well-known forecasters. Simply put, the data in Table 12.2 suggest that the Fed staff has little information advantage over other forecasters and that, taken as a whole, the Fed's forecasts are "state of the art."[4]

The forecasts we examined covered a period that saw two oil price shocks, two serious recessions, widespread financial innovation and deregulation, several changes in monetary policy operating procedures, increased globalization of the real and financial sectors of the U.S. economy and historically large fluctuations in money growth, interest rates, and exchange rates. Accordingly, aggregating over the entire period may obscure important information on within-period characteristics of the forecasts. Table 12.3, therefore, examines the cyclical characteristics of the staff's forecasts. In general, the staff's forecasts tended to be less accurate and more biased during recessions than during expansions.

Table 12.3. *Cyclical characteristics of fourth-quarter-ahead forecast errors: Fed staff, 1973–82*

Variable and error	Contractions	Expansions
Real GNP		
Mean error	−4.72	1.0
Mean absolute error	4.87	3.2
Deflator		
Mean error	1.67	1.0
Mean absolute error	3.34	1.6

Notes: Contractions (including troughs) were 1974:2–1975:1, 1980:2–1980:3, and 1981:4–1982:4. Expansions (including peaks) were 1975:2–1980:1, 1980:4–1981:3, and 1983:1–1983:4. All data are in percentage points at seasonally adjusted annual rates. See also the notes to Table 12.1.

Because that finding mirrored the results reported by Zarnowitz (1986, p. 8) in his examination of private forecasts, we computed the correlation coefficients between the Fed staff's year-ahead forecast errors and the median year-ahead forecast errors examined by McNees (1985) for real GNP and the GNP deflator (see the notes to Table 12.2). The results – 0.86 for real GNP and 0.89 for the deflator – suggest that forecasters are similarly proficient in exploiting the systematic information contained in past data and are similarly afflicted with large cyclical errors.

Such difficulties, along with the tendency for the staff to overestimate inflation in the 1980s, in contrast to the tendency to underestimate inflation in the 1970s, suggest that the information content of the forecasts is rather limited.[5] The data presented in Table 12.4 support this indication. In general, the forecasting errors are at least as large as the spread encompassing the staff's forecasts of the economic implications of alternative monetary policy strategies. These comparisons, and the implied confidence intervals, strongly suggest that forecast uncertainty limits the information value of the staff's forecasts and their alleged usefulness in the design of an activist monetary policy.

How good are the staff's financial forecasts?

The staff's financial forecasts of monetary and reserve aggregates (e.g., M1, M2, and nonborrowed-reserve growth) and money-market conditions (e.g., the federal funds rate and discount-window borrowing) are

Table 12.4. *Information content of Fed staff forecasts, 1973–82*

Real GNP	
Year-ahead mean absolute error	2.0
Typical "spread"	1–2
Deflator	
Year-ahead mean absolute error	1.5
Typical "spread"	½–1

Notes: Numbers are percentage points at seasonally adjusted annual rates. "Spread" refers to the typical differences between the staff's forecasts of, say, real GNP a year ahead under the "easiest" policy alternative presented to the FOMC (say 6% M1 growth) and the "tightest" policy alternative presented to the FOMC (say 4% M1 growth). The typical range of policy alternatives was 2 percentage points of monetary growth. Year ahead figures are from Table 12.1.

the connecting link between the FOMC's inflation and real-growth objectives and day-to-day policy actions, particularly open-market operations. More specifically, once the FOMC has agreed to a longer-run (yearly) plan for monetary policy, as indexed by the growth rates of the monetary aggregates and the path for the economy that the FOMC believes is implied by the policy plan, the plan must be translated into shorter-run (daily, weekly, monthly, and quarterly) guides for the actual conduct of policy.

Given the staff's income forecast and the FOMC's longer-run monetary aggregate targets, the staff's task, discharged in the "bluebook" prepared for each FOMC meeting, is to develop an internally consistent set of shorter-run alternatives that will guide the conduct of policy over the next one to three months and that will be consistent with achieving the longer-run monetary aggregate targets and, presumably, the FOMC's economic objectives. A hypothetical set of alternatives that the staff typically prepared for the FOMC, with the aid of both econometric and judgmental projection techniques, is shown in Table 12.5.[6] Each alternative is accompanied by analysis of the financial repercussions likely to emerge if it is adopted and is tied explicitly to the FOMC's longer-run policy objectives.[7]

Following mainstream theory, higher (lower) rates of monetary growth require lower (higher) short-term interest rates, as indexed by the federalfunds rate, in order to induce the requisite changes in money demand, and higher (lower) rates of reserve growth in order to produce the implied changes in money supply. With short-term rates falling (ris-

Table 12.5. *Hypothetical Bluebook menu of short-run policy alternatives*

Variable	A	B	C
(1) M1 growth	6%	5%	4%
(2) M2 growth	8%	$7\frac{1}{2}$%	7%
(3) Federal funds rate	6%	7%	8%
(4) Nonborrowed-reserve growth	7%	6%	5%
(5) Discount-window borrowing	$100 million	$500 million	$900 million

Table 12.6. *Monetary aggregate forecast errors, 1973–82*

Variable	Mean error	Mean absolute error	Root-mean-square error
M1 (monthly)	0.54	5.17	7.02
M2 (monthly)	0.42	3.05	3.99
M1 (quarterly)	0.24	2.44	3.58

Notes: Data are actual minus predicted values at seasonally adjusted annual rates. "Final" revised data for the definitions of M1 and M2 in place at the time were used to compute the actual numbers.

ing) relative to the Fed's discount rate, the volume of discount-window borrowing, which depends on the spread between the funds rate and the discount rate, will fall (rise).

Against this background, the data available in the bluebook can be used to measure the accuracy of the staff's short-run forecasts of the monetary aggregates. The results are shown in Table 12.6. The monthly projection errors are sizable, presumably reflecting to a large degree the considerable "noise" – that is, transitory variation – in short-run data.[8] Clearly, there is very little information in the monthly projections or in the monthly data.

Not surprisingly, the FOMC and the staff were painfully aware of the difficulties associated with projecting, monitoring, interpreting, and reacting to the monthly data. Accordingly, by the late 1970s, policy discussions increasingly focused on a quarterly rather than a monthly horizon. The last row of Table 12.6 shows the quarterly forecast errors for M1. Reflecting the smaller degree of transitory variation in quarterly data, and the partially offsetting monthly projection errors, the various error statistics fall by about 50 percent. Nonetheless, the $2\frac{1}{2}$ percentage point mean absolute error is large relative to the 2–3 percentage point range of policy options typically considered by the FOMC. Here again, it would seem that forecast uncertainty is large relative to information content.

Forecasts, analysis, and actions: What drives FOMC decisions?

Various shortcomings in the economic analysis underlying policy-making have undoubtedly contributed somewhat to an erratic policy record. The fact that policy-makers operate in an environment characterized by considerable uncertainty over structural relationships and the path of the economy is undeniable. The key issues, of course, are two: What is the "best" policy to follow in the face of such uncertainty, and what in fact do policy-makers do?

Experts on policy analysis have long argued that the economist's ideal, scientific approach to policy-making – specify objectives, develop alternatives, assess the costs and benefits of options, choose "optimal" policy – is unreasonable, unnecessary, and unattainable, for within the context of complex policy problems, all analysis will be "incomplete."[9] Thus, "disjointed incrementalism" – a kind of enlightened "muddling through" – is perhaps the most that can be hoped for, and the call for complete policy processes firmly grounded in economic analysis must be viewed as naive.

If "good" policy-making consists only in being able to make decisions, the virtues of ambiguity and incompleteness follow. However, if the standard against which policy actions are to be judged is defined in terms of the economic outcomes that such actions help to produce or propagate, then ambiguity, a shifting compromise among multiple goals, and the associated confusion of means and ends would seem to impede rather than facilitate the making of "good" policy.

Of course, it would be naive to imply that even "second-best" policies are always feasible and identifiable. As Woolley argues, the environment within which the Fed acts is

> marked by a tension between its nominal political independence and the kind of tasks it is called upon to perform in the economic system. It is asked to be politically neutral while regulating an economic system that is not neutral in results. It is expected to act on the basis of reflective scientific judgment in an environment that stresses political responsiveness. It is asked to make technically correct decisions despite conditions of economic uncertainty that make it difficult to avoid errors and despite a highly conflictual scientific debate as to what correct policy is. (1984, p. 12)

Against this background, it is not surprising that the Fed frequently has vacillated on the analytical significance of the money stock – that is, whether money should be controlled or simply used as an "information variable" – and, given the limited information contained in the staff's forecasts, has tended to utilize a "flexible" approach to the formulation of policy.[10] Reflecting such flexibility, there have been several changes in the Fed's operating procedures over the past 20 years (Gilbert 1985; Sellon and Teigen 1981a, b; Wallich 1984; Melton and Roley, this volume) and thus a changing emphasis accorded the variables shown in the various rows of Table 12.5. More specifically, over the 1970–late-1979 period the settings for the funds rate and M1 growth dominated policy discussions, whereas over the late-1979–mid-1982 period, nonborrowed-reserve growth, along with M1 and M2 growth, was at center stage. Since mid-1982, borrowings, the funds rate, and M2 growth appear to have been the focus of policy discussions and actions. Despite these changes, and the eminently defensible technical and structural considerations that may have motivated them, there have been several noteworthy and closely related "constants" that have characterized the formulation and implementation of policy over the past 20 years.

Interest-rate smoothing adjustments to the bluebook alternatives and paths

Over the 1971–late-1979 period, the short-run targets adopted by the FOMC often did not coincide with any one of the particular M1-growth–funds-rate alternatives in the bluebook. Rather, the FOMC "adjusted" the menu presented by the staff; the predominant adjustments were to lower the staff's projected federal-funds rate for a given money stock [e.g., taking alternative B in Table 12.5 for M1 growth (5%), but alternative A for the funds rate (6%)] or to lower both the funds rate and M1 growth. Such adjustments, assuming the staff's forecasts were internally consistent (which our research suggests was in fact the case), along with a demonstrated reluctance to move the federal-funds rate very much between FOMC meetings, will virtually guarantee that actual money growth will exceed targeted money growth, on average.

For the October 1979–December 1981 period, Feinman (1987, p. 54) reports that the Fed "adjusted" its reserve paths and borrowing assumptions in 39 percent of the weeks. Of these adjustments, 93 percent served to reduce the weekly fluctuation in the funds rate relative to what it otherwise would have been. As Feinman argues, such alternatives "effectively weakened the interest rate response to off-path money growth" (1987, p. 55). In fact, over the 1973–82 period as a whole, actual money growth exceeded targeted money growth by about $1\frac{1}{2}$ percentage points per quarter at an annual rate, with the excess money growth positively correlated with the deviation of actual GNP growth from that forecast by the staff. Such outcomes, which are symptoms of an inflationary and pro-cyclical policy rather than the activist stabilization policy supposedly in place, suggest that the Fed's adjustments, however well motivated, produced costs as well as alleged benefits.

Adjusting the funds rate: a study of "flexible" monetary targeting

More than any other issue, the appropriate setting and adjustment of the federal funds rate dominated discussions at FOMC meetings, especially through October 1979, and dominated discussions of how best to adjust the weekly reserve paths and borrowing assumptions after October 1979. Moreover, as was noted earlier, the Fed's operating strategy for implementing monetary policy passed through several stages over the 1973–82 period, and the role of the monetary aggregates in guiding policy actions fluctuated over time. To get some feel for how empirically significant such changes have been, we have adopted the "reaction-function" approach.[11] More specifically, to check for the temporal stability of the Fed's reaction to deviations of money growth from target, we estimated a simple equation using the TVARYING procedure with the Kalman filter algorithm in RATS, wherein the quarterly average of the federal funds rate is regressed on the lagged funds rate and the difference between the preceding quarter's actual growth of M1 (as first published) and the M1 target.

The resulting time-varying coefficient on the deviation of money from target is plotted in Figure 12.1. The results suggest that the Fed did indeed adjust the funds rate in response to deviations of money growth from target, with the initial response averaging about 30 basis points for each percentage point deviation of money from target, and that the magnitude of such adjustments varied considerably relative to this average response across time in a manner broadly consistent with the Fed's announced changes in its operating strategy.[12] Clearly, flexibility is an enduring characteristic of U.S. monetary policy.

Adjusting the funds rate: forecasts versus current conditions

We also estimated equations over the 1973–82 period that included various measures of current economic conditions (e.g., the growth of real GNP in the preceding quarter, the prevailing unemployment rate, the trade-weighted exchange rate, and the rate of change in the GNP deflator in the preceding quarter) and future economic conditions (e.g., the current quarter, the next quarter, and year-ahead staff forecasts for real GNP, unemployment and prices). In general, we could not uncover

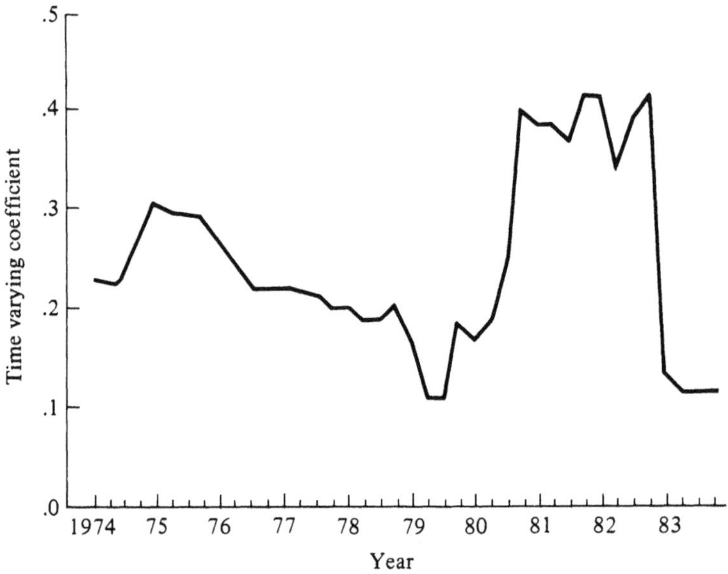

Figure 12.1. Time-varying coefficient on money

any systematic, durable relationship between the funds rate and the prevailing exchange rate (or changes therein) or forecasts of real GNP, prices, and unemployment for the next quarter or for a year ahead.[13] We did, however, find a strong response of the funds rate to the current unemployment rate – the Fed appears to lower the funds rate by about 0.5 percentage points, on average, for every 1 percentage point rise in the unemployment rate – and some response to prevailing inflation in the post-1979 period.

Taken together, these results strongly suggest that current economic conditions, rather than forecasts, drive FOMC behavior. Of course, this is not terribly surprising, given the limited information contained in the staff's forecasts of real GNP growth and inflation. However, in a world characterized by lags between policy actions and their subsequent effects on economic activity, such a backward-looking, reactive policy can easily turn out to be unduly pro-cyclical.

Unstable money demand plus static price expectations plus poor nonfinancial forecasts equal observed Fed behavior

The enduring characteristics of the Fed's behavior outlined earlier – interest-rate smoothing, flexibility, and an emphasis on responding to current economic conditions – should now be somewhat clearer. What remains to be done, however, is to expand on the several rationales discussed earlier, focusing, in particular, on the common threads running through and thus binding together the various aspects of Fed behavior. At a minimum, the modifications to the staff's bluebook alternatives usually helped to secure a clear consensus among FOMC members; politically astute, they could go on record as desiring lower money growth and lower interest rates! More to the point, however, as revealed unmistakably in the various policy documents and staff papers, the FOMC and the staff believed that the demand for money was extremely unstable and that inflationary expectations were essentially static, adjusting very slowly over time. The latter implied that, as a first approximation, such expectations could be treated as fixed over the relevant policy horizon. Taken together, such beliefs, within Poole's familiar optimal-policy framework (Poole 1970), imply that deviations of monetary growth from targeted and projected rates should more often than not be accommodated, with a stable nominal interest rate serving as proxy for a stable real interest rate, given the assumption of static inflationary expectations. The fact that interest-rate volatility per se was viewed as "costly" to the financial system and the economy (Lombra and Struble 1979) simply reinforced the economic and political arguments and pressures weighing in against interest-rate volatility in general and interest-rate increases in particular.

As Kane argues elsewhere in this volume, "a central bank is inescapably a political institution." Accordingly, given that "in the popular mind and in the financial press, the Fed is a politically beleaguered institution whose chief task is to act as the arbiter of nominal interest rates" (Kane 1980, p. 200), the political milieu constrains and conditions Fed policy in ways that buttress purely economic considerations and together produce the enduring characteristics of policy we observe.

Conclusion

Research on American monetary policy is prompted by many concerns. Among the most prominent is the considerable evidence supporting the conjecture that monetary policy has not consistently prevented money itself from being an important source or propagation mechanism for economic fluctuations and inflation.

Although in principle monetary policy should be able to stabilize aggregate demand, the evidence presented in this chapter on the policy process at the Fed suggests that there is "many a slip twixt cup and lip." More specifically, the linkages between the staff's analysis and policy-makers' choices of feasible paths for the economy, longer-run monetary targets, short-run monetary targets, operating procedures, and daily policy actions are loose at best. The resulting inconsistencies help to explain the lack of correspondence between the Fed's rhetoric and its record. Moreover, the realities of Fed policy do not correspond closely to assumptions about policy typically embedded in theoretical and empirical work in monetary economics.

Without denying that there have been monetary policy "successes" from time to time, or that randomness exists and that financial innovation and deregulation have been associated with transitory and permanent portfolio shifts from time to time, or that forecasts are often quite unreliable, the potential problems with the Fed's policy process and resulting "flexibility" are obvious. In particular, as Milton Friedman argued 20 years ago, if the monetary authority uses nominal interest rates as its primary guide for policy actions, "it will be like a space vehicle that has taken a fix on the wrong star. No matter how sensitive and sophisticated its guiding apparatus, the space vehicle will go astray. And so will the monetary authority" (1968, p. 15).

Notes

1 The former U.S. senator from Tennessee helped galvanize and focus the congressional investigation of the Watergate scandal in 1974 by stating the key questions: What did the president know, and when did he know it?

2 Full details, including illustrations from the "greenbook" and "bluebook," which contain the forecasts and analysis, are available in Karamouzis and Lombra (1989).

3 The Fed imposes a five-year lag on access to the documents used in the policy process, from which we extracted the data utilized in this chapter.

4 This finding mirrors that of Lombra and Moran (1980) for the 1970–3 period. William Poole and Joshua Feinman, in comments on Karamouzis and Lombra (1989), take issue with the "state of the art" evaluation. They argue that, other things being the same, we should expect the Fed's nonfinancial forecasts to be somewhat better than other forecasts because the Fed staff has inside knowledge about the course of monetary policy. Offsetting this informational advantage, however, is the fact that the Fed staff is constrained: It must assume that the Fed hits the monetary targets that condition the forecasts; forecasters outside the Fed are free to assume whatever set of values for the monetary aggregates and interest rates they believe to be likely to emerge.

5 Karamouzis and Lombra (1989) present evidence on the change in the pattern of the inflation forecast errors. They argue that the staff's handling of inflationary expectations played an important role in contributing to the size and pattern of the forecast errors.

6 In actuality, many of the figures appeared as ranges, say $5\frac{1}{2}$–$6\frac{1}{2}$M1 growth for

alternative A, with the midpoint of the range representing the staff's point estimate.

7 For example, if it is April and the money stock has grown by 1 percentage point more than the longer-run target over the year to date, each alternative will specify the rate of "reentry" for the money stock – that is, the time it will take under each alternative to bring actual money growth back down to its longer-run target trajectory. The reentry problem is typically dominant because of the FOMC's focus on the implications for short-term interest rates. A fast reentry, alternative C, for example, would require a higher federal-funds rate than the slower reentry implied by alternative A.

8 See Pierce (1980) and Siegel and Strongin (1986) for details.

9 See, for example, Lindbloom (1979) and Wildavsky (1979) and the references cited therein.

10 See Lombra (1988) for elaboration. The chapters by Kane and Hetzel in this volume link Fed flexibility to distributional concerns and pressures.

11 See Lombra and Moran (1980) and McNees (1986) and the literature cited therein. One must be cautious in interpreting the results from such equations because, among other things, the estimated coefficients are complex combinations of the weights in policy-maker objective functions and the "structural" parameters. Moreover, to the extent that the structural parameters themselves depend on policy parameters, and changes therein (the "Lucas critique"), the interpretation is fraught with even more difficulty. See also Khoury in this volume.

12 At a minimum, such results (the details of which are available from the authors) suggest that the variance–covariance structure linking reserves, money, and interest rates is not stable across time and is dependent in part on the particular operating regime employed by the Fed. Put another way, the Fed's approach to the short-run implementation of policy affects the way in which shocks are absorbed and transmitted within the financial system. The implications for monetary economics, including the learning that rational agents are presumed to engage in, are obvious. As for political economy, it is entirely possible that the varying coefficient shown in Figure 12.1 is itself a dependent variable explainable by the forces and factors emphasized elsewhere in this volume; see the chapters by Kane, Hetzel, and Willett.

13 McNees (1986) found that the current-quarter forecast over a longer sample period had some explanatory power. Although we also found that relationship, the high correlation between the preceding quarter's data employed in the regression discussed in the text and the current quarter's forecasts makes it difficult to distinguish empirically between them. More important, the spirit of the exercise is consistent with classifying funds-rate movements in response to current-quarter forecasts as responses to "current conditions."

References

Brunner, Karl (1985). "The Limits of Economic Policy," *Schweizerische Zeitschrift für Volkswirtschaft und Statistik*, pp. 213–35.

Feinman, Joshua (1987). "An Analysis of the Federal Reserve System's Nonborrowed Reserves Operation Procedure," Ph.D. thesis, Brown University.

Friedman, Milton (1968). "The Role of Monetary Policy," *American Economic Review,* 58(March):1–17.

Gilbert, Alton (1985). "Operating Procedures for Conducting Monetary Policy," *Federal Reserve Bank of St. Louis Review* 66(February):13–21.

Kane, Edward (1980). "Politics and Fed Policymaking: The More Things Change the More They Remain the Same," *Journal of Monetary Economics,* 6(April):199–211.

Karamouzis, Nicholas, and Lombra, Raymond (1989). "Federal Reserve Policymaking: An Overview and Analysis of the Policy Process," in K. Brunner and A. Meltzer (eds.), *Carnegie-Rochester Conference Series on Public Policy, Vol. 30,* pp. 7–62. Amsterdam: North Holland.

Lindbloom, Charles (1979). "Still Muddling, Not Yet Through," *Public Administration Review,* 39(November–December):517–26.

Lombra, Raymond (1988). "Monetary Policy: The Rhetoric vs. the Record," in T. Willett (ed.), *Political Business Cycles,* pp. 337–65. Durham, N.C.: Duke University Press.

Lombra, Raymond, and Moran, Michael (1980). "Policy Advice and Policymaking at the Federal Reserve," in K. Brunner and A. Meltzer (eds.), *Monetary Institutions and the Policy Process,* pp. 9–68. (*Vol. 13, Carnegie-Rochester Series on Public Policy*). Amsterdam: North Holland.

Lombra, Raymond, and Struble, Frederick (1979). "Monetary Aggregate Targets and the Volatility of Interest Rates: A Taxonomic Discussion," *Journal of Money, Credit and Banking,* 11(August):283–300.

McNees, Stephen (1985). "Which Forecast Should You Use?" *Federal Reserve Bank of Boston New England Economic Review* (July/August):36–42.

McNees, Stephen (1986). "Modeling the Fed: A Forward-Looking Monetary Policy Reaction Function," *Federal Reserve Bank of Boston New England Economic Review* (November–December):3–8.

Meltzer, Allan (1987). "Limits of Short-Run Stabilization Policy," *Economic Inquiry,* 25(January):1–14.

Pierce, David (1980). "Trend and Noise in the Monetary Aggregates," staff memorandum, Board of Governors of the Federal Reserve System, December.

Poole, William (1970). "Optimal Choice of Monetary Policy Instruments in a Simple Stochastic Macro Model," *Quarterly Journal of Economics,* 84:197–256.

Sellon, Gordon, and Teigen, Ronald (1981a). "The Choice of Short-Run Targets for Monetary Policy. Part I: A Theoretical Analysis," *Federal Reserve Bank of Kansas City Economic Review,* 66(April):3–16.

(1981b). "The Choice of Short-Run Targets for Monetary Policy. Part II: An Historical Analysis," *Federal Reserve Bank of Kansas City Economic Review,* 66(May):3–12.

Siegel, Diane, and Strongin, Steven (1986). "M1: The Ever-Changing Past," *Federal Reserve Bank of Chicago Economic Perspectives,* 22(March–April): 3–12.

Wallich, Henry (1984). "Recent Techniques of Monetary Policy," *Federal Reserve Bank of Kansas City Economic Review,* 69(May):21–30.

Wildavsky, Aaron (1979). *The Politics of the Budgetary Process.* Boston: Little, Brown.

Woolley, J. (1984). *Monetary Politics: The Federal Reserve and the Politics of Monetary Policy.* Cambridge University Press.

Zarnowitz, Victor (1986). "The Record and Improvability of Economic Forecasting," National Bureau of Economic Research working paper no. 2099.

CHAPTER 13

A theory of FOMC dissent voting with evidence from the time series

THOMAS HAVRILESKY AND ROBERT SCHWEITZER

The main purpose of this chapter is to develop and test a theory that predicts the voting of individual Federal Open Market Committee (FOMC) members who dissent, on the side of either tightness or ease, from the Committee's regular monetary policy directives. It is initially assumed that such a directive reflects the monetary policy desired by a majority of the Committee and that the Committee controls monetary policy. It is further assumed that the central government, specifically the administration, has a strong influence on monetary policy (Havrilesky 1987, 1988) through ongoing communication with the Committee (or its chair) and through FOMC appointments (Havrilesky and Gildea 1989).

The theory predicts individual dissenting votes as a function of the difference between each of the dissenter's "characteristics" and the mean value for that characteristic for all FOMC members. Each characteristic is a measure of the member's "career proximity" to the central government. The desired monetary stabilization policy of the central government is assumed to have a time-consistent inflationary bias. Presidential appointments of 7 of the 12 members of the FOMC are assumed to reflect several objectives. These objectives include attaining politically optimal stabilization policy, paying political debts, building antiinflationary credibility, and satisfying the representational demands of constituents (Woolley 1984; Havrilesky and Gildea 1989). Because of these multiple objectives, the FOMC as a whole will have a lesser inflationary bias than will the central government. Therefore, members whose career-proximity characteristics are closer to the central government than are the FOMC means for those characteristics will tend to dissent on the side of ease.[1] The more proximate the member's career characteristics are to central government, the greater the number of his or her dissenting votes on the side of ease. Members with career-

We are grateful to William Barnett, Thomas Mayer, and John Gildea for helpful suggestions.

proximity characteristics that are further from central government than the FOMC mean for those characteristics will tend to dissent on the side of tightness. The less proximate such a member's career characteristics are to central government, the greater the number of his or her dissenting votes on the side of tightness.

Though owing much to the earlier work of Yohe (1966), Canterbery (1967), Puckett (1984), Woolley (1984), and Gildea (this volume), this chapter has a number of novel and important aspects. It rigorously models the FOMC as a self-protective but diverse "committee" having a smaller inflationary bias than does the central government.[2] By focusing on measurable indicators of each member's critical independence of central government relative to the Committee's, it breaks with the (official Federal Reserve) practice of alluding to unmeasurable preferences and unspecified structural models as causes of dissent voting.

This chapter examines a sizable population of individual dissenting votes over time, each vote reflecting a unique set of member-versus-committee-mean career characteristics. In contrast, Gildea's chapter in this volume considers each member's voting record (dissents as a percentage of total voting opportunities) in a cross-sectional analysis.

Successful prediction of dissent voting patterns based on these indicators would be valuable, because dissenting votes may occasionally presage changes in FOMC directives (*Wall Street Journal,* June 4, 1984) and shifts in money-supply growth. For example, during the 1984–6 period, Ronald Reagan's new supply-side appointees dissented nine times on the side of monetary ease, and ease eventually prevailed (*Wall Street Journal,* December 11, 1987).

A model of dissent voting

The utility of dissent

The characteristics for the ith member are increasing measures of that member's career proximity to the central government: $X_{i1}, X_{i2}, \ldots, X_{iN}$. Where $\bar{X}_j$ is the FOMC's mean for the jth characteristic, as $X_{ij} - \bar{X}_j$ increases, the ith member's career is more proximate to the central government. All $X_{ij} > \bar{X}_j$ promote member dissents on the side of ease; all $X_{ij} < \bar{X}_j$ promote member dissents on the side of tightness. As $X_{ij} - \bar{X}_j > 0$ increases, the magnitude of the increase in ease dissents depends on how the jth characteristic is weighted; as $X_{ij} - \bar{X}_j < 0$ decreases, the magnitude of the increase in tightness dissents depends on how the jth characteristic is weighted.

Let the utility of the dissent voting of the ith member be

$$U_i(D_i) = U(D_i \mid X_{ij} - \bar{X}_j, \quad j = 1, \ldots, N) \tag{13.1}$$

where optimization occurs through the number of the member's ease or tightness dissenting votes, and where $X_{ij} - \bar{X}_j$, $j = 1, \ldots, N$, are the career-proximity parameters that condition those votes, as described earlier. Assume that U_i possesses a global maximum at $\bar{D}_i$ and that there is only one such optimum. As the actual number of dissents, D_i, differs from the utility-maximizing number of dissents, $\bar{D}_i$, total utility for the member, $U(D_i)$, decreases at an increasing rate. As shown in Figure 13.1, $\partial U/\partial(D_i - \bar{D}_i) < 0$ and $\partial^2 U/\partial(D_i - \bar{D}_i)^2 > 0$. There is decreasing utility to an FOMC member dissenting more or less than his or her global maximum. This occurs because each member has a conscience and moral values. For example, consider the words of Governor Nancy Teeters:

> Once a consensus is formed there is a very strong temptation to fall into line. Nobody pressured me but I wanted to be on record. I wanted to be able to say I voted against it. (Greider 1988, p. 221)

As the utility-maximizing number of dissents is approached, the marginal utility of dissenting more or less than the utility-maximizing level decreases. There is a diminishing marginal utility of "voting" (closer to) one's conscience.

The disutility of dissent

The Federal Reserve System is a bureaucracy whose transactions with the administration, Congress, and its constituencies in the financial-services sector are made more beneficial, more advantageous to it, when FOMC members do not dissent. This is dramatically captured in Governor and Vice-Chairman Frederick Schultz's attempt in 1980 to muzzle the president of the St. Louis Federal Reserve Bank:

> Look, we're in a helluva battle now and we're all in the same boat. We at the Board in Washington may not be as monetarist as you would like, but we're all on the same side. We should argue in the Board meetings but close ranks in public. (Greider 1988, p. 390)

Given that appeal to unity, it is reasonable to posit that the System would punish dissenters. As two former Fed staff members observed 26 years ago,

> A board member not deemed a contributor to the welfare of the System is likely to be shunted aside. (Hastings and Robertson 1962, p. 99)

And as Paul Samuelson testified 25 years ago,

I am sure there were such people in the Reserve System who felt themselves silenced because of feared reprisals. (U.S. Congress 1984, p. 1119)

The threat of punishment is also clear in the candid commentaries of several FOMC members. For example, consider the observation of Governor Charles Partee:

I would not take dissent lightly. (Greider 1988, p. 212)

Or consider that of Bank President David Eastburn:

There's a tremendous centripetal force of cohesion and esprit within the FOMC. It tends to make you think very hard about being a maverick. (*Wall Street Journal,* December 7, 1984)

From Governor Henry Wallich:

It is not a pleasant thing to have to keep dissenting. . . . One dissents less often than you would think. After all you are a member of a group and you want to get along with the other members. (Greider 1988, p. 201)

The disutility of dissent arises from private opprobrium and scorn, as well as from disapproving or derisive public comments. Consider Partee's comments on his colleague, Governor Preston Martin:

He doesn't seem to be trying to bring a group of people with him. He just doesn't structure his arguments in a way that could capture votes. (Greider 1988, p. 611)

Martin's view:

Unless you were there, an "insider," you cannot comprehend the power at play in consensus building, the frustration at times in accepting those decisions for the sake of market stability, and the compelling case at other times for dissent and even for taking your vote public for reasons of conscience. (*Wall Street Journal,* August 5, 1987)

The manifestations of such disutility range from the mere discomfort in interactions with colleagues to alienation from the committee, loss of self-esteem, and perceived erosion of future career opportunity sets. As Lawrence Roos, president of the St. Louis Federal Reserve Bank, put it,

If one is a young, career-oriented president who's got a family to feed, he tends to be more moderate in his opposition to governors. (Greider 1988, p. 205)

Therefore, it is reasonable to assume that a reputation of not being cooperative, of not presenting a "united front,"[3] of being an ideologue or a grandstander, or of having excessive or egoistic ambitions is believed to be damaging by potential dissenters.

Thus, the disutility of dissent is an important consideration. Let the disutility of the dissent voting of the ith member be

$$V_i(D_i) = V(D_i \mid X_{ij} - \bar{X}_j, \quad j = 1, \ldots, N) \tag{13.2}$$

where optimization occurs through the number of the member's dissenting votes conditioned on the $X_{ij} - \bar{X}_j$ (career-proximity) parameters, as described earlier. Assume that V_i possesses a global minimum at $D_i = 0$. As the actual number of dissents, D_i, differs from zero, the total disutility for the member, $V(D_i)$, increases at an increasing rate. As shown in Figure 13.1, $\partial V/\partial D_i > 0$ and $\partial^2 V/\partial D_i^2 > 0$.

Optimization of (net) utility

Where a (net) utility function has additive terms, the convention is to write it in the general form

$$W(D_i) = F[U(D_i \mid X_{ij} - \bar{X}_j, \quad j = 1, \ldots, N) - V(D_i \mid X_{ij} - \bar{X}_j, \quad j = 1, \ldots, N)] \tag{13.3}$$

where $F' > 0$, and F is a monotonically increasing function to assure ordinality. Differentiating $W(D_i)$ with respect to D_i and setting it equal to zero,

$$U'(D_i) = V'(D_i)$$

The first-order condition for an unconstrained maximum is satisfied where the marginal disutility of increasing one's dissent is equal to the marginal utility of increasing one's dissent (i.e., where the marginal net utility is zero).

Now we consider the condition under which there is a monotonic transformation from the (weighted) differences between a member's career characteristics and the FOMC means for those characteristics to the actual number of dissenting votes. Although the globally optimal number of dissents, $\bar{D}_i$, increases monotonically with these differences, because of the rising marginal disutility, $V'(D_i)$, and falling marginal utility, $U'(D_i)$, of increasing the number of dissenting votes toward the global optimum, the actual number of dissents, D_i^*, need not map monotonically onto career characteristic differences, $X_{ij} - \bar{X}_j$. For example, in Figure 13.1 we assume for illustrative simplicity a common disutility function across all members. It can be seen that in order for actual dissents, D_i^*, to be ordered in the same way as globally optimal dissents, $\bar{D}_i$, at all levels of dissent the marginal utility of the ith member increasing dissent toward his or her global optimum, $\bar{D}_i$, must always be less than the marginal utility of the $(i + k)$th member increasing dissent toward his or her global optimum, $\bar{D}_{i+k}$, where k measures a greater number of globally optimal dissents.

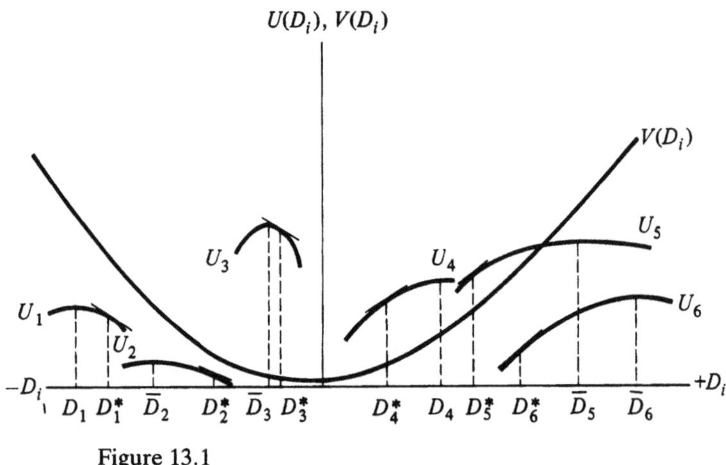

Figure 13.1

In the more general case, where the disutility of dissent is not the same across members, the condition for a monotonic transformation is that the marginal net utility of the *i*th member increasing dissent toward his or her global optimum must be less than the marginal net utility of the $(i + k)$th member increasing dissent toward his or her global optimum. This restriction says that for any level of dissent, if one member is further away from his or her bliss point than another member, he or she cannot have a smaller marginal net utility of moving toward it.[4] In other words, a member with marginally stronger moral convictions in favor of dissenting cannot be marginally more easily cowed by group (System) disapproval.[5]

This sets the stage for estimating the ease and tightness dissent votes by each member over time as a function of the difference between each of the member's career characteristics and the FOMC mean for that characteristic at the time of the vote. However, before that is done, it will be useful to discuss our data set.

Dissenting votes, career characteristics, and empirical tests

Dissenting votes

During the period from 1960 to 1983 there were 365 FOMC directives issued involving 185 split decisions and 322 dissenting votes. Prior to 1960, changes in directives were less incremental in nature. Therefore, dissenting votes did not have the same meaning, and earlier years could not be included. Table 13.1 is a tabulation of all FOMC members who dissented more than four times from 1960 to 1983. The bifurcation of

Table 13.1. *FOMC members with more than four dissenting votes, 1960–83*

Ease number		Tightness number	
Mitchell	21	Hayes (P)	26
Robertson	18	Wallich	20
Mills	18	Francis (P)	13
Teeters	13	Mills	10
Bucher	11	Coldwell	11
Maisel	8	Black (P)	7
Sheehan	8	Willes (P)	7
Morris (P)[a]	6	Winn	7
Partee	5	Balderston	6
Swan (P)	5	Shepardson	6
		Ford (P)	5
22 others	40	26 others	44
Total	153	Total	162

[a]P denotes Federal Reserve Bank president.

members into ease and tightness groups is striking and provides support for our hypothesis. The correlation coefficient between members' ease and tightness dissents is only −.04.[6] Only one person, Governor Mills, dissented more than three times on either side, but in his case the shift to ease occurred in the middle of his long tenure in Washington, at the height of the Kennedy-Johnson romantic centralism. From 1962 to 1965, Mills dissented only twice on the side of tightness, but dissented 17 times on the side of ease.[7]

Another interesting fact is that there were neither significant time trends in aggregate absolute, ease or tightness, dissents nor significant shifts in aggregate dissents during any chairmanship or any presidency.[8] The latter fact falsifies the widespread conjectures that Arthur Burns suppressed and Paul Volcker encouraged dissents during their tenures. The fact that Federal Reserve chairmen are believed to have such legendary dictatorial qualities attests to the bureaucratically self-serving image of the oracular "sound-money chairman" (Havrilesky 1988).

Career characteristics

Eight measures of members' career proximity were used. Each measure is the algebraic difference between the member's characteristic and the mean for that characteristic for the FOMC as a whole at the time of the member's dissenting vote. Positive values for four measures were conjectured as indicating close proximity to the central government and hence dissenting votes on the side of ease. These measures were years employed in government, years employed at the Federal Reserve Board, years employed as an economist, and years employed as a lawyer. The rationale for selecting the latter two measures may not be obvious. Over the entire sample, many of the economists and lawyers on the Board had prior experience as "Washington" (Board, congressional, or Council of Economic Advisors) staff members (see note 1). In addition, it was felt that professional economists and lawyers, educated during the halcyon days of the Keynesian revolution, would have had, over the entire sample period, an activist bent, despite the countervailing theoretical advances of the 1970s, of which economists were surely aware.[9] Finally, the conjecture that the economists were ease-oriented appears frequently in the earlier literature; see Canterberry (1967), Whitlesey (1963), and Woolley (1984).

Positive values for four other measures were conjectured as indicating less proximity to the central government and hence dissenting votes on the side of tightness. These measures were years employed in private industry, years employed in private banking, years employed as an academic, and years employed at a Federal Reserve Bank. The first three measures are justified simply because they indicate distance from the center of governmental power. The rationale for selecting the latter measures may not be as obvious. Federal Reserve Banks have supportive constituencies in the financial-services sector. In addition, the Bank directorates who select Bank presidents are required by law to be representative of diverse interests (Havrilesky 1986). Finally, many of the Banks have given succor to critics of monetary activism, as, of course, have academic institutions.

There were significant time trends in the mean values for seven of the eight aggregate career characteristic variables. Years as an economist, years as a lawyer, years in academics, years in government, and years at a Federal Reserve Bank all had positive time trends that were significant at the .04 level or better. Years employed in private industry and years in private banking had negative trend coefficients that were significant at the .01 level. Only years employed at the Board had no statistically significant trend over the sample period. The decline in private-sector representation, a pattern first detected in the early 1960s (*Wall Street Journal,* March 9, 1964), may be of some concern.

Methods

The individual ease and tightness dissenting votes by each member from 1960 to 1983 were regressed, using binary probit analysis, on the difference between each of the member's eight career characteristics and the Committee mean for that characteristic at the time of the vote. Ease dissents were measured as +1, tightness dissents as 0.

Data points were included conditional on a member's dissenting. If a member went along with the majority in a split decision, the vote was not counted in the data set. Therefore, when an individual sided with the consensus, it meant that his or her characteristics had no impact on the results, except insofar as they affected the Committee means at the time. Thus, the greater the number of a member's dissents, the greater the impact of his or her characteristics as a dissenter. This truncation of the data set possibly could bias the results.

This possible selectivity bias could be avoided by using only cross-section data and measuring dissenting votes as a percentage of total voting opportunities (Gildea, this volume). However, that approach would, of necessity, neglect the effect of changing Committee characteristics over time. The best way to determine whether or not there was a selectivity bias in the results reported here would be, in future research, to include data on nondissenters and to explain how members voted, not just why they dissented.

Results

Regressions are reported in Table 13.2 for all FOMC members, governors, and presidents, and for governors alone. In the equations for all members, a binary variable (Pres) was added, with a value of 1 if the member was a Federal Reserve Bank president, and 0 otherwise. Table 13.2 indicates that while controlling for career characteristics, the position of Bank president generates dissent on the side of tightness. This is consistent with the data in Table 13.1 as well as the findings of Puckett (1984) and Woolley (1984).

The results for governors only are more impressive. All of the estimated coefficients have the predicted signs and are statistically significant, except for years in government and years on the staff of the Federal Reserve Board.

The results for all members have a higher log likelihood ratio because a variable, the president dummy, was added. However, in contrast to the governors-only results, the estimated coefficients for years as an economist, years in industry, years in law, and years in government are not statistically significant, while the estimated coefficient for the years on the Federal Reserve Board staff is statistically significant. This overall deterioration in the results probably occurs because there is less variance between the mean characteristics of ease dissenters and tightness dissent-

Table 13.2. *FOMC members' ease and tightness dissenting votes explained by differences between their career characteristics and Committee means for those characteristics, 1960–83*

Intercept	Pres	Years as an economist	Years in industry	Years in law	Years in banking	Years in academe	Years in gov't.	Years on Fed Board staff	Years at Fed Bank
All members[a]									
−0.667	−1.118	−0.002	−0.242	0.004	−0.049	−0.061	0.008	0.283	−0.237
(−4.941)[b]	(−5.688)	(−0.203)	(−0.885)	(0.074)	(−3.841)	(−4.890)	(0.423)	(3.597)	(−1.645)
Governors only[c]									
−0.805		0.095	−0.071	0.722	−0.630	−0.158	−0.281	0.124	−0.161
(−3.733)		(2.823)	(−1.652)	(2.549)	(−3.471)	(−4.668)	(−1.016)	(1.067)	(−3.782)

[a]Log likelihood ratio 152.8.
[b]t statistics in parentheses.
[c]Log likelihood ratio 110.3.

ers when presidents are included. The mean career characteristics of presidents are more homogeneous than those of governors.[10]

Our model predicts dissents on the side of tightness quite well. The results challenge Woolley's assertion that occupational background makes no difference in FOMC dissent voting (Woolley 1984). Estimates for variables conjectured to predict tightness dissents are significant, with the predicted sign, in eight of nine cases. The model fares less well in predicting dissents on the side of ease. Estimates for variables conjectured to predict ease dissents are significant, with the predicted sign, in three of eight cases. This disparity may occur because the ideological sentiments that cause members to identify with the inflationary bias of the central government are not readily captured by the career characteristics used in this study.[11]

Concluding comment

This chapter is premised on the notion that all administrations have a time-consistent inflationary bias, but because of constituency/representational objectives, they cannot "pack" the FOMC with members who will always conform to that bias (Havrilesky and Gildea 1989). As a result, FOMC members whose career characteristics reflect greater proximity to the central government than the FOMC means for those characteristics are predicted, via a utility-maximizing model of committee voting, to cast dissenting votes on the side of ease. Those whose career characteristics reflect lesser proximity to the central government than the Committee means are predicted to cast dissenting votes on the side of tightness.

Probit regressions provide a good deal of support for the theory, especially when Federal Reserve Bank presidents are excluded from the sample. Only one of the eight career characteristic variables consistently failed to have the predicted effect on dissent voting. The model performed much better in predicting tightness dissenting votes than in predicting ease dissenting votes. Future work will expand the data set to include nondissenting votes. It will also test the hypothesis that dissent is motivated by differences in career characteristics between the dissenter and the chairman, rather than between the dissenter and the Committee as a whole. The expanded data set will be used to estimate reaction functions for individual FOMC members (Havrilesky and Chappell 1990).

Notes

1 The pliability of career Washingtonians to the will of the central government has been noted by several observers. See, for example, Harry Johnson's testi-

mony in the 1964 congressional hearings (U.S. Congress 1964) and Preston Martin's comments in the August 5, 1987, *Wall Street Journal.* Moreover, it is not a recent phenomenon; see *Banker's Magazine* (1925).

2 This view was thoroughly aired long ago by Wright Patman and others in congressional hearings (U.S. Congress 1964). For an alternative perspective, see Toma (1982).

3 As suggested by Thomas Mayer in this volume, "group think" may be a way of easing the latent disutility of dissenting.

4 This may not be an unreasonably severe restriction. Individuals with stronger consciences typically become accustomed to group pressure and are not as easily intimidated by it.

5 If utility is assumed not to rise with the number of dissents as rapidly as disutility, total net utility decreases with dissent, and the absolute number of dissenting votes may be an indicator of the erosion of human psychological capital. Under these conditions, increases in the absolute number of dissents per period should be associated, while controlling for career opportunity costs, with reductions in a member's tenure in office. Ordinary-least-squares regression analysis indicates a statistically insignificant relationship between a member's months in office, M, and the absolute number of his or her dissent votes per month $|D|$:

$$M = \underset{(5.59)}{125.76} + \underset{(-0.49)}{100.82|D|} + \underset{(2.39)}{100.15B}, \qquad \bar{R}^2 = .21$$

where B is the percentage of time in office that the member served under Arthur Burns; t statistics are in parentheses. The results falsify our conjecture and also tend to debunk the belief that Arthur Burns hastened the resignation of many FOMC members when he was chairman (Newton 1985).

6 Members with a proclivity for ease tend to dissent when the FOMC directive calls for tightness or for no change. Over the entire 24-year period, among the 154 ease dissents within 365 directives, only 19 occurred in the 56 times that the directive called for ease. Members with a proclivity for tightness tend to dissent when the FOMC directive calls for ease or for no change. Among 168 tightness dissents, there were only 29 in the 61 times that the directive called for tightness.

		Individual dissents	
Committee directives		Ease	Tightness
No change	248	79	94
Ease	56	19	45
Tightness	61	56	29
Total	365	154	168

7 The only other significant dissent mugwumps from these groups were 11-time tightness dissenter Coldwell, who had three ease dissenting votes, 6-time ease dissenter Morris, who cast three tightness dissenting votes, and 6-time tightness dissenter Balderston, who cast two ease dissenting votes.

8 For example, where x_{a_t} is total absolute dissents per year, t is time, and B is a binary variable equal to 1 for years when Burns was chairman,

$$x_{a_t} = \underset{(4.94)}{16.03} - \underset{(-0.39)}{0.09\ln t} - \underset{(-1.33)}{4.48B}, \qquad \bar{R}^2 = .09, \qquad \text{DF} = 21$$

Puckett (1984) also found no trends in dissents.

When total ease x_{e_t} and total tightness x_{t_t} dissents per year were dependent variables and the change in the inflation rate, $\Delta\dot{P}$, and the change in the unemployment rate, ΔU, were added, the results were

$$x_{t_t} = \underset{(1.64)}{3.88} + \underset{(2.98)}{1.113\Delta\dot{P}_t} + \underset{(1.75)}{1.78\ln t} - \underset{(-1.39)}{3.37B}, \qquad \bar{R}^2 = .29, \qquad \text{DF} = 17$$

$$x_{e_t} = \underset{(3.32)}{11.98} + \underset{(0.47)}{0.54\Delta U_t} - \underset{(-1.44)}{2.28\ln t} - \underset{(-0.47)}{1.27B}, \qquad \bar{R}^2 = .18, \qquad \text{DF} = 17$$

Except for the change-in-inflation variable, none of the coefficients is significant, and the $\bar{R}^2$ values are quite low for time-series data; t statistics are in parentheses. In comparison, Luckett and Potts (1980) found significant responses of an index of FOMC directives to state-of-the-economy variables.

9 Consider, for example, Thomas Mayer's observation in this volume: "From reading the FOMC minutes, one would hardly know that many of the participants are professional economists."

10 The following mean comparisons are illustrative:

	Presidents		Governors	
Mean years:	Tightness dissenters	Ease dissenters	Tightness dissenters	Ease dissenters
as economist	17.33	17.27	18.10	12.79
in industry	1.19	2.03	1.36	1.02
in law	0.56	0.85	0	0
in banking	8.06	2.15	6.89	6.42
in academics	3.55	5.36	14.53	2.84
in gov't.	1.17	1.57	2.86	6.35
at board	0	0.0606	0.15	2.28

11 There is evidence that Democratic presidential administrations engage in easier money than Republican ones (Havrilesky 1987) and that governors appointed by Democrats dissent more on the side of ease than do governors appointed by Republicans (Woolley 1984).

References

Abrams, Richard K., Froyen, Richard, and Waud, Roger N. (1980). "Monetary Policy Reaction Functions, Consistent Expectations, and the Burns Era," *Journal of Money, Credit and Banking,* 12(February):30–42.

Banker's Magazine (1925). 110:3 (editorial).

Canterbery, E. Ray (1967). "A New Look at Federal Open Market Voting," *Western Economic Journal,* 6(December):25–38.

Friedman, Milton, and Schwartz, Anna (1963). *A Monetary History of the United States, 1867–1960.* Princeton University Press.

Greider, William (1988). *Secrets of the Temple.* New York: Simon & Schuster.

Hastings, Delbert C., and Robertson, Ross M. (1962). "The Mysterious World of the Fed," *Business Horizons,* pp. 15–63.

Havrilesky, Thomas (1986). "The Effect of the Federal Reserve Reform Act on the Economic Affiliation of Directors of Federal Reserve Banks," *Social Science Quarterly,* 67(2):393–401.

(1987). "A Partisanship Theory of Monetary and Fiscal Policy Regimes," *Journal of Money, Credit and Banking,* 19:308–25.

(1988). "Monetary Policy Signaling from the Administration to the Federal Reserve," *Journal of Money, Credit and Banking,* 20:83–101.

(1990). "The Influence of the Federal Advisory Council on Monetary Policy," *Journal of Money, Credit and Banking* (February).

Havrilesky, Thomas, and Chappell, Henry (1990). "Reaction Functions for Individual FOMC Members," Duke University working paper, February.

Havrilesky, Thomas, and Gildea, John (1989). "Reliable and Unreliable Partisan Appointees to the Board of Governors," Duke University working paper, October.

Luckett, Dudley, and Potts, G. (1980). "Monetary Policy and Partisan Politics," *Journal of Money, Credit and Banking,* 12(November):540–6.

Newton, Maxwell (1985). *The Fed.* New York: Times Books.

Potts, Glenn T., and Luckett, Dudley G. (1978). "Policy Objectives of the Federal Reserve System," *Quarterly Journal of Economics,* 82(August):525–34.

Puckett, Richard (1984). "Federal Open Market Committee Structure and Decisions," *Journal of Monetary Economics,* 12(July):97–104.

Toma, Mark (1982). "Inflationary Bias of the Federal Reserve System," *Journal of Monetary Economics,* 10:163–90.

U.S. Congress (1964). *Hearings, The Federal Reserve after Fifty Years.* House Subcommittee on Domestic Finance and Committee on Banking and Currency. Washington, D.C.: U.S. Government Printing Office.

Whitlesey, C. R. (1963). "Power and Influence in the Federal Reserve System," *Economica,* 45:123–35.

Woolley, John (1984). *Monetary Politics: The Federal Reserve and the Politics of Monetary Policy.* Cambridge University Press.

Yohe, William P. (1966). "A Study of Federal Open Market Committee Voting, 1955–1964," *Southern Economic Journal,* 12(April):369–405.

(1971). "Federal Open Market Committee Decisions in a Markov Process," *Public Choice* (Fall):89–109.

CHAPTER 14

Explaining FOMC members' votes

JOHN A. GILDEA

The controversy over the effectiveness of monetary policy has raged on for decades despite the fact that the first link in the monetary policy chain has been virtually ignored – the link between the individuals who compose the FOMC and the resulting open-market policy directive.[1] The sixth edition of *The Federal Reserve System: Purposes and Functions* (1974, p. 57) describes FOMC members as first having to "individually interpret the available statistical and qualitative macroeconomic data in order to evaluate the state of the economy." Second, "each attending FOMC member is asked to give his or her own policy recommendation." Finally, "committee members have to deliberate in order to reach a consensus of their individual viewpoints." The purpose of this chapter is to incorporate this discretionary behavior into an analysis of the voting records of individual FOMC members. The hypothesis to be tested is that FOMC members attempt to implement their personal preferences subject to certain imposed constraints. Career and social-background variables will reflect preferences, whereas relevant political and economic variables will enter as effective constraints.

Preferences: political voting theory

Political scientists have long tried to explain the voting behavior of Supreme Court justices. The question they have tried to answer is this: Why do various Supreme Court justices vote differently when confronted by the same facts and the same history of legal precedents? That question is strikingly similar to the question of interest in this chapter: Why do FOMC members vote differently when confronted by the same economic data and the same economic history? The explanation that political scientists developed and studied was that "the different life experiences of individuals play a role in the formation of predispositions that in turn shape behavior" (Ulmer 1970, p. 585).

I would like to thank Thomas Havrilesky, Thomas Mayer, Henry Wallich, William Yohe, Dudley Wallace, and Jerome Waldron for helpful suggestions.

The absence of a comparable sociological study of FOMC voting seems peculiar in light of the many similarities to the Supreme Court. As one author described it, "both have tried to define its expertise as technical, its criteria as non-partisan, and its goals as 'above politics' but both the Court and the Fed have neither avoided nor been impervious to public opinion and political pressures" (Borins 1972, p. 185). Just as the Supreme Court interprets controversial legal precedents, FOMC members interpret the relevant economic data. And just as the justices differ in citing legal precedents, FOMC members differ regarding which economic facts are more important. Both groups are able to disguise their preferences within objective criteria. Thus, in order to explain FOMC voting behavior, it becomes necessary to incorporate individual members' preferences, as reflected by various career and social-background variables.

The constraint: bureaucracy theory

An increasingly popular explanation for the erratic behavior of monetary policy and the economy lies in the economic theory of bureaucracy and the symbiotic relationships that have developed between the Fed and the president and, to a lesser extent, the Fed and Congress; see, for example, Acheson and Chant (1973) and Kane (1980). Evidence of the former relationship is not hard to come by. William McChesney Martin, who served as Federal Reserve chairman longer than anyone else, openly admits that presidents influence Fed policy-making (Cordtz 1982).

Federal Reserve critics try to explain the relationship between the president and the Federal Reserve by pointing out the benefits each can bestow on the other. A president seeking reelection for himself or his party, or seeking passage of a controversial program, needs a strong economy to win public support. The Federal Reserve, realizing that its continued existence is at the mercy of Congress, needs a strong political ally in its corner in times when Federal Reserve authorities are threatened. Because the president's short-run preferences concerning monetary policy are no secret, advantageous terms of trade usually can be found between the desired level of, say, nominal interest rates and continued administration support for Fed authorities.

Similarly, the Federal Reserve also enjoys a symbiotic relationship with Congress. Using public dissonance as evidence of mass support, politically adept members of Congress have been able to translate antipathy to rising interest rates and to large exchange-rate fluctuations into criticism of the Fed, the perennial scapegoat for unpopular economic conditions (Kane 1980, 1982). It is believed that Fed officials willingly accept this scapegoat role in tacit exchange for the continuance of long-term relative autonomy and for a budget that is insulated from congressional review. This relationship, however, is thought to be weaker than the relationship between the president and the Fed, because the benefits of monetary policy are more diffuse than the benefits of the conventional pork-barrel activities of members of Congress.

The model

Politicoeconomic constraints

The model being proposed simply assumes that FOMC members will seek to maximize their utility subject to a politically signaled short-run inflation–unemployment trade-off.[2] This constraint will be contingent on the current state of the economy and on the desires of the president and incumbent legislators for levels of unemployment and inflation that will enhance their support and chances for reelection. Mounting political pressures for monetary accommodation are seen to shorten the time horizon of politicians and thereby flatten the signaled inflation–unemployment trade-off to which FOMC members are to respond. Conversely, as politicians' desires for favorable movements in real variables weaken, their time horizon lengthens, and the apparent short-run Phillips curve imposed on the FOMC becomes steeper.

By viewing this politically signaled trade-off as measuring the perceived relative "prices" of inflation and unemployment and by allowing FOMC members' preferences to yield concave indifference curves in inflation and unemployment space, members' individual voting demand functions can be derived. A member's desire for lower unemployment (more expansionary monetary policy) may then be reasoned to be negatively related to the perceived price of lower unemployment (the perceived increase in inflation the economy suffers).

We can begin to broaden this model by interpreting a desire on the part of a policy-maker for more expansionary policies as also a desire to lower the price of credit – the ex ante real interest rate.[3] Members' desires to manipulate the ex ante real interest rate will depend on the perceived cost of doing so. The cost or price of a short-run change in the ex ante real interest rate is the associated change in inflation that will necessarily occur within the time horizon of politicians. Within our theoretical framework, this new trade-off represents a related price variable. The higher this price, ceteris paribus, the lower will be a member's demand for more expansionary monetary policy.

Although we cannot directly measure these relevant short-run constraints, we can adduce variables that are likely to influence their slope. The average presidential approval rating (APPRVL), the average presidential disapproval rating (DISAPP), and the average congressional disapproval rating (CONDIS) are hypothesized to be such variables.[4] The smaller the approval rating (or the larger the disapproval rating), the shorter the time horizon of politicians, and the flatter the signaled short-run trade-offs will be to FOMC members. The flatter these trade-offs are, the smaller the perceived costs of expansionary policies will be, and thus the greater the likelihood of expansionary monetary policy.

Another important consideration that needs to be explicitly modeled within a member's voting behavior is the average endowment position during a member's tenure (AEND). The state of the economy when an FOMC member votes constitutes the endowment position. This new explanatory variable may account for the different voting behaviors of members who served over different time periods. Incorporating this endowment variable into our voting demand function and formulating it as the inflation rate divided by the sum of the unemployment rate and the ex ante real interest rate, the demand for lower unemployment (more expansion) will now be said to be a negative function of the endowment variable.[5]

The final consideration that needs to be explicitly modeled within a member's voting behavior is the desire for Federal Reserve credibility. If the Federal Reserve is perceived by the public to be extremely credible, monetary policy-makers will be better able to exploit existing short-run economic trade-offs and thereby affect real economic variables through surprise accelerations of money growth. Whatever benefits monetary policy-makers gain through this action will be offset, however, by the future worsening of economic trade-offs as economic agents lose faith in the announced intentions of monetary authorities. Because econometric forecasts do not account for the effects that changing expectations have on the structure of the economy, a direct measure of future trade-offs is impossible (Lucas 1976). Instead, a variable measuring recent deviations in money growth will be employed as a proxy measure for the expected worsening of the economic trade-offs (MSDEV). This variable will be calculated by taking the sum of the last six months of money-supply (M1) growth deviations from its long-run (60-month) trend. If large unexpected swings in money are left unchecked, expected inflation will tend to differ from actual inflation and thus erode the Fed's credibility and make future trade-offs much more unfavorable. Our hypothesis will be that the Fed's short-run policy focus will necessitate a very high rate of discount, so that large unexpected swings in money growth will be left unchecked, thus making the expected relationship between the desire for monetary expansion and money growth deviations positive.

Individual preferences

Political scientists have identified certain attributes in a judge's social background that they believe to reflect that judge's predispositions, attitudes, values, and preferences; see, for example, Tate (1981). In accounting for FOMC members' preferences, a similar approach will be taken. The variables believed to be relevant are classified into two categories: career variables and social-background variables. Those variables that suggest a member's preference for more expansionary monetary policy may be characterized as increasing the marginal rate of substitution of inflation for unemployment.

Career variables

1. Appointing president (APP and APPF).[6] These variables allow for the ideological latitude presidents have in their selection of Fed governors. It is believed that Democratic presidents prefer a point on the short-run Phillips curve northwest of the target of Republican presidents (Stein 1978).

2. Partial-term appointment (PART). This dummy variable attempts to single out those members whose continued service on the FOMC is dependent on reappointment and thus may be more susceptible to short-run political pressures for accommodative monetary policy.

3. Years in government (YRSGOV). The length of time a member serves within the bureaucracy of federal government may increase his or her likelihood of nurturing an acceptance of central-government goals, which tend to be chronically expansionary.

4. Years on the Federal Reserve Board staff (YRSFRB). This variable attempts to account for a staffer's sense of loyalty and long-standing defense of a system that is consistently bombarded by short-run political pressures for accommodative monetary policies.

5. Years in industry (YRSIND). Members who have had prior associations with private industry may be more susceptible to industry's concerns over high and rising borrowing costs.

6. President or governor (PREGOV).[7] This variable identifies those members who served as Federal Reserve Bank presidents. The geographical separation between Washington and the Federal Reserve Banks and the regional focus of these Banks may better insulate Bank

presidents from the chronic pressures for monetary accommodation from the central government.

7. Ph.D. in economics (PHDE) and years in academe (YRSACA). These variables attempt to measure a member's level of expertise in economic affairs and propensity for independent thinking, which might render a member less susceptible to accommodating short-run political pressures. Additionally, formal training in economics may enlighten members as to the long-run consequences of expansionary monetary policy and thus make trained economists less accommodating.

8. Chairman. Of the four chairmen who served between 1960 and 1982, the two whose terms were sufficiently long to permit study were William Martin (CMAR) and Arthur Burns (CBUR). The Federal Reserve under Chairman Martin was considered to be strongly conservative, whereas the Federal Reserve under Chairman Burns was seen to have lost that antiinflationary militance (Havrilesky, Sapp, and Schweitzer 1977). Because a chairman has never been on the losing side of a split FOMC decision vote, a member's voting record might be influenced by the leadership ability of the chairman under whom the member served.

Social-background variables

1. Political affiliation (POLAF). The inclusion of this variable allows for the commonly held belief that Democrats will favor the interests of low- and middle-income groups and will be more adverse to unemployment than to inflation, whereas Republicans will favor the interests of upper-income groups and will be more concerned about inflation than about unemployment.

2. Prestige of education (PRED). The political scientists' conjecture is that graduates from schools with low tuitions might be expected to be more liberal in their views, because students at those schools frequently come from lower-socioeconomic backgrounds; see, for example, Nagel (1961).

The dependent variables

The primary dependent variable (NCTSD) used in this study is the percentage of noncontractionary votes a member registered in nonunanimous decisions during his or her tenure on the FOMC. This variable was calculated by assigning a plus, minus, or zero to each member's vote. A plus categorized the more expansionary side of a split decision, a minus categorized the more contractionary side of a split decision, and a zero classified the majority votes that occasionally were in between expansionary and contractionary dissents. The dependent variable was then derived by dividing the number of zeros and pluses by the sum of all zeros, pluses, and minuses.[8]

In addition to this dependent variable, it was thought that it might be enlightening to analyze the differences between the two groups that make up the FOMC – those members characterized by a more liberal voting record and those members characterized by a more conservative voting record. The continuous dependent variable (NCTSD) was transformed into a binary variable (CNCTSD) appropriate for discriminant and logit analysis by choosing a dividing line between the members' voting scores (40%) that roughly cut the total sample in half (45%/55%). Those members who scored 40 percent or less were given a 0; those members scoring above 40 percent were given a 1. If a member failed to participate in at least five split-decision votes during his or her tenure, he or she was excluded from the analysis.

Empirical results

The model was tested on a cross-sectional basis for the period January 1960 to August 1982. The statistical techniques employed were stepwise ordinary least squares, stepwise logistic analysis, and stepwise discriminant analysis. The stepwise procedures were modified so as to first introduce a member's political-affiliation variable or appointing president's party variable when that information was available. The results are reported for four different samples: those members who completed a confidential questionnaire, the Federal Reserve governors, the Federal Reserve Bank presidents, and the entire FOMC.[9]

Survey sample

The 21 members whose political affiliations were ascertained from a survey compose the first sample to be analyzed. The basis for selecting this sample comes from evidence of the important role that political affiliation plays in Supreme Court justices' voting behavior (Tate 1981). The results for this sample are reported in Table 14.1.

As one can see, the statistical results for the three techniques for this sample suggest that a member's social background does indeed influence his or her voting behavior. The significance of the partisan variable, political affiliation (POLAF), lends support to the notion that monetary policy is a partisan process. Members describing themselves as Democrats tended to view noncontractionary monetary policy as more desirable over their tenure than did their Republican counterparts. Addition-

Table 14.1. *Survey sample*

Ordinary least squares

$$NCTSD = 2.06 + 7.03POLAF + 1.00DISAPP + .702YRSFRB - 17.13PHDE$$
$$\quad (2.43) \quad (4.56) \quad (2.29) \quad (-2.71)$$

$R^2 = .69$, $F = 8.75$, $N = 21$
The figures in parentheses are t statistics.

Logistic regression

$$CNCTSD = 22.29 + 1.47POLAF - .35APPRVL - 1.12PRED$$
$$(3.29) \quad (2.39) \quad (3.42) \quad (2.08)$$

Model chi-square = 17.36
The figures in parentheses are chi-square statistics.
Predictive accuracy = 90.5%

Discriminant analysis

$$CNCTSD = .714POLAF - .966\ APPRVL - .647PRED$$

$F = 6.51$, canonical $R^2 = .53$
Predictive accuracy = 90% (19/21)

Note: The discriminant function for the first 14 members appointed correctly classified 6 of the remaining 7 members (86%).

ally, the significant negative coefficient on a social-background variable, prestige of education (PRED), appears to support political scientists' contention that an Ivy League education is likely to impart a preference for more conservative policies.

Within the career category, high levels of significance and correct signs were found on these variables: years on the Federal Reserve Board staff (YRSFRB) and Ph.D. in economics (PHDE). As expected, Federal Reserve Board staff experience tended to have a liberalizing impact on members' voting behavior, whereas a Ph.D. in economics imparted a conservative policy approach.

Of the politicoeconomic constraint variables tested, presidential popularity (APPRVL and DISAPP) appeared as the most significant explanatory variable for members' voting behavior. What this suggests is a response to the politically imposed economic constraint implied by presidential pressure. As presidential popularity decreased, the time frame perceived by these FOMC members shortened, and the implied prices of lower unemployment and lower ex ante real interest rates declined. As the perceived prices declined, members in this sample tended to prefer more expansionary monetary policies.

This last conclusion, however, needs to be qualified by the high correlation (.90) between presidential popularity and the current state of the

Table 14.2. *Governors*

Ordinary least squares

NCTSD = 1.48 + 7.84APP + .12 DISAPP + 1.40YRSIND + .39CBUR
(2.12) (1.79) (5.78) (4.81)

R^2 = .78, F = 21.67, N = 29

Logistic regression

CNCTSD = −4.74 + 1.00APPF + .20DISAPP − 3.08PHDE
(3.47) (2.54) (5.01) (3.55)

Model chi-square = 13.78
Predictive accuracy = 79.3%

Discriminant analysis

CNCTSD = 1.19APPF + .71DISAPP − .49PHDE + .47PART + 1.31CBUR

F = 10.38, canonical R^2 = .69
Predictive accuracy = 96.6%

Note: The discriminant function for the first 19 governors appointed correctly classified 8 of the remaining 10 governors (80%).

economy, as measured by the average endowment (AEND) variable. This fact suggests that presidential popularity may be a proxy for economic conditions. The significance of both these variables suggests that members may be responding to the perceived slopes of the constraints as well as the economy's current positions on them. Although the former variable is slightly more significant, either of these interpretations would seem to highlight the short-run concerns of FOMC members.

Federal Reserve governors

The 29 governors who served between 1960 and 1982 make up this sample. Only information that was available for every governor was used in the statistical tests for this sample. That eliminated the political-affiliation information the questionnaires provided for some governors. However, the prior expectation for this sample was that the appointing president's party variable would likely provide information about a governor's own political inclination, as well as possible bureaucratic tendencies to accommodate the preferences of the president's party.[10] The results for this sample are presented in Table 14.2.

Consistent with the findings for the first sample, governors' voting behavior also seems to have been affected by constraint and preference variables. The significance of the constraint variable measuring presidential popularity (DISAPP) provides further evidence of the Fed's desire to respond to short-run political or economic fluctuations. Also consistent with the prior expectation for this sample, a career variable, appointing president's party (APP or APPF), indicates that governors appointed by Democratic presidents tended to prefer more expansionary monetary policies than did their Republican counterparts.

The sign of one of the career variables, percentage of votes during Chairman Burns's tenure (CBUR), would seem to suggest that Chairman Burns's preference for less contractionary monetary policy was heavily imposed upon his fellow governors with whom he had frequent contact. This variable's lack of significance for other samples suggests that Federal Reserve Bank presidents may have successfully distanced themselves from his influence, because they came to Washington only once every four to six weeks, possibly with a policy choice already decided.

In addition to those career variables, the significance and positive coefficients of two career variables, years in industry (YRSIND) and partial-term appointment (PART), seem to support the conjecture that members with business backgrounds and reappointment opportunities tend to view noncontractionary monetary policy as more desirable. Finally, the negative coefficient on one career variable, Ph.D. in economics (PHDE), as in the first sample, seems to support the contention that formal economic training imparts a more conservative approach to monetary policy-making.

Federal Reserve Bank presidents

Forty Federal Reserve Bank presidents and three vice-presidents of the Federal Reserve Bank of New York composed this sample. The prior conjecture for this sample was that the results would be weakened by the lack of information about political affiliation. The results for this sample are reported in Table 14.3.

As can be seen from the various summary statistics, the explanatory power and predictive capability of these equations do indeed fall substantially. However, there is still consistency with earlier results. In addition to the prestige of education (PRED) variable being significant, the short-run focus of FOMC policy-making is still evidenced by the significance of the congressional disapproval (CONDIS) variable. As the time frame was shortened by mounting congressional pressures, Federal Reserve Bank presidents appear to have responded to the lower perceived costs of reducing unemployment and real interest rates by voting for more expansionary policies. This interpretation, however, needs to be qualified by the high correlation (.60) between the congressional disap-

Table 14.3. *Presidents*

Ordinary least squares

NCTSD = 23.58 − 1.99PRED + 1.13YRSIND + .46CONDIS
(−2.10) (1.90) (1.81)

R^2 = .23, F = 3.82, N = 43

Logistic regression

CNCTSD = −2.82 + .06CONDIS + .20YRSGOV
(3.57) (2.79) (2.32)

Model chi-square = 7.24
Predictive accuracy = 63%

Discriminant analysis

CNCTSD = .75CONDIS + .71YRSGOV + .55YRSIND

F = 3.04, canonical R^2 = .20
Predictive accuracy = 68%

Note: The discriminant function for the first 21 presidents appointed correctly classified 18 of the remaining 20 presidents (60%).

proval (CONDIS) rating and the average endowment (AEND) variable. It could very well be that the presidents' preferences for more expansionary policies are reactions to increases in unemployment and ex ante real interest rates relative to inflation, instead of the shorter time horizon imposed by Congress.

Finally, the significances and signs of two career variables, years in industry (YRSIND) and years in government (YRSGOV), appear to indicate that those presidents with substantial experience in private industry or government service are likely to prefer policies that tend to be more expansionary.

Entire FOMC

Seventy FOMC members who served between 1960 and 1982 made up this last group to be analyzed. The results were expected to be somewhat weaker than those for either of the first two samples, because a political-affiliation variable and a presidential-appointment variable were unavailable. The empirical findings for this sample are presented in Table 14.4.

As in the previous three samples, the results for this sample attest to the short-run focus of monetary policy. The significance and sign of the presidential disapproval rating (DISAPP) indicate that the FOMC has tended to respond to politically imposed shorter-term trade-offs and/or increases in the endowment variable. In either case, the description

Table 14.4. *All FOMC members*

Ordinary least squares

$$NCTSD = 1.49 + 1.12DISAPP + 13.92PART - 12.3PHDE$$
$$\qquad (5.79) \qquad (2.45) \qquad (-2.06)$$

$R^2 = .39$, $F = 14.34$, $N = 70$

Logistic regression

$$CNCTSD = -2.01 + .08DISAPP + .91PART - .97PREGOV - .05YRSACA$$
$$(2.65) \quad (6.03) \qquad (2.64) \qquad (2.80) \qquad (2.47)$$

Model chi-square = 15.98
Predictive accuracy = 73.6%

Discriminant analysis

$$CNCTSD = .71DISAPP + .48PART - .48PREGOV - .44YRSACA$$

$F = 4.79$, canonical $R^2 = .22$
Predictive accuracy = 75%

Note: The discriminant function for the first 40 members appointed correctly classified 18 of the remaining 30 members (60%).

would suggest a monetary policy that is aimed at the most politicized economic problem of the day.

The significance and sign of the career variable that distinguishes Bank presidents from Fed governors (PREGOV) would seem to provide further testimony of the less accommodating preference of Federal Reserve Bank presidents. This result would seem clearly to support Puckett's findings (1984), which portray Federal Reserve Bank presidents as voting much like Republican Fed governors.

The significance of one career variable, years in academe (YRSACA), appears to be related to the prior significance of another variable: Ph.D. in economics (PHDE). Of the 28 members with Ph.D.s in economics, all but four had experience in teaching. Moreover, of the 328 teaching years logged by FOMC members, 246 (75%) had been taught by those with Ph.D.s in economics.

Finally, the inclusion of one of the career variables, partial-term appointment (PART), for this sample would seem to be related to its significance for the sample of governors. Its lack of significance in the first sample may have been due to the small number of governors in that sample.

Conclusion

The purpose of this study has been to develop and test a model of FOMC voting behavior. Unlike past models, the approach taken in this chapter is consistent with both economic theory and the political-science literature. It directly models preferences by incorporating sociological variables as well as politicoeconomic variables in a demand theoretic framework attempting to explain FOMC voting outcomes. The rationale for this approach lies in the belief that the men and women who make monetary policy do so subjectively, individually weighing the many economic and political costs and benefits associated with their policy choices.

The results of testing this model are summarized in Appendix Table 14.1 and appear to strongly support the basic framework that a politically imposed economic constraint and members' preferences seem to consistently influence the voting behavior of FOMC members. Specifically, it appears that members are quite responsive to the constraint imposed on them by the president and/or the current state of the economy. As presidential popularity declined, and/or as unemployment and the ex ante real interest rate rose relative to inflation, members tended to respond by voting for more expansionary monetary policies. Within the category of preference variables, evidence of the partisan nature of monetary policy-making was uncovered. Governors tended to cast their split-decision votes in accordance with the appointing president's party, whereas a sample of FOMC members voted according to their political affiliations.

Also unique to this study was the inclusion and subsequent significance of other preference variables previously ignored as being unimportant in explaining monetary policy-making. Fulfilling a partial-term appointment, Federal Reserve Board and government experience, along with a background in private industry tended to impart a relatively liberal voting behavior. Conversely, an Ivy League education, a Ph.D. in economics, and being a Federal Reserve Bank president tended to describe those FOMC members who voted more conservatively over their tenure.

These results appear to paint a significantly different picture of FOMC members than the one officially put forward. Despite their technical expertise, FOMC members seem to be unable to avoid the subjectivity that inherently accompanies policy-making. As Kane (1982, p. 222) described it, "some opinions may be better informed and less self-serving than others, but all of them are affected by the owner's perspective as an interested member of various political and economic groups." It is from this perspective that monetary policy-making should be judged. Continued failure on the part of Congress to enact meaningful guidelines for FOMC members to follow will perpetuate discretionary monetary policies. Further attempts by Congress to encourage greater disclosure of monetary policy-making should include a better understanding of the discretionary role individual FOMC members play. Just as fiscal policy-makers outline their preferences in their campaigns and as Supreme Court justices' preferences are revealed by their prior voting records, FOMC members' preferences and suspected biases, relative to likely political constraints, should be made as explicit as possible. This would provide more and better information to understand and anticipate future Federal Reserve policies.

Notes

1 Notable exceptions have been Canterbery (1967), Yohe (1966), Woolley (1984), and Puckett (1984). Havrilesky and Schweitzer (this volume) analyze FOMC members' individual dissents over time as functions of the differences between an individual's characteristics and the averages for all FOMC members.
2 A short-run time frame was chosen because many Fed-watchers would agree with Lombra (1979, p. 26) that "the confluence of uncertainty and political pressure encourages the Fed to focus on the short-run and, like fiscal policy-makers, to ignore the long-run cumulative effects of its policy decisions."
3 In an open economy, a case can be made for the importance of a terms-of-trade variable. Although that variable will not explicitly be included in the model, the inclusion of the real interest rate may be thought of as a proxy for the terms-of-trade variable. With a free flow of financial capital, the terms-of-trade variable will be related to the real interest rate.
4 The presidential approval and disapproval ratings were obtained from *The Gallup Poll* (1960–82). Unfortunately, no such index was available for congressional ratings. Instead, for the period of time in which the president was of the same political party as the majority of the House of Representatives, the presidential disapproval rating was used. And for the period of time in which the president was of a different political party than the majority of the House, the presidential approval rating was used.
5 The ex ante real interest rate was approximated by subtracting a moving average of the most recent 12 months' annualized inflation rates from the current month's average federal-funds rate. As measured, a very simple adaptive expectations formulation is assumed.
6 The variable APP assigns a +1 to a Democratic appointee and a −1 to a Republican appointee. The variable APPF differs from APP by assigning a 0 to all of President Ford's appointees. The reason for this modification is that the circumstances surrounding President Ford's appointments may have led to more moderate appointments than otherwise would have been the case.
7 The dummy variable PREGOV assigned a 0 to a governor and a 1 to a president.
8 A correction for heteroscedasticity was made for the continuous variable

(NCTSD) by dividing raw percentages by the number of votes a member cast during his or her tenure.

9 The questionnaire consisted of 11 questions and was sent up to three times to nonresponding members. The questions ranged from inquiries about members' political affiliations to inquiries about their parents' backgrounds. Twenty-one responses were attained from 54 inquiries.

10 This expectation is supported by the work of Woolley (1984) and Puckett (1984).

References

Acheson, Keith, and Chant, John (1973). "Bureaucratic Theory and the Choice of Central Bank Goals," *Journal of Money, Credit and Banking* 5 (May):637–55.

Borins, Sanford (1972). "The Political Economy of the Fed," *Public Policy,* 20:175–98.

Canterbury, E. Ray (1967). "A New Look at Federal Open Market Voting," *Western Economic Journal,* 6(December):25–38.

Cordtz, Dan (1982). "ABC News Closeup – The Money Master." (December).

Havrilesky, Thomas, Sapp, Robert, and Schweitzer, Robert (1977). "Tests of the Federal Reserve's Reaction to the State of the Economy: 1964–74," *Social Science Quarterly,* 55(March):835–52.

Kane, Edward (1980). "Politics and Fed Policymaking," *Journal of Monetary Economics,* 6(April):199–211.

(1982). "External Pressure and the Operations of the Fed," in R. Lombra and W. Witte (eds.), *Political Economy of International and Domestic Monetary Relations,* pp. 211–32. Iowa State University Press.

Lombra, Raymond (1979). "Policy Advice and Policy-Making: Economic, Political, and Social Issues," in Michael Dooley, Herbert Kaufman, and Raymond Lombra (eds.), *The Political Economy of Policy-Making* pp. 13–34. Beverly Hills: Sage.

Lucas, Robert E., Jr. (1976). "Econometric Policy Evaluation: A Critique," in Karl Brunner and Allan H. Meltzer (eds.), *The Phillips Curve and Labor Markets,* pp. 19–46. Amsterdam: North Holland.

Nagel, Stuart S. (1961). "Political Party Affiliations and Judges' Decisions," *American Political Science Review,* 55(December):843–50.

Puckett, Richard (1984). "Federal Open Market Committee Structure and Decisions," *Journal of Monetary Economics,* 14(July):97–104.

Stein, Jerome (1978). "Inflation, Employment, and Stagflation," *Journal of Monetary Economics,* 4(April):193–228.

Tate, C. Neal (1981). "Personal Attribute Models of the Voting Behavior of U.S. Supreme Court Justices," *American Political Science Review,* 75 (June):355–66.

The Federal Reserve System: Purposes and Functions (1974). Washington, D.C.: Board of Governors of the Federal Reserve System.

The Gallup Poll (1960–82). Wilmington, Del.: Scholarly Resources, Inc.

Ulmer, S. Sidney (1970). "Dissent Behavior and the Social Background of Supreme Court Justices," *Journal of Politics,* 32(August):580–97.

Woolley, John (1984). *Monetary Politics: The Federal Reserve and the Politics of Monetary Policy.* Cambridge University Press.

Yohe, William (1966). "A Study of Federal Open Market Committee Voting, 1955–64," *Southern Economic Journal,* 12(April):396–405.

Appendix Table 14.1. *Estimated effects*

Category and variable	Expected effect	Survey		Governors		Presidents		Total	
		NCTSD	CNCTSD	NCTSD	CNCTSD	NCTSD	CNCTSD	NCTSD	CNCTSD
Politicoeconomic									
APPRVL	−		−						
DISAPP	+	+		+	+			+	+
CONDIS	+					+	+		
AEND	−								
MSDEV	+								
Career									
APP	+			+					
APPF	+				+				
PART	+				+			+	+
YRSGOV	+						+		
YRSFRB	+	+							
YRSIND	+			+		+	+		
PREGOV	−								−
PHDE	−	−			−			−	
YRSACA	−								−
CMAR	−								
CBUR	+			+	+				
Social background									
POLAF	+	+	+						
PRED	−		−			−			

CHAPTER 15

Fed behavior and X-efficiency theory: toward a general framework

HARINDER SINGH AND ROGER FRANTZ

In this chapter a conceptual framework developed from the insights of X-efficiency (XE) theory is employed to analyze the behavior and performance of the Fed. Our analysis makes two major points of departure. First, the extreme public-choice and neoclassical perspectives are regarded as limiting cases. In our framework, the Fed attempts to strike a trade-off between (1) increasing its own organizational welfare (public-choice perspective) and (2) increasing public welfare (neoclassical perspective). Second, from the perspective of XE theory, we regard completely optimal behavior by the Fed as a limiting case, because this perspective allows for the existence of behavior that is less than completely optimal behavior, or X-inefficient behavior. However, this contention does not imply that Fed policy-makers are selfish or incompetent. X-inefficiency is a ubiquitous phenomenon that exists (at least to some degree) in almost all organizations, in spite of best intentions and vigilance. The precise extent of X-inefficiency in an organization may be controversial. Its potential existence should not be ruled out on a priori grounds.

Ideally, this assertion should be backed by numerous examples of X-inefficiency in the Fed. However, because there is always considerable controversy about the precise optimal monetary response in a specific situation, it is difficult to assert with certainty that a given Fed response or behavior is X-inefficient. Janis and Mann (1977) concede that within an organization, frequently it is impossible to carry out adequately controlled field experiments that permit unambiguous determination of the causal impact of alternative decision-making styles and procedures. Our problem is even more intractable because the responses themselves are controversial. One solution adopted by Janis and Mann is to analyze the quality of decision-making and operational procedures employed by an

We gratefully acknowledge extensive comments by Tom Mayer regarding the first draft of this manuscript.

organization. The implied presumption is that "good" procedures are likely to result in relatively optimal decision-making ability. Following this line of argument, we view the quality of decision-making and operational procedures of the Fed as providing indirect evidence about the ability to make optimal decisions. Another form of indirect evidence that we analyze consists of econometric studies, which tend to show that there is considerable slack in not only the operation of firms but also in public-sector undertakings and commercial banks. The third form of indirect evidence is the existence of various types of dysfunctional behaviors in the decision-making processes of groups and organizations. We discuss some empirical results to show the widespread prevalence of this phenomenon. If X-inefficiency is prevalent in different types of organizations, its potential existence in the Fed becomes more likely.

Finally, it may be noted that X-inefficiency may exist in the Fed because of another important determinant: the role of pressure in determining performance. A major postulate of XE theory is that initially the quality of decision-making performance improves with additional pressure, at least up to a point, beyond which additional pressure may actually reduce performance. This pressure–performance relationship is corroborated by a modern interpretation of the Yerkes-Dodson law, which has been empirically verified in a wide variety of experimental contexts. This psychological law stipulates that stress or pressure improves performance up to a point, beyond which increases in pressure reduce performance (Broadbent 1971). In this context, Friedman (1982) contends that the basic problem with the Fed is the absence of a bottom line (i.e., it is not answerable to an electorate or subject to a budget constraint). If the Fed is not under adequate pressure to perform, there is potential for greater X-inefficiency.

In the first section we develop a general framework for analyzing Fed behavior. The second section analyzes various forms of empirical evidence about the existence of X-inefficiency.

XE theory and a general framework

Leibenstein's XE theory (1966) focuses on nonallocative efficiency: Its origins are nonmarket phenomena prevalent inside the firm. The basic source of X-inefficiency is that an individual exhibits both optimal (maximizing) and nonoptimal behavior. Maximizing behavior – the assumption of traditional neoclassical theory – is regarded as a limiting case (Frantz, 1988; Leibenstein, 1986). Consequently, maximizing behavior is one extreme point along a continuum of behavior, ranging from com-

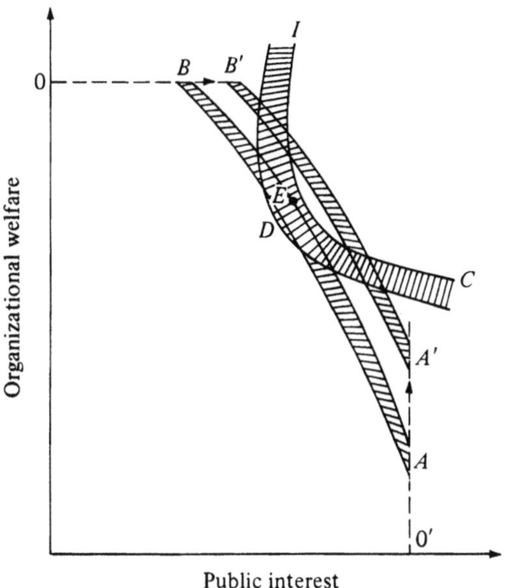

Figure 15.1. Organizational welfare versus public interest

pletely optimal to completely nonoptimal. The actual operation on this continuum depends on the pressures to be rational. There is always a certain amount of slack in the activity inside the firm (i.e., intrafirm activity), particularly because contracts are incomplete. Time can be contracted, but individual effort and motivational level are subject to considerable discretion. As pointed out earlier, a major implication of XE theory is that the level of slack inside the firm depends on the level of pressure exerted on the individuals and the organization.

The basic tools of microeconomics can be employed to show how the Fed "adjusts" to an acceptable mixture of both objectives (i.e., attempting to maximize its own organizational welfare as well as the public interest). We do not believe that the Fed should be viewed as an optimizing agent, in the rigid neoclassical sense. Consequently, instead of employing the normative notion of "optimizing," we prefer to use the descriptive term "adjusting."

Consider Figure 15.1. The Fed conceivably can spend all its time and effort in increasing either its own organizational welfare or the public interest. However, this does not imply that if the Fed solely pursues one objective, it does not make some progress toward the other objective.

Even if the Fed devotes all its time and effort to improving the public interest, it also partly increases its own welfare (given by the distance $0'A$ in Figure 15.1). Striving for and achieving public goals may bring a sense of accomplishment (especially to the public-spirited), popular acclaim, and even material benefits (depending on the prevailing reward structure). Conversely, to the extent that its own organizational welfare is intertwined with the general welfare of the economy, solely attempting to achieve its own interest will also imply enhancing the public interest (given by $0B$ in Figure 15.1). The curve AB expresses the environmental constraint: given the social, political, economic, and administrative conditions prevailing at a particular time, what the Fed can do to strike a trade-off between the two sets of goals. XE theory implies that the thickness of the AB line depends on the amount of slack in the organization. Traditional neoclassical theory views AB as a thin line, implying that the firm is always on the production-possibility frontier.

The proponents of the public-choice approach contend that a "revised" monetary constitution should be such that the goals of public interest and organizational welfare are more congruent, so that the Fed will be inclined to pursue both goals simultaneously. In our framework, this implies a change in the basic environment, so that the AB curve shifts rightward to $A'B'$.

What the Fed can do, given the environmental constraints, and what it wants to do are two different things. The "tastes" of the Fed, in terms of attempting a trade-off between the two objectives, are captured by an indifference curve: On this curve the Fed is indifferent between incremental increases in public interest and organizational welfare (the IC curve in Figure 15.1). The psychic trade-off between the two objectives may depend on factors such as organizational traditions and conventions, the background profiles of its management personnel, and subtle biases in its research programs. A Fed composed of personnel who are highly public-service-oriented will have an indifference curve that is relatively flat, resulting in a "stable comfort level" weighted in favor of public-interest goals, within the context of an AB curve specified by the prevailing environment. The indifference curve is also thick, because psychological and perceptual difficulties may lead to a lack of sensitivity (inertia) in the trade-off between the two objectives.

This framework allows the possibility of operational inefficiency (thick AB curves) as well as perceptual and psychological difficulties experienced by the decision-makers (thick indifference curves). In the next section we discuss a variety of empirical evidence to demonstrate that such X-inefficiencies are likely to be prevalent in the Fed, at least to some degree.

Does X-inefficiency exist?

Since Leibenstein's seminal paper (1966) on XE theory, at least 60 empirical investigations have confirmed the existence of some form of X-inefficiency in both public-sector and private-sector organizations. A detailed evaluation of these empirical results is available (Frantz 1988). Our first form of indirect evidence comes from discussing some representative empirical studies, particularly of public-sector undertakings and the commercial banking industry. The existence of X-inefficiency in these undertakings provides a pertinent clue concerning its potential existence in the Fed. Our second form of indirect evidence derives from analyzing major findings regarding group and organizational decision-making abilities. The existence of suboptimal decision-making procedures in groups and organizations implies that some form of dysfunctional behavior may exist in the Fed. Finally, we discuss the quality of operational and decision-making procedures adopted by the Fed. The presumption is that if these procedures are suboptimal, the Fed is likely to make decisions in a suboptimal manner, resulting in potentially greater X-inefficiency.

Econometric evidence

Medoff and Fay (1985) analyzed the short-run labor–output relationships in 168 U.S. manufacturing plants. One of the major findings of that extensive study was that labor is not paid according to the value of its marginal product. A typical plant paid 8 percent more "blue-collar hours" than were needed for regular production. This result implies that these firms were not on their production-possibility frontiers. Fair (1985) made an aggregate test of a similar hypothesis and found results consistent with the Medoff and Fay (1985) results. Several studies of public-sector undertakings have demonstrated the existence of considerable slack in these organizations. Silkman and Young (1982) studied the costs of (1) providing local school transportation among 1,317 school districts and (2) local library services for 749 local public libraries. Estimation of the cost frontier and deviations from the frontier revealed that the cost of providing school transportation per student per year was $67.07 for the most efficient provider and $142.72 for the average provider. Similarly, the most efficient local libraries provided volume-hours at $0.24, whereas the cost for average libraries was $0.78. They found that schools and libraries that received a higher share of their funds from local sources had significantly lower costs of production, implying that one tends to monitor local (own) money expenditure more carefully.

Similarly, Tyler (1979) found that large amounts of effective protection for domestic and publicly owned plastics and steel firms, in various countries, made them relatively inefficient compared with foreign firms. For instance, in the plastics industry, the average efficiency rating for public firms was 0.56, whereas for foreign firms the corresponding number was 0.72. One of Tyler's interpretations of the results was that domestic and publicly owned firms had relatively larger X-inefficiencies than did foreign firms. Gillis (1982), on the basis of firsthand reports of activities within firms, also found a relatively large amount of X-inefficiency among publicly owned tin-mining firms in both Bolivia and Indonesia.

In the commercial banking industry, several studies have demonstrated the existence of slack, which is consistent with the implications of XE theory. Edwards's empirical analyses (1977) of the banking industry in 44 metropolitan areas supported the expense-preference hypothesis, implying that monopolistic banks have relatively higher labor expenses and larger staffs than do comparable profit-maximizing organizations. Glassman and Rhoades (1980) analyzed the largest banks of 1,406 bank holding companies for 1975 and 1986. They found that at every level of market share, owner-controlled banks had significantly higher profit rates than did manager-controlled banks. In a similar vein, Fraser and Rose (1972) showed that the entry of 56 independent-unit banks in 49 towns (each with 1–3 banks) during the period 1962–4 significantly improved the performances of existing banks: Loan–asset ratios increased, greater emphasis was placed on business and consumer loans, and better service and increased output were achieved with no change in costs. These types of empirical findings provide some indirect evidence about the possible existence of X-inefficiency in the Fed.

Psychological dysfunction in organizations

Lindbloom (1959) has suggested that organizations sometimes adopt a "successive limited comparisons" method of decision-making, also termed "muddling through." This procedure is particularly relevant when the comprehensive method (in which all possible alternatives are objectively evaluated) is difficult to implement. The specific circumstances in which the muddling-through approach is likely to be employed require detailed elaboration, because the Fed's decision-making appears to be undertaken in similar conditions. First, a comprehensive analysis is difficult, because policy-makers are confronted with values that conflict with each other and are not amenable to any unequivocal ranking procedure. Second, the ranking of these values, at least at the margin, changes over time. Third, the selection of values or goals and the empirical analysis needed for action are hopelessly intertwined, so that decision-making cannot follow in a logical sequence. Finally, in the absence of clear theoretical guidelines, we may be compelled to employ a method of comparative analysis whereby successive incremental changes allow movements toward more distant objectives.

When we consider the circumstances, particularly the informational constraints under which the Fed makes policy decisions, it appears that all five of these conditions apply to some extent. Consider the Fed's basic dilemma: simultaneously attempting to avoid the risk of a recession and inflationary pressure. These two goals conflict and are difficult to rank, and information about their realization is initially always tentative and incomplete. Consequently, the Fed attempts to strike a tradeoff by a series of sequential, consensus decisions that are made as new information about the risks of inflation and recession becomes available. With these information constraints, a comprehensive evaluation of all possible alternatives usually is difficult to implement, and a muddling-through approach sometimes is the only available alternative.

This does not, however, imply that decision-making at the Fed is always performed in an optimal (although sequential) manner. There is persuasive evidence indicating that policy-making groups and organizations can regress into suboptimal decision-making in spite of their best intentions (Weiss et al. 1985). Hackman, Brousseau, and Weiss (1985), analyzing the task performances of experimental groups, found that strategy discussion occurred rarely. Most groups routinely applied an initial strategy (which had been successful in the past) without considering alternatives. A persuasive study by Gersick (1984) of real task groups working under deadlines suggested that groups may have natural tendencies to change behavior under certain circumstances. Gersick found that the task groups she studied went through a period of strategy reevaluation when one-half of the group's project time had been exhausted. Janis and Mann (1977) described the flawed decision process of policy-making groups engaged in "group-think." Their symptoms of flawed decision-making – poor information search, incomplete survey of alternatives, failure to examine the risks of the preferred course of action – were consequences of the group's concurrence-seeking tendencies, arising from such antecedent conditions as group cohesiveness and stress. McClelland (1984) showed that groups required to make repetitive judgments developed the same set of symptoms in the absence of stress and high cohesiveness. Groups engaged in a judgment task showed reductions in strategy discussion, information search, and reaction periods as a result of engaging in the task over repeated trials.

Within this context, XE theory has emphasized the role of "inert areas" in determining inefficiency. Inertia is a ubiquitous administrative and social phenomenon. The obvious form of inertia is not doing anything. A less obvious form of inertia is doing something according to a well-organized, timeworn pattern. Both are examples of invariant behavior. Inertia can manifest itself in routinization of responses. Initially a procedure or a convention may imply efficiency. Because a successful response tends to be applied repeatedly, eventually a routine may imply an inability to cope with changing environmental demands (Weiss et al. 1985). Starbuck and Hedberg (1977) have described this process in their "success breeds failure" explanation of organizational decline. Organizations tend to focus only on those salient features of the environment that suggest the use of well-established programs. These programs remain in force long after the situation they fit has faded away. Gilad, Kaish, and Loeb (1985) provided a detailed analysis of recent business failures (Atari and Continental Illinois Bank). They found that the primary cause of such failures was that for a relatively long period of time, environmental information that was contrary to the leaders' beliefs was simply ignored, until it was too late. Danning Miller and Manfred Vries (1984), two psychologists with extensive research experience in organizational problems, have pointed out the strong similarity between the dysfunctional neurotic behavior of individuals and that of organizations. Actual profiles of firms depicting paranoid, compulsive, repressive, and schizoid tendencies have been derived to illustrate the similarities.

Operational and decision-making procedures of the Fed

The pertinent question arises: To what degree are these empirical results applicable to the Fed's behavior and performance? Although the question cannot be answered definitely, consider the following indirect evidence. From reading the FOMC minutes, it becomes clear that there is a weak link between the technical research in the Fed and the actual utilization of that research as an important input for decision-making. The economists at the Fed have an incentive to write highly technical papers that generate professional prestige. However, in spite of the technical backgrounds of most members, the FOMC discussions are remarkably casual and general. One possible explanation for this phenomenon proposed by Hetzel (this volume) is that it allows the FOMC members to bend to political pressures. According to Janis and Mann (1977), empirical investigations have demonstrated that highly cohesive groups tend to have an excessive concurrence-seeking tendency. The collective cognitive resources of a cohesive group are employed to develop rationalizations about shared illusions and to generate a collective pattern of defensive avoidance. Some of this group-think activity may be prevalent in Fed policy-making, because FOMC members generally have had similar economic and financial experiences. This does not, however, imply that relevant background characteristics of the decision-makers are not important.

John Gildea (this volume) has demonstrated that background variables such as the number of years on the Federal Reserve Board, political affiliation, educational background, and so forth, significantly affect the voting behavior of FOMC members. Similarly, Havrilesky and Schweitzer (this volume) have shown that FOMC members who dissent on the side of ease are close, in terms of "career proximity," to the central government. Conversely, those who dissent on the side of tightness do not have close career proximity to the central government. These investigations provide indirect evidence implying that decision-making is not based solely on objective facts, but is also affected by the subjective evaluations of policy-makers.

Following Janis and Mann (1977), we believe that the quality of the procedures employed by the decision-maker provides indirect evidence about the extent of vigilant (optimal) decision-making. We have commented on the quality of some of the decision-making procedures, such as the inadequate utilization of technical research and the tendency to adopt a muddling-through approach. An analysis of the operational procedures also shows some proclivity toward unsuitable and/or obsolete procedures. Friedman (1982) discusses three such procedures: (1) the use of lagged-reserves accounting (in spite of the resulting volatility of free reserves and the federal-funds rate); (2) the excessive amount of "churning" by defense open-market operations (leading to greater uncertainty in money-market conditions); (3) applying a shifting base, that is, employing the actual (not targeted) level of the previous quarter for computing the projections of various money-stock growth rates (thereby essentially burying, in the base, any failure to achieve the target).

In two insightful papers, Tom Mayer (1987, 1988) has provided various examples of Fed behavior that are consistent with cognitive-dissonance theory and other behavioral heuristics, such as anchoring and representativeness. For instance, the Fed has preferred to target interest rates rather than monetary aggregates, partly because the former can be precisely targeted, in spite of the general criticism that interest-rate targeting results in a pro-cyclical monetary policy. We are not in a position to assert that these procedures definitely reflect suboptimal decision-making, because the benefits of these procedures are controversial. However, the preponderance of the evidence indicates that they are not entirely optimal.

Conclusion

On the basis of the insights obtained from XE theory, we have developed a general model of Fed behavior that incorporates the public-choice and neoclassical perspectives as limiting cases and also allows for suboptimal behavior.

The broad picture of the Fed that emerges is that of an administrative organization striving to attain a "comfort level" between organizational and public-interest objectives, constrained by the prevailing economic situation and the institutional arrangement, as well as by its own perceptual and organizational difficulties. In a sense, the framework does not tell us anything we do not already know. However, it does help in developing a balanced perspective and providing an integrated view of a complex issue. Judgments about the emphasis placed on different factors within this general framework may differ, but we should not continue to ignore the various dimensions implied by the framework.

We have provided indirect empirical evidence regarding the potential existence of X-inefficiency in public-sector undertakings and in the banking industry. Experimental evidence also indicates the existence of considerable dysfunctional behavior when groups or organizations make decisions. Moreover, Fed decision-making and operational procedures do not appear to be completely optimal. These three sources of indirect evidence lead us to believe that there is considerable potential for X-inefficiency to exist in the Fed. The precise extent of X-inefficiency, however, will continue to be controversial.

References

Broadbent, D. E. (1971). *Decisions and Stress*. London: Academic Press.

Edwards, Franklin (1977). "Managerial Objectives in Regulated Industries: Expense-Preference Behavior in Banking," *Journal of Political Economy*, 85(1):147–62.

Fair, Ray C. (1985). "Excess Labor and the Business Cycle," *American Economic Review*, 75(1):239–45.

Frantz, R. (1988). *X-Efficiency: Theory, Evidence and Applications*. Boston: Kluwer.

Fraser, Donald, and Rose, Peter (1972). "Bank Entry and Bank Performance," *Journal of Finance*, 27:65–77.

Friedman, Milton. (1982). "Monetary Policy: Theory and Practice," *Journal of Money, Credit and Banking,* 14:98–118.

Gersick, C. (1984). "The Life Cycles of Ad Hoc Groups: Time, Transition and Learning in Teams," unpublished doctoral dissertation, Yale University.

Gilad, B., Kaish, S., and Loeb, P. D. (1985). "A Theory of Surprise and Business Failure," *Journal of Behavioral Economics,* 14:35–53.

Gillis, Malcolm (1982). "Allocative and X-Efficiency in State Owned Mining Enterprises: Comparisons between Bolivia and Indonesia," *Journal of Comparative Economics,* 6(March):1–23.

Glassman, Cynthia, and Rhoades, Stephen (1980). "Owner vs. Manager Control Effects on Bank Performance," *Review of Economics and Statistics,* 62(May):263–70.

Hackman, J. R., Brousseau, K. R., and Weiss, J. A. (1985). "The Interaction of Task Design and Group Performance Strategies in Determining Group Effectiveness," *Organizational Behavior and Human Performance,* 16:350–65.

Janis, Irving, and Mann, Leon (1977). *Decision Making: A Psychological Analysis of Conflict, Choice and Commitment.* New York: Free Press.

Leibenstein, H. (1966). "Allocative Efficiency vs. X-Efficiency," *American Economic Review,* 56(June):392–415.

(1986). "On Relaxing the Maximization Postulates," *Journal of Behavioral Economics,* 15(Winter):2–16.

Lindbloom, C. E. (1959). "The Science of Muddling Through," *Public Administration Review,* 19:79–99.

McClelland, C. L. (1984). "The Development and Persistence of Routinized Group Decision Making," unpublished master's thesis, Purdue University.

Mayer, Thomas (1987). "Minimizing Regret as an Explanation of Fed Policy: An Application of Cognitive Dissonance Theory," working paper no. 49, University of California, Davis.

(1988). "Interpreting Federal Reserve Behavior," working paper no. 52, University of California, Davis.

Medoff, James, and Fay, John (1985). "Labor and Output over the Business Cycle: Some Direct Evidence," *American Economic Review,* 75:638–55.

Miller, Danning, and Vries, Manfred (1984). *The Neurotic Organization.* San Francisco: Jossey-Bass.

Silkman, R., and Young, D. (1982). "X-Inefficiency and State Formula Grants," *National Tax Journal,* 35(September):383–97.

Starbuck, W., and Hedberg, B. (1977). "Saving an Organization from Stationary Environment," in H. Thorelli (ed.), *Strategy + Structure = Performance,* pp. 110–32. Bloomington: Indiana University Press.

Tyler, W. (1979). "Technical Efficiency in Production in a Developing Country: An Empirical Examination of the Brazilian Plastics and Steel Industries," *Oxford Economic Papers,* 31(November):77–95.

Weiss, Howard, and Ilgen, Daniel (1985). "Routinized Behavior in Organizations," *Journal of Behavioral Economics,* 14(Winter):57–68.

CHAPTER 16

Minimizing regret: cognitive dissonance as an explanation of FOMC behavior

THOMAS MAYER

The case against discretionary monetary policy rests on two bases. One is technical: Monetary policy has long and variable lags, and forecasts are inaccurate. The second is that monetary policy is not made by a philosopher-king who efficiently uses all available information and always puts the public interest ahead of his own interest. Friedman argues that one need not attribute evil intent to Fed officials to conclude that they often put the Fed's self-interest ahead of the public interest.

> I am not saying that people in the [Federal Reserve] system deliberately pursue these measures for these reasons. Not at all. . . . I am trying to analyze the forces at work, and not to describe the detailed motivation or personal behavior of the people involved. All of us know that what is good for us is good for the country. . . . We all know that what we are doing is important, that it performs a real and useful function. . . . I am not criticizing specific individuals. . . . I have often argued that the human species is distinguished from animals much more by its ability to rationalize than to reason. (Friedman 1982, p. 116)

Nonetheless, many economists seem to interpret the monetarist's belief that the Fed does not wholeheartedly pursue the public interest as an attack on the integrity of Fed policy-makers. Many economists know these policy-makers personally and know them to be devoted public servants. Hence, they find any attack on the Fed's intentions entirely implausible.

But Friedman cites several examples of Fed behavior that many of these same economists might find hard to explain as rational choices by a central bank that is concerned only with the public interest. A promising solution to this puzzle is to qualify – though not to reject – the rationality assumption. Many economists treat the Fed as an agent who evaluates all the available information entirely uninfluenced by wishes, fears,

I am indebted to Richard Thaler for the basic idea for this chapter – that Fed policy-makers try to minimize regret – and to John Gildea, Robert Hetzel, and Stephen Sheffrin for helpful comments.

and other emotions. I shall argue here, as well as in a companion paper (Mayer 1989), that this "well-intentioned robot" hypothesis of Fed behavior is invalid, that the thinking of Fed officials is, like the thinking of others, influenced by a subjective factor: the fear of having occasionally to confront the realization that one has made a mistake. This takes the sharp edge off the dichotomy between pursuing the public interest and self-interest. If policy-makers did not care about the public interest, they would not care about their mistakes that never became known to others. But at the same time, by favoring policies whose failures, if they do fail, will not become apparent, they act (unconsciously) in their self-interest.

The policy-maker's utility function

The utility functions of Fed policy-makers contain three arguments. The first, which may play only a small role, is the personal welfare of the officials and their agency irrespective of the public welfare. The second is the public welfare, regardless of whether or not a loss experienced by the public is due to the Fed's action. The third is the policy-makers' perception of the effects of their actions on the public welfare. It seems plausible that a given loss to the public will be much more painful for policy-makers if they realize that it is due to their actions. Hence, they have an incentive to adopt policies whose failures, if failures there be, cannot be laid at their door. They do this not only because they wish to avoid criticism by others but also (and perhaps to a greater extent) because they want to avoid self-criticism. In other words, they unconsciously act to minimize regret.[1] Along these lines, while crediting monetary policy with what went right, they will tend to blame other developments for what went wrong.

A regret-avoidance theory is the mirror image of standard public-choice theory. The latter sees policy-makers as driven in large part by a wish to enhance the power they exercise, whereas the former sees them as trying to reduce their feelings of responsibility when a policy turns sour. In actuality, policy-makers are, of course, driven by both motives. Those who do not enjoy exercising power usually do not become policy-makers, but probably few policy-makers are indifferent to feelings of guilt.

Is regret avoidance consistent with rational behavior? This depends on whether or not one considers the wish to avoid confronting one's mistake to be a "taste." If so, it is neither rational nor irrational. But regardless of whether or not it is rational, as Thaler (1980), Thaler and Shefrin (1981), and Akerlof and Dickens (1982) have shown, several otherwise puzzling types of behavior, such as the frequent absence of deductibles in medical insurance and the existence of many precommitting contracts, can be explained by the wish to avoid feelings of regret.

Cognitive-dissonance theory

The hypothesis that people act so as to avoid having to realize that they have made mistakes rests on a psychological theory called cognitive-dissonance theory. Aronson (1980, pp. 102–3) described the basis of this theory as follows:

> Cognitive dissonance is a state of tension that occurs whenever an individual simultaneously holds two cognitions (ideas, attitudes, beliefs, opinions) that are psychologically inconsistent. . . . Two cognitions are dissonant if, considering these cognitions alone, the opposite of one follows from the other. Because the occurrence of cognitive dissonance is unpleasant, people are motivated to reduce it. . . . How do we reduce cognitive dissonance? By changing one or both cognitions in such a way as to render them more compatible (more consonant) with each other, or by adding new cognitions that help bridge the gap between the original cognitions.

Aronson (1980, pp. 125, 143) reformulated the theory in a way that suggested that

> dissonance is most powerful in situations in which the self-concept is threatened. Thus for me the important aspect of dissonance [in an experiment in which the subjects were induced to lie] is not that the cognition that "I said *X*" is dissonant with the cognition that "I believe 'not *X*.' " Rather the crucial fact is that I have misled people. The cognition "I have said something I don't believe and it could have bad consequences for people" is dissonant with my self-concept; that is, it is dissonant with my cognition that "I am a decent, reasonable, truthful person." . . . Those individuals with the highest self-esteem experience the most dissonance when they behave in a stupid or cruel manner.

An important implication of cognitive-dissonance theory is that people seek out information that will justify their previously made decisions. Hence,

> once a small commitment is made it sets the stage for ever-increasing commitments. The behavior needs to be justified, so attitudes are changed. One of the key determinants of whether . . . a person engages in distortion . . . after a decision is the irrevocability of the decision. (Aronson 1980, pp. 114, 116)[2]

Another implication is the occurrence of "group-think," that is, pressure on each member of the group to agree with the group's consensus.

There exists much experimental evidence for cognitive-dissonance theory.[3] Here are some of the experiments cited by Aronson (1980): In one experiment in which people were presented with good arguments and poor arguments on both sides of an issue, they tended to remember not only the plausible arguments on their side but also the poor arguments on the other side. Another experiment showed that people rate a boring job they have agreed to do as more interesting if their pay is low than if they are paid better for it. Similarly, once people have actually placed their bets on their horses, they are more convinced that they will win than they were before they irrevocably placed their bets.[4] Although specific aspects of cognitive-dissonance theory have been challenged by some psychologists (White 1982), this theory is widely accepted by psychologists.

Implications for policy-making

Cognitive-dissonance theory implies that policy-makers try to protect themselves from feeling regret. An obvious way is to avoid responsibility by surrendering autonomy. For example, the Fed could ask the president to make hard decisions it now makes.

An alternative is for policy-makers to (falsely) deny to themselves that they are really making decisions. They may assert that they are merely ratifying decisions imposed by external events – the classic justification for painful decisions under the gold standard. Such a claim that the policy is inevitable and is not a matter of choice can be rationalized in either of two ways. One is to argue that it is required by a theory that is "obviously" correct. The other is to deny that the decision is based on any theory at all and to claim that it is the required pragmatic response to events. The latter claim has two advantages. First, it can be used where, as is true for monetary policy, there often is no generally accepted theory. Second, if the policy-makers rely explicitly on a theory, and that theory is subsequently shown to be wrong, they feel guilty for having followed the wrong policy for so long. By contrast, with a pragmatic approach the policy-maker reduces risk by diversifying. Thus, a former governor, Henry Wallich (1982, p. 243), wrote that when Keynesians and monetarists disagree, the "Board and the FOMC will be reasonably safe in the middle. If they duck in between, the two sides will be shooting at each other."

Moreover, policy-makers can reduce cognitive dissonance by the choice of their goals. One way is to select goals that are strongly affected by the actions of others, who can then be blamed in case of failure. Alternatively, policy-makers can select targets that are easy to attain, even though these targets may have little relevance for the ultimate goals that they are supposed to achieve. Still another way is to focus on unimportant targets, where failure will cause little harm.

Policy-makers can also reduce feelings of guilt by employing numerous capable experts, so that they can claim that any damage their policies do is not their fault – "We followed the best available advice." But experts can be dangerous. If they disagree among themselves, policy-makers still face the responsibility of making the decision, but in addition, whichever side they choose, they may be confronted with sophisticated arguments for the other side, arguments that may well be stronger than any they would have thought of on their own. Often, the more one knows about a problem, the less strong is one's conviction about its solution. To obtain the best of both worlds, policy-makers have an incentive to do either of two things. One is to filter the staff's work through a small group of senior staff members, or perhaps just one person. This group then either presents a single recommendation or, if it does present various options, comes down clearly in favor of one of these options. The other "out" is to have the staff engage primarily in those types of research that have little relevance for policy-making, such as elaborate descriptions of institutional details, or highly abstract models. Policy-makers can then tell themselves that they have taken the precaution of acquiring a first-rate staff, more or less ignoring that they have not made effective use of it.

In addition, cognitive dissonance can be reduced by shutting out information that shows the policy to be wrong. This is often accomplished by what Janis (1982) has called "group-think," that is, by bringing pressure to bear on any member of the group who opposes the consensus of the group. Hence, policy-makers tend to stay too long with policies that events have shown to be wrong.

One way that the Fed can shut out unwelcome information is to blame bad macroeconomic developments on factors other than monetary policy (e.g., OPEC or fiscal policy), though taking credit when macroeconomic performance is good.

Moreover, policy-makers can try to avoid basing policy on information that can subsequently be refuted by new evidence. Thus, they are tempted to give excessive preference to relatively solid but less relevant information.

Does regret avoidance explain some aspects of Fed behavior?

One would not expect the Fed to use all of these devices for avoiding cognitive dissonance. Anyone who shuts out all conflicting information is not likely to be successful enough to become a policy-maker. Moreover, if minimizing regret means exercising less power, policy-makers may be willing to accept some regret rather than relinquish power. Only those who enjoy power tend to become policy-makers. Cognitive-dissonance theory suggests only that there are *some* aspects of Fed behavior that can be explained better by a wish of human policy-makers to avoid feelings of guilt than as rational choices by a well-intentioned robot.

The first-mentioned implication of cognitive-dissonance theory, that the Fed might abdicate its policy-making responsibilities, is not borne out. The Fed has jealously protected its powers. To be sure, it rarely, if ever, opposes the main thrust of the monetary policy that the president desires (Weintraub 1978; Woolley 1984; Havrilesky 1987; Havrilesky and Schweitzer, this volume), but one does not need cognitive-dissonance theory to explain that. In part it is explained by the belief that unelected Fed officials do not have the right to deny the president the overall monetary policy he or she desires, and in part it is a rational response to the Fed's relative lack of political power (Maisel 1973).

As previously mentioned, policy-makers can reduce cognitive dissonance either by adhering to a theory dogmatically or, at the other extreme, by an atheoretical pragmatism. The Fed clearly has chosen the latter. It makes policy by intuitive feel and pays little attention to more formal economic reasoning; from reading the FOMC minutes, one would hardly know that many of the participants are professional economists.[5]

Does the Fed choose those tasks for itself that make it hard to blame the Fed when things go wrong, or those that are easy to achieve? One must distinguish here between goals and targets. The Fed's goals – high employment, low inflation, and appropriate exchange rates – are certainly difficult to reach. But many other factors besides monetary policy impinge on employment and exchange rates (and, in the short run, on inflation), and so the Fed can claim that it is not responsible for failure to attain these goals. Moreover, having multiple goals allows policy-makers to think that failure to reach one goal results from the need to take care of some conflicting goal. The Fed has fought legislative attempts, dating back to the 1920s, to make it concentrate on a single goal: price stability (Hetzel 1985). Its opposition may be due in part to the policy-makers' fear that if they had only a single goal, they would have less excuse for failing to achieve it. This is a familiar point when looked at as an attempt by the Fed to minimize accountability to others, but it is also accountability to themselves that bothers Fed policy-makers.

The Fed's uses of experts is generally consistent with cognitive-dissonance theory. The Fed has a large and excellent staff, but if rumors and general impressions can be trusted, that staff seems to have disappointingly little influence on policy. Much of its work consists of sophisticated and often esoteric analyses that are not likely to have much effect on day-to-day policy.[6] Moreover, at least until recently, if rumors can be believed, the staff's work was channeled through a filter that made its results seem more nearly unanimous, and in accord with the FOMC's current policy, than was justified. Cobb (1978, p. 16) has described the staff's morning briefings of the governors as follows:

> junior members of the staff . . . tell an interesting story of how official business is conducted. . . . The Monday briefings are tightly orchestrated by the senior staff to ensure that none of the more junior economists, who are present to make reports or answer questions, are likely to disagree with one another – or with their superiors. . . . There is only one acceptable point of view and it is usually that of staff director Steve Axilrod.

However, in one important way, the Fed's use of its staff does not conform to the predictions of cognitive-dissonance theory. By allowing the Federal Reserve Banks to have strong research departments, the Board of Governors provided leeway for dissenting voices to be heard.[7]

Does the FOMC shut out disconcerting information and indulge in "group-think"? Within the FOMC there seems to be some group-think. There is strong pressure not to dissent from the Directive. Jerry Jordan, a former economist at the St. Louis Bank, in discussing the FOMC's minutes, stated that

> the President of the St. Louis Federal Reserve Bank was definitely influenced in a very positive way by the existence of a permanent record. . . . It helped him and his staff to maintain intellectual honesty, *sometimes in the face of great pressure to bend.* (U.S. Congress 1979, p. 216, emphasis added)

The chapter by Havrilesky and Schweitzer in this volume provides additional evidence on the pressure not to dissent at FOMC meetings. Much, probably most, of that pressure occurs because the Fed's political stature is enhanced if it presents a unified front. But it is plausible that some of that pressure occurs because of the desire to reduce cognitive dissonance.

The Fed has a definite tendency – not all of which need be a matter of public relations – to take credit when things go well and to blame others when things go badly. As Friedman (1982, pp. 115–16) put it,

> statements by the chairman of the Federal Reserve to congressional committees have a common script. If things have gone well in the economy . . . the chairman explains that it was all due to the wise policies followed by the Fed. If things have gone badly . . . the reason was the limited powers of the Fed to offset external disturbances.[8]

The FOMC has also shown a strong tendency to stick with its policies. Thus, in the 1970s it persisted in trying to stabilize the funds rate, even though that policy both caused inflation and resulted in a pro-cyclical growth rate for the money supply. That policy cannot be explained by saying that targeting interest rates was a reasonable policy, with much support among academic economists, because the Fed was not *targeting* interest rates in the sense of selecting the appropriate funds rate – usually it was stabilizing the funds rate around whatever level it happened to occupy.[9]

The FOMC's response to the lag of monetary policy also seems like an attempt to reduce cognitive dissonance. Estimates of the lag diverge widely, with small models usually showing short lags, whereas big econometric models – including the Fed's own model – generally show long lags. In many of the model simulations tabulated by Christ (1975), the mean impact of monetary policy comes only after 10 quarters.[10] If these models are right, then the Fed needs to forecast far ahead. But according to James Pierce, a former senior FOMC staff economist, long-run forecasts played little role in FOMC decision-making:

> It is difficult if not impossible to produce judgmental forecasts with a horizon much beyond a year. . . . As a result, only the model was available. Some senior staff and many FOMC members had a great distrust of models. As a result, longer-run forecasts were viewed as highly untrustworthy. . . . On several occasions longer-run forecasts were presented to the Federal Reserve Board and the FOMC. These forecasts were not treated seriously by the policy-makers. (Pierce 1980, p. 80)

In principle, one should be able to tell how far ahead the FOMC looks by examining those Fed reaction functions that include current and projected values of the independent variables. But quite apart from the problems with Fed reaction functions discussed by Khoury in this volume, this evidence is mixed. The reaction functions of Lombra and Moran (1980), and of Lombra and Karamouzis in Chapter 12 of this volume, suggest that policy was based more on current conditions than on a forecast. But in the McNees (1986) reaction function, the one-quarter-ahead forecast values of the independent variables performed somewhat better than the observed values of those variables in the previous quarter. Moreover, four-quarter-ahead estimates of the independent variables (which is as far as McNees's study went) performed about as well as one-quarter-ahead forecasts (S. McNees, personal communication, 1987).

Suppose that monetary policy is made on the basis of current conditions or a four-quarter-ahead forecast. If the lag of monetary policy is as great as the big models show, then countercyclical monetary policy may well be destabilizing.

Hence, the FOMC is charged with a task that may be beyond its capacity. How would a well-intentioned robot respond to this dilemma?[11] One possible response would be to undertake an exhaustive study of the lag of monetary policy and of the reliability of long-run forecasts and then, if necessary, announce that countercyclical monetary policy is infeasible. Another possibility might be to take advantage of probable variations in the lag of monetary policy, by undertaking countercyclical policy only in those cases in which the lag is likely to be unusually short.

But cognitive-dissonance theory implies that human policy-makers will respond differently. They will tend to push the problem out of awareness. In addition, they may shift the focus of their attention away from stabilizing GNP toward tasks for which lags are less of a problem, such as stabilizing the monetary growth rate or interest rates.

These responses suggested by cognitive-dissonance theory seem to describe Fed behavior. It is highly unlikely that the Fed has undertaken an exhaustive analysis of the lags of monetary policy.[12] FOMC minutes generally do not include discussions of what the lag of policy is likely to be in the particular case. And the Fed often has been criticized for myopically focusing on the money market (Brunner and Meltzer 1964).

Has the Fed allowed its choices of target variables to be influenced by its wish to avoid cognitive dissonance? It probably has. In selecting its targets, the Fed usually has preferred interest rates to the growth rate of some monetary aggregate. One reason may be that interest-rate targets are easier to attain than monetary-growth-rate targets. The Fed can set the funds rate precisely, but not the monetary growth rate. Hence, the Fed can avoid some apparent failures by using an interest-rate target rather than an aggregates target. This may not be the major reason why the Fed prefers an interest-rate target, but it may be a significant factor.[13]

Another way in which avoiding cognitive dissonance may bias the Fed toward favoring an interest-rate target over a money-stock target is that the current money-stock data available at FOMC meetings are subsequently revised substantially. Suppose that the FOMC is told that money growth is exceeding its target, and it therefore adopts a more restrictive policy. Afterward, when the money data are revised, the FOMC might realize that its restrictive policy and the costs it inflicted on the economy were unnecessary. Interest-rate targeting presents no such danger.

Alternative explanations

Most of the characteristics of Fed behavior explained here as attempts to avoid regret can also be explained by other theories. Thus, in another chapter in this volume, Hetzel traces the FOMC's lack of an underlying theory to political pressures. Similarly, the way the FOMC uses its staff might, at least in part, be explained as a device that helps the chairman to dominate the FOMC. The Fed's focus on current rather than future conditions could be due to the fact that the public and Congress do not know much about the lag of monetary policy, and therefore they tend to object to a policy that seems inappropriate for the current state of the economy. Moreover, public-choice theory can explain the Fed's emphasis on stabilizing interest rates.

When faced with several possible explanations for empirical observations, the standard procedure is to claim that one's own theory yields the better fit, or that it is the more general theory. Neither is appropriate here. The observations are qualitative, and crude at that, so that one cannot readily decide how well each theory fits them. And it is far from clear how to judge the generality of various explanations of Fed behavior.

Moreover, the standard rule of choosing the simplest theory that "explains" the observations is not appropriate here. We observe the Fed doing something, and it seems a logical action if the Fed is motivated by *X*, but it also seems a logical action if the Fed is motivated by *Y*. If it seems plausible that the Fed has both motives, then neither explanation should be dismissed. The crux of the matter is that we cannot quantify the extent of the influences of *X* and *Y* and hence cannot make statements such as this: "If motivation *Y* did not exist, to a first approximation the Fed still would behave just as it does now." Hence, one should not insist on a single explanation.

Conclusion

Cognitive-dissonance theory implies that the Fed will tend to abdicate responsibility, will either adhere rigidly to a theory or go to the other extreme of thoroughgoing pragmatism, will choose goals that either are easy to attain or else are not well under the Fed's control, will use experts as cover, will indulge in group-think, will be slow to abandon failed policies, will pay insufficient attention to the lag of monetary policy, and will have a bias in favor of an interest-rate target. Two of these implications are not borne out. The Fed does not try to reliquish responsibility for macroeconomic policy, and it allows much independence to the research staffs of the Federal Reserve Banks. But the other implications are supported. These characteristics of the Fed can also be explained in other ways, but insofar as the wish to minimize regret has a significant role in explaining them, the Fed should not be treated as though it were a well-intentioned robot.

Hence, there is something more to be said in favor of a stable-monetary-growth-rate rule than just the usual litany of poor forecasts, long and variable lags, the potential for political pressure, and possible self-seeking behavior by the Fed. The psychological pressures that impinge on FOMC members may prevent effective stabilization policy, despite Fed policy-makers being highly capable and having good intentions. It is difficult to determine if these pressures actually prevent the Fed from stabilizing aggregate demand or if they degrade the quality of discretionary policy only to a small extent. But given the existence of the other problems of stabilization policy, the additional problems that result when policy-makers minimize regret may well be sufficient to tip the balance and make countercyclical policy destabilizing.

None of this should be interpreted as Fed-bashing. As the chapter by Singh and Frantz in this volume shows, X-inefficiency is ubiquitous. Moreover, if cognitive dissonance causes the Fed to adopt inappropriate policies, it is precisely because policy-makers do care about the public welfare. Moreover, if to a significant extent Fed policy can be explained by cognitive-dissonance theory, this does not mean that the Fed is less efficient than others. Cognitive-dissonance theory helps to explain the behavior of households (Thaler 1980; Thaler and Shefrin 1981; Tversky and Kahneman 1981), and the greater efficiency of firms may be due to a Darwinian mechanism, not to any greater rationality of their decision-makers.[14]

Notes

1 Minimizing regret differs from the minimax principle of game theory. Here, someone who had a chance to buy a winning ticket in a lottery, but did not do so, is worse off than someone who never had the chance.

2 Such factors might help to explain why empirical studies undertaken by monetarists always seem to elicit monetarist results, whereas those done by Keynesians always generate Keynesian results.

3 The subjects in these experiments usually were students; but it is doubtful that policy-makers show more rationality (Janis 1982; Stockman 1987).

4 For additional examples, see Akerlof and Dickens (1982).

5 See Hetzel's chapter in this volume, and see Brunner and Meltzer (1964), Lombra and Moran (1980), and Mayer (1982a,b).

6 Prior to the quantitative revolution of the 1960s, the Fed's staff seemed to devote an excessive proportion of its efforts to the details of the financial structure, such as the flow-of-funds accounts.

7 Could the Fed suppress or at least reduce these criticisms? It probably could, through its control over the budgets of the Federal Reserve Banks. On whether or not it did use such pressure, see Toma and Toma (1985a,b) and Rolnick (1985).

8 See also Kane (1974). For an example of a former Fed official blaming inflation on external events, see Burns (1987).
9 For a long time, academic critics of interest-rate targeting missed the point that the Fed was stabilizing the funds rate, rather than using it as a target in the sense of setting it at the level that would generate the correct growth rate of GNP. But Fed policy-makers should have realized much sooner than outsiders the peculiar sense in which they "targeted" interest rates.
10 See Christ (1975). The models discussed by Christ were simulated for periods during the 1960s and 1970s, and simulations over more recent years might show different results. However, this is not relevant for explaining the FOMC's behavior at that time.
11 In interviews that I conducted with Fed officials in 1981 about monetary policy in 1973–5, several of them referred to this problem as a "dilemma."
12 Had the Fed undertaken a large-scale study of the lags of monetary policy, one would, in all probability, have heard about it.
13 However, this cannot be the entire explanation of the Fed's preference for interest-rate targets, because the Fed could also hit a total-reserves target (a target recommended by many monetarists) quite accurately. Here the explanation must run differently. If policy is made efficiently, the growth rate of the base is an inferior target to the monetary growth rate because of fluctuations in the money multiplier. The case for using the base rate rather than the monetary growth rate is that the former deprives the Fed of discretion. But Fed policy-makers do not want to admit to themselves that they are not to be trusted with discretion.
14 Academic economists, too, are not immune from problems such as groupthink. What else explains the widespread acceptance of the upside-down use of significance tests, the assumption that failure to reject a hypothesis at the 5% level implies that it should be accepted?

References

Akerlof, George, and Dickens, William (1982). "The Economic Consequences of Cognitive Dissonance," *American Economic Review,* 82:307–19.

Aronson, Elliot (1980). *The Social Animal.* San Francisco: Freeman.

Brunner, Karl, and Meltzer, Allan (1964). *Some General Features of the Federal Reserve's Approach to Policy.* Washington, D.C.: Committee on Banking and Currency, House of Representatives, 88th Congress, 2nd session.

Burns, Arthur (1987). "The Anguish of Central Banking," *Federal Reserve Bulletin,* 73:687–98.

Christ, Carl (1975). "Judging the Performance of Econometric Models of the U.S. Economy," *International Economic Review,* 16:52–74.

Cobb, Joe (1986). "What Makes the Fed Tick?" *Wall Street Journal,* June 2, p. 16.

Friedman, Milton (1982). "Monetary Policy: Theory and Practice," *Journal of Money, Credit and Banking,* 14:98–118.

Havrilesky, Thomas (1987). "A Partisanship Theory of Fiscal and Monetary Regimes," *Journal of Money, Credit and Banking,* 19:308–26.

Hetzel, Robert (1985). "The Rules vs. Discretion Debate over Monetary Policy in the 1920s," Federal Reserve Bank of Richmond *Economic Review,* 71:3–14.

Janis, Irving (1982). *Groupthink.* Dallas: Houghton-Mifflin.

Kane, Edward (1974). "All Is for the Best: The Federal Reserve Board's 60th Annual Report," *American Economic Review,* 74:835–50.

Lombra, Raymond, and Moran, Michael (1980). "Policy Advice and Policy-making at the Federal Reserve," *Carnegie-Rochester Conference Series on Public Policy,* 13:9–68.

McNees, Stephen (1986). "Modeling the Fed: A Forward-Looking Monetary Policy Reaction Function," Federal Reserve Bank of Boston, *New England Economic Review,* pp. 3–8.

Maisel, Sherman (1973). *Managing the Dollar.* New York: Norton.

Mayer, Thomas (1982a). "Federal Reserve Policy in the 1973–75 Recession: A Case Study of Fed Behavior in a Quandary," in Paul Wachtel (ed.), *Crises in the Economic and Financial Structure,* pp. 41–84. Lexington, Mass.: Lexington Books.

(1982b). "Regulation Q in 1966: A Case Study of Federal Reserve Policymaking," *Journal of Monetary Economics,* 10:259–71.

(1989). "Interpreting Federal Reserve Behavior," *Journal of Behavioral Economics,* 17:264–77.

Pierce, James (1980). "Comments on the Lombra-Moran Paper (1980)," *Carnegie-Rochester Conference Series on Public Policy,* 13:79–86.

Rolnick, Arthur (1985). "Research Activities and Budget Allocations among Federal Reserve Banks: Comment," *Public Choice,* 45:193–5.

Stockman, David (1987). *The Triumph of Politics.* New York: Avon Books.

Thaler, Richard (1980). "Towards a Positive Theory of Consumer Choice," *Journal of Economic and Organizational Behavior,* 1:39–60.

Thaler, Richard, and Shefrin, H. M. (1981). "An Economic Theory of Self-Control," *Journal of Political Economy,* 89:392–405.

Toma, Eugenia, and Toma, Mark (1985a). "Research Activities and Budget Allocations among Federal Reserve Banks," *Public Choice,* 45:175–91.

(1985b). "Research Activities and Budget Allocations among Federal Reserve Banks: Reply," *Public Choice,* 45:197–8.

Tversky, Amos, and Kahneman, Daniel (1981). "The Framing of Decisions and the Psychology of Choice," *Science,* 21:453–8.

U. S. Congress (1979). *Maintaining and Making Public Minutes of Federal Reserve Meetings, Hearings* (October 27, 28, November 17). House Subcommittee on Domestic Monetary Policy, 95th Cong., 2nd sess. Washington, D.C.: U.S. Government Printing Office.

Wallich, Henry (1982). "Policy Research, Policy Advice and Policymaking," in Raymond Lombra and Willard Witte (eds.), *Political Economy of International and Domestic Monetary Relations,* pp. 237–46. Ames: Iowa State University Press.

Weintraub, Robert (1978). "Congressional Supervision of Monetary Policy," *Journal of Monetary Economics*, 4:341–62.

White, C. J. M. (1982). *Consistency in Cognitive Social Behavior.* London: Routledge & Kegan Paul.

Woolley, John (1984). *Monetary Politics: The Federal Reserve and the Politics of Monetary Policy.* Cambridge University Press.

CHAPTER 17

The discount window

WILLIAM POOLE

Any Federal reserve bank may make advances for periods not exceeding 15 days to its member banks on their promissory notes secured by the deposit or pledge of bonds, notes, certificates of indebtedness, or Treasury bills of the United States . . . at rates to be established by such Federal reserve banks, such rates to be subject to the review and determination of the Board of Governors of the Federal Reserve System. Federal Reserve Act, Sec. 13(8)

As a student, I did not know where the term "discount window" came from. Why not "discount facility"? When I joined the staff of the Federal Reserve Bank of Boston in 1973, the mystery was solved. The bank was still housed in its old building, which had a grand banking lobby. And in the lobby was a teller's window with the word "Discount" above. It used to be that bankers would bring their collateral to the window and arrange their loans. The Boston Fed's new building does not have a teller's discount window, but the facility survives.

President Wilson signed the Federal Reserve Act into law on December 23, 1913, "to provide for the establishment of Federal reserve banks, to furnish an elastic currency, to afford means of rediscounting commercial paper, to establish a more effective supervision of banking in the United States, and for other purposes" (preamble, Federal Reserve Act). In 1913 the discount rate was the principal policy instrument, and the gold standard was taken for granted. Open-market operations had been invented, but not yet discovered.[1] Few economists considered bank deposits to be "money." The relation of what we now call the "monetary base" to the volume of bank deposits was not understood. The conception of central banking today is as far removed from the 1913 conception as is modern medical practice from bloodletting. Why does

This chapter was written at the end of the author's tenure as a member of the Council of Economic Advisers and was originally published in a memorial volume for Robert Weintraub. (Joint Economic Committee, Congress of the United States, Joint Committee Print, *Monetarism, Inflation, and the Federal Reserve,* June 27, 1985, pp. 28–40.) That publication has been shortened and changed slightly for publication in this volume. Marvin Goodfriend and Charles Shorin provided helpful comments and research assistance, but the views expressed do not necessarily reflect their own, and they should not be held responsible for any errors that may remain in this chapter.

the discount window live on? My purpose in this chapter is to outline the simple economics of the discount window and to show that discount-rate changes since the Korean War have had announcement effects that have been poorly timed with respect to the business cycle. The real purpose of the discount window today is to serve the political and bureaucratic needs of the Federal Reserve. Perhaps these are the "other purposes" referred to in the preamble to the Federal Reserve Act.

The simple economics of the discount window

Both critics and defenders of the discount window accept two elementary points. First, in meeting reserve requirements, bank reserves supplied by the Federal Reserve through the discount window are perfect substitutes for reserves supplied through open-market operations. For given reserve requirements, extra bank reserves can support extra bank deposits, but the amount of extra deposits does not depend on the source of the reserves. Given the volume of bank reserves, the effects, if any, of discount-rate changes on market interest rates occur through changing market expectations. With certain qualifications that will be discussed later, the discount window should be analyzed in terms of expectational effects, not in terms of any direct channels arising from the provision of reserves through the window rather than through open-market operations.

A second agreed point is that if short-run policy is viewed as determining interest rates, rather than the quantity of bank reserves, then the discount window could be a perfect substitute for open-market operations conducted to control interest rates. The Federal Reserve can peg the federal-funds rate day to day by supplying (absorbing) reserves through open-market operations when the funds rate tends to rise (fall). The discount window could achieve exactly the same result if the Fed were to lend to banks freely, without administrative rationing, at the discount rate. A change in the discount rate would then change the federal-funds rate by the same amount.

A generalization of this proposition applies directly to a Fed operating procedure involving a free-reserves target or a borrowed-reserves target, which the Federal Open Market Committee (FOMC) pursued from the time of the 1951 Accord to the mid-1960s and again starting in the fall of 1982. Suppose the Fed's administration of the discount window combines with bank borrowing behavior to yield a stable bank borrowing function. Then, discount-rate adjustments will be the exact equivalents of adjustments in a pegged federal-funds rate. The analysis is simple: With a stable bank borrowing function, in which the amount of borrowing depends on the spread between the federal-funds rate and the discount rate, a change in the discount rate with an unchanged FOMC borrowing target will yield an equal change in the federal-funds rate. However, because the borrowing function is not perfectly stable, a free-reserves (or borrowed-reserves) target is in practice only the approximate equivalent of a pegged federal-funds rate.

Federal Reserve lending through the discount window may be divided into two basic categories: adjustment assistance and lender-of-last-resort assistance. Historically, most discount-window borrowing has been for adjustment assistance. Individual banks sometimes find themselves short of required reserves, and in such cases they then borrow from the Fed to meet their reserve requirements. There is, however, no reason to maintain a discount window for this purpose, because banks ordinarily borrow using government-securities collateral. There is a ready market for government securities; banks running short of reserves can easily sell the securities to obtain the needed funds.

At the very end of a reserve settlement period, banks might find that they need reserves at a time when the government-securities market is essentially closed, or that the amounts needed are too large to be obtained on short notice by selling government securities. Also, if all banks together are short of reserves, then they cannot all simultaneously obtain reserves by selling government securities. In that case, it might seem reasonable for banks to borrow reserves from the Federal Reserve to meet their reserve requirements. However, that justification for the discount window fails because there is an obviously superior alternative. Rather than lending banks reserves, the Federal Reserve could simply charge a small penalty when banks do not meet their reserve requirements. That procedure would have several advantages. One would stem from the fact that because of inevitable accounting delays, the amount of any reserve deficiency is known accurately only after the end of a reserve period. The current procedure requires banks to decide on the amount of discount-window borrowing before the size of a reserve deficiency is accurately known. Another advantage to simply assessing a penalty on reserve deficiencies would arise from the fact that in recent years the Fed usually has set the discount rate below the federal-funds rate. Under these circumstances the discount window provides a subsidy rather than a penalty for banks that fail to meet their legal reserve requirements on their own. It is surely peculiar to enforce a regulation by providing a subsidy to those not in compliance.

The discount window serves one indispensable function: The central bank can provide funds as the lender of last resort. Sometimes a bank suffering a run can obtain the funds through the market, and the run is soon over. However, the same news that triggers a run may make others in the market nervous about providing loans or buying assets from the bank for fear that the bank will fall or that the assets will not be good assets. If the Federal Reserve decides that the bank is in fact solvent – that the value of its assets exceeds its liabilities – then it makes sense to provide emergency support through the discount window. These emergency funds enable the bank to meet its obligations and to survive. If the banking authorities decide that a bank should be closed, the emergency funds provide breathing time to arrange for an orderly merger with a stronger institution or an orderly liquidation of the bank. More important, the emergency support calms the market and reduces the probability that one bank's difficulties will trigger runs on other banks, thereby creating widespread financial disorder.

The logic of the lender-of-last-resort function requires that the discount rate be at least as high as the prevailing market rate for riskless loans. If a bank is solvent, it will be able to pay an above-market interest rate for a time and still survive. A bank that can survive only through access to subsidized funds from the central bank – funds provided at a discount rate below the market rate – ought to be closed promptly.

Resorting to the discount window may in some circumstances accelerate a run on a bank. The Federal Reserve and the borrowing bank are not always successful in maintaining the confidentiality of discount-window borrowing; knowledge that the bank must use the discount window discloses the severity of its difficulties. Moreover, discount-window borrowing is secured by a bank's best assets, which increases the size of any possible loss to uninsured depositors if the bank fails. Because the Fed takes the best assets as collateral, discount-window lending has about the same effect as depositors who engage in a run. Such depositors are successful in realizing 100 cents on the dollar, and they leave the losses for those who are slow to act. The difference between a run and emergency discount-window borrowing is that a bank borrowing at the window is not forced to sell assets at prices that may, because of incomplete market information, be below their true values.

Announcement effects

Changes in the discount rate have for many years been interpreted as signals or announcements of monetary policy intentions. Critics of the Federal Reserve's use of discount-rate changes to make announcements have long argued that the announcements frequently are unclear and that the Fed could more efficiently make announcements in such forms as press releases, statements before Congress, or articles in the *Federal*

Reserve Bulletin. However, debates over the value of announcement effects have not, to my knowledge, been based on a systematic examination of the announcements the Federal Reserve has actually made. Table 17.1 is based on an examination of every discount-rate change from 1953 through 1984 as announced and explained in the *Federal Reserve Bulletin.*

Table 17.1 reports my interpretation of the reasons offered in the *Federal Reserve Bulletin* when the discount rate was changed. As can be seen from the entries in the "None" column, in the 1950s the Federal Reserve typically reported discount-rate changes without offering reasons. The rate change had to speak for itself, a matter to be addressed after completing discussion of the table.

The reason the Fed most often offers for changing the discount rate is alignment with market interest rates. For example, in the "National Summary of Business Conditions" in the *Federal Reserve Bulletin* for April 1956, the discount-rate change is explained in this way: "Partly in response to these yield developments, the discount rate was raised to $2\frac{3}{4}$ percent at nine Federal Reserve Banks and to 3 percent at two of the banks effective April 13."

If the discount rate were tied by formula to market rates of interest, as many economists have urged, discount-rate adjustments would occur automatically and match the explanation that the Federal Reserve itself has most often offered for changing the rate. However, the discussion in the preceding section pointed out that alignment may or may not occur, depending on other policies. If the Federal Reserve is operating with a federal-funds-rate target, then an adjustment of the funds-rate target equal to the adjustment of the discount rate will keep the spread between the two rates from changing. If the Fed employs a borrowed-reserves target, failure to adjust that target will lead to a federal-funds-rate change equal to the discount-rate change, assuming the borrowing function is stable.

As indicated by the "Alignment only" column in the table, there are occasions when the Federal Reserve is at pains to explain that the discount-rate action has no purpose other than to align the discount rate with market rates of interest. In the "Announcements" section of the *Federal Reserve Bulletin,* the discount-rate increase effective January 15, 1973, was explained this way: "The present increase of the discount rate is merely a passive adjustment to what has already happened to market interest rates, and it, therefore, should not be the occasion for a further increase in interest rates." Another example of the "Alignment only" statement appears in the "Announcements" section of the *Federal Reserve Bulletin* for September 1977: "The Board stated that this action is intended as a technical move for the purpose of bringing the discount

Table 17.1. *Federal Reserve System discount-rate changes by reason, 1953–84*

Effective date of new rate	New Rate (%): First FRB to change	New Rate (%): FRB New York	Reasons offered: None	Reasons offered: Alignment	Reasons offered: Alignment only	Reasons offered: Policy 1	Reasons offered: Policy 2	Federal Reserve Bulletin reference
1953:								
January 16	2	2	×					Feb. 1953
1954:								
February 5	$1\frac{3}{4}$	$1\frac{3}{4}$	×					Feb. 1954
April 14	$1\frac{1}{2}$		×					April 1954
April 16		$1\frac{1}{2}$	×					April 1954
1955:								
April 14	$1\frac{3}{4}$		×					April 1955
April 15		$1\frac{3}{4}$	×					April 1955
August 4	2		×					Aug. 1955
August 4	$2\frac{1}{4}$		×					Aug. 1955
August 5		2	×					Aug. 1955
September 9		$2\frac{1}{4}$	×					Sept. 1955
November 18	$2\frac{1}{2}$	$2\frac{1}{2}$	×					Dec. 1955
1956:								
April 13	$2\frac{3}{4}$	$2\frac{3}{4}$		×				April 1956
April 13	3			×				April 1956
August 24		3	×					Sept. 1956
1957:								
August 9	$3\frac{1}{2}$		×					Aug. 1957
August 23		$3\frac{1}{2}$	×					Aug. 1957
November 15	3	3	×					Nov. 1957
1958:								
January 22	$2\frac{3}{4}$		×					Feb. 1958
January 24		$2\frac{3}{4}$	×					Feb. 1958
March 7	$2\frac{1}{4}$	$2\frac{1}{4}$	×					March 1958
April 18	$1\frac{3}{4}$	$1\frac{3}{4}$	×					April 1958
August 15	2		×					Aug. 1958
September 12	2		×					Sept. 1958
October 24	$2\frac{1}{2}$			×				Nov. 1958
November 7	$2\frac{1}{2}$			×				Nov. 1958
1959:								
March 6	3	3	×					March 1959
May 29	$3\frac{1}{2}$	$3\frac{1}{2}$	×					June 1959
September 11	4	4	×					Sept. 1959

Table 17.1. *(cont.)*

Effective date of new rate	New Rate (%)		Reasons offered					Federal Reserve Bulletin reference
	First FRB to change	FRB New York	None	Alignment	Alignment only	Policy 1	Policy 2	
1960:								
June 3	$3\frac{1}{2}$		×					June 1960
June 10		$3\frac{1}{2}$	×					June 1960
August 12	3	3	×					Aug. 1980
1963:								
July 17	$3\frac{1}{2}$	$3\frac{1}{2}$		×			×	July 1963
1964:								
November 24	4	4					×	Dec. 1964
1965:								
December 6	$4\frac{1}{2}$	$4\frac{1}{2}$	×					Dec. 1965
1967:								
April 7	4	4	×					April 1967
November 20	$4\frac{1}{2}$	$4\frac{1}{2}$					×	Nov. 1967
1968:								
March 15	5		×					March 1968
March 22		5	×					April 1968
April 19	$5\frac{1}{2}$	$5\frac{1}{2}$	×					April 1968
August 16	$5\frac{1}{4}$			×				Aug. 1968
August 30		$5\frac{1}{4}$	×					Sept. 1968
December 18	$5\frac{1}{2}$	$5\frac{1}{2}$		×			×	Dec. 1968
1969:								
April 4	6	6					×	May 1969
1970:								
November 11	$5\frac{3}{4}$			×		×		Nov. 1970
November 13		$5\frac{3}{4}$		×		×		Nov. 1970
December 1	$5\frac{1}{2}$			×				Dec. 1970
December 4		$5\frac{1}{2}$		×				Dec. 1970
1971:								
January 8	$5\frac{1}{4}$	$5\frac{1}{4}$		×				Jan. 1971
January 19	5		×					Jan. 1971
January 22		5		×				Feb. 1971
February 13	$4\frac{3}{4}$			×				Feb. 1971
February 19		$4\frac{3}{4}$		×				Feb. 1971
July 16	5	5		×			×	July 1971
November 11	$4\frac{3}{4}$			×				Nov. 1971
November 19		$4\frac{3}{4}$		×				Nov. 1971
December 13	$4\frac{1}{2}$			×			×	Dec. 1971
December 17		$4\frac{1}{2}$		×			×	Dec. 1971

Table 17.1. *(cont.)*

Effective date of new rate	New Rate (%) First FRB to change	FRB New York	Reasons offered None	Alignment	Alignment only	Policy 1	Policy 2	Federal Reserve Bulletin reference
1973:								
January 15	5	5			×			Jan. 1973
February 26	$5\frac{1}{2}$	$5\frac{1}{2}$		×			×	March 1973
April 23	$5\frac{3}{4}$		×					May 1973
May 4		$5\frac{3}{4}$	×					May 1973
May 11	6	6		×				May 1973
June 11	$6\frac{1}{2}$	$6\frac{1}{2}$		×		×		June 1973
July 2	7	7					×	July 1973
August 14	$7\frac{1}{2}$	$7\frac{1}{2}$		×				Aug. 1973
1974:								
April 25	8	8		×		×		May 1974
December 9	$7\frac{3}{4}$	$7\frac{3}{4}$		×				Dec. 1974
1975:								
January 6	$7\frac{1}{4}$						×	Jan. 1975
January 10		$7\frac{1}{4}$					×	Jan. 1975
February 5	$6\frac{3}{4}$	$6\frac{3}{4}$		×				Feb. 1975
March 10	$6\frac{1}{4}$	$6\frac{1}{4}$		×		×		March 1975
May 16	6	6		×				May 1975
1976:								
January 19	$5\frac{1}{2}$	$5\frac{1}{2}$		×				Jan. 1976
November 22	$5\frac{1}{4}$	$5\frac{1}{4}$		×				Dec. 1976
1977:								
August 30	$5\frac{3}{4}$				×			Sept. 1977
August 31		$5\frac{3}{4}$			×			Sept. 1977
October 26	6	6		×				Nov. 1977
1978:								
January 9	$6\frac{1}{2}$	$6\frac{1}{2}$				×		Jan. 1978
May 11	7	7		×				May 1978
July 3	$7\frac{1}{4}$	$7\frac{1}{4}$		×				July 1978
August 21	$7\frac{3}{4}$	$7\frac{3}{4}$				×		Sept. 1978
September 22	8	8		×			×	Oct. 1978
October 16	$8\frac{1}{2}$	$8\frac{1}{2}$		×		×		Oct. 1978
November 1	$9\frac{1}{2}$	$9\frac{1}{2}$					×	Nov. 1978
1979:								
July 20	10	10		×			×	Aug. 1979
August 17	$10\frac{1}{2}$	$10\frac{1}{2}$				×		Sept. 1979
September 19	11	11		×				Oct. 1979
October 8	12	12					×	Oct. 1979

Table 17.1. *(cont.)*

Effective date of new rate	New Rate (%) First FRB to change	FRB New York	Reasons offered None	Alignment	Alignment only	Policy 1	Policy 2	Federal Reserve Bulletin reference
1980:								
February 15	13	13					×	March 1980
May 29	12	12			×			June 1980
June 13	11	11			×			July 1980
July 28	10	10			×			Aug. 1980
September 26	11	11		×			×	Oct. 1980
November 17	12	12		×		×		Dec. 1980
December 5	13	13		×			×	Dec. 1980
1981:								
May 5	14	14		×			×	May 1981
November 2	13	13		×			×	Nov. 1981
December 4	12	12		×				Dec. 1981
1982:								
July 20	$11\frac{1}{2}$	$11\frac{1}{2}$		×		×		Aug. 1982
August 2	11	11		×		×		Aug. 1982
August 16	$10\frac{1}{2}$	$10\frac{1}{2}$		×		×		Sept. 1982
August 27	10	10		×				Sept. 1982
October 12	$9\frac{1}{2}$	$9\frac{1}{2}$		×				Nov. 1982
November 22	9	9		×		×		Dec. 1982
December 14	$8\frac{1}{2}$	$8\frac{1}{2}$				×		Jan. 1983
1984:								
April 9	9	9		×				April 1984
November 21	$8\frac{1}{2}$	$8\frac{1}{2}$				×		Jan. 1985
December 24	8	8		×		×		Feb. 1985

rate into better alignment with other short-term interest rates and that it has no monetary policy implications."

A clear statement of a policy reason for changing the discount rate did not occur until the change effective July 17, 1963. In the "Announcements" section of the *Federal Reserve Bulletin* the reasoning behind the increase in the discount rate and reserve requirements is provided at some length:

> On July 16, the Federal Reserve System acted on two fronts to aid the United States efforts to combat its international balance of payments problem. . . .
>
> Both actions are aimed at minimizing short-term capital outflows prompted by higher interest rates prevalent in other countries. Preliminary information indi-

cates that short-term outflows contributed materially to the substantial deficit incurred once again in the balance of payments during the second quarter of this year.

Recently, market rates on U.S. Treasury bills and other short-term securities have risen to levels well above the 3 percent discount rate that had prevailed for nearly 3 years, making it less costly for member banks to obtain reserve funds by borrowing from the Federal Reserve Banks rather than by selling short-term securities.

The increased discount rates will reverse that circumstance, making it once again more advantageous for member banks seeking reserve funds to obtain them by selling their short-term securities rather than by borrowing from the Federal Reserve Banks. Sales so made should have a bolstering effect on short-term rates, keeping them more in line with rates in other world financial markets. . . .

These actions to help in relieving the potential drain on U.S. monetary reserves associated with the long persistent deficit in the balance of payments do not constitute a change in the System's policy of maintaining monetary conditions conducive to fuller utilization of manpower and other resources.

The last paragraph of that passage provides a good example of why discount-rate announcements are ambiguous. The earlier paragraphs point to a policy of maintaining higher interest rates than before, but the last paragraph seems to say either that the higher interest rates will have no effect on the domestic economy or that the domestic policy will be unchanged and that interest rates will not in fact be pushed up to the higher levels. If the policy was indeed one of pushing interest rates up, then the last paragraph would seem to be designed simply to provide an assertion that the policy would not set back the efforts of the Kennedy administration to reduce unemployment. Conversely, if domestic interest rates were not going to be maintained at the new higher levels, then the discount-rate action and the accompanying explanation would seem designed to provide the appearance of doing something about the balance-of-payments deficit, which was viewed as a substantial problem in 1963, without in fact doing anything. In Table 17.1, that discount-rate change has been listed in the column marked "Policy 2." That designation means that the Federal Reserve explained the discount-rate change in terms of achieving a particular policy objective.

The meaning of the "Policy 1" column can be explained by quoting from the announcement of the discount-rate decrease effective November 11, 1970. In the "Announcements" section of the *Federal Reserve Bulletin,* the Fed explained that "the reduction in the discount rate, made within the framework of the moderately expansive monetary policy that was initiated earlier this year, is the first since August 1968." An entry is made in the "Policy 1" column when statements say that the discount-rate change was taken "in the light of," or "in recognition of," or "in the framework of," or similar phrases. Language of this kind provides hints, but seems considerably less strong than language that says, in effect, that the discount-rate change was made "for the purpose of" achieving a certain end.

If the words accompanying discount-rate adjustments frequently are ambiguous, as they are, the market is likely to concentrate on the action itself. Instead of attempting the complicated task of trying to measure the expectational effects of discount-rate changes, I shall pursue a different approach. Based on the assumptions that the market interprets a discount-rate decrease (increase) as a sign of an easier (tighter) policy and that the expectation of an easier (tighter) policy causes interest rates to fall (rise) without there being any immediate change in the level of bank reserves and the money stock, it is possible to explore the appropriateness of the discount-rate changes for the cyclical position of the economy. To prevent this discussion from being too long and tedious, the review of discount-rate adjustments will be confined to those in the neighborhood of business-cycle peaks.

The discount-rate history reported in Table 17.1 begins with 1953. A business-cycle peak occurred in July of that year, but the discount rate was not lowered until February 1954. The next cycle peak was August 1957. The Fed increased the discount rate that month and did not reduce it until November. The timing was better in 1960; the discount rate was reduced in early June, following the cycle peak in April. The long 1960s expansion ended with the cycle peak of December 1969. The discount rate had been increased in April 1969 and was not lowered until November 1970, the month of the cyclical trough. Leading up to the cyclical peak in November 1973, the Fed increased the discount rate in January, February, April, May, June, July, and August, and also in April 1974. During that recession, which extended to the trough in March 1975, the first discount-rate decrease did not occur until December 1974. That late response reflected both the fact that the discount rate had not been increased enough to remain in line with rising market rates in the first half of 1974 and the Fed's determination not to provide any signal that it was reversing a restrictive policy to fight inflation.

The record of poor timing continued with the two recessions in the early 1980s. Preceding the January 1980 cycle peak, the Fed increased the discount rate four times in 1979 – in July, August, September, and October. The rate was also increased in February 1980, after the recession had begun. The first decrease occurred in late May, shortly before the cycle trough in July. In 1981, the discount rate was increased in May, shortly before the cycle peak in July. The first decrease in the rate occurred in November.

From this review of 32 years of discount-rate announcements it is difficult to believe that the announcement effects provide a constructive feature of U.S. monetary policy. The timing record reflects two inevitable features of discount-rate administration. First, discount-rate adjustments are, and should be, motivated by an effort to keep the rate reasonably aligned with market rates of interest. But discount-rate changes are also viewed by the Fed and by the market as statements of policy. In 1957, 1969, 1973, 1980, and 1981 the business-cycle peaks occurred at times of widespread concern about inflation. In none of those cases was the existence of a cycle peak clear at the time it occurred. To maintain a stance of "fighting inflation," the Federal Reserve was concerned in each case not to give a signal that it had adopted a less restrictive policy.

Other functions of the discount window

From 1955 through 1964 the federal-funds rate was always below the discount rate on a monthly average basis. The funds rate rose above the discount rate in early 1965 and has remained above for almost the entire period since. Thus, the Fed has been subsidizing banks through the discount window almost continuously since 1965. I argued earlier that a subsidy discount rate serves no monetary policy purpose, and so it is worth exploring the advantages to the Fed of providing subsidies to banks through the discount window.

Beyond the obvious point that subsidies provide any agency an opportunity to maximize its political support, the subsidy discount window enables the Federal Reserve to establish regulatory constraints that might not otherwise exist. In granting last-resort loans, the discount officers at the various Federal Reserve banks must be satisfied that the borrowing bank is sound. To survive, the borrowing bank must correct the problems that led to its troubles, and Federal Reserve supervision is fully appropriate in these cases. But these arguments do not apply when a sound bank is borrowing for short-run adjustment. There is absolutely no risk to the Federal Reserve to lending to such a bank, because the loans ordinarily are collateralized by government securities. Supervision by a discount officer is the price a bank pays for obtaining the subsidy when the discount rate is below the federal-funds rate. Under a penalty-discount-rate system, the bank would have no motivation to borrow from the Fed rather than from the federal-funds market, and so the Federal Reserve would lose that avenue of supervision.

This system might have considerable advantage to the Federal Reserve because of the wide discretion available to the discount officer. In contrast, other banking supervision takes place within a formal system of written regulations. Both the regulations and actions under the regulations are subject to court challenge. Of course, any bank that finds the supervision by the discount officer onerous can escape by forgoing the discount-window subsidy.

Another function of the discount window is that it permits the Federal Reserve to express its concern about obvious problems such as rising unemployment or rising inflation without necessarily taking any substantive action. I discussed a particularly clear example of this phenomenon in a paper published in 1975.[2] Interest rates fell as unemployment rose rapidly after the middle of 1974. The federal-funds rate, at its peak in July 1974, was almost 5 percentage points above the discount rate, providing a very substantial incentive for banks to borrow through the discount window. By February 1975 the funds rate was more than half a percentage point below the discount rate. The Federal Reserve expressed its concern about the recession by three discount-rate cuts in January, February, and March 1975. But the federal-funds rate declined even more rapidly, and so the incentive for banks to borrow through the discount window actually declined. The Federal Reserve used another inconsequential policy instrument – reserve requirements – in the same way. Reserve requirements were cut in January 1975, but open-market operations then absorbed almost all of the reserves released by cutting reserve requirements.

Minimal recommendations

It would be desirable for the discount window to be abolished, except for its use in a lender-of-last-resort context at a penalty discount rate. Federal Reserve lending in these circumstances would have to be combined with close supervision of the activities of the borrowing banks. But given that this "radical" proposal has been advocated by many economists for years and ignored by the Congress, a minimal set of reforms should be considered.

First, the Federal Reserve Act should be amended to require that the Federal Reserve System maintain the discount rate above money-market rates of interest. The Federal Reserve System could be permitted to adjust the rate according to current practice, except that the adjustments would refer to the spread over market rates. The discount rate would, therefore, follow the market rate of interest, except when Fed action changed the spread. Adjustment borrowing, which should be collateralized by U.S. government securities, should be rationed by the discount rate only, not through application of nonprice rationing criteria.

Second, the Federal Reserve Act should be amended to require that the FOMC release its policy Directive at the end of the day on which it is adopted. Current practice permits the Federal Reserve to announce changes in the inconsequential policy instruments – the discount rate and reserve requirements – while maintaining secrecy over important policy decisions made by the FOMC. As emphasized earlier, the policy significance of changes in the discount-rate spread cannot be assessed without knowledge of the FOMC Directive. The effects of a discount-rate change depend critically on FOMC policies toward providing reserves – policies relating to the nonborrowed- or borrowed-reserves target or to the federal-funds rate. No public-policy purpose is served by the Federal Reserve releasing partial information about its policy stance; incomplete information can mislead the markets and mislead the Congress. Although there is ample reason to protect the confidentiality of policy deliberations, a "truth-in-policy act" should require immediate disclosure of Federal Reserve policy actions.

Notes

1 That is, the mechanics, but not the significance, of open-market operations were known.

2 William Poole, "Monetary Policy During the Recession," *Brookings Papers on Economic Activity,* 1(1975):123–39.

CHAPTER 18

Leaning against the wind: the behavior of the money stock in recession and recovery, 1953–8

ELMUS WICKER

"Leaning against the wind" is a distinctively telling metaphor that communicates to an audience of laypeople and nonprofessionals what the Federal Reserve is up to in a way that the phrase "contracyclical monetary policy" cannot. The metaphor was introduced by Chairman William McChesney Martin in congressional testimony just after the famous Accord in 1951. According to Ralph Young (private communication, August 6, 1976), he used it frequently for dramatic expository effect in informal colloquy before large groups, and its main purpose was "[Fed] *political* and *public relations*." The phrase appears only rarely in the official minutes of the Federal Open Market Committee (FOMC). Nevertheless, I think that so apt a metaphor deserves a permanent place in the literature that attempts to describe Federal Reserve monetary policy. The connotation of the phrase "leaning against the wind" is clear enough. The policy response of the Fed to cyclical disturbances is to moderate disturbances in output, employment, and prices.

The performance of the U.S. economy during the 1950s was blemished by the occurrence of two recessions (1953–4 and 1957–8), interspersed by a mild inflationary boom (1954–7). Some Federal Reserve critics, such as Brunner and Meltzer (1964, pp. 51–2), Lombra and Torto (1973, pp. 48–9), and Guttentag (1966), regarded the Fed's responses to those cyclical disturbances as suboptimal. They ascribed the Fed's unsatisfactory behavior solely to a defective policy strategy attributable to an alleged discrepancy between policy action and policy intent. Presumably, the intent of the policy-makers was strongly countercyclical, whereas their understanding of how monetary policy was to work was defective. Lombra (1980, p. 289) concluded: "In fact, since there is persuasive evidence that over the postwar period the Fed has leaned *with* rather than *against* the wind, reserves are more properly viewed as a result rather than cause of changes in the money stock."

And Meltzer (1982, p. 634) wrote that "About twenty years ago a series of studies by Meigs, Dewald, Friedman and Schwartz, Brunner and Meltzer, and Weintraub contributed an explanation in which Federal Reserve procedures fostered procyclical monetary growth." As we shall see, both of these statements contain half-truths. Gordon (1983, p. 9) in a recent survey of U.S. recession experience since World War II, concluded that the recessions between 1949 and 1961 "displayed the expected procyclical movement." He noted a consistent tendency for monetary growth to be lower in recessions.

The purpose of this chapter is to reexamine the behavior of the money stock in two recessions and one economic recovery in the 1950s. What the evidence reveals is that there was negligible growth in currency and demand deposits (M1) in both recessions and in the latter half of the recovery. Moreover, there were negligible changes in the reserve aggregates: total reserves, unborrowed reserves, and the monetary base. And although the 1948–9 and 1959–60 recessions are not examined here, the behavior of M1 in those recessions was similar to that described for the 1950s.

The Fed's monetary strategy contributed to the asymmetrical policy response, that is, a weak procyclical response in recession and a strong contracyclical response in the latter half of the recovery. The behavior of M1 can be attributed to (1) a serious flaw in the free-reserves strategy, (2) the avoidance of a money-market state described somewhat picturesquely by members of the FOMC as "sloppy," and (3) strong restrictions placed on the growth of unborrowed reserves during economic recovery. Despite the alleged massive easing action by the Fed, the money stock failed to grow in the pre-1960 recessions in the U.S. economy. The monetary authorities succeeded only in preventing the money stock from receding, but there was no significant expansion of M1.

Behavior of the money stock and reserves during two recessions and one recovery: 1950s

A contracyclical response of the money stock implies that the money stock should increase during recession and decelerate during expansion. The decade of the 1950s contained two clearly demarcated recessions (1953–4 and 1957–8) and one full recovery (1954–7). An examination of the behavior of M1 during those three episodes reveals an asymmetrical contracyclical response, that is, negligible change in M1 during both the recession and expansion phases of the business cycle.

According to the National Bureau of Economic Research (NBER) chronology of business cycles, M1, seasonally adjusted, expanded less

Table 18.1 *Behavior of various reserve aggregates in two recessions and one recovery: 1953–8 ($ million)*

Episode	Excess reserves	Borrowed reserves	Free reserves	Total reserves	Unborrowed reserves	Monetary base
Recessions						
1. July 1953	784	428	356	21,483	21,055	49,300
May 1954	716	155	561	21,523	21,368	49,100
2. August 1957	534	1005	−471	20,599	19,594	48,900
April 1958	623	130	493	20,382	20,252	48,700
Recovery						
June 1954	858	146	712	21,968	21,322	49,100
July 1957	917	534	−383	20,747	20,213	49,100

Source: Board of Governors of the Federal Reserve System (1976). *Banking and Monetary Statistics 1941–1970*. Washington, D.C.: Board of Governors of the Federal Reserve System.

than 1 percent from July 1953 to the trough in May 1954 (10 months). During the first six months of the 1953–4 recession, M1 remained virtually unchanged. Between December and the cyclical trough in May, M1 increased by only .78 percent. During the 1957–8 recession, M1 remained virtually unchanged from a peak in August 1957 to the trough in April 1959 (8 months). In contrast to the 1953–4 episode, however, M1 declined continuously during the first six months of the recession. The level of the money stock in January 1958 was 1.2 percent below what it had been in August of the preceding year. The decline was almost exactly offset by a 1.1 percent increase between January and the cyclical trough in April. During both of the recession episodes the Fed was pursuing what it called a policy of "Active ease," with free reserves moving from zero to the $600–700 million range. During the 1954–7 economic expansion the FOMC moved gradually from a policy of "neutrality" to "restraint." The money stock increased 2 percent during the first six months of the recovery from the 1953–4 recession. The increase slowed to 1.65 percent in 1955, slowed to less than 1 percent between January and November 1956, and ground to a halt between December 1956 and July 1957. Unmistakably, the Fed was "leaning against the wind," as measured by the behavior of the money stock, almost with a vengeance, beginning in January 1956 and continuing to August 1957.

The behaviors of the various reserve aggregates – free reserves, total reserves, unborrowed reserves, the monetary base – during each of the two recessions and one recovery episode are set out in Table 18.1. Changes in the money stock can be attributed to changes in the monetary base or some relevant reserve aggregate and/or to changes in the components of the money multiplier. The data in Table 18.1 reveal quite clearly that changes in the monetary base in both recession and recovery were negligible. In each of the two recessions the monetary base (high-powered money) declined by $200 million, less than one-half of 1 percent. The monetary base decreased by $100 million during the 1954–7 expansion.

Total reserves showed practically no change in the 1953–4 recession and a 1 percent decrease in 1957–8; they decreased 1 percent during the 1954–7 recovery.

The behavior of unborrowed reserves paints a slightly more optimistic picture, but not much more, of contracyclical monetary policy during the two recessions. Unborrowed reserves increased 1.5 percent in 1953–4 and more than twice that – 3.4 percent – in 1957–8. However, unborrowed reserves seriously constrained money-stock growth. A $1 billion decrease in free reserves was accompanied by a 5 percent decline in unborrowed reserves. Total reserves, unborrowed reserves, and the monetary base decreased in the precise direction called for by contracyclical monetary policy.

One further word must be said about the various reserve aggregates as effective barometers for measuring the thrust of FOMC policy. Because these aggregates have not been adjusted for changes in reserve requirements, they do not capture all of the action taken by the Fed to stimulate or to retard economic activity, especially changes in reserve requirements. Reserve requirements were lowered in July 1953 and in June/July 1954. They were also reduced in February, March, and April 1958.

Free reserves increased $200 million in the first recession and almost $1 billion in the second. But the magnitude of the Fed's response in 1953–4 was seriously distorted by the fact that in May 1953, Fed officials reacted swiftly and strongly to a disturbance in the bond market that had nothing to do with the state of the economy. The effect of the policy-makers' actions increased free reserves from −$364 million in May to +$355 million in June. Therefore, at the outset of the first recession, free reserves were positive by accident of a money-market disturbance, not any adverse readings on the condition of the economy. Nevertheless, the increase in free reserves had little perceptible effect on total reserves, on the monetary base, or on the money stock. Free reserves increased by almost $1 billion during the second recession, but the so-called flood of free reserves did not prevent a decline of 1 percent or less in total reserves and the monetary base. Likewise, during the economic recovery (June 1954 to July 1957), free reserves decreased $1 billion. The decrease in free reserves was attended by reductions in total reserves, unborrowed reserves, and the monetary base. The Fed appeared to be pursuing a successful contracyclical monetary policy, perhaps too successful, as measured by the performance of the reserve aggregates.

Summing up, a review of the record of the behavior of reserve aggregates tells us that during the 1953–4 recession the official policy state designated "active base" was barely sufficient to prevent either total reserves or the monetary base from declining. The performance of Fed officials was slightly worse in 1957–8, when total reserves and the monetary base contracted.

The conclusion from the evidence of the 1950s seems unambiguous. Judged solely on the basis of peak-to-trough data, the behavior of some reserve aggregates, and the money stock, the Fed did not "lean against the wind" in either recession. There may have been substantial increases in free reserves for the deliberate purpose of lowering unemployment, but the increase in free reserves failed to induce an increase in total reserves, in the monetary base, or in the stock of M1.

During the first six months of the 1953–4 recession, M1 remained virtually unchanged, whereas the money stock decreased by 1.2 percent in a similar period in 1957–8. In the remaining months of both recessions, M1 increased – less than 1 percent in the earlier episode, and slightly more than 1 percent in the later episode. If there are moderate lag lengths in monetary policy, the acceleration of money-stock growth in the late stages of both recessions would begin to exert an impact on output and employment only after economic recovery had begun.

The record is equally clear that in the 1954–7 recovery the Fed did vigorously and perhaps overenergetically "lean against the wind." The Fed resisted any tendency for either reserves or the money stock to increase endogenously with an expansion of output, except in the very early stages of the boom. The monetary policy strategy in effect was a strategy to inhibit the growth of unborrowed reserves by keeping reserve injections through open-market operations to a bare minimum.

Explanations of the observed money-stock response

What explanations, if any, do we have for the observed weak procyclical money-stock response during the 1953–4 and 1957–8 recessions and the contracyclical money-stock response during the 1954–7 recovery? Why did the Fed's monetary policy strategy (the so-called free-reserves strategy) perform so poorly during recession and perform too effectively, perhaps, during recovery? There are at least three factors that may account for some aspects of the observed cyclical money-stock response: (1) the FOMC's free-reserves strategy was fatally flawed. (2) The avoidance of a money-market state described as "sloppy" by members of the FOMC constrained the Committee from selecting target levels of free reserves that would have induced an expansion of the money stock. (3) The monetary policy states of "neutrality" and "restraint" placed strong restrictions on the growth of unborrowed reserves, thus dampening the growth of total reserves and the monetary base. However, before we undertake to explain the observed money-stock response, we give a brief account of the origins of the free-reserves guide and the role of free reserves in overall monetary strategy.

Only in February 1954 did free reserves emerge as an operational guide to the Open-Market Account Manager. Between the time of the Accord in 1951 and the emergence of free reserves as a policy guide, the Fed had as its main task the revival of the discount mechanism and the development of an efficient market for government securities. For more than 10 years, interest-rate pegging had been its chief objective. Reserves had been supplied at the initiative of the commercial banks through sales of government securities to the Fed. The discount mechanism had atrophied from disuse, and open-market operations had not been used to achieve stabilization objectives since the 1920s and the 1930s. So strong was the revulsion from the pre-1951-Accord policy of pegged rates that the FOMC staunchly rejected interest rates as an operating guide for the Account Manager. The rejection of an interest-rate guide, however, did not necessarily mean that Federal Reserve officials attached any less significance to the behavior of interest rates, nor did the eventual choice of a free-reserves guide imply more concern about the behavior of total bank credit and the money stock.

The first stage in the revival of a freer market for government securities was the adoption of a policy state labeled "Neutrality" in August 1951. Neutrality did not mean the absence of monetary effects; it meant that during a period of economic expansion the FOMC would sharply reduce its intervention in the government-securities market and would induce banks to rely more heavily on member-bank borrowing to meet seasonal and growth demands for reserves. Winfield Riefler (1952, p. 197), a staff economist, told the Executive Committee of the FOMC in October 1952 that the Committee "had taken the position that it was preferable for banks to borrow to adjust their reserves rather than to sell securities which the Federal Reserve would have to purchase." Therefore, the renewal of interest in the discount mechanism did not stem from any nostalgia about how monetary control was exercised in the decade of the twenties. Policy-makers required a mechanism for injecting reserves while keeping open-market operations to a minimum. The existence, at that time, of an excess-profits tax ensured that the banks had a stronger incentive to borrow than to dispose of government securities.

For the 2.5 years following the Accord, borrowing, not free reserves, was the principal guide to FOMC policy. At first, borrowing was permitted to drift upward in response to seasonal and growth demands for reserves, but during the latter half of the period the Committee attempted to constrain the maximum amount of borrowing by setting a borrowing ceiling. If borrowed reserves tended to exceed $1.5 billion, the Account Manager was authorized to acquire securities. Staff officials were aware of the expansionary consequences of setting a borrowing ceiling, but the desire to avoid money-market stringency took precedence over other objectives.

The FOMC had officially shifted its policy from "Neutrality" and "Restraint" to one of "Active Ease" in September 1953. "Active Ease" referred to a policy state where interest rates at all maturity levels were low, where there was a large volume of excess reserves, and where borrowings were small and intermittent; that is, free reserves were large. The necessary conditions were large excess reserves and minimum borrowing. The level of free reserves was merely an indicator of the policy state labeled "Active Ease." The indicator function was more prominent than the target function. Chairman Martin, at the time a free-reserves guide was adopted in February 1954, stated "That he did not think the Committee wished to have any particular figure as a guide but that he would like to know whether any of the members of the Committee felt this figure offered a reasonable indication of what 'Active Ease' meant" (FOMC 1964, p. 34).

The FOMC minutes clearly reveal that FOMC policy-makers rarely, if ever, associated the thrust of monetary policy solely with the level of free reserves; the level and term structure of interest rates and the relationship of the discount rate to open-market rates were equally important.

Each of the policy states (Active Ease, Ease, Neutrality, and Restraint) identified by the FOMC implied, as we have indicated, a particular relationship between excess reserves and borrowing. "Active Ease" meant large excess reserves, minimum borrowing, and positive free reserves. "Restraint" implied minimum excess reserves, large amounts of borrowing, and negative free reserves. Attention was directed at the quantity of excess reserves and the quantity of borrowing, not free reserves per se. Hence, free reserves were an indicator, albeit not a very good one, of the desired policy state described by the FOMC. When Fed officials recognized the necessity for one of the desired policy states, the direction, if not the exact level, of the movement of free reserves was determined.

Some of the appeal of free reserves resided in its alleged usefulness as a guide to the Account Manager in determining the amount of open-market operations. From the identities

$$\text{total reserves} = \text{required reserves} + \text{excess reserves} \quad (18.1)$$

$$\text{total reserves} = \text{borrowed reserves} + \text{unborrowed reserves} \quad (18.2)$$

$$\text{free reserves} = \text{excess reserves} - \text{borrowed reserves} \quad (18.3)$$

we obtain

$$\text{free reserves} = \text{unborrowed reserves} - \text{required reserves} \quad (18.4)$$

Equation (18.4) was used to project anticipated changes in free reserves, assuming zero open-market operations, that is, no offsetting purchases or sales of government securities by the FOMC. Weekly changes in unborrowed reserves were projected by estimating changes in the technical factors causing unborrowed reserves to change (currency in circulation, U.S. Treasury deposits, float, etc.) and by estimating changes in required reserves.

Estimates of required reserves were made by the Federal Reserve Board's staff based on fairly rigid assumptions of only customary seasonal variations and an allowance for the annual growth rate of demand deposits. The assumed growth rates of demand deposits was 2 percent at first, and 3 percent later. The minutes of every meeting of the Executive Committee, and, after it was abolished in 1955, the full FOMC, between 1952 and 1957 contain staff projections of free reserves. Free reserves were estimated biweekly for one to two months into the future. Once a year, in either May or June, staff officials prepared free-reserves projections for the final six months of the year in anticipation of the large year-end seasonal increase in the demand for reserves (Wicker 1974).

The discrepancy, if any, between the desired level of free reserves and the free-reserves projection provided a guide for the conduct of open-market operations. Explicit, therefore, in the free-reserves projections was an allowance for an assumed growth of demand deposits.

Critics of the Fed's free-reserves strategy, such as Brunner and Meltzer (1964) and Meigs (1962), have stressed that the maintenance of any given level of free reserves has no implications per se for the growth rate of the money stock; that is, any level of free reserves is compatible with a positive, negative, or zero growth rate of the money stock. To make any valid inferences about changes in the money stock, a clear distinction must be drawn between the demand for free reserves and the supply of free reserves. Changes in the stock of money can be induced by the creation of an excess demand or excess supply of free reserves.

Given a targeted level of free reserves, unexpected changes in the demand for free reserves will induce changes in the equilibrium money stock. For example, suppose actual free reserves have increased from $500 to $600 million. If the banks' demands for free reserves have remained unchanged at $500 million, the banks will have $100 million of free reserves that they do not desire to hold, and they will proceed to expand their earning assets, thereby increasing checking-account deposits. However, if the banks' demands for free reserves increase by $100 million, perhaps because of greater uncertainty about deposit withdrawals (the demand for excess reserves has increased), there will be no earning-assets response and no change in checkable deposits.

The Fed's explicit desire to avoid a "sloppy" money market is an explanation for its failure to have increased free reserves in recession sufficiently to have increased the money stock. The Manager of the Open-Market Account was specifically directed by the FOMC to prevent two money-market states described as "sloppy" and "knots." A "knot" was described as a situation so tight that credit was almost unavailable. In later years, a similar condition was described as a "credit crunch." A "sloppy" money market was identified with the presence of large excess reserves and a reluctance of banks to invest in the short-term securities market. The avoidance of knots had the effect at specific times, such as 1952, of putting an upper bound on the level of net borrowed reserves and, in May and June 1953, of increasing securities purchases, and a "sloppy" money market constrained any further expansion of free reserves. The fear of creating a money-market disturbance in the latter stages of economic recovery led policy-makers to substitute "feel and tone of the market" for free reserves as the Account Manager's operating guide. The fear of creating a "sloppy" money market constrained additional open-market operations to increase free reserves in the early stages of the 1957–8 recession; it also constrained the increase in the range of free reserves above $400–700 million. Money-market considerations influenced FOMC conduct by the selection of free-reserves guides that may have prevented a more satisfactory growth rate of the money stock.

William McChesney Martin, chairman of the FOMC, asked the Account Manager in March 1954 what the probable effects would be of a $1 billion free-reserves target as compared with the current amount ($500 million) (FOMC 1964, pp. 114–15). The latter replied that the market would be very sloppy. The Account Manager tended to associate a sloppy money market with the willingness of the large money-market banks to allow excess reserves to accumulate temporarily. Allan Sproul, president of the Federal Reserve Bank of New York, in March 1954 identified it as a condition of "excessive" excess reserves: "With excessive excess reserves you can drive down interest rates on money market instruments and you can drive nonbank investors out of the market, but you can't make banks lend" (FOMC 1964, p. 116). Later, in May, 1954, Sproul expanded on his earlier statement: "You drive up prices but don't increase output – in this case you drive down yields on liquidity instruments but don't increase the kind of bank lending and capital investment which facilitates recovery" (FOMC 1964, pp. 164–5). Martin agreed with Sproul that an increase in free reserves that would lead to a reduction in short-term rates but would not promote investment was not desirable.

At times, the Committee came dangerously close to assuming the existence of some sort of temporary short-term liquidity trap. That is, short-term rates having fallen to very low levels (as three-month Treasury bills fell to .782% in May 1954 and bottomed out in June at .65%), some banks, including the large money-market center banks, might have preferred holding excess reserves to acquiring alternative interest-bearing assets.

The view of Federal Reserve officials in the latter months of the 1954 recession was that additional increases in free reserves would reduce further short-term rates, but probably would not have much of an effect on the level of bank credit. Therefore, there was no reason to move outside the $400–700 million targeted range for free reserves.

The Fed's response to the 1957–8 recession was delayed at least two months, if we accept the NBER's timing of the cycle peak as August 1957. There was no indication that Federal Reserve officials had recognized a turning point in economic activity before the FOMC meeting in early November. Ralph Young, economic advisor to the Committee, confirmed that there was a moderate downward adjustment taking place. However, unlike the FOMC's response in May 1953 when there was a marked increase in free reserves, there was no urgent clamor for a drastic switch in policy. Chairman Martin, in December 1957, warned that the Committee should not attempt "to throw reserves in with the reckless abandon that we did then [1953]" (FOMC 1964, p. 48). Alfred Hayes, president of the Federal Reserve Bank of New York, who replaced Sproul in 1956, in December 1957 wanted to "avoid creating the impression that the System is moving rapidly to a policy of Active Ease" (FOMC 1964, p. 14). He told the FOMC in January 1958 that it should "avoid creating a sloppy money market or a needlessly low structure of interest rates that would have adverse longer-run effects on savings and investment returns" (FOMC 1964, p. 23). Moreover, there was the precaution to be taken in not creating a sloppy money market at the same time as a Treasury debt operation was under way – what has been termed "even-keeling." Chairman Martin agreed with Hayes: "He did not wish any overt move that would make it appear that the System was trying to flood the market with reserves." Moving in the direction of zero free reserves, he thought, was adequate.

The contrast with the 1953 episode is striking. Between May and June 1953, free reserves, for whatever reason, had shifted dramatically from −\$364 million to +\$355 million, that is, two months before the NBER cycle peak in July 1953. The Fed had entered the downturn with a substantial amount of free reserves, whereas in 1957 free reserves were still negative in early January, five months after the onset of the recession (August 1957).

President Hayes, in January 1958, called the Committee's attention to the fact that the maintenance of a free-reserves target might entail a shrinkage of total reserves and the money stock. He said that the System's action to date had not gone far enough to provide for a year-to-year increase in the money stock, and it was time that policy "be directed at supplying sufficient reserves in coming weeks and months to establish a clear upward trend in the reserve base and the money supply on the basis of year-age comparisons. Net free reserves would be of secondary interest in the achievement of this primary objective" (FOMC 1964, p. 9). The policy, he said, could be implemented by an additional infusion of reserves by a reduction of reserve requirements. He repeated his request at the next meeting of the Committee (February 11).

Beginning on February 26, the Federal Reserve Board reduced reserve requirements in four steps, releasing approximately \$1 billion of reserves. Free reserves responded by increasing to well over \$500 million. The downward trend in the M1 was reversed. M1 increased by 1 percent between January and April. Nevertheless, the action taken by the FOMC to reduce reserve requirements was not sufficient to affect materially the behavior of M1 during the recession. The full impact, moreover, was not felt until after the cycle trough in April. M1 increased 3.4 percent during the remainder of the year.

To explain why monetary policy became so tight during the expansion phase of the cycle we must recall our earlier description of the monetary policy states labeled "Neutrality" and "Restraint." The policies of "Neutrality" and "Restraint" differed primarily from the policies of "Ease" and "Active Ease" in the method employed by the FOMC to inject or absorb reserves. Under "Neutrality" and "Restraint," banks were expected to meet the seasonal and cyclical growth demands for bank credit and deposits via the discount window in lieu of open-market operations. During the 1950s, seasonal demands for reserves were not automatically accommodated by defensive open-market operations. Robert Roosa (1956, p. 9), who coined the term, never implied that they were. Although he had classified both increased borrowing and security purchases to meet seasonal drains as defensive, he acknowledged that seasonal drains, when met through the discount window, could be of genuine importance in the implementation of a dynamic policy. "Neutrality" and "Restraint" represented monetary policy states in which the discount window was the chief instrument for the conduct of a dynamic policy. We are not saying that the Fed refrained from engaging in open-market operations – though, on occasion, it did so for extended periods. For example, no outright purchases or sales were made for the Fed open-market account during the nine-week period ending April 27, 1955. But what we are saying is that the FOMC policy seriously constrained the increase in unborrowed reserves during economic recovery, and thereby constrained the growth of the money stock. The policy was so effective that unborrowed reserves actually decreased by 5.2 percent between June 1954 and July 1957.

Federal Reserve officials were beguiled by a reserve-supply mechanism that would respond automatically to changes in the banks' demands for reserves. Sproul described this characteristic as allowing "market factors" to express themselves in the reserve positions of the banks. Banks should come to the Fed for reserves, rather than the Fed attempting to estimate reserve demand and supplying reserves through open-market operations. The latter was referred to as "forcing reserves." Sproul attempted to define the passive role of the FOMC in February 1955 as follows:

> I would like to see us feel our way down further toward zero free reserves, letting member bank borrowing play more of a role in meeting seasonal swings in reserve needs . . . I would like to get back to a situation where the market is ordinarily coming to us for reserves, rather than our going to the market with reserves on the basis of unreliable projections of free reserves. (FOMC 1964, p. 63)

What mattered most was the direction of the trend, rather than the speed with which any target level was achieved. A plausible interpretation of the monetary policy states of "Neutrality" and "Restraint" is that the FOMC deliberately constrained the growth of unborrowed reserves, which goes some way toward explaining the constrained growth rate of M1 during the 1954–7 recovery.

Summary and conclusions

One conspicuous fact has emerged from the cyclical experience of the 1950s: the failure of the money stock to have increased significantly in either recession or recovery. And the predominant cause is to be found in the behavior of the various reserve aggregates – the monetary base, total reserves, and unborrowed reserves. The monetary base had changed less than 1 percent between July 1953 and April 1958, an interval encompassing two recessions and one full recovery.

Money-stock behavior during the two recessions is difficult to reconcile with the view that Federal Reserve policy-makers pursued successfully the contracyclical objectives of maintaining stable prices, high employment, and economic growth. The failure of the money stock to have increased in recession may be interpreted in either of two ways: as a weak policy-maker attachment to the objectives of stabilization, or as a defective policy strategy.

The failure of the money stock to have increased in the latter stages of the recovery is evidence of a strong contracyclical response.

The explanation for the Fed's asymmetrical policy response in recession and in recovery is to be found, I believe, in its strategy that identified free reserves as a guide to open-market policy. Less credence can be given to an interpretation that suggests that stabilization objectives were weak in recession and strong in recovery!

It should be clear that there are no logical flaws per se in the free-reserves guide to monetary policy. The weakness resides in how the policy was administered. The policy-makers' failure in the 1950s to have distinguished carefully between the demand for free reserves and the supply of free reserves rendered the impact on the money stock nugatory. Moreover, constraining the movement of free reserves beyond a clearly defined level to prevent an undesirable money-market state labeled "sloppy" guaranteed that the discrepancy, if any, between desired and actual free reserves would be held to a minimum and thereby would slow the growth of the money stock.

On the other hand, the emphasis attached by the FOMC to supplying reserves in recovery mainly, though not entirely, through the discount window rather than through open-market operations inhibited the growth of unborrowed reserves and the monetary base and thus contributed to the contracyclical behavior of the money stock.

References

Board of Governors of the Federal Reserve System (1976). *Banking and Monetary Statistics 1941–1970.* Washington, D.C.: U.S. Government Printing Office.

Brunner, Karl, and Meltzer, Allan (1964). *The Federal Reserve's Attachment to the Free Reserve Concept.* Washington, D.C.: Committee on Banking and Currency, House of Representatives, 88th Congress, 2nd session.

Christian, James W. (1968). "A Further Analysis of the Objectives of American Monetary Policy, 1952–61," *Journal of Finance,* 23(June):465–77.

Dewald, W. G., and Johnson, Harry (1963). "An Objective Analysis of the Objectives of American Monetary Policy," in D. Carson (ed.), *Banking and Monetary Studies,* pp. 171–89. Homewood, Ill.: Richard D. Irwin.

FOMC (1964). Minutes of the Federal Open Market Committee, 1936–60, and of its Executive Committee, 1939–55. Washington, D.C.: National Archives microfilm publications.

Gordon, Robert J. (1983). "Using Monetary Control to Dampen the Business Cycle: A New Set of First Principles," National Bureau of Economic Research working paper no. 1210.

Guttentag, Jack (1966). "The Strategy of Open Market Operations," *Quarterly Journal of Economics,* 80(February):1–30.

Knight, Robert (1970). *Federal Reserve System Policies and Their Effects on the Banking System.* Federal Reserve Bank of Boston research report no. 45.

Lombra, Raymond (1980). *Controlling Monetary Aggregates III.* Federal Reserve Bank of Boston.

Lombra, Raymond, and Torto, Raymond. (1973). "Federal Reserve Defensive Behavior and the Reverse Causation Argument," *Southern Economic Journal,* 40:47–55.

Meigs, James (1962). *Free Reserves and the Money Supply.* University of Chicago Press.

Meltzer, Allan (1982). "Comment on Federal Reserve Control of the Money Stock," *Journal of Money, Credit and Banking,* 14(November):632–40.

Riefler, Winfield (1952). *Minutes of the Federal Open Market Committee.* Washington, D.C.: National Archives microfilm publications, p. 197.

Roosa, Robert (1956). *Federal Reserve Operations in the Money and Government Securities Market.* Federal Reserve Bank of New York.

Wicker, Elmus (1974). "Open Market Money Supply Strategy, 1952–56," *Quarterly Journal of Economics,* 88(February):170–9.

CHAPTER 19

Bureaucratic self-interest as an obstacle to monetary reform

EDWARD J. KANE

To appreciate the textures and aromas of exquisitely flavored foods and sauces, one needs to cultivate an educated palate. Similarly, to appreciate the Federal Reserve's complex role in the evolution of U.S. monetary and regulatory policies and policy structures, one needs to cultivate an informed political-economic perspective on the Fed's evolving bureaucratic interest and on the various battles for turf in which this agency becomes involved.

Top Federal Reserve officials portray monetary stabilization and financial regulation as multidimensional services that, because of potentially valuable informational spillovers, are best produced together and run by their agency. Implicit in that conception is a presumption that Fed officials operate a politically inert and farsighted enterprise, passionately dedicated to the goals of economic efficiency and macroeconomic stability. Far from acquiescing in that presumption, this chapter emphasizes that efforts to protect the Fed's bureaucratic self-interest introduce myopia and distributional politics into Fed policy decisions and public statements.

The analysis offered here is intended as an antidote to traditional writings on the U.S. Federal Reserve System. Most macroeconomists portray the Fed as a politically inactive institution whose virtually only business is to use its "big three" policy weapons (open-market operations, reserve requirements, and the discount rate) to fight the excesses of the business cycle. This chapter depicts the Fed as a politically sensitive bureaucracy whose marketing activity and capacity for financing continuing clientele subsidies are at least as important as its production of stabilization services.

Unfortunately, outmoded statutory formulas enshrined in the Federal Reserve Act make it easy for Fed officials to nurture a naively narrow view of what they do and why they do it. Framers of that Act conceived

I wish to thank Thomas Havrilesky, Robert Hetzel, Thomas Mayer, and a seminar audience at De Paul University for helpful comments on an earlier draft.

of the Fed as a passive entity located beyond the reach of partisan political influences, so that it could respond more or less automatically to the "legitimate" needs of trade. That the Fed has evolved into an aggressively discretionary manager of the national economy would surprise (if not horrify) its creators.

The concept of a policy framework and its constituent elements

Monetary and financial policies have two dimensions:

1. *Decisions meant to establish a policy framework:* statutory and discretionary decisions that structure the policy framework of goals and instruments within which government officials operate.
2. *Policy implementation:* strategic and tactical policy decisions made about goals, intermediate targets, and instruments within a given policy framework.

Policy-framework decisions designate a particular set of control instruments (e.g., open-market operations, the discount rate, reserve requirements, and capital requirements) for achieving various policy goals and assign control over the instrumental keyboard to a particular set of government officials. In effect, policy-framework decisions seek, over long periods, to divide up in hard-to-revise ways what may broadly be called "regulatory turf." Policy implementation involves manipulating specific control instruments in pursuit of intermediate targets and policy goals selected at a particular time. It consists of a series of short-run and easily reversed decisions about which targets and goals to emphasize and the levels at which to set the designated control instruments.

By definition, proposals for policy reform seek to replace an existing policy framework with a better one. To understand the ways in which one policy framework can improve on another, it is instructive to disaggregate the domains of monetary and financial reform into three separate subsystems of institutional arrangements that a reformer could propose to change:

The information subsystem

Reforms in this part of the monetary and financial policy-making system focus on *reducing asymmetries of information* between the federal regulators and deposit institutions, between federal regulators and elected politicians, and between federal regulators and the voting public. Applicable rules cover the frequency and character of agency and private institutions' financial and performance reports, the extent to which those reports are double-checked and disclosed to politicians or the public, and how those and other data are analyzed by agency staff members.

The control subsystem

This is the subsystem over which Keynesian and monetarist economists, as well as collectivists and free-marketeers, have waged their main battles. Reforms of this part of the policy process deal with issues of rules versus discretion and alternative views of how to choose and arrange different sets of policy instruments, intermediate targets, and ultimate goals.

The political- and bureaucratic-incentive subsystem

This part of the policy-making process looks at contingent benefits and costs that accrue to potential voters and campaign contributors in different sectors of the economy and to federal agencies and particular government officials from different configurations of the control and information subsystems. Although monetary and financial reformers typically neglect these distributional and bureaucratic issues, political economy focuses predominantly on such questions.

With this conceptual background, it is possible to summarize briefly the analysis developed in this chapter. First, important defects exist in the control and information subsystems of monetary and financial policy. This is a point on which economists of all schools agree. Alternative schools of thought differ principally in the ways they propose to make Fed officials and/or elected politicians more accountable for policy mistakes. Second, this chapter contends that defects in control policy and reporting survive not because of policy-makers' ignorance or ineptitude but because these defects serve policy-makers' political and bureaucratic interests. They trace to defects in the political and bureaucratic incentive subsystem that governs how policy-framework decisions are made. Third, to understand why monetary and financial reform occurs infrequently and generally only in response to crises and scandals that greatly distress the populace at large, it is necessary to appreciate how in ordinary times the self-interest of politicans and bureaucrats tends to squelch proposals for reform.

Until now, the discussion has treated monetary reform and financial reform as components of a single problem. However, clarifying the political dimensions of U.S. monetary arrangements is tough enough. The range of choices to be considered in restructuring U.S. financial markets and institutions is too extensive to review effectively at the same time.

Hence, the rest of this presentation focuses exclusively on problems of monetary reform.

Monetary policy-making as a series of games within games

To spice up the exposition, it is instructive to view Fed policy-makers and elected politicians as repeatedly playing a game against each other. In playing this game, the Fed's objectives are to improve the performance of the national eçonomy and to improve the agency's standing as a public enterprise. Politicians engage in "Fed-bashing" to make sure that these two objectives come into conflict when they either want a change in current policy or want to avoid blame for previous policy moves that have turned out to be unpopular. In this way, Fed personnel are made to face difficult trade-offs.

In any round of play, the Fed's moves consist of public statements and various adjustments in its vector of designated control instruments: reserve requirements, capital requirements, the discount rate, and open-market operations. Round by round, politicians like some of the Fed's potential moves and dislike others. The goal of their play is to influence the Fed to make moves they favor and to avoid moves they disfavor. However, for politicians the skillful part of the game is to wield this influence in a hidden rather than overt way. Politicians' moves consist of delivering various kinds of political and bureaucratic rewards and punishments to Fed officials. Politicians' rewards and punishments range from verbal praise and chastisement to supporting changes in the rules of the game that are preferred or disliked by Federal Reserve officials.

From this perspective, the policy-control framework that encompasses a country's monetary arrangements constitutes a strategic long-period equilibrium solution to some essential aspects of this repeated game. Individual plays of the game focus on what to do about problems in political economy that currently annoy voters, would-be campaign contributors (or financial supporters), foreign central bankers, and elected government officials. In the United States, society authorizes citizens elected to the presidency and Congress to control jointly the framework of monetary policy. Politicians may at any time change the policy-making arrangements that define the rules that apply in future plays of the game. This ability to redefine the rules of the game reinforces politicians' ability to influence the central bank's monetary policy choices in the control and information arenas. It extends the range of potential bureaucratic rewards and punishments to items that are not easy to list completely in advance.

It is reasonable to presume that each player knows how to calculate the benefits and costs that attend his or her various potential moves, as well as what would constitute the best response to each move by opposing players. This assumption lets us use Paul Samuelson's principle of revealed preference to interpret the moves actually made in a given situation as "revealed" to be preferred to all moves that are not made. This tells us that, at least for the next few plays, the chosen set of monetary arrangements is conditionally preferred to all other feasible arrangements by those who effectively control them.

Inference is restricted to the next few plays to recognize that transition costs frequently slow the adoption of reforms that are known to be advantageous for the long run. However, if we define the long run as a period long enough for transition costs to become negligible, the observed long-period stability of these arrangements tells us that elected officials and the Fed must conditionally prefer the current framework to the various alternative systems regularly proposed by reformers (Kane 1975). The manifestly imperfect nature of existing arrangements for achieving society's ostensible goals implies that they must promote hidden goals of the Fed and politicians (i.e., they must deliver valuable options and privileges to the Fed and to elected players). Any reform threatens to curtail these options and privileges in some way. Hence, to make reform attractive to controlling officials, beneficiaries of the reform in the society at large have to find ways to compensate officials explicitly or implicitly in appropriate amounts for the losses that reform threatens to impose on them. This compensation may be seen to be the missing ingredient in economists' various proposals for monetary reform.

Linking the Fed and politicians' private game to the public game of Fed-bashing

The private game played between elected politicians and the Fed has a public extension that is staged for an audience of potential voters at various critical points in unfolding business and electoral cycles. This sporadic three-handed game may be called Fed-bashing.

In politically or economically difficult times, incumbent U.S. politicians indulge in a bipartisan practice of blaming the economic ills of the country on the "misguided" monetary policies of an "independent" Federal Reserve System. Far from acknowledging a prior role in encouraging Fed officials to select the very policies they currently wish to disavow, Fed-bashers seek to distance themselves from policies that are currently unpopular with potential campaign contributors and swing voters. Holding other things equal, the more dissatisfied that the polls show contributors and swing voters to be with any aspect of the national economy, the closer the date of the next election, and the tighter a Fed-basher's election campaign, the more abuse he or she tends to heap upon the Fed.

What makes the game work is that Fed officials take their bashings graciously. Rather than shifting guilt by clarifying the role that their politician-critics may have played in choosing the policies under attack, Fed officials' prototypical defense is to point out that fiscal policy and such unforecastable events as financial innovations or oil shocks cause monetary policy-makers insuperable difficulties. This ready acceptance of blame supports the perception that monetary policy is a delicate (even arcane) art and increases the credibility of Fed-bashers' collective efforts to heap political guilt for questionable policies onto the Fed.

In turn, Fed officials profess an unswerving resistance to political influence and accept the role of scapegoat for two reasons: because the structure of decision-making at their agency depersonalizes blame and because serving as scapegoats lets them preserve a series of valuable bureaucratic privileges that make scapegoating credible in the first place. These privileges include budgetary autonomy for the agency, potentially long terms of office for agency leaders, an extraordinary degree of public recognition, and a broader turf and policy keyboard than competitive financial regulators enjoy at the Office of the Comptroller of the Currency, the Federal Deposit Insurance Corporation, and the Securities and Exchange Commission.

Because U.S. political parties lack discipline, and different parties may control the presidency and one or both houses of Congress, the resulting incentive system is designed to favor not one party over the other but incumbent politicians over their challengers. In a system in which a well-disciplined party with a parliamentary majority rules all phases of a country's national government, incumbents in the "out" party have little reason to scapegoat officials of the central bank. Instead, they have a clear interest in pinning the blame for unpopular policies squarely on the opposing party.

The tendency for incumbent politicians to distract the public's attention from the consequences of their actions is an age-old tendency. It has its parallel in the Roman emperors' reliance on "bread and circuses." In *Fahrenheit 451,* Ray Bradbury argues that a government would rather tranquilize its populace than serve it efficiently:

> If the government is inefficient, top-heavy, and tax-mad, better it be all those than that people worry over it. . . . Give the people contests they win by remembering the words to more popular songs or the names of state capitals or how much corn Iowa grew last year. Cram them full of noncombustible data, chock them so damned full of "facts" they feel stuffed, but absolutely "brilliant" with

information. Then they'll feel they're thinking, they'll get a *sense* of motion without moving. And they'll be happy, because facts of that sort don't change. Don't give them any slippery stuff like philosophy or sociology to tie things up with. That way lies melancholy. (1953, pp. 55–6)

How can an economically imperfect control system survive the criticism of observing economists?

Contemporary economists characteristically think of themselves as specialists in positive economics: calculators *extraordinaire* of individual and institutional benefits and costs. To focus on economic problems per se, they determinedly strip away normative and political dimensions of policy problems. This predilection undermines the policy relevance of economic research whenever (as in monetary-policy-framework decisions) normative and political aspects of the problem fail to be surgically separable issues.

Focusing exclusively on the "positive economics" of the control subsystem, economist reformers typically attempt only to show that a particular change in the performance criteria or structure of Federal Reserve decision-making would lead to better macroeconomic policy performance (Hafer, Hein, and Kool 1983). The catch is that, evaluated over a full business cycle, a great many different changes in the monetary control system can be shown to lead to better policy. The deeper question is why the Fed and elected politicians did not choose to adopt one of these socially better arrangements years ago.

The answer is twofold. First, one function of monetary arrangements is to provide ways for sectoral interests to influence policy decisions. Important segments of the electorate perceive particular reforms as compromising their distributional interest in being able to influence monetary policy in the short run. This creates a constituency for the status quo. Even if the potential losers from reform were offered explicit compensation, it is reasonable for beneficiaries of current arrangements to fear that explicit compensation may be harder to defend in the long run than the well-hidden subsidies they currently enjoy. Second, supporters of different reforms often let efforts to promote their particular idea of the "best" become the enemy of the good. By not addressing the effects of political and bureaucratic incentives, advocates of monetary or credit growth rules, of strict price-level or national-income targeting, or of returning to the gold standard permit their various schemes to cancel each other out. Efforts to erect competitive reform frameworks generate a kind of lobbying turbulence that makes it hard for any single reform scheme to make more than token headway.

Virtually all reform proposals seek to impose stricter accountability on Fed officials for the monetary policy they choose to follow. If such proposals are to have a substantial chance for success, their sponsors must find a way to undo the political and bureaucratic incentives that make current arrangements so cozy both for incumbent politicians and for the Fed. The Fed minimizes its accountability to the electorate and to politicians in two ways: by accepting contradictory goals and by making discretionary use of a self-selected bevy of intermediate policy targets such as the federal-funds rate, nonborrowed reserves, and various monetary growth rates. The resulting vagueness in the institution's aims and methods lets Fed officials reverse their economic priorities suddenly in response to the ebb and flow of political pressure, with minimal embarrassment. FOMC secrecy and the carefully crafted structural ambiguity of Fed decision-making permit Fed officials to fuzz over the important political compromises they effect between goals desired by different political constituencies and let those compromises be made with minimal short-term political stress for elected politicians. Moreover, the large staff of professional economists whose research on policy issues is directed by the Fed serves the institution's leadership in two ways. First, staff analysis helps Fed officials to maintain an informational advantage over other players. Second, by manipulating the size of this staff and the activities for which they are rewarded and penalized, Fed officials help to shape the agenda of contemporary economic research on monetary policy. Unless Fed staff members are willing to risk career penalties, they are induced to devote their research to bureaucratically approved issues. Such issues focus on the control subsystem – topics such as the effects of using different arrays of intermediate targets or of moving from contemporary to lagged accounting for reserves and back again – rather than on the broader principal–agent conflicts comprised in the information and incentives subsystems of monetary policy-making.

The incentive subsystem

It is not necessary to assume that top Fed officials deliberately calculate the political benefits and costs of the decisions they make. Animal trainers are known to control the actions of nonrational animals by continually delivering rewards and punishments for desired and undesired behaviors. The preselection candidate-screening process for potential Fed officials, in which their previous attitudes and behaviors (including past party service and susceptibility to political appeals) are examined, may force them to make some quasi-promises and should help to sensitize them to the subtle dimensions of political horse trading. This sensitization and the role that the popular standing of the agency plays in generating subsequent job opportunities for top Fed officials who step down make it hard for agency leaders to avoid calculating political costs and benefits, at least subconsciously.

Political rewards and punishments represent congressional and presidential plays in the game of monetary policy-making. Potential moves can range from private and public expressions of approval or disapproval to support for or opposition to legislative changes that Fed officials do or do not want enacted. Legislative rewards can focus on expanding the Fed's policy turf and instrumental keyboard, as exemplified by the 1980 extension of Fed reserve-requirement authority to nonbank deposit institutions and the Fed's perennial request for the right to pay interest on reserve balances. Legislative punishments can consist of withholding keenly desired rewards and imposing various restrictions that threaten either the Fed's inherited turf and span of instrumental control or its budgetary and short-run policy autonomy.

If we assume that structural adjustments in the Fed's powers are perceived as politically optimal by those empowered to make them, Congress and the president have repeatedly reaffirmed the political value to them of the Fed's lack of accountability. It is no accident that throughout the Fed's 75 years of existence Congress and the president usually have remained content not to force the Fed to submit openly to their wills. By leaving the Fed's high command a substantial amount of ex ante discretion, elected politicians leave themselves room to blame the Fed ex post for whatever aspects of its policies happen to go wrong. This conception supports a scapegoat theory of the bureaucratic structure of the Fed (Kane 1980, 1982b).

Empirical research has yet to assess quantitatively how much the operation of myopic and redistributional politics fostered by looseness in monetary policy reporting and decision-making damages macroeconomic and financial performance. Lack of accountability facilitates sudden shifts in the central thrust of monetary policy actions by taking embarrassment out of the process. Reformers hold that rapidly shifting, stop–go monetary policies increase macroeconomic and financial volatility in ways that lessen consumer welfare on average over time. Although only a minority of contemporary economists would explicitly recommend a policy rule, it is widely believed that incentive reforms designed to induce more time-consistent policies would reduce the average severity of inflation, unemployment, and balance-of-payments difficulties (Mullineaux 1985).

The special case of Fed efforts to resist monetarist criticism

Top Federal Reserve officials find it useful to portray monetary policy as an eclectic and multitargeted business requiring delicate back-and-forth adjustments in the values assigned to achieving interest-rate, reserves, and money-stock targets (Hetzel 1988). In contrast, monetarists see monetary policy as mainly a matter of maintaining a relatively smooth and controlled expansion in a single variable, such as the money supply or the monetary base. In particular, monetarists deny that smoothness in interest-rate movements is valuable per se.

Monetarist criticism combines three separable constituent hypotheses:

1. *A proxy-variable hypothesis:* The rate of growth of a nation's money stock or monetary base can serve as a good proxy measure of the effects that monetary policy has on society's macroeconomic-goal variables.
2. *A feasibility hypothesis:* Growth in the nation's money stock or monetary base could in fact be controlled within sufficiently close limits by the central bank if only it were to try hard enough.
3. *An observability hypothesis:* Shifts in the demand for money (and its components) can be observed closely enough to be offset, at least in the long run.

Monetarists' basic model of monetary control conceives of each alternative monetary-aggregate target, M, as the produce of an uncontrolled "multiplier," m, and a controllable reserve aggregate, which we can call the control "handle," H. To acknowledge that M is also subject to random variation, it is appropriate to add a stochastic-error term, u_t. The key control equation expresses the money-supply process as follows: $M_t = m_tH_t + u_t$. The recommended control procedure is to view m_t as the sum of a term that can be forecast from past data and a stochastic-error term, v_t. Through time, the control handle H_t needs only to be moved along a time path that implies a macroeconomically optimal rate of monetary growth.

Although the thrust of the monetarist attack on the Fed has remained essentially unchanged for at least 30 years, Federal Reserve defenses have rallied around different arguments in different eras. During the 1950s and early 1960s, Fed officials dismissed the monetarists' proxy hypothesis out of hand. They treated monetarism as an eccentric and quasi-religious belief system that no responsible macroeconomist or public official could possibly take seriously. Fed officials insisted implicitly that, as self-appointed critics, monetarists had to solve the problem of designing and conducting unambiguous econometric tests of alternative versions of the constituent subhypotheses before the Fed should even acknowledge any scientific standing for their position. As a result, monetarists found themselves forced to function not merely as empirical scientists but also as missionaries.

By the late 1960s, sufficient empirical evidence favorable to the monetarist case had accumulated to render simple skepticism an untenable Fed defense. During the 1970s, the proxy hypothesis was accepted and progressively incorporated into the FOMC's monetary policy planning and evaluation framework (Hetzel 1984; Kaufman 1983). At the same time, Fed officials shifted the force of their objections from the proxy hypothesis to the feasibility and observability hypotheses. They maintained that two unsettled econometric issues rendered the interpretation of monetarist estimates of reduced-form monetary-control parameters linking monetary targets to the Fed's policy instruments too unreliable to serve as a complete foundation for a practicable system of monetary control. For convenience, we may call these issues

1. *the endogeneity issue,* which asks whether or not Fed efforts to control either the money stock or the monetary base generate substantially offsetting responses by private decision-makers in either the economic or the political arena, and
2. *the shifting-parameter issue,* which asks whether or not whatever links exist between Fed policy instruments and specific monetary targets remain fixed long enough for the Fed's staff to construct reliable projections of the effects of its actions.

Both issues concern potentially important econometric complications that are rooted in the concept of policy-induced financial innovation and whose presence or absence cannot be observed either directly or immediately.

No matter how small or how large econometric studies show these sophisticated econometric difficulties to be, observing economists should see that acceptance or rejection of any monetarist subhypothesis by Fed officials is predominantly a political decision (Mayer 1987). As an institution that is regularly buffeted by conflicting political pressures, the Fed finds it extremely useful to deny the feasibility of effective monetary control. Whether or not a many-goal conception of its task helps Fed officials to perform their macroeconomic missions, the idea that they have to make trade-offs makes it easier for them to handle criticism. Accepting the feasibility hypothesis would make it much harder for Fed officials to reconcile their quasi-monetarist conception of monetary policy-making with their continuing failure to prevent pro-cyclical variation in the money supply. If the task of monetary control is a fully feasible one, movements in the money supply reflect Fed decisions one for one. Alternative explanations for poor Fed performance cast its employees into one of three uncomfortable roles: Poor performance must be the result of bureaucratic incompetence, of problems with the proxy subhypothesis (e.g., reflecting unobservable changes in money demand or in the composition of the truly relevant monetary aggregate induced by Fed control efforts), or of the existence of other goals whose influences on Fed decision-makers have been kept hidden.

Under the leadership of Karl Brunner and Allan Meltzer, the Shadow Open Market Committee (SOMC) has been in the forefront of the fight to undercut statistical objections to the feasibility and shifting-parameter hypotheses. In particular, extending work begun by Johannes and Rasche (1979), Brian Motley and SOMC member Robert Rasche (1986) have developed evidence that the endogeneity and shifting-parameter problems raise mainly short-period complications that could be surmounted if the Fed wanted to make monetary-aggregate control its sole long-period objective. But this evidence would mean a great deal more to the Fed if someone could also show that singleminded pursuit of a monetary-aggregate goal would be in the Fed's bureaucratic self-interest, either currently or under a politically feasible set of reforms that could be introduced into the Fed's statutory charter. Following the lead of Friedman (1982) and Mayer (1987), it would move the debate to a new level if the political costs and benefits that alternative reforms imply for Fed officials could be brought explicitly into reformers' models of monetary control.

What is wrong with related proposals to establish policy rules?

Fed leaders make uncomfortable compromises between their need to respond to immediate political pressure and their desire to improve the long-run performance of the national economy (Kane 1982b; Grier 1985; Lombra 1988; Mayer 1987; Woolley 1984). Political goals and constraints complicate the dilemmas inherent in the Fed's economic policy mission. Over short accounting periods, macroeconomic goals such as high employment and low inflation require contradictory actions. Nondiscretionary policy rules (such as gold-standard or monetary-growth rules) are naive brute-force ways of reducing the myopic bias that day-to-day political pressure and macroeconomic lags tend to impart to monetary policy.

A policy rule establishes consistency in policy priorities over time, both by forestalling myopic policies for redistributing income to curry votes and by undermining inherited procedures for responding to distributional grievances. Policy rules are intended to retard reversals of policies that sectoral interests suffering foreseeable and especially unforeseeable policy burdens would otherwise possess the political clout to effect. By focusing on narrow indices of policy performance, a policy rule would serve as a mechanism for ensuring consistent control decisions across business and electoral cycles. At the same time, a rule would drastically alter the bureaucratic- and political-incentive system. It would require Congress to commit itself both to review on a secular basis the appropriateness of the policy rule in place and of the levels at which associated policy triggers are formally set and to monitor systematically Fed compliance with the rule. These oversight responsibilities would implicate congressional authorities in monetary policy selection, greatly reducing their ability to duck the blame for unpopular policies after the fact.

To accept a policy rule, Congress would have to surrender two options whose vote-gaining power it has valued in the past: (1) the option of scapegoating Fed officials for problems of macroeconomic performance and (2) the option of responding quickly at various stages of the business cycle to changes in the electorate's consensus view of what monetary policies are appropriate. Advocates of rules need to recognize that continual divergences between the current thrust of monetary policy and consensus views of the economy's short-run need for monetary stimulus or restraint would lessen incumbent politicians' chances for reelection.

A policy rule would prove difficult to sustain, because over time political frustration would accumulate against it. Over a typical business cycle, it would engender political costs that professional politicians and Fed officials could not be expected to ignore. Procedures that threaten to leave aggrieved parties feeling powerless endanger the careers of elected politicians. Any rule that Congress could bring itself to adopt would be likely to be full of loopholes. Those loopholes would be meant to forestall the buildup of political pressure not only against the rule but especially against the larger political system of which it is a part. Without compensation, and reliable compensation at that, why should Congress choose to deprive itself of opportunities to disclaim unpopular policies after the fact and to perform "constituent services" for those who feel themselves impacted by monetary policy. Without compensation, why should vulnerable sectors give up the power to use the political system to protect themselves against anticipated and unanticipated losses that changes in monetary policy can occasion? Without compensation, why should the Fed surrender the special bureaucratic privileges that its scapegoat role earns for it?

The need for reliable schemes for compensating or overcoming those who would lose from reform

Real-world systems of taxation and governmental regulation, production, and income redistribution are riddled with hidden subsidies. It is naive to believe that government officials' simultaneous concealment of so many subsidies is merely a coincidence. Presumably, recipients prefer hidden subsidies to open ones, because their existence is difficult for political opponents to prove, let alone to eliminate. Proponents of policy reform need to recognize that the existence of aggregate welfare gains from adopting new monetary arrangements is merely a *necessary* condition for rational reform. The harder condition is to determine what level of compensation is needed, for whom, and what particular forms the compensation ought to take.

Instead of treating political feasibility as a wholly noneconomic problem, economists could usefully analyze alternate ways in which compensation to various participants might reduce barriers to socially beneficial reforms and assess the role that hidden compensation may have played in past U.S. monetary reforms. My own cursory review of past reforms suggests that occurrences of serious crises and scandals have first at least partly delegitimized the existing policy framework. Crises and scandals promote reform precisely because the sense of urgency abroad at such times greatly reduces the need to compensate those who lose from reform.

A central bank is inescapably a political institution. Its macroeconomic mission has important distributional overtones. With the major exceptions of West Germany and Switzerland (countries whose postwar constituencies against inflation have proved unusually strong), politicians in advanced countries have chosen to bind their central banks into the formal political process far more tightly than U.S. politicians have secured the Fed.

Although limited autonomy was given to the Fed ostensibly as a way to assure less inflationary monetary policies, the fragility of the Fed's special bureaucratic privileges has turned its quasi-independent status into a political leash. If U.S. politicians' only goal was to give our country better macroeconomic performance over the representative business cycle, they would long ago have made themselves and Federal Reserve officials more directly accountable for short-run central-bank behavior. Among the simpler ways to accomplish this would be to give the Fed chairman cabinet status or to make the secretary of the Treasury and the chairman of the Council of Economic Advisers full-fledged members of the FOMC. Putting the Fed under more explicit short-run political pressure would greatly lessen politicians' ability to disclaim responsibility for past policy decisions. For political parties and would-be career politicians who seek to advance in office or to stay in place for several terms, enhanced responsibility for the consequences of monetary policy would establish incentives to look past the boundaries of the current swing in the business cycle.

Most incumbent politicians revel in the political benefits of Fed-bashing. Presidents and congressional leaders will keep the game running as long as the political benefits of Fed-bashing exceed its political costs. The balance of benefits and costs improves slightly whenever voters place the same party in control of the presidency and both houses of Congress. However, even at these times, presidential politics and the lack of discipline in the congressional wings of U.S. parties make scapegoating attractive to incumbents in the majority party. To achieve substantial and permanent progress, voters must develop and communicate sufficient concern about weaknesses in national economic performance to overcome the symbiotic relation that now exists between elected politicians and the Fed. For this to occur, either the public must learn (perhaps with the help of essays such as this one) to see through biennial and quadrennial efforts to scapegoat the Fed or critics of the Fed must agree on a unified plan for making the Fed clearly accountable to politicians so that, in turn, politicians become accountable for Fed behavior. As it is now, macroeconomists squander too much of their energies trying to show that the performance criteria and reporting requirements that they would impose on the Fed would be better than those proposed by competitive reformers. Internecine squabbling among sponsors of sensible alternative central-bank arrangements serves perversely to shorten the political leash under which the Fed operates. This squabbling also helps Fed officials to keep the voting public in a state of confusion about the nature of monetary policy decision-making, a confusion that effectively expands the Fed's capacity both to act eclectically and to serve as an after-the-fact scapegoat for unpopular macroeconomic events. As long as would-be monetary reformers passionately shout down one another's ideas, their efforts serve to mystify the task of monetary policy-making and to keep Fed officials battling politically to preserve their special bureaucratic status. Sadly, the level of the noise they make about alternative targeting schemes and performance criteria tends to drown out these critics' far more telling concerns about the wisdom of drawing clear lines of political accountability for Fed actions.

References

Bradbury, Ray (1953). *Fahrenheit 451.* New York: Ballantine.

Friedman, Milton (1982). "Monetary Policy: Theory and Practice," *Journal of Money, Credit and Banking,* 14(February):98–118.

Grier, Kevin B. (1985). "Congressional Preference and Federal Reserve Policy," Center for the Study of American Business working paper no. 95, Washington University, St. Louis.

Hafer, R. W., Hein, S. E., and Kool, C. J. M. (1983). "Forecasting the Money Multiplier: Implications for Money Stock Control and Economic Activity," *Federal Reserve Bank of St. Louis Review,* 65(October):22–33.

Hetzel, Robert (1988). "The Formulation of Monetary Policy," Federal Reserve Bank of Richmond.

(1980). "The Political Economy of Monetary Policy," Federal Reserve Bank of Richmond.

Johannes, James M., and Rasche, Robert H. (1979). "Predicting the Money Multiplier," *Journal of Monetary Economics,* 5(July):301–25.

Kane, Edward J. (1975). "New Congressional Restraints and Federal Reserve Independence," *Challenge* (November–December):37–44.

(1980). "Politics and Fed Policymaking: The More Things Change the More They Remain the Same," *Journal of Monetary Economics,* 6(April):199–211.

(1982a). "External Pressure and the Operations of the Fed," in R. Lombra and W. Witte (eds.) *Political Economy of International and Domestic Monetary Relations,* 211–32. Ames: Iowa State University Press.

(1982b). "Selecting Monetary Targets in a Changing Financial Environment," pp. 181–206. Federal Reserve Bank of Kansas City.

Kaufman, George G. (1983). "Monetarism at the Fed," *Journal of Contemporary Studies,* 12(Winter):27–36.

Lombra, Raymond (1982). "Discussion," in *Monetary Policy Issues in the 1980s,* pp. 215–22. Federal Reserve Bank of Kansas City.

(1988). "Monetary Policy: The Rhetoric *vs.* the Record," in T. Willett (ed.), *Political Business Cycles: The Political Economy of Money, Inflation, and Unemployment,* pp. 337–65. San Francisco: Pacific Institute for Public Policy Research.

Mayer, Thomas (1987). "The Debate About Monetarist Policy Recommendations," *Kredit und Kapital,* 20(January):281–302.

Motley, Brian, and Rasche, Robert H. (1986). "Predicting the Money Stock: A Comparison of Alternative Approaches," *Federal Reserve Bank of San Francisco Economic Review,* 2(Spring):38–54.

Mullineaux, Donald J. (1985). "Monetary Rules and Contracts: Why Theory Loses to Practice," *Federal Reserve Bank of Philadelphia Business Review* (March–April):13–19.

Woolley, John (1984). *Monetary Politics: The Federal Reserve and the Politics of Monetary Policy.* Cambridge University Press.

Index

For EU product safety concerns, contact us at Calle de José Abascal, 56–1°,
28003 Madrid, Spain or eugpsr@cambridge.org.

www.ingramcontent.com/pod-product-compliance
Ingram Content Group UK Ltd.
Pitfield, Milton Keynes, MK11 3LW, UK
UKHW012157180425
457623UK00018B/249

* 9 7 8 0 5 2 1 4 4 6 5 1 8 *